LIFE from DEATH

The Organ and Tissue Donation and Transplantation Source Book with Forms

Phillip G. Williams

Contemporary Public Health Issues
Volume 2

The P. Gaines Co.
PO Box 2253, Oak Park, Illinois 60303

Copyright © 1989 by Phillip G. Williams

All rights reserved. No part of this book may be reproduced or transmitted in any form or by any means, electronic or mechanical, including photocopying, recording or by any information storage or retrieval system without written permission from the author, except for the inclusion of brief quotations in a review.

Since laws are subject to differing interpretations, neither the publisher nor the author offers any guarantees concerning the information contained in this publication or the use to which it is put. Although this publication is designed to provide accurate and authoritative information concerning anatomical gift laws, it is sold with the understanding that neither the author nor the publisher is engaged in rendering legal or other professional advice. If legal or other expert assistance is required, the services of a competent professional should be sought.

Library of Congress Cataloging in Publication Data

Williams, Phil, 1946-
   Life from death : the organ and tissue donation and transplantation source book, with forms / Phillip G. Williams.
     p.   cm. -- (Contemporary public health issues ; v. 2)
   1. Donation of organs, tissues, etc.--Law and legislation--United States--States.   2. Transplantation of organs, tissues, etc.--Law and legislation--United States--States.   3. Dead bodies (Law)--United States--States.   I. Title.
KF3827.D66Z958 1989
344.73'0419--dc19
[347.304419]   88-24461
ISBN 0-936284-44-7   CIP

Manufactured in the United States of America

Copyright is not claimed in any reprinted material obtained from official U.S. Government or state sources.

ACKNOWLEDGMENTS

We gratefully acknowledge the assistance of the numerous individuals working in the field of organ donation and transplantation who generously provided time, information, and support: Patricia Kolff of the National Heart Assist and Transplant Fund, Betty Perls of the Regional Organ Bank of Illinois, Arthur Harrell of the American Council on Transplantation, Fran Weiss of the American Liver Foundation, Barbara O'Reilly of the Eye-Bank for Sight Restoration, Teri Romo of the Living Bank, Kim Coreil of the National Kidney Foundation, Joyce Brown of the Division of Organ Transplantation, The Department of Health and Human Services, and Karen Kirsch of the Eye Bank Association—to name but a few of the many who have helped.

We extend special thanks to Amy Godinez for her unflagging attention to the nuances of the written word.

Table of Contents

Introduction — 1

Chapter 1: An Overview — 3
    Severe Organ Shortages: The Case of Kidneys — 3
    The Broad Scope of Uses for Anatomical Gifts — 3
    The Emerging Field of Brain Implants — 4
    Religious Considerations — 4
    Organ Donation and the Black Community — 5
    Hispanic Outreach Programs — 6
    Contrasting Approaches to Organ Donation in France and the United States — 7
    Organ Donation and the Human Community — 8
    Children's Right to Make Anatomical Gifts — 8
    Every Donor as a Potential Recipient — 8

Chapter 2: The Uniform Anatomical Gift Act — 9
    Text of 1968 Uniform Anatomical Gift Act — 11
    Overview and Commentary — 14

Chapter 3: The Legacy of the National Organ Transplant Act of 1984 — 17
    Recommendations of Task Force — 18
        Immunosuppressive Medications — 18
        Organ and Tissue Donation And Procurement — 18
        Organ Sharing — 21
        Equitable Access to Organ Transplantation — 22
        Diffusion of Organ Transplantation Technology — 24
        Research in Organ Transplantation — 25
        Establishment of an Advisory Board on Organ Transplantation — 26

Chapter 4: State Anatomical Gift Laws — 27
    ALABAMA — 27
    ALASKA — 30
    ARIZONA — 32
    ARKANSAS — 36
    CALIFORNIA — 39
    COLORADO — 42
    CONNECTICUT — 47
    DELAWARE — 50
    DISTRICT OF COLUMBIA — 53
    FLORIDA — 56
    GEORGIA — 61
    HAWAII — 66
    IDAHO — 69

ILLINOIS	71
INDIANA	74
IOWA	78
KANSAS	81
KENTUCKY	83
LOUISIANA	87
MAINE	92
MARYLAND	96
MASSACHUSETTS	100
MICHIGAN	104
MINNESOTA	108
MISSISSIPPI	113
MISSOURI	116
MONTANA	120
NEBRASKA	124
NEVADA	127
NEW HAMPSHIRE	131
NEW JERSEY	133
NEW MEXICO	136
NEW YORK	139
NORTH CAROLINA	144
NORTH DAKOTA	148
OHIO	151
OKLAHOMA	156
OREGON	159
PENNSYLVANIA	162
RHODE ISLAND	166
SOUTH CAROLINA	169
SOUTH DAKOTA	172
TENNESSEE	175
TEXAS	179
UTAH	181
VERMONT	183
VIRGINIA	185
WASHINGTON	189
WEST VIRGINIA	192
WISCONSIN	197
WYOMING	200

Appendix A — 205

Uniform Donor Card	205
Anatomical Gift by Next of Kin or Other Authorized Person	206
Anatomical Gift by a Living Donor	207
Anatomical Gift by a Living Minor Donor	208

Appendix B	**209**
Amended Uniform Anatomical Gift Act (1987)	209
Appendix C	**215**
National Organ Transplant Act	215
Appendix D	**224**
Omnibus Budget Reconciliation Act of 1986 (Selected Sections)	224
Hospital Protocols for Organ Procurement and Standards for Organ Procurement Agencies	224
Appendix E	**226**
Glossary	226
Appendix F	**229**
Directory of Support Services	229
Bibliography	**239**
Index	**243**

Introduction

Today, more than ever, efforts to increase public awareness about organ donation are sorely needed. Transplant operations that remained largely experimental until a few years ago have now become standard medical procedure, thanks to the development of effective immunosuppressive drugs and new advances in surgical techniques. As a result, transplant procedures can now benefit many more people than previously was thought possible.

These advances in medical science have created a tragic dilemma, however. On the one hand, they have given hope to the seriously or terminally ill. On the other, these hopes often remain unfulfilled, since they are completely dependent upon the generosity of anonymous donors. The need for transplantable organs and tissues is greatly outstripping donations at present and will undoubtedly continue to do so for the foreseeable future.

Every effort is being made to expand the donor pool. The maximum age for donors of hearts, for example, has been repeatedly revised upward as the number of available organs has dwindled. Whereas thirty once constituted the upper age limit for heart donors, it is not unusual for gifts from forty-five or even fifty-year olds to be accepted for transplants today. Organs from donors suffering from diseases such as diabetes are now being transplanted in emergencies when the only alternative is immediate death. The possibility of the use of *xenographs* (across-the-species transplants, say, from baboons to humans) is even being seriously considered by some as a last resort.

"Required request" legislation, passed by 44 states to date as well as the federal government, mandates that hospitals routinely ask for donations from all families of dying patients. In some areas, this practice has helped, to a degree, to alleviate organ and tissue shortages, but it has not achieved the dramatic increase in donations originally expected. After a swell in donations in 1986, the rate of anatomical gifting has reached a plateau.

According to the detailed report of the Task Force created by the National Organ Transplant Act, the first major federal legislation addressing organ and tissue donation and transplantation, public and professional education is a necessary route to fill the present need for anatomical gifts. No project or organization by itself can accomplish the goal of assuring the availability of transplants for those whose lives depend on them. Only a multi-pronged educational approach carried out through the coordinated efforts of primary and secondary schools, public libraries, medical and nursing schools, hospital staffs, community organizations, churches, synagogues and other religious groups, as well as the business community, can insure success.

To this end, the present volume may serve as a source book of information on the various issues pertaining to anatomical gifts. Chapter 1 provides an overview. More than 50,000 persons a year currently benefit from some form of organ or tissue transplant. By the year 2000, given present rates of growth in such procedures, many tens of thousands of individuals can be expected to be recipients of heart, kidney, and liver transplants annually, while hundreds of thousands will become the benefactors of skin, bone, and cornea grafts. In addition to focusing on current uses of organ and tissue donations in transplants, restorative surgery, hormonal therapy, research, and teaching, Chapter 1 looks at the newly emerging technologies of brain "implants" to treat Parkinson's and Huntington's disease and, potentially, Alzheimer's, brain injury, and stroke; the growing crisis in the availability of organs, tissues, and body parts; the key role of public and professional education in meeting this crisis; the unique transplant needs of the black community; Hispanic outreach programs; the stance of twenty-two major religions or religious denominations in America, from the Amish to Jehovah's Witnesses and Judaism, on organ donation and transplantation; children and anatomical gifts. Common misconceptions are answered.

Chapter 2 focuses on the Uniform Anatomical Gift Act. Originally approved by the American Bar Association and the National Conference of Commissioners on Uniform State Law in 1968, this Act has provided the model for all state legislation on anatomical gifts for the past twenty years. The actual text of this formative model is included in this chapter, along with clear analysis and commentary. A concise overview of all fifty states' anatomical gift laws is presented in light of this common reference point.

Chapter 3 examines the significance of the National Organ Transplant Act and the report of the Task Force created by the Act in regard to current legal, public policy, and educational trends in this area. Highlighted are the commendations of the Task Force for a national education program on organ donation and transplantation, targeting primary and secondary schools, minority groups, family units, and churches. Its professional guidelines advise the incorporation of organ and tissue procurement and transplantation in medical and nursing school curricula, the requiring of knowledge of organ and tissue donation and transplantation for certification, and the establishment of educational programs on donor referral and the donation process for professional organizations of physicians and nurses.

Chapter 4 provides a state-by-state compilation of current anatomical gift laws in the fifty states and the District of Columbia, with state-mandated forms included.

Six appendices attach Uniform Donor forms and instructions for both adults and minors, the reprint of the complete text of the recently amended (August 1987) Uniform Anatomical Gift Act, the unabridged text of the National Organ Transplant Act, Sections 1138 and 9335 of the Omnibus Budget Reconciliation Act of 1986 (covering hospital protocols for organ procurement and standards for organ procurement agencies and Medicare coverage of immunosuppressive drugs), a glossary of key terms, and an annotated directory listing support services for both donors and transplant recipients as well as organizations active in public policy and those offering opportunities for volunteerism in this field.

The focus of Life from Death *falls squarely on the legal framework supporting our system of so-called "encouraged voluntarism" in this country, whereby anatomical gifts, with certain exceptions, must come through voluntary acts of conscience. Our legal system governing anatomical gifts was established—and is continually being rethought and recast—in order to promote, to the maximum degree, organ and tissue donation by individuals and their next of kin. Many other countries, by contrast, such as Greece, Israel, and France, have a completely different legal approach than ours, one of "presumed consent," which presupposes implied permission to utilize, after death, for medical purposes, any needed organs and tissues, unless specifically forbidden by the deceased or next of kin.*

Given the focus of the present study on the key role played by state and federal law in our system of donation and transplantation in the United States, it is not the primary intent of this work to illuminate either the human side of the donor and transplant process or, for that matter, the more technical aspects of donation and transplantation procedures, for those faced with immediate do-or-die choices, issues previously treated in various other publications. Recently, the frantic and fascinating experiences of the patients, the donors, the transplant surgeons, and the transplant coordinators at the world's largest transplant center, Pittsburgh's Presbyterian-University Hospital, has been eloquently brought to life in Lee Gutkind's Many Sleepless Nights *(New York: W.W. Norton and Company, 1988), to mention but one book that has narratively dramatized the sufferings and triumphs of those involved in the realities of transplantation. Numerous articles and books, furthermore, deal with every conceivable aspect of the medical issues. The annotated bibliography at the end of* Life from Death *points to additional readings that present significant aspects of the world of donation and transplantation other than those covered in this book.*

Chapter 1: An Overview

Is there anyone who has not heard about the dramatic heart and kidney transplant operations performed at hospitals throughout the country today? Even ten years ago, such transplants were highly experimental. Today, they have become almost routine as well as much more effective, due, in large part, to the development of the powerful immunosuppressive drugs cyclosporine and prednisone that help prevent organ rejection. At present, 82 per cent of heart transplant recipients survive one year, some 76 per cent for at least four years. The operative procedures themselves no longer seem shrouded in mystery. The often frantic search for matching organ donations nowadays comprises the chief dramatic element of the transplant process. There never seems to be a lack of stories of lives hanging in the balance, particularly those of young lives.

Severe Organ Shortages: The Case of Kidneys

On any given day, some 13,000 persons in the United States are waiting for a suitable kidney donation alone. The total number of individuals on waiting lists for all types of organs and tissues is, of course, much higher. Many of these will die waiting. Many more children who need kidney transplants, for example, die without receiving an organ than those who do receive one. It is estimated that, only about 20 per cent of the organs needed for transplants are presently being donated.

Whereas children's transplants in general and heart transplants in particular tend to get the lion's share of public attention, it is unglamorous kidney transplants which comprise the great bulk of transplant operations. The 8,972 kidneys transplanted in 1987 dwarf the number of heart and liver transplants (each approximately a thousand annually). Only eye and skin transplants outnumber those involving kidneys. Kidney donations, unlike most other transplants, may come from either living or dead donors. Since the body only needs one kidney to function, a living relative with a compatible tissue type who is able and willing to give up a kidney can make a donation. About two thousand living persons annually donate one of their kidneys to someone else needing a transplant, usually a blood relative. Not surprisingly, the greatest success rate results from this kind of transplant, obtained from a living blood relative, with approximately a 96 per cent one-year survival rate. The next best tissue matches come from other unrelated individuals of the same race as the recipient.

The Broad Scope of Uses for Anatomical Gifts

There are other, equally important stories about organ and tissue donations besides major organ transplantations, which captured newspaper headlines throughout the 1970s. These other accounts quietly testify to the almost miraculous yet little known opportunities for healing which anatomical gifts provide. Some twenty-five kinds of tissues and organs presently can be utilized in transplant procedures. Every day donated human skin, for example, is saving the lives of burn victims. Bones extracted from the dead are enabling individuals stricken with cancer or other diseases or injured in accidents to walk again. Pituitary glands removed from the dead are correcting serious pituitary deficiencies in some of the many thousands of children afflicted each year. The dura, the covering of the brain, provides repair tissue for extensive head injuries resulting from accidents or surgical

4 Life from Death

removal of tumors. Donated eyes, in addition to their role in various types of transplant surgery, are also used in research and medical education. Clearly, the human body's vast storehouse of tissues and organs can allow the dead, through advance planning, to bestow new life in almost countless ways.

The Emerging Field of Brain Implants

In addition to major organ transplants and restorative surgeries utilizing such tissues as skin and bones, a completely new area of transplantation has emerged in the past few years. Employing brain "implants" consisting either of fetal brain cells derived from spontaneously aborted fetuses or of adrenal tissue taken from the patient's own body, these transplants evidently are reversing many of the effects of Parkinson's and Huntington's disease. It is still too early to tell if the long-term results of these techniques will fully justify the early excitement aroused by them. But more than twenty transplant centers around the country are now following the lead of Vanderbilt University and Rush-Presbyterian-St. Luke's Medical Center in entering this field. The possibility of using brain implants to treat Alzheimer's and other neurological diseases, brain injury, stroke, and even mental retardation is already being seriously explored. In the coming years, this field will undoubtedly yield many revolutionary discoveries.

Religious Considerations

Many individuals appear uncertain as to whether their religion allows organ and tissue donation. Although they may sincerely desire to donate, their uncertainty makes them hesitant to commit themselves. *Faith of Our Patients,* a handbook of religious beliefs prepared by the Committee on Medicine and Religion of the Texas Medical Association, and a statement on this issue prepared by the National Kidney Foundation both confirm that the views of almost all religions in America not only permit but strongly encourage anatomical gifts. The following religious denominations do support such donations, provided the physical sanctity and moral integrity of both donor and recipient are respected: the Amish, the Baptists, the Christian Church (Disciples of Christ), Christian Scientists, the Church of Christ (Independent), the Church of Jesus Christ of Latter-Day Saints (Mormons), the Episcopal Church, the Greek Orthodox Church, the Independent Conservative Evangelical Church, the Lutheran Church, Orthodox and Reform Judaism, Presbyterians, the Roman Catholic Church, Seventh-Day Adventists, the United Church of Christ, and the United Methodists.

The beliefs of Jehovah's Witnesses do not specifically forbid organ donation or transplantation. The church views such procedures as a matter of individual conscience. Because of their prohibition against blood transfusion, however, any organs and tissues so employed must be completely drained of blood prior to transplantation into the body of a Jehovah's Witness. Such a requirement may, in reality, preclude certain types of transplant operations.

While Buddhism has no written policy on the issue and leaves the matter up to individual conscience, all acts of charity, including anatomical gifts, are in keeping with the basic tenets of Buddhist teaching. Hinduism likewise regards donation as an individual decision. Islam in the past did not permit organ donation by its followers. That official policy has now been reversed, provided that (1) donors consent in writing in advance and that (2) the organs of Moslem donors be transplanted immediately upon removal from the body and not be stored in organ banks.

Gypsies comprise one of the few ethnic or religious groups in the United States that oppose all forms of organ and tissue donation. Because of their belief in the physicality of the soul, which is said to retrace its steps for one year after the person dies, the bodies of gypsies must be preserved whole in keeping with their traditions.

If you remain in doubt about the teachings of your religion on organ donation and transplantation, plan to discuss the issue with your priest, minister, rabbi, or other religious leader.

Organ Donation and the Black Community

A number of studies have documented that the rate of organ donation by blacks, as well as by other ethnic minorities, is considerably lower percentagewise than that for whites. (Reports from organ procurement agencies show a 9.7 per cent black donation rate for 1986, as compared with a 5.5 per cent rate for Hispanics.) As a result, blacks and other racial minorities who need organ or tissue donations are far less likely than whites to receive a favorable tissue match. Due to subtle differences between black and white immune systems, the best choice for a black kidney transplant, for example, is an organ from a living related black donor (the second best is an organ from a living or dead unrelated black donor).

In general, this principle applies to all ethnic minorities: the best tissue matches will tend to come from a pool of donors of the same ethnic background. Since a very high percentage of transplant donors are white(some 84 per cent at present), most black and other ethnic transplant recipients receive organs from whites, with a less than ideal tissue match. The success rate for black and other ethnic transplant recipients is consequently much lower than that for whites.

The causes of this significantly lower donation rate on the part of blacks and other minorities are complex. According to ongoing studies of Dr. Clive Callender and his associates at Howard University Hospital's Transplant Center in Washington, D.C., five major factors account for the reluctance of blacks to make anatomical gifts. In ascending order of frequency and importance, these are as follows: (1) fear of the racist use of anatomical gifts; (2) mistrust of the medical profession; (3) fear that organs will be taken prematurely, before death; (4) religious beliefs; (5) lack of information.

While "racism" is not often cited as a cause of unwillingness to donate, it does crop up. Some blacks express the fear of a conspiracy to use their organs solely to benefit whites. Just the reverse is true. Only about 20 per cent of the organs needed by blacks actually come from black donors at present; thus the other four-fifths of transplants needed by blacks must come from white donors. Organ donation can and should become a cause of racial pride. There are few ways of better investing in one's ethnic heritage than by making and encouraging others to make anatomical gifts. When one begins to look upon one's body as a real physical resource which can be passed on to others, one enhances one's own sense of worth while benefiting the life of the community as well.

The second reason cited, mistrust of doctors, is deeply ingrained and related to the fear that organs will be removed prior to death. The matter of mistrust of the medical profession is perhaps the hardest factor to address because it is sometimes rooted in legitimate apprehensions which are not unique to the black community, from the daily cases of blatant malpractice and other abuses of authority to the simple failures on the part of medical professionals to communicate well.

Hospital administrative and legal safeguards have been set in place to prevent organ or body snatching like that portrayed in Robin Cook's *Coma*, the fictional thriller about a hospital that killed patients in order to harvest their organs. Such a story does appeal to that often unconscious mistrust people feel when confronted by a medical bureaucracy which seems to have lost touch with the human element to such a degree that they begin to suspect it of being yet another agent of death. As a matter of standard procedure, to alleviate such suspicions and prevent such abuses, the laws governing anatomical gifts in each of the fifty states and the District of Columbia, with the notable exception of Wyoming, specify that the physicians who care for patients cannot be involved in the transplant procedures. The medical team and the transplant team operate independently, and only after death has been certified by the attending physician, according to the legal definition of death in that particular state (in most cases, now defined as brain death), can the transplant team step in. Because donated organs go to those who (1) have been waiting the longest and (2) have the best tissue compatibility with the donated organ in question, the donation process normally remains anonymous in the best sense and not open to manipulation.

Concerning the issue of religious beliefs, few religions specifically forbid transplant procedures, as noted above. Almost all religions counsel love of neighbor as a first principle. And there may be no more generous and unique way to express concern for others than through an anatomical gift.

The final and most important reason cited for failure to donate, the lack of information, calls for the development of effective educational programs by leaders in the field and the implementation of these programs by community leaders, educational and religious institutions, and libraries.

Nowhere does the relative lack of black organ donations pose a greater problem than in the area of kidney transplants. The black community has a special need for donated kidneys. Kidney disease affects members of all races, to be sure, but it is now well documented that blacks experience chronic kidney failure to a much larger degree than any other racial group in America. High blood pressure is the chief culprit. Its occurrence has reached astronomical proportions in the black population, appearing many times more frequently among blacks than whites. Because blacks at present are much less willing than whites to donate organs, even those of deceased relatives, for the reasons cited above, concerted community efforts to promote black donation are needed to increase the pool of suitable organs for black recipients. Some 50 per cent of kidney patients are black, according to one estimate, while the typical organ procurement agency report shows that only about one in ten of the organ donors is black. Progress is being made, however; the number of black organ donations today is about ten per cent higher than what it was four years ago.

Hispanic Outreach Programs

Other ethnic communities in the United States are also becoming more involved in organ and tissue donation programs through outreach programs. Spanish-speaking individuals comprise the largest ethnic group (or constellation of related ethnic groups sharing a common language) in many large American cities. In New York City, for example, the Eye-Bank for Sight Restoration, Inc. has established a model program. Its new Hispanic Outreach program encourages eye donation among Spanish-speaking people in the Greater New York area. Other American cities and states with large Hispanic populations are in the process of creating similar programs. Illustrative of the way in which all such educational efforts must appeal to the shared cultural values of its intended audience, the Eye-Bank produced and now makes available a Spanish-language video, "Ilumina Una Vida." This video features the stories of five Hispanic corneal transplant recipients told in their own words, from a 15-year-old youth suffering from an eye injury to an older woman with a degenerative eye disease. It is narrated by a well-known New York radio talk-show hostess, Gilda Mirós, who also appears in tie-in public service announcements sent to Spanish-language radio and television stations. Also appearing in the video are the mother of an organ donor, who discusses her decision to donate her son's eyes and other organs after his death, a priest who talks about the support of the Catholic Church for organ and tissue donation, and an ophthalmologist who answers medical questions about transplant operations. The video was first previewed by community leaders and thereafter was made available for Hispanic community groups.

Contrasting Approaches to Organ Donation in France and the United States

The necessity for such grass roots programs to achieve needed gifts depends upon the history of the way in which anatomical gifts have been perceived from the beginning in this country, as voluntary acts of conscience. All appeals for anatomical donations must rest upon the sense of altruism and community spirit of individuals in order to succeed. Persons in the United States must make a choice to donate their bodies or body parts as anatomical gifts and so indicate their wishes in writing. In addition, the next of kin can also make a donation, providing the deceased did not expressly forbid it during life. In France and several other countries, by contrast, this element of individual decision-making is not operable. Presumed consent laws there permit automatic removal of organs and tissues after death unless the deceased or a family member expressly has objected. As a result, no shortage of tissues and organs for transplant purposes exists in France.

New state and federal donor laws. In the past two years, many states have legislated a new donor protocol: at the time of death, the next of kin *must* be asked by the hospital administrator to consider making an anatomical donation from the decedent's body. A new federal law to take effect October 1, 1987, likewise requires all hospitals that receive Medicare or Medicaid payments (which includes about 97 per cent of the nation's public and private hospitals) to identify potential organ donors and to notify those patients' relatives of their right to approve organ donations.

Education the key to increased anatomical donation in the United States. These new state and federal laws should increase the quantity of organs and tissues available for medical purposes, although severe shortages still exist at present. Some have advocated introducing financial incentives in order to alleviate such shortages, a procedure which has been used in the procurement of blood products for a number of years. Payments to individuals who agree to donate their bodies after death would undoubtedly increase the pool of anatomical gifts. It appears unlikely at present, however, that such a system will win acceptance. Because our society's approach, unlike that of France, depends upon the prior consent of the individual or the next of kin and tends to abjure financial incentives, the emphasis in this country must fall on education.

The promotion of education by the Florida Anatomical Gift Act. The Florida Anatomical Gift Act *is* exemplary in this respect. It establishes a continuing program of education for medical professionals, law enforcement agencies, and the public regarding the laws relating to anatomical gifts and the need for anatomical gifts. Because of the particular difficulties of making minority communities aware of the laws (and the particular needs of minorities for anatomical gifts, as noted above), the educational program specifically targets nonwhite, Hispanic, and Caribbean populations of the state.

The ongoing educational process. The purpose of this book is to further public and professional awareness about organ and tissue donation and transplantation. A knowledge of the laws governing anatomical gifts comprises one important aspect of this awareness. A complete account of the legal procedures that one must follow in each of the fifty states and the District of Columbia in order to make or to receive anatomical gifts is provided. An understanding of the laws governing anatomical gifts is no substitute, of course, for the generosity of spirit which motivates persons to make such gifts in the first place. But since many misconceptions do still exist in this area, such information may remove the first impediment to giving.

Organ Donation and the Human Community

In the final analysis, donation does not merely involve the question of the disposition of organs and tissues after death. Beneath the surface, what is at stake are certain fundamental beliefs and attitudes about the nature of human society, its solidarity and sense of community. The me-generation has had its say. At a time when selfishness and individual isolation no longer seem fashionable, organ donation represents one compelling mode of expression of the realization that we are intimately tied to our fellows; my well-being depends on yours, and yours on mine.

Children's Right to Make Anatomical Gifts

Participation in anatomical gift-giving has in the past been limited primarily to the adult domain. Many state legislatures, however, in recognition of children's rights as persons and the growing medical need for such donations have recently rewritten their laws, giving minors the stated right to make anatomical gifts as well. Those states which still have not legally recognized this right nevertheless generally follow the common law practice of allowing gifts from minors, with written parental consent. See the appropriate form in Appendix A.

Every Donor as a Potential Recipient

It is perhaps worth noting that the single group with the highest rate of card-carrying organ donors consists of those persons who have already received transplants from others. Those whose lives have been extended or whose quality of life has been improved through the foresight of others do not need to be reminded of the value of such donations. Each new day of their lives is a reminder of the importance of such thoughtfulness in advance planning. Many of us will require organ or tissue transplants of some type during the future. The best way to insure that transplantable tissues and organs will be available to all who need them is to become donors ourselves and to encourage others to do likewise.

Many states make organ donation as simple as filling out a short form on the back of your driver's license. If your state does not have this provision or you do not have a license, you may use the Uniform Donor Card in Appendix A, which is recognized as a legal document in every state. If you are under eighteen and your state does not make explicit provisions for your donation (see your state laws in chapter 4), you may use the "Anatomical Gift by a Living Minor Donor" form in the same Appendix in order to convey your wishes. Whether you are an adult or minor donor, make a photocopy of the appropriate form, fill it out and have it witnessed, and always carry it in your wallet or purse. Inform your family and friends and your personal physician, if you have one, of your decision. Even though you have filled out a donor card, family consent is still normally asked before donated organs are removed. If you wish to donate your entire body to a medical school, see the listing "Anatomical Gift Association" in Appendix F. You may decide to register your donation with one of the registry services listed in Appendix F. Additional support networks for potential donors and transplant recipients are also included in this same Appendix. There exist many voluntary and non-profit organizations in this field that can use your help. If you want to become involved in educating the public about organ donation or providing counseling or support to families who have donated or have a member in need of an organ transplant or wish to participate in volunteer work in some other area relating to anatomical gifts, agencies which can use your abilities are also listed in Appendix F.

Chapter 2: The Uniform Anatomical Gift Act

Originally approved by the American Bar Association and the National Conference of Commissioners on Uniform State law in 1968, the Uniform Anatomical Gift Act has provided the model for all state legislation on anatomical gifts for the past twenty years. Prior to 1968, most states already had some form of law addressing this issue, but these laws in most cases consisted of a bewildering hodgepodge of statutes which failed to offer consistent, systematic guidelines. Even with the eventual adoption of this model act in succeeding years by all fifty states and the District of Columbia, each state's uniform anatomical gift laws emerged in part as a reflection of the character of that particular state. Customized according to the wishes of the individual state legislatures, no two are exactly alike, and some deviate rather markedly from this standard. Although the Act has not, despite its name, succeeded in introducing complete uniformity in this area, it has served a valuable function. By providing a comprehensive framework for states to follow in rethinking and redrafting their anatomical gift laws, it has brought a degree of order out of chaos. The Act can serve as a common reference point for the consideration of the similarities and differences of the various state anatomical gift laws.

Analysis of and commentary on the Uniform Anatomical Gift Act appear in this chapter, along with the actual text of the Act itself. The chapter concludes with an overview of all fifty states' anatomical gift laws in light of this model.

The main questions which this model Act addresses are the following:

1. Who, during his or her lifetime, may legally make advance directives regarding the gift of his or her body or body parts after death?

2. What relative rights do the next of kin have in making anatomical gifts from the body of the deceased when the deceased has made no advance directives in this regard?

3. Whose rights shall prevail in the event that the next of kin and the decedent's expressed wishes are in conflict?

4. Who may legally become donees (recipients) of anatomical gifts, and for what purposes may these gifts be used?

5. What form may the execution of such gifts take, whether by will, by a card carried on the person, or by other written document, or, in the case of the next of kin, by telegraphic, recorded telephonic, or other recorded message?

6. Where may the document of the gift be kept, whether sent to and held by a specified donee or deposited in a hospital, bank or storage facility, or registry office that accepts it for safekeeping and for facilitation of procedures to implement it after the occurrence of death?

7. How may a gift be amended or revoked during the lifetime of the donor, whether by a signed statement or an oral one or by cancellation, destruction, or mutilation of a previously executed donor document?

8. What rights do the next of kin possess in the body of the deceased, and what provisions are made for the survivors' wishes for memorial services?

9. How shall the time of death of the donor be determined for the purposes of this Act?

10. How may a conflict of interest between the attending physician and the transplant team be avoided?

11. What safeguards from legal liability may be provided a person who acts in good faith in accord with the tenets of this Act or the anatomical gift laws of another state or country?

12. How can this Act be reconciled with the laws governing autopsies in a particular state?

In an effort to make donation simpler and procurement more effective, in light of an insufficient supply of organs and tissue available to meet current demands, the National Conference of Commissioners passed an amended version of this Uniform Anatomical Gift Act in August 1987, the first revision in almost twenty years. Since most states are still operating under the provisions of the old Act and the old Act forms the basis for the new, the text of the original Act is given below. The text of the revised version appears in Appendix B. In the coming years, more and more state legislatures are expected to amend their anatomical gift laws to bring them in line with the new, amended model.

The chief changes in the amended Uniform Anatomical Gift Act, which distinguish it from the old, are the following:

A. The group of individuals authorized to remove a part has been expanded to include nonphysician specialists properly trained and certified, namely, eye enucleators and other technicians.

B. The requirement of two witnesses signing a donor card or other document of gift has been eliminated.

C. A provision specifying the method of making a refusal of gift, in the case of individuals definitely opposed to donation for any purpose, is now included.

D. It is now clearly stated that an anatomical gift not revoked by a donor cannot be revoked after the donor's death by any other person.

E. In cases in which a donee is not specified, the hospital, not the attending physician, will now be regarded as the donee.

F. Donor cards circulated by various organizations that appear to limit the anatomical gift to only one organ, e.g., eyes, kidneys, etc., are not now to be construed as limiting the anatomical gift to that organ only, in the absence of a refusal to give other organs or of other contrary indications.

G. Revocation or amendment of a previous anatomical gift, in the absence of any other action or contrary indication by that individual before his death, does not now indicate an intention of the donor to refuse to make an anatomical gift.

H. "Grandparent" has been added to the list of survivors who may make a donation from the body of the deceased.

I. If a person defined as of a higher priority of relationship to the decedent is available and does not make a decision either to make a gift or to refuse to do so, a person of a lower class of relationship to the decedent may make a gift from the body.

J. In cases in which a body is in custody of the coroner or medical examiner, the removal of a part from the body for transplantation or therapy is now permitted under specific circumstances, provided no refusal or contrary indication by the decedent or objection by the next of kin is known.

K. In addition to the routine questions asked each individual upon admission to a hospital, a routine inquiry must now be made as to whether the patient is an organ or tissue donor. If so, the admitting person shall request a copy of the document of gift. If not, a person designated by the hospital shall discuss with the patient the option to make or refuse to make an anatomical gift. All such information is to be documented in the patient's medical record. So-called "required request" procedures are also mandated; the next of kin of patients who have not made or refused to make an anatomical gift must be asked to make a donation from the body of their deceased relative upon death. (Most states have already passed some form of required request statute, because of federal law requiring written protocols in this area by hospitals participating in Medicare or Medicaid.)

L. A reasonable search for a document of gift is to be conducted in the case of persons dead or near death when found by law enforcement officers, firemen, paramedics, or other emergency rescuers, or by hospitals in the case of admission of an individual at or near the time of death.

M. Each hospital is to establish an affiliation with an organ procurement agency for coordination of procurement and use of human bodies and parts.

N. The sale or purchase of human body parts from cadavers for transplantation or therapy is forbidden under force of fine and imprisonment.

Hereafter follows the actual text of the 1968 Uniform Anatomical Gift Act.

Text of 1968 Uniform Anatomical Gift Act

An act authorizing the gift of all or part of a human body after death for specified purposes.

Sec.
1. Definitions.
2. Persons Who May Execute an Anatomical Gift.
3. Persons Who May Become Donees; Purposes for Which Anatomical Gifts May be Made.
4. Manner of Executing Anatomical Gifts.
5. Delivery of Document of Gift.
6. Amendment or Revocation of the Gift.
7. Rights and Duties at Death.
8. Uniformity of Interpretation.
9. Short Title.

1.[Definitions]
  (a) "Bank or storage facility" means a facility licensed, accredited, or approved under the laws of any state for storage of human bodies or parts thereof.
  (b) "Decedent" means a deceased individual and includes a stillborn infant or fetus.
  (c) "Donor" means an individual who makes a gift of all or part of his body.
  (d) "Hospital" means a hospital licensed, accredited, or approved under the laws of any state; includes a hospital operated by the United States government, a state, or a subdivision thereof, although not required to be licensed under state laws.
  (e) "Part" means organs, tissues, eyes, bones, arteries, blood, other fluids, and any other portions

of a human body.

(f) "Person" means an individual, corporation, government or governmental subdivision or agency, business trust, estate, trust, partnership or association, or any other legal entity.

(g) "Physician" or "surgeon" means a physician or surgeon licensed or authorized to practice under the laws of any state.

(h) "State" includes any state, district, commonwealth, territory, insular possession, and any other area subject to the legislative authority of the United States of America.

2. [Persons Who May Execute an Anatomical Gift]

(a) Any individual of sound mind and 18 years of age or more may give all or any part of his body for any purpose specified in Section 3, the gift to take effect upon death.

(b) Any of the following persons, in order of priority stated, when persons in prior classes are not available at the time of death, and in the absence of actual notice of contrary indications by the decedent or actual notice of opposition by a member of the same or a prior class, may give all or any part of the decedent's body for any purpose specified in Section 3:

(1) the spouse,
(2) an adult son or daughter,
(3) either parent,
(4) an adult brother or sister,
(5) a guardian of the person of the decedent at the time of his death,
(6) any other person authorized or under obligation to dispose of the body.

(c) If the donee has actual notice of contrary indications by the decedent or that a gift by a member of a class is opposed by a member of the same or a prior class, the donee shall not accept the gift. The persons authorized by subsection (b) may make the gift after or immediately before death.

(d) A gift of all or part of a body authorizes any examination necessary to assure medical acceptability of the gift for the purposes intended.

(e) The rights of the donee created by the gift are paramount to the rights of others except as provided in Section 7 (d).

3. [Persons Who May Become Donees; Purposes for Which Anatomical Gifts May be Made]

The following persons may become donees of gifts of bodies or parts thereof for the purposes stated:

(1) any hospital, surgeon, or physician, for medical or dental education, research, advancement of medical or dental science, therapy, or transplantation; or

(2) any accredited medical or dental school, college or university for education, research, advancement of medical or dental science, or therapy; or

(3) any bank or storage facility, for medical or dental education, research, advancement of medical or dental science, therapy, or transplantation; or

(4) any specified individual for therapy or transplantation needed by him.

4. [Manner of Executing Anatomical Gifts]

(a) A gift of all or part of the body under Section 2(a) may be made by will. The gift becomes effective upon the death of the testator without waiting for probate. If the will is not probated, or if it is declared invalid for testamentary purposes, the gift, to the extent that it has been acted upon in good faith, is nevertheless valid and effective.

(b) A gift of all or part of the body under Section 2(a) may also be made by document other than a will. The gift becomes effective upon the death of the donor. The document, which may be a card designed to be carried on the person, must be signed by the donor in the presence of 2 witnesses who must sign the document in his presence. If the donor cannot sign, the document must be signed for him at his direction and in the presence of 2 witnesses who must sign the document in his presence. Delivery of the document of gift during the donor's lifetime is not necessary to make the gift valid.

(c) The gift may be made to a specified donee or without specifying a donee. If the latter, the gift may be accepted by the attending physician as donee upon or following death. If the gift is made to a specified donee who is not available at the time of death, the attending physician upon or following death, in the absence of any expressed indication that the donor desired otherwise, may accept the gift as donee. The physician who becomes a donee under this subsection shall not participate in the procedures for removing or transplanting a part.

(d) Notwithstanding Section 7(b), the donor may designate in his will, card, or other document of gift the surgeon or physician to carry out the appropriate procedures. In the absence of a designation or if the designee is not available, the donee or other person authorized to accept the gift may employ or authorize any surgeon or physician for the purpose.

(e) Any gift by a person designated in Section 2(b) shall be made by a document signed by him or made by his telegraphic, recorded telephonic, or other recorded message.

5. [Delivery of Document of Gift]

If the gift is made by the donor to a specified donee, the will, card, or other document, or an executed copy thereof, may be delivered to the donee to expedite the appropriate procedures immediately after death. Delivery is not necessary to the validity of the gift. The will, card, or other document, or an executed copy thereof, may be deposited in any hospital, bank or storage facility or registry office that accepts it for safekeeping or for facilitation of procedures after death. On request of any interested party upon or after the donor's death, the person in possession shall produce the document for examination.

6. [Amendment or Revocation of the Gift]

(a) If the will, card, or other document or executed copy thereof, has been delivered to a specified donee, the donor may amend or revoke the gift by:

(1) the execution and delivery to the donee of a signed statement, or

(2) an oral statement made in the presence of 2 persons and communicated to the donee, or

(3) a statement during a terminal illness or injury addressed to an attending physician and communicated to the donee, or

(4) a signed card or document found on his person or in his effects.

(b) Any document of gift which has not been delivered to the donee may be revoked by the donor in the manner set out in subsection (a), or by destruction, cancellation, or mutilation of the document and all executed copies thereof.

(c) Any gift made by a will may also be amended or revoked in the manner provided for amendment or revocation of wills, or as provided in subsection (a).

7. [Rights and Duties at Death]

(a) The donee may accept or reject the gift. If the donee accepts a gift of the entire body, he may, subject to the terms of the gift, authorize embalming and the use of the body in funeral services. If

14 Life from Death

the gift is of a part of the body, the donee, upon the death of the donor and prior to embalming, shall cause the part to be removed without unnecessary mutilation. After removal of the part, custody of the remainder of the body vests in the surviving spouse, next of kin, or other persons under obligation to dispose of the body.

(b) The time of death shall be determined by a physician who tends the donor at his death, or, if none, the physician who certifies the death. The physician shall not participate in the procedures for removing or transplanting a part.

(c) A person who acts in good faith in accord with the terms of this Act or with the anatomical gift laws of another state [or a foreign country] is not liable for damages in any civil action or subject to prosecution in any criminal proceeding for his act.

(d) The provisions of this Act are subject to the laws of this state prescribing powers and duties with respect to autopsies.

8. [Uniformity of Interpretation]

This Act shall be so construed as to effectuate its general purpose to make uniform the law of those states which enact it.

9. [Short Title]

This Act may be cited as the Uniform Anatomical Gift Act.

Overview and Commentary

All fifty states and the District of Columbia have passed some form of anatomical gift law. These statutes differ from one another in many respects. The following discussion, using the above cited 1968 Uniform Anatomical Gift Act as a point of reference, will highlight some of the major similarities and differences in these laws from state to state.

Section 1: "Definitions." The numerous variations in different states are, in most cases, of little or no consequence. One noteworthy addition to this section by several states, including Illinois and West Virginia, is a formal definition of "death" as "the irreversible cessation of total brain function." Since death has been legally defined in forty states and the District of Columbia as "brain death," this particular definition of death is implied although not explicitly stated in most state anatomical gift laws. Also worthy of note is the inclusion of stillborn infants or fetuses in the definition of "the decedent" in the Uniform Act. Today, the potential medical uses of tissues from aborted fetuses and the possibility of raising fetuses in order to "harvest" such tissues raises a host of troubling ethical issues still to be addressed by state and federal legislatures. It is already becoming standard practice, for example, for parents of doomed fetuses that will die soon after birth to donate their babies' organs to other babies. Much less common and more controversial is the use of tissues derived from fetuses to treat such illnesses as Parkinson's disease. Both the 1968 and 1987 versions of the Uniform Anatomical Gift Act are conservative in this regard, only taking into consideration the use of such tissues taken from stillborn fetuses.

Section 2: "Persons Who May Execute an Anatomical Gift." Most states require donors to be of "sound mind and eighteen years of age or older." Alaska and Nebraska specify "a person of sound mind who is nineteen years of age or more." At present, six states, Connecticut, Delaware,

Minnesota, North Dakota, Utah, and Wisconsin, make explicit provisions for minors to make anatomical gifts, with written parental permission. In Delaware, a married minor may make a donation without parental consent. In Utah, by contrast, a minor donor must not only have written parental or guardian approval but also be legally married. In Wisconsin, a parent may revoke a gift made by a minor unmarried decedent if the gift specifies donation of the entire body. Florida, Louisiana, Mississippi, and Texas require competence to execute a will under state law as the criterion of making a donation. Illinois specifies "any individual of sound mind and being an adult"; Maine, "any person of sound mind and of legal age"; Vermont, "any individual of sound mind who has attained the age of majority." Wisconsin allows "any individual of sound mind" to make a gift, with two exceptions, one already noted above: a gift by a minor, unmarried decedent of the entire body may be revoked by a parent; likewise, a gift by a married decedent of the entire body may be revoked by the surviving spouse unless the surviving spouse gave consent to the donation in writing prior to the donor's death.

Section 2, Subsection (b): "Donations by Next-of-Kin." All states provide survivors the right to make anatomical gifts from the body of the deceased. Only small variations in the statement of this right and the priorities among the survivors appear from state to state. All states allow for the next-of-kin to make gifts of tissues and organs from the bodies of deceased minors. Florida law is atypical in that the spouse cannot make a gift of the body of the deceased if any adult son or daughter of the dead person objects.

Section 3: "Persons Who May Become Donees; Purposes for Which Anatomical Gifts May be Made." Each state defines the "persons" who may be designated to receive anatomical gifts, with a broad definition of person which encompasses medical and dental schools, storage banks, and hospitals, as well as specifically named individuals, such as your sister Myrna or your friend Kanellas. Some state statutes provide a more detailed list of conceivable recipients (donees), as well as the purposes for which anatomical gifts may be employed; others offer briefer guidelines. Several states mandate that storage banks be non-profit organizations.

Section 4: "Manner of Executing Anatomical Gifts." All states specify donation by will or by other written document, in spite of the fact that donations made by will alone may not always be implementable, because of the short time after death that some organs remain viable for transplant purposes. Many states provide for written documentation of gift by means of a donor card, either on the back of a driver's license or a separate card. Almost all states at present require two witnesses to the execution of the document of gift. Utah specifies only one witness; California requires none. Whereas the role of witnesses in most states is simply to testify to the validity of the donor's signature, witnesses in Illinois, by signing the document of gift, certify that the donor "was of sound mind and memory and free from any undue influence and knows the objects of his bounty and affection." The Uniform Act makes allowance for the next of kin to make a gift of the decedent's body by means of written as well as telegraphic or telephonic message. This provision is intended to facilitate donation by survivors who are out of town or out of the country, allowing them to consent to donation via telephone or telegraph. This section also names the attending physician as donee in the absence of a designated donee or in the event the specified donee is not available. The attending physician may thereafter transfer the gift to a third party for transplantation or other accepted medical purpose.

Section 5: "Delivery of Document of Gift." This section, which Connecticut law poetically refers to as "Perfection of the Gift," covers the manner of filing or storage of the written documentation of anatomical gifts, i.e., record-keeping. The great majority of states make allowance for filing of the document with a hospital, bank or storage facility, or registry office or with a particular state office such as the department of health services, the anatomical board, the registrar of vital statistics, the county clerk's office, or the department of highway safety and motor vehicles. All such filings are voluntary and are merely for the purpose of facilitating donation after death. The laws of every state indicate that "delivery (that is, filing) is not necessary to the validity of the gift." In the event the document is filed, the person or institution in possession must produce the document for examination on request of any interested party upon or after the donor's death. Donations made via a driver's license application or renewal in New Mexico are automatically microfilmed and filed in the statewide organ and tissue registry.

Section 6: "Amendment or Revocation of the Gift." All fifty states and the District of Columbia make allowance for amendment or revocation, generally by either a written or an oral statement, in the case of a document of gift which has been delivered to a specified donee, or by destruction, cancellation, or mutilation, in the instance of a document of gift which has not been delivered to the donee.

Section 7: "Rights and Duties at Death." This section defines the donee as possessing absolute ownership in the gift, which he may use or transfer to another person. Many state laws declare the donee's rights as paramount to the rights of others; in other words, the donee's rights are superior to and take precedence over the rights of other interested parties. Certain particular limitations are placed on the donee's rights in all states, in order to allow the survivors to provide memorial or funeral services for the deceased. It is generally specified that a body part designated for donation must be removed without mutilation, whereupon the remainder of the body vests in the next of kin. This section also leaves open the question of the time of death, stating that it shall be determined by the attending physician or, in his absence, by the certifying physician. Some states, as noted above, have attempted to close any indeterminacy in this area through a formal definition of death, added in Section 1, "Definitions." Furthermore, the attending physician is expressly forbidden to participate in the transplant procedures in all states except Wyoming. This section, in addition, states that a person who acts in good faith in accord with the terms of this Act shall not be liable for damages in any civil or criminal proceeding. Finally, in those instances involving death by a suspected criminal action, the provisions of the anatomical gift act are subject to the laws of the state governing autopsies.

Section 8: "Uniformity of Interpretation"; Section 9: "Short Title." These last two sections simply state the general purpose of the act, namely, to make state anatomical gift laws more uniform, and the title by which the Act is to be known, the Uniform Anatomical Gift Act.

Chapter 3: The Legacy of the National Organ Transplant Act of 1984

The Congress enacted the National Organ Transplant Act of 1984 (Public Law 98-507) in response to increasing public concern about and involvement in the field of organ and tissue transplantation. Major provisions of the act included prohibition of the purchase of organs, the establishment of federal grants to organ procurement agencies in order to improve the overall organ procurement system in the United States, and the creation of a national organ-sharing system. (The actual text of the National Organ Transplant Act appears in Appendix C.) Perhaps the most significant of all the provisions of the Act, however, was the setting up a 25-member Task Force on Organ Transplantation, to consist of representatives from the fields of science and medicine, law, theology, ethics, health care financing, the social and behavioral sciences, and human organ procurement. Members of the general public and the health insurance industry also participated. The Surgeon General of the United States, the Commissioner of the Food and Drug Administration, and the Administrator of the Health Care Financing Administration served as ex officio members.

The Act commissioned the Task Force to conduct comprehensive examinations of the medical, legal, ethical, economic, and social issues presented by human organ procurement and transplantation, as well as to assess the safety, effectiveness, and costs of immunosuppressive medications used to prevent organ rejection in transplant patients. The report of the findings of the Task Force was to include a series of recommendations regarding major aspects of organ donation and transplantation.

Five work groups within the Task Force were formed to study the concerns identified by Congress. Relevant data were gathered through a variety of means: surveys, literature reviews, commissioned studies, consultations, and public testimony.

The final report of the Task Force represents the most comprehensive and wide-ranging study ever done in the United States on the field of organ procurement and transplantation. These highly influential recommendations are determining the future direction of thought on the subject of anatomical gifts. They are included hereafter in their entirety (with the exception of "immunosuppressive drugs," which is a summary of the full assessment). This report demands careful consideration by the general public, federal and state legislators, public health officials, the organ and tissue transplantation community, organized medicine, nursing, and the federal government. Included among its topics of study are: factors which diminish the number of organs available for transplant; recommendations for assuring equitable access by patients to organ transplantation, without regard to economic means; difficulties in coordinating procurement of viable organs for transplant purposes, including skin and bones; identification of barriers to organ and tissue donation; recommendations for the fostering and encouragement of research in all areas of organ donation and

18 Life from Death

transplantation; analysis of factors in reimbursement for transplant procedures by private insurers and the public sector; analysis of the process of diffusion and adaptation of transplantation technology by medical centers.

Although these recommendations of the Task Force do not have the force of law, they will clearly shape all laws and practices in this field for years to come. Since this is a book designed to promote education about anatomical gifts, the topic of public and professional education addressed in these recommendations demands special attention. In its regard for public education about organ and tissue donation as a top national priority, the Task Force has recommended that a national education program be established. Such a program would include development of curricula and materials for use in primary and secondary schools throughout the nation and of programs directed to special target populations, for example, minority groups, family units, and churches. Regarding professional education, the Task Force report suggests that medical and nursing schools (1) incorporate organ and tissue procurement and transplantation in the curriculum; (2) require demonstration of knowledge of organ and tissue donation and transplantation for certification; (3) establish programs to educate and encourage members of professional organizations of physicians and nurses both to participate in the referral of donors and to cooperate in the organ donation process.

RECOMMENDATIONS OF TASK FORCE

IMMUNOSUPPRESSIVE MEDICATIONS

The new immunosuppressive regimens, although expensive, proved to be cost-saving due to improvement in outcome; for this reason, and in order to ensure equitable access, the Task Force recommends that the federal government establish a mechanism to provide immunosuppressive drugs to recipients otherwise unable to pay for these drugs, when Medicare paid for the transplantation procedure.(See Appendix D for the amended text of Section 9335 of Title XI of the Social Security Act, which provides for payment of such drugs after January 1, 1987.)

ORGAN AND TISSUE DONATION AND PROCUREMENT

The serious gap between the *need* for organs and tissues and the *supply* of donors is common to all programs in organ transplantation, as well as to tissue banking and transplantation. The Task Force believes that substantial improvement in organ donation would ensue through new, innovative, and expanded programs in public and professional education and the coordination of efforts of the many organizations and agencies that engage in these activities. In particular, we support both the enactment of legislation in states that have not clarified determination of death based on irreversible cessation of brain function (the Uniform Determination of Death Act), and the enactment of legislation requiring implementation of routine hospital policies and procedures to provide the next-of-kin with the opportunity of donating organs and tissues. In addition, we found both a serious lack of uniform standards of accountability and quality assurance in organ and tissue procurement and a spectrum of effectiveness of procurement activities. Therefore, the Task Force supports the development both of minimum performance and certification standards, and of monitoring mechanisms.

Recommendations
1. To facilitate organ donation, the Task Force recommends:

- The Uniform Determination of Death Act be enacted by the legislatures of states that have not adopted this or a similar act.
- Each state medical association develop and adopt model hospital policies and protocols for the determination of death based upon irreversible cessation of brain function that will be available to guide hospitals in developing and implementing institutional policies and protocols concerning brain death.
- States enact legislation requiring coroners and medical examiners to give permission for organ and tissue procurement when families consent unless the surgical procedure would compromise medicolegal evidence. Further, the legislation should (1) require coroners and medical examiners to develop policies that facilitate the evaluation of all nonheart-beating cadavers under their jurisdiction for organ and tissue donation, and (2) provide the next-of-kin with the opportunity to consider postmortem tissue donation. The Task Force further recommends that coroners develop agreements with local tissue banks to help implement these policies.

2. To facilitate the identification of potential donors and provide the next-of-kin with appropriate opportunities to donate organs and tissues, the Task Force recommends that:

- All health professionals involved in caring for potential organ and tissue donors voluntarily accept the responsibility for identifying these donors and for referring such donors to appropriate organ procurement organizations.
- Hospitals adopt routine inquiry/required request policies and procedures for identifying potential organ and tissue donors and for providing next-of-kin with appropriate opportunities for donation.
- The Joint Commission on the Accreditation of Hospitals develop a standard that requires all acute care hospitals to both have an affiliation with an organ procurement agency and have formal policies and procedures for identifying potential organ and tissue donors and for providing next-of-kin with appropriate opportunities for donation.
- The Department of Defense and the Veterans Administration require their hospitals to have routine inquiry policies.
- The Health Care Financing Administration incorporate into the Medicare conditions of participation for hospitals certified under subpart U of the Code of Federal Regulations, a condition that requires hospitals to have routine inquiry policies.
- All state legislatures formulate, introduce, and enact routine inquiry legislation.
- The Commission for Uniform State Laws develop model legislation that requires acute care hospitals to develop an affiliation with an organ procurement agency and to adopt routine inquiry policies and procedures.

3. In regard to living donors and the donor pool, the Task Force recommends that:

- A study of the potential donor pool be conducted using data available through the National Hospital Discharge Survey, supplemented by regional retrospective hospital record reviews.
- Living donors be fully informed about the risks of kidney donation. Health care professionals must guarantee that the decision to donate is entirely voluntary. In the case of all living donors, special emphasis should be placed on histocompatibility.
- A national registry of human donors *not* be established.

4. To improve public education in organ and tissue donation, the Task Force recommends that:

- Educational efforts aimed at increasing organ donation among minority populations be developed and implemented, so that the donor population will come to more closely resemble the ethnic profile of the pool of potential recipients in order to gain the advantage of improved donor and recipient

immunologic matching.
• At the regional level, single consortia, composed of public, private, and voluntary groups that have an interest in education on organ and tissue donation should develop, coordinate, and implement public and professional education to supplement, but not replace, activities undertaken by local programs.
• A single organization, such as the American Council on Transplantation, composed of public, private, and voluntary groups that are national in scope and have an interest in education for organ and tissue donation, should develop and coordinate broad scale public and professional educational programs and materials on the national level. This umbrella organization would both develop and distribute model educational materials for use by national and local organizations and plan, coordinate, and develop national efforts using nationwide electronic and print media.
• A national educational program should be established, similar to the High Blood Pressure Education Program of National Institutes of Health's National Heart, Lung, and Blood Institute, aimed at increasing organ donation. This program should include development of curricula and instructional materials for use in primary and secondary schools throughout the nation, and of programs directed to special target populations, e.g., minority groups, family units, and churches.

5. To improve professional education in organ and tissue donation, the Task Force recommends that:
• Medical and nursing schools incorporate organ and tissue procurement and transplantation in the curriculum.
• The Accreditation Council of Graduate Medical Education, the body responsible for accrediting residency programs, include requirements for exposure to organ and tissue donation and transplantation in relevant programs in graduate medical education, such as emergency and critical care medicine and the neurological sciences.
• Each appropriate medical and nursing specialty require demonstration of knowledge of organ and tissue donation and transplantation for certification.
• All professional associations of physicians and nurses involved in caring for potential organ and tissue donors (especially neurosurgeons, trauma surgeons, emergency physicians; and critical care, emergency room, and trauma team nurses), establish programs to educate and encourage their members both to participate in the referral of donors and to cooperate in the organ donation process.
• Organizations of physician specialists who frequently come in contact with organ and tissue donors should establish mechanisms, such as a committee on transplantation, to facilitate communication and cooperation with physicians in the transplantation specialties.

6. The Task Force recommends that organ procurement agencies and procurement specialists be certified:
• Professional peer group organizations, e.g., the North American Transplant Coordinators Organization, should establish mechanisms for certification of nonphysician organ and tissue procurement specialists and standards for evaluation of performance at regular intervals.
• The Department of Health and Human Services should certify no more than one Organ Procurement Agency in any standard metropolitan statistical area or existing organ donor referral area, whichever is larger.
• The Department of Health and Human Services should use the criteria developed by the Association of Independent Organ Procurement Agencies as a guideline to develop consistent certification standards for Independent Organ Procurement Agencies and Hospital-Based Organ Procurement Agencies.
• The Department of Health and Human Services should establish minimal performance produc-

tivity standards as part of a recertification process that could be conducted at regular intervals. Such standards should address procurement activity, organizational structure and programs, staff training and competence, and fiscal accountability.
• Appropriate peer organizations should develop standards for certifying tissue banks and for conducting performance evaluations at regular intervals. Such standards should include assessment of quality and quantity of performance, organizational structure and programs, staff training and competency, and fiscal responsibility.

7. The Task Force recommends that the Department of Health and Human Services collect uniform data on organ procurement activities of all Organ Procurement Agencies, including, at a minimum, the number of kidneys procured, kidneys transplanted, kidneys procured but not transplanted, kidneys exported abroad, and relevant cost data. (The data could be collected through the Organ Procurement and Transplantation Network or from each Organ Procurement Agency.)

• The Department of Health and Human Services require all Organ Procurement Agencies to have, as a minimum, a form of governance that would be similar to that described for the national Organ Procurement and Transplantation Network, i.e., it should include adequate representation from each of the following categories: transplant surgeons from participating transplant centers, transplant physicians from participating transplant centers, histocompatibility experts from the affiliated histocompatibility laboratories, representatives of the Organ Procurement Agencies, and members of the general public. Representatives of the general public should have no direct or indirect professional affiliation with the transplant centers or the Organ Procurement Agency. Not more than 50 percent of the Board of Directors may be surgeons or physicians directly involved in transplantation, and at least 20 percent should be members of the general public. Where the governing boards of existing Organ Procurement Agencies differ from this composition, it is desirable that those boards be modified over a maximum of two years to achieve this distribution. The Task Force believes that all Organ Procurement Agency boards should consider immediate steps to include public representatives.

8. To facilitate more effective collaboration between organ and tissue banks, the Task Force recommends that formal cooperative agreements be established among eye, skin, and bone banks.

• All Organ Procurement Agencies evaluate all potential donors for multiple organ and tissue donation.
• Organ procurement agencies and tissue banks enter into formal agreements for collaborative programs to educate the public and health professionals and to coordinate donor identifications, discussions with next-of-kin, and the procurement process.

ORGAN SHARING

The Task Force believes that establishment of a unified national system of organ sharing that encompasses a patient registry and coordinates organ allocation and distribution will go far in assuring equity and fairness in the allocation of organs. In addition, a national network organization, through adoption of agreed upon standards and policies, may serve as the vehicle both for improving matching of donors and recipients and for improving access of groups at special disadvantage (the sensitized and small pediatric recipients); thus, the outcome of organ transplantation in this country will surely improve. The development of a national network will permit the gathering and analysis of comprehensive data and, through the establishment of a scientific registry, will facilitate the exchange of new information vital to progress in the field. We assisted the Office of Organ Transplantation in developing specifications for a model network, and urge the National Organ Procurement and Transplantation Network be established promptly; in addition, we urge Congress to appropriate the funds necessary to initiate the development of the scientific registry.

Recommendations

1. The Task Force recommends that a single national system for organ sharing be established; that its participants agree on and adopt uniform policies and standards by which all will abide; and that its governance include a broad range of viewpoints, interests, and expertise, including the public.

• The national network establish a method to systematically collect and analyze data related to both kidney and extrarenal organ procurement and transplantation. Further, to provide an ongoing evaluation of the scientific and clinical status of organ transplantation, a scientific registry of the recipients of kidney and extrarenal organ transplants should be developed and administered through the national network, and the Task Force urges the Congress to appropriate funds to initiate this activity.

• Organ sharing be mandated for perfectly matched (HLA A, B, and DR) donor-recipient pairs and for donors and recipients with zero antigen mismatches (assuming that at least one antigen has been identified at each locus for both donor and recipient).

• A system of serum sharing and/or allocation of organs based on computer-determined prediction of a negative crossmatch, be developed to increase the rate of transplantation in the highly sensitized patient group by increasing the effective size of the donor pool.

• Blood group O organs be transplanted only into blood group O recipients.

• Because of the limited local and regional donor pools available to small pediatric patients, the national organ-sharing system should be designed to provide pediatric extrarenal transplant patients access to a national pool of pediatric donors.

• The national organ-sharing network, when established, should conduct ongoing reviews of organ procurement activities, particularly organ discard rates, and develop mechanisms to assist those agencies and programs with high discard rates. In the meantime, we recommend that the Department of Health and Human Services conduct a study to identify why procured kidneys are not transplanted and why the discard rates vary widely from one organ procurement program to another.

2. The Task Force recommends regional centralization of histocompatibility testing where it is geographically feasible, and standardization of key typing reagents and crossmatching techniques.

3. The Task Force recommends that the Congress appropriate funds to establish a national ESRD registry that would combine a renal transplant registry with a dialysis registry. The Task Force further recommends that the national organ-sharing network be represented on any committee responsible for management and data analysis of a national ESRD registry.

EQUITABLE ACCESS TO ORGAN TRANSPLANTATION

The process of selecting patients for transplantation, both in the formation of the waiting list and in the final selection for allocation of the organ, is generally fair and for the most part has succeeded in achieving equitable distribution of organs. However, the Task Force believes that these processes must be defined by each center and by the system as a whole, and that the standards for patient selection and organ allocation must be based solely on objective medical criteria that are applied fairly and are open to public examination. Moreover, as vital participants in the process, the public must be included in developing these standards and in implementing the policies. We recognized the complex conflict between need for an organ (medical urgency) and the probability of success of the transplant, and did not presume to make recommendations in this sphere; rather we believe that a thoughtful process of development of policies for organ allocation, which takes into account both medical utility and good stewardship, must take place within a broadly representative group.

The Task Force condemns commercialization of organ transplantation and the exploitation of living unrelated donors. The Task Force also addressed the difficult problem of offering organ transplantation to non-immigrant aliens. Because transplantable organs are scarce, we have recommended that no more than 10 per cent of all cadaveric kidney transplants in any center be performed in non-immigrant aliens and that extrarenal transplants be offered only when no suitable recipient who is a resident of this country can be found. The Task Force also concluded that equitable access of patients to extrarenal organ transplantation is impeded unfairly by financial barriers, and recommends that all transplant procedures that are efficacious and cost effective be made available to patients, regardless of their ability to pay, through existing public and private health insurance or, as a last resort, through a publicly funded program for patients who are without insurance, Medicare, or Medicaid who could not otherwise afford to obtain the organ transplant.

Recommendations

1. The Task Force recommends that each donated organ be considered a national resource to be used for the public good; the public must participate in the decisions of how this resource can be used to best serve the public interest.

2. In order that patients and their physicians be fully informed, the Task Force recommends that:

• Health professionals provide unbiased, timely, and accurate information to all patients who could possibly benefit from organ transplantation so that they can make informed choices about whether they want to be evaluated and placed on a waiting list.

• Information be published annually for patients and physicians on the graft and patient survival data by transplant center. A clear explanation of what the data represent should preface the presentation of data. A strong recommendation should be made in the publication that each patient discuss with his or her attending physician the circumstances of medical suitability for transplantation and where that patient may best be served.

3. The Task Force recommends that selection of patients both for waiting lists and for allocation of organs be based on medical criteria that are publicly stated and fairly applied.

• The criteria for prioritization be developed by a broadly representative group that will take into account both need and probability of success. Selection of patients otherwise equally medically qualified should be based on length of time on the waiting list.

• Selection of patients for transplants not be subject to favoritism, discrimination on the basis of race or sex, or ability to pay.

• Organ-sharing programs that are designed to improve the probability of success be implemented in the interests of justice and the effective and efficient use of organs, and that the effect of mandated organ sharing be constantly assessed to identify and rectify imbalances that might reduce access of any group.

4. The Task Force recommends that non-immigrant aliens not comprise more than 10 percent of the total number of kidney transplant recipients at each transplant center, until the

Organ Procurement and Transplantation Network has had an opportunity to review the issue. In addition, extrarenal organs should not be offered for transplantation to a non-immigrant alien unless it has been determined that no other suitable recipient can be found.

5. The Task Force emphatically rejects the commercialization of organ transplantation and recommends that:

- Exportation and importation of donor organs be prohibited except when distribution is arranged or coordinated by the Organ Procurement and Transplantation Network and the organs are to be sent to recognized national networks. Even then, when an organ is to be exported from the United States, documentation must be available to demonstrate that all appropriate efforts have been made to locate a recipient in the United States and/or Canada. The Task Force has every expectation that these international organ sharing programs will be reciprocal.
- The practice of soliciting or advertising for non-immigrant aliens and performing a transplant for such patients, without regard to the waiting list, cease.
- Transplanting kidneys from living unrelated donors should be prohibited when financial gain rather than altruism is the motivating factor.
- To the extent federal law does not prohibit the intrastate sale of organs, states should prohibit the sale of organs from cadavers or living donors within their boundaries.
- As a condition of membership in the Organ Procurement Transplant Network (OPTN), each transplant center be required to report every transplant or organ procurement procedure to the OPTN. Moreover, transplantation procedures should not be reimbursed under Medicare, Medicaid, CHAMPUS, and other public payers, unless the transplant center meets payment, organ-sharing, reporting, and other guidelines to be established by the OPTN or another agency administratively responsible for the development of such guidelines. Failure to comply with these guidelines will require that the center show cause why it should not be excluded from further organ sharing through the OPTN.
- In order to insure that patients in need of an extrarenal organ transplant can obtain procedures regardless of ability to pay, the Task Force recommends that private and public health benefit programs, including Medicare and Medicaid, should cover heart and liver transplants, including outpatient immunosuppressive therapy that is an essential part of post-transplant care.
- A public program should be set up to cover the costs of people who are medically eligible for organ transplants but who are not covered by private insurance, Medicare, or Medicaid and who are unable to obtain an organ transplant due to lack of funds.

DIFFUSION OF ORGAN TRANSPLANTATION TECHNOLOGY

The number of organ transplant centers in this country is rapidly increasing. As the technical aspects of the procedures have been mastered and patient management has become better understood and standardized, it is not surprising that diffusion of this technology has taken place. The issue of designating centers for reimbursement purposes requires careful consideration of many factors, including cost, criteria for facilities, resources, staffing, and the training and experience of personnel. After lengthy debate, the majority of the Task Force agreed with the widely accepted principle within surgery that the volume of surgical procedures performed is positively associated with outcomes and inversely related to cost and believe that this principle applies to organ transplantation procedures as well. Therefore, we recommend that a minimum volume criterion be enforced, together with other criteria defining the minimal outcome of transplantation procedures. In the context of scarcity of donor organs, we strongly support regulating diffusion of transplantation technology.

Recommendations

1. The Task Force recommends that transplant centers be designated by an explicit, formal process using well-defined, published criteria.

2. The Task Force recommends that the Department of Health and Human Services designate centers to perform kidney, heart, and liver transplants, and that the centers be evaluated against explicit criteria to ensure that only those institutions with requisite capabilities are allowed to perform the procedures.

3. The Task Force recommends that the Department of Health and Human Services adopt minimum criteria for kidney, heart, and liver transplant centers that address facility requirements, staff experience, training requirements, volume of transplants to be performed each year, and minimum patient and graft survival rates.

RESEARCH IN ORGAN TRANSPLANTATION

Organ transplantation continues to evolve and improve at a fast pace. Strong research programs in basic and applied clinical sciences have been vital to this fortunate development. As is clearly evident in the concerns of the public that resulted in the enactment of the National Organ Transplant Act, research also is needed in the social, ethical, economic, and legal aspects of organ donation and transplantation. The Task Force acknowledges the important role played by the NIH in transplantation research, and encourages the NIH to coordinate the free flow of information regarding transplant-related research through an interinstitutional council on transplantation. Moreover, we strongly urge that research on all aspects of transplantation be fostered and encouraged and that funding for this vital effort be increased. Therein lies the future of transplantation.

Recommendations

1. The Task Force recommends that basic research continue to receive high priority.

2. The Task Force recommends that both laboratory and clinical research of an applied nature directly related to transplantation also be fostered, encouraged and increasingly funded. For the immediate benefit of patients, the Task Force further recommends that research be aggressively pursued in organ preservation and optimal immunosuppression techniques. The Task Force also wishes to emphasize the importance of sponsoring prospective clinical trials, involving multiple institutions, to solve certain problems in patient management.

3. The Task Force recommends that continuing attention be devoted to collecting complete information on the status and efficacy of transplantation treatments.

4. The Task Force recognizes that the interaction and exchange of information between the agencies involved in transplantation research and its funding must be encouraged. Therefore, we recommend that the National Institutes of Health be provided with resources to establish an interagency and interinstitute Council on Transplantation that will serve as a focus for this activity.

ESTABLISHMENT OF AN ADVISORY BOARD ON ORGAN TRANSPLANTATION

At the final meeting of the Task Force, where this report was adopted, a recommendation was made to establish a National Organ Transplantation Advisory Board. The Task Force agreed in concept that a national group to advise the Secretary of Health and Human Services would continue to be needed to monitor implementation of the Task Force's findings and serve in an advisory capacity on organ procurement and transplantation issues. Therefore we adopted the following recommendation:

The Task Force recommends that a National Organ Transplantation Advisory Board be authorized and funded to review, evaluate, and advise with regard to the implementation of the recommendations of the Task Force on Organ Transplantation, to serve in an advisory capacity to the Office of Organ Transplantation and to other transplant-related activities of the Department of Health and Human Services, and that this board be established in the Office of the Secretary.

Chapter 4: State Anatomical Gift Laws

This chapter consists of a point-by-point presentation of each state's anatomical gift laws. All fifty states and the District of Columbia are covered, in alphabetical order.

ALABAMA

§ 22-19-40. Short title. This article may be cited as the Alabama Uniform Anatomical Gift Act.

§ 22-19-41. Definitions. For the purposes of this article, the following terms shall have the meanings respectively ascribed to them by this section:

(1) BANK OR STORAGE FACILITY. A facility licensed, accredited or approved under the laws of any state for the storage of human bodies, or parts thereof.

(2) DECEDENT. A deceased individual and includes a stillborn infant or fetus.

(3) DONOR. An individual who makes a gift of all, or part of, his body.

(4) HOSPITAL. A hospital licensed under the laws of the state of Alabama, or any subdivision thereof, or under the laws and regulations of the United States government, or any agency thereof.

(5) PART. Organs, tissues, eyes, bones, arteries, blood or other fluids and any other portions of a human body.

(6) PERSON. An individual, corporation, government or governmental subdivision or agency, business trust, estate trust, partnership or association or any other legal entity.

(7) PHYSICIAN OR SURGEON. A physician or surgeon licensed or authorized to practice under the laws of any state.

§ 22-19-42. Who may donate all, or part of, body; rights of donees. (a) Any individual of sound mind and 18 years of age or older may give all, or any part of, his body for any purposes specified in section 22-19-43, the gift to take effect upon death.

(b) Any of the following persons, in order of priority stated, when persons in prior classes are not available at the time of death, and in the absence of actual notice of contrary indications by the decedent or actual notice of opposition by a member of the same or a prior class, may give all, or any part of, the decedent's body for any purpose specified in section 22-19-43:

   (1) The spouse;
   (2) An adult son or daughter;
   (3) Either parent;
   (4) An adult brother or sister;
   (5) A guardian of the person of the deceased at the time of his death; or
   (6) Any other person authorized or under obligation to dispose of the body.

(c) If the donee has actual notice of contrary indications by the decedent or that a gift by a member of a class is opposed by a member of the same or of a prior class, the donee shall not accept the gift. The persons authorized by subsection (b) of this section may make the gift after or immediately before death.

(d) A gift of all, or part of, a body authorizes any examination necessary to assure medical acceptability of the gift for the purposes intended.

(e) The rights of the donee created by the gift are paramount to the rights of others, except as provided by subsection (d) of section 22-19-47.

§ 22-19-43. Institutions or persons who may become donees; purposes for which anatomical gifts may be made. The following persons may become donees of gifts of bodies, or parts thereof, for the purposes stated:

(1) Any hospital, surgeon or physician for medical or dental education, research, advancement of medical or dental science, therapy or transplantation.

(2) Any accredited medical or dental school or college or university for education, research, advancement of medical or dental science or therapy;

(3) Any bank or storage facility for medical or dental education, research, advancement of medical or dental science, therapy or transplantation; or

(4) Any specified individual for therapy or transplantation needed by him.

§ 22-19-44. Modes of executing gift. (a) A gift of all or part of the body under subsection (a) of section 22-19-42 may be made by will. The gift becomes effective upon the death of the testator without waiting for probate. If the will is not probated, or if is declared invalid for testamentary purposes, the gift, to the extent that it has been acted upon in good faith, is nevertheless valid and effective.

(b) A gift of all or part of the body under subsection (a) of section 22-19-42 may also be made by document other than a will. The gift becomes effective upon the death of the donor. The document, which may be a card designed to be carried upon the person, must be signed by the donor in the presence of two witnesses, who must sign the document in his presence. If the donor cannot sign, the document may be signed for him at his direction and in his presence and in the presence of two witnesses, who must sign the document in his presence. Delivery of the document of gift during the donor's lifetime is not necessary to make the gift valid.

(c) The gift may be made either to a specified donee or without naming a donee. If the donee is not named, the attending physician may accept as donee upon or following death. If the gift is made to a specified donee who is not available at the time and place of death, the attending physician may, in the absence of any expressed indication that the donor desired otherwise, accept the gift as donee. The physician who becomes a donee under this subsection shall not participate in the procedures for removing or transplanting a part.

(d) The donor may designate in his will, card or other document of gift the surgeon or physician to carry out the appropriate procedures. In the absence of a designation, or if the designee is not available, the donee or other person authorized to accept the gift may comply or authorize any surgeon or physician for the purpose.

(e) Any gift by a person designated in subsection (b) of section 22-19-42 shall be made by a document signed by him or made by his telegraphic, recorded telephonic or other recorded message.

§ 22-19-45. Delivery or deposit of gift document. If the gift is made by the donor to a specified donee, the will, card or other document, or an executed copy thereof, may be delivered to the donee to expedite the appropriate procedures immediately after death. Delivery is not necessary to the validity of the gift. The will, card or other document, or an executed copy thereof, may be deposited in any hospital, bank or storage facility or registry office that accepts it for safekeeping or for facilitation of procedures after death. On request of any interested party upon, or after, the donor's death, the person in possession shall produce the document for examination.

§ 22-19-46. Amendment or revocation of gift. (a) If the will, card or other document, or executed copy thereof, has been delivered to a specified donee, the donor may amend or revoke the gift by:

(1) The execution and delivery to the donee of a signed statement;

(2) An oral statement made in the presence of two persons and communicated to the donee;

(3) A statement during a terminal illness or injury addressed to an attending physician and communicated to the donee; or

(4) A signed card or document found on his person or in his effects.

(b) Any document of gift which has not been delivered to the donee may be revoked by the donor in the manner set out in subsection (a) of this section or by destruction, cancellation or mutilation of the document and all executed copies thereof.

(c) Any gift made by a will may also be amended or revoked in the manner provided for amendment or revocation of wills or as provided in subsection (a) of this section.

§ 22-19-47. Powers, duties and liabilities upon death. (a) The donee may accept or reject the gift. If the donee accepts a gift of the entire body, he may, subject to the terms of the gift, authorize embalming and the use of the body in funeral services. If the gift is of a part of the body, the donee, upon the death of the donor and prior to embalming, shall cause the part to be removed without unnecessary mutilation. After removal of the part, custody of the remainder of the body vests in the surviving spouse, next of kin or others under obligation to dispose of the body.

(b) The time of death shall be determined by a physician who attends the donor at his death or, if none, the physician who certifies the death. The physician shall not participate in the procedures for removing or transplanting a part.

(c) A person who acts in good faith in accord with the terms of this article or with the anatomical gift laws of another state or a foreign country is not liable for damages in any civil action or subject to prosecution in any criminal proceeding for his act.

(d) The provisions of this article are subject to the laws of this state prescribing powers and duties with respect to autopsies.

Alabama has also enacted the following section which is not technically part of its uniform anatomical gift act but has direct bearing on it:

§ 22-19-60. Gift made by execution of affidavit to be filed with department of public safety; notice of intent and specific gift to be noted on driver's license or nondriver identification card; when gift effective; execution and acknowledgment of affidavit; effect of expiration, revocation, renewal, etc. of license or card. (a) A gift of all or part of the body may also be made by the holder of a valid Alabama driver's license or nondriver identification card by the execution of a sworn affidavit to be filed with the department of public safety.

(b) Notice of intent to make a gift shall be noted on the driver's license or nondriver identification card of the donor in a manner to be determined by the department of public safety and there shall also be noted thereon the specific gift of the donor in accordance with the following legend:

E--Eye
K--Kidney
H--Heart
Li--Liver
L--Lungs
A--All (everything)

(c) The gift shall become effective on the death of the donor without any formal requirements of delivery.

(d) The affidavit shall be signed by the holder of the driver's license or nondriver identification card in the presence of two witnesses who shall acknowledge the affidavit in the presence of the donor.

(e) The gift shall become invalidated upon the expiration, cancellation, revocation or suspension of a driver's license or nondriver identification card.

(f) The gift shall not become invalidated if the driver's license or nondriver identification card is properly renewed before the expiration date.

(g) The amendatory provisions of subsection (b) of this section shall commence on the date of renewal of the driver's license or nondriver identification card of the donor.

ALASKA

§ 13.50.010. Persons who may execute an anatomical gift. (a) A person of sound mind who is 19 or more years of age may make a gift to take effect upon death, of all or a part of the person's body for a purpose specified in Section 13.50.020.

(b) When persons in prior classes are not available at the time of death, and in the absence of actual notice of contrary indications by the decedent or actual notice of opposition by a member of the same or a prior class, any of the following persons, in order of priority listed, may give all or a part of the decedent's body for a purpose specified in Section 13.50.020:

(1) the spouse;
(2) an adult son or daughter;
(3) either parent;
(4) an adult brother or sister;
(5) a guardian of the decedent at the time of death;
(6) any other person authorized or under obligation to dispose of the body.

(c) The persons authorized by (b) of this section may make the gift after or immediately before death.

(d) If the donee has actual notice of contrary indications by the decedent or that a gift by a member of a class is opposed by a member of the same or a prior class, the donee may not accept the gift.

(e) A gift of all or a part of a body authorizes any examination necessary to assure medical acceptability of the gift for the purposes intended.

(f) The rights of the donee created by the gift are superior to the rights of others except as provided in Section 13.50.060(d).

§ 13.50.020. Potential donees and purposes for which anatomical gifts may be made. The following persons may become donees of gifts of a decedent's body or a part of a decedent's body for the purposes stated:

(1) a hospital, surgeon, or physician, for medical or dental education, research, advancement of medical or dental science, therapy, or transplantation;

(2) an accredited medical or dental school, college or university for education, research, advancement of medical or dental science, or therapy;

(3) a bank or storage facility, for medical or dental education, research, advancement of medical

or dental science, therapy or transplantation; or

(4) a specified individual for therapy or transplantation needed by the individual.

§ 13.50.030. Manner of executing anatomical gifts. (a) A gift of all or a part of the body under Section 13.50.010(a) may be made by will. The gift takes effect upon the death of the testator before probate. If the will is not probated, or is declared invalid for testamentary purposes, the gift, to the extent that it has been acted upon in good faith, is valid and effective.

(b) A gift of all or part of the body under Section 13.50.010(a) may be made by a document other than a will. The gift takes effect upon the death of the donor. The document, which may be a card designed to be carried on the person, shall be signed by the donor in the presence of two witnesses who shall sign the document in the donor's presence. If the donor cannot sign, the document may be signed for the donor at the donor's direction and in the donor's presence in the presence of two witnesses who must sign the document in the donor's presence. Delivery of the document of gift during the donor's lifetime is not necessary to make the gift valid.

(c) A gift may be made to a specified donee or without specifying a donee. If a donee is not specified, the gift may be accepted by the attending physician as donee upon or after death. If the gift is made to a specified donee who is not available at the time and place of death, the attending physician upon or following death, in the absence of any express indication that the donor desired otherwise, may accept the gift as donee.

(d) The donor may designate in a will, card, or other document of gift the surgeon or physician to carry out the appropriate procedure for removing or transplanting a part of the decedent's body. In the absence of a designation or if the designee is not available, the donee or other person authorized to accept the gift may employ or authorize any surgeon or physician for the purpose of removing or transplanting a part of the decedent's body.

(e) A gift by a person designated in Section 13.50.010(b) shall be made by a document signed by the person or made by the person's telegraphic, recorded telephonic, or other recorded message.

§ 13.50.040. Delivery of document of gift. If the gift is made by the donor to a specified donee, the will, card, or other document, or an executed copy of it, may be delivered to the donee to expedite the appropriate procedure for removing or transplanting a part of the decedent's body immediately after death. Delivery is not necessary for a valid gift. The will, card, or other document, or an executed copy of it, may be deposited in a hospital, bank or storage facility, or registry office to facilitate the procedure for removing or transplanting a part of the decedent's body after death. On the request of any interested person upon or after the donor's death, the person in possession of the document shall produce the document for examination.

§ 13.50.050. Amendment or revocation of gift. (a) If the will, card, or other document or executed copy of it is delivered to a specified donee, the donor may amend or revoke the gift by

(1) the execution and delivery to the donee of a signed statement;

(2) an oral statement made in the presence of two persons and communicated to the donee;

(3) a statement during a terminal illness or injury addressed to an attending physician and communicated to the donee; or

(4) a signed card or document found on the donor's person or in the donor's effects.

(b) A document of gift which is not delivered to the donee may be revoked by the donor as provided in (a) of this section or by destruction, cancellation, or mutilation of the document and all executed copies of it.

(c) A gift made by a will may be amended or revoked in the manner provided for amendment or revocation of wills or as provided in (a) of this section.

§ 13.50.060. Rights and duties at death. (a) The donee may accept or reject the gift. If the donee accepts a gift of the entire body, the donee may, subject to the terms of the gift, authorize embalming and the use of the body in funeral services. If the gift is of a part of the body, the donee, upon the death of the donor and before embalming, shall have the part removed without unnecessary mutilation. After removal of the part of the body, custody of the remainder of the body vests in the surviving spouse, next of kin, or a person other than the spouse or next of kin who is authorized to dispose of the body.

(b) The time of death shall be determined by a physician who attends the donor at death, or, if no physician attends, by the physician who certifies the death. The physician may not participate in the procedures for removing or transplanting a part of the body, except as provided in Section 13.50.030(d).

(c) A person who acts in good faith in accordance with the terms of this chapter or the anatomical gift laws of another state is not liable for damages for the act in any civil action or subject to prosecution in any criminal proceeding for the act.

(d) The provisions of this chapter are subject to the state autopsy laws under Section 12.65.

§ 13.50.070. Definitions. In this chapter

(1) "bank or storage facility" means a facility licensed, accredited, or approved under the laws of any state for storage of human bodies or parts of them;

(2) "decedent" means a deceased individual, stillborn infant, or fetus;

(3) "donor" means an individual who makes a gift of all or a part of the individual's body;

(4) "hospital" means a hospital licensed, accredited, or approved under the laws of any state; or a hospital operated by the United States government, or a subdivision thereof, although not required to be licensed under state laws;

(5) "part" means organs, tissues, eyes, bones, arteries, blood, other fluids and any other portions of a human body;

(6) "physician" or "surgeon" means a physician or surgeon licensed or authorized to practice under the laws of any state;

(7) "state" includes any state, district, commonwealth, territory, insular possession, and any other area subject to the legislative authority of the United States.

§ 13.50.080. Uniformity of interpretation. This chapter shall be construed and interpreted so as to carry out its general purpose to make uniform the laws in those states which enact it.

§ 13.50.090. Short title. This chapter may be cited as the Uniform Anatomical Gift Act.

ARIZONA

§ 36-841. Definitions. In this article, unless the context otherwise requires:

(1) "Bank or storage facility" means a facility licensed, accredited, or approved under the laws of any state for storage of human bodies or parts thereof.

(2) "Decedent" means a deceased individual and includes a stillborn infant or fetus.

(3) "Donor" means an individual who makes a gift of all or part of his body.

(4) "Hospital" means a hospital licensed, accredited, or approved under the laws of any state and includes a hospital operated by the United States government, a state, or a subdivision thereof, although not required to be licensed under state laws.

(5) "Part" means organs, tissues, eyes, bones, arteries, blood, other fluids and any other portions of a human body.

(6) "Person" means an individual, corporation, government or governmental subdivision or agency, business trust, estate, trust, partnership or association, or any other legal entity.

(7) "Physician" or "surgeon" means a physician or surgeon licensed or authorized to practice under the laws of any state.

(8) "State" includes any state, district, commonwealth, territory, insular possession, and any other area subject to the legislative authority of the United States of America.

§ 36-842. Persons who may execute an anatomical gift. (A) Any individual of sound mind and eighteen years of age or more may give all or any part of his body for any purpose specified in Section 36-843, the gift to take effect upon death.

(B) Any of the following persons, in order of priority stated, when persons in prior classes are not available at the time of death, and in the absence of actual notice of contrary indications by the decedent or actual notice of opposition by a member of the same or a prior class, may give all or any part of the decedent's body for any purpose specified in Section 36-843:

(1) The spouse;

(2) an adult son or daughter;

(3) either parent;

(4) an adult brother or sister;

(5) a guardian of the person of the decedent at the time of his death;

(6) any other person authorized or under obligation to dispose of the body.

(C) If the donee has actual notice of contrary indications by the decedent or that a gift by a member of a class is opposed by a member of the same or a prior class, the donee shall not accept the gift. The persons authorized by subsection (B) of this section may make the gift after or immediately before death.

(D) A gift of all or part of a body authorizes any examination necessary to assure medical acceptability of the gift for the purposes intended.

(E) The rights of the donee created by the gift are paramount to the rights of others except as provided by Section 36-847, subsection (D).

§ 36-843. Persons who may become donees; purpose for which anatomical gifts may be made. The following persons may become donees of gifts of bodies or parts thereof for the purposes stated.

(1) Any hospital, surgeon or physician, for medical or dental education, research, advancement of medical or dental science, therapy or transplantation.

(2) Any accredited medical or dental school, college or university for education, research, advancement of medical or dental science, or therapy.

(3) Any bank or storage facility, for medical or dental education, research, advancement of medical or dental science, therapy or transplantation.

(4) Any specified individual for therapy or transplantation needed by him.

(5) The department of health services, for delivery to any of the institutions or persons listed in paragraphs 1 through 4 which have registered with the department and have requested in writing to be notified by the department of the availability of such gifts of bodies or parts thereof. All expenses of delivery of bodies or parts thereof to such person or institution pursuant to this paragraph shall be paid by the person or institution receiving the body or parts thereof.

§ 36-844. Manner of executing anatomical gifts. (A) A gift of all or part of the body under Section 36-842, subsection (a), may be made by any of the following:

(1) A will. The gift becomes effective upon the death of the testator without waiting for

probate. If the will is not probated, or if it is declared invalid for testamentary purposes, the gift, to the extent that it has been acted upon in good faith, is nevertheless valid and effective.

(2) A sworn affidavit provided by and filed with the motor vehicle division of the department of transportation at the time of application for an operator's or chauffeur's license. Such affidavit shall be in a form prescribed by the director of the department of transportation. The gift becomes effective upon the death of the donor. A gift made under this paragraph shall become invalid upon surrender of the license or execution of the gift revocation signed by the licensee on the reverse of the license. A new affidavit shall be filed upon application for renewal or duplicate issuance of a license. The affidavit shall not be construed to be a last will and testament.

(3) A document other than a will or a license. The gift becomes effective upon the death of the donor. The document, which may be a card designed to be carried on the person, must be signed by the donor in the presence of two witnesses who must sign the document in his presence. If the donor cannot sign, the document may be signed for him at his direction and in his presence in the presence of two witnesses who must sign the document in his presence. Delivery of the document of gift during the donor's lifetime is not necessary to make the gift valid.

(B) The gift may be made to a specified donee or without specifying a donee. If the latter, the gift may be accepted by the attending physician as donee upon or following death. If the gift is made to a specified donee who is not available at the time and place of death, the attending physician upon or following death, in the absence of any expressed indication that the donor desired otherwise, may accept the gift as donee. The physician who becomes a donee under this subsection shall not participate in the procedures for removing or transplanting a part.

(C) Notwithstanding Section 36-847, subsection (B), the donor may designate in his will, card or other document of gift the surgeon or physician to carry out the appropriate procedures. In the absence of a designation or if the designee is not available, the donee or other person authorized to accept the gift may employ or authorize any surgeon or physician for the purpose.

(D) Any gift by a person designated in Section 36-842, subsection (B), shall be made by a document signed by him or made by his telegraphic, recorded telephonic, or other recorded message.

§ 36-845. Delivery of document of gift. If the gift is made by the donor to a specified donee, the will, card, license or other document, or an executed copy thereof, may be delivered to the donee to expedite the appropriate procedures immediately after death. Delivery is not necessary to the validity of the gift. The will, card, license or other document, or an executed copy thereof, may be deposited in any hospital, bank or storage facility or registry office that accepts it for safekeeping or for facilitation of procedures after death. On request of any interested party upon or after the donor's death, the person in possession shall produce the document for examination.

§ 36-846. Amendment or revocation of the gift. (A) If the will, card, license or other document or executed copy thereof, has been delivered to a specified donee, the donor may amend or revoke the gift by any of the following methods:

(1) The execution and delivery to the donee of a signed statement.

(2) An oral statement made in the presence of two persons and communicated to the donee.

(3) A statement during a terminal illness or injury addressed to an attending physician and communicated to the donee.

(4) A signed card or document found on his person or in his effects.

(B) Any document of gift which has not been delivered to the donee may be revoked by the donor in the manner set out in subsection (A) of this section or by destruction, cancellation or mutilation of the document and all executed copies thereof.

(C) Any gift made by a will may also be amended or revoked in the manner provided for amendment or revocation of wills, or as provided in subsection (A) of this section.

§ 36-847. Rights and duties at death. (A) The donee may accept or reject the gift. If the donee accepts a gift of the entire body, he may, subject to the terms of the gift, authorize embalming and the use of the body in funeral services. If the gift is of a part of the body, the donee, upon the death of the donor and prior to embalming, shall cause the part to be removed without unnecessary mutilation. After removal of the part, custody of the remainder of the body vests in the surviving spouse, next of kin, or other persons under obligation to dispose of the body.

(B) The time of death shall be determined by a physician who tends the donor at his death, or, if none, the physician who certifies the death. The physician shall not participate in the procedures for removing or transplanting a part.

(C) A person who acts in good faith in accord with the terms of this article or with the anatomical gift laws of another state or a foreign country is not liable for damages in any civil action or subject to prosecution in any criminal proceeding for his act.

(D) The provisions of this article are subject to the laws of this state prescribing powers and duties with respect to inquests and autopsies.

(E) Any person who does not have actual notice of an anatomical gift made under this article or the anatomical gift laws of another state or a foreign country and acts in good faith shall not be liable for damages in any civil action or subject to prosecution in any criminal proceeding for an otherwise lawful act which may render a body or parts thereof unusable to a donee.

§ 36-848. Short title. This article may be cited as the uniform anatomical gift act.

§ 36-849. Organ and tissue procurement protocol; notification of death to organ or tissue procurement agency; consent to donate; waiver of confidentiality; definition. (A) The person in charge of a hospital, or his designated representative, shall establish an organ and tissue procurement for transplant protocol which includes the notification of an appropriate organ or tissue procurement agency pursuant to subsection B of this section, defining who may obtain any and all consents pursuant to subsection C of this section and requiring specified training for the person who requests such consent in proper and appropriate procedures.

(B) At or near the occurrence of death in a hospital, the person in charge of the hospital or his designated representative, other than the physician connected with the determination of death, shall notify an appropriate organ or tissue procurement agency within a period of time to permit a viable donation.

(C) At or near the occurrence of death in a hospital, a person who is authorized to obtain consent by the protocol required by subsection A of this section shall, in conformity with the protocol established pursuant to subsection A of this section, attempt to obtain consent to donate pursuant to § 36-842, subsection B, such consent to be the gift of all or any part of the decedent's body for any purpose specified in § 36-843.

(D) If, pursuant to § 11-594, subsection A, the county medical examiner must conduct an investigation of the facts surrounding death, the organ or tissue procurement agency shall obtain the consent of the county medical examiner before seeking consent to donate pursuant to § 36-842, subsection B. This section does not relieve a hospital of its duty to report certain deaths to the county medical examiner pursuant to § 11-593.

(E) A person authorized pursuant to this section may obtain the consent to donate from a patient or from a minor patient's parent on admission to the hospital as part of its standard admitting procedure.

(F) No hospital, person or entity is subject to civil damages or legal action as a consequence of good faith acts or omissions related to procurement of organs or tissue in compliance with this article. All acts and omissions are presumed to be in good faith unless the acts or omissions are done with intent to maliciously cause injury.

(G) A consent to donate constitutes a limited waiver of a patient's confidentiality provided by § 12-2235 to the extent that the appropriate organ or tissue procurement agency has access to and may obtain a copy of all or any portion of a medical record necessary to determine whether a person is a suitable organ or tissue donor. A hospital shall release copies of records on request if the agency agrees to pay reasonable copying charges. An organ or tissue procurement agency shall keep the records as confidential and privileged to the same extent as required of the hospital from which they are released.

(H) For purposes of this section, "attempt to obtain consent" means reasonable efforts to contact the appropriate person pursuant to § 36-842, subsection B.

ARKANSAS

§ 20-17-601. Definitions. (a) "Bank or storage facility" means a facility licensed, accredited, or approved under the laws of any state for storage of human bodies and parts thereof;

(b) "Decedent" means a deceased individual and includes a stillborn infant or fetus;

(c) "Donor" means an individual who makes a gift of all or part of his body.

(d) "Hospital" means a hospital licensed, accredited, or approved under the laws of any state and includes a hospital operated by the United States government, a state, or a subdivision thereof, although not required to be licensed under state laws;

(e) "Part" means organs, tissues, eyes, bones, arteries, blood, other fluids and any other portions of a human body;

(f) "Person" means an individual, corporation, government or governmental subdivision or agency, business trust, estate, trust, partnership or association, or any other legal entity;

(g) "Physician" or "surgeon" means a physician or surgeon licensed or authorized to practice under the laws of any state;

(h) "State" includes any state, district, commonwealth, territory, insular possession, and any other area subject to the legislative authority of the United States of America.

§ 20-17-602. Persons who may execute an anatomical gift.

(a) Any individual of sound mind and eighteen (18) years of age or more may give all or any part of his body for any purpose specified in § 20-17-603, the gift to take effect upon death.

(b) Any of the following persons, in order of priority stated, when persons in prior classes are not available at the time of death, and in the absence of actual notice of contrary indications by the decedent or actual notice of opposition by a member of the same or a prior class, may give all or any part of the decedent's body for any purpose specified in § 20-17-603:

(1) the spouse;

(2) An adult son or daughter;

(3) Either parent;

(4) An adult brother or sister;

(5) A guardian of the person of the decedent at the time of his death;

(6) Any other person authorized or under obligation to dispose of the body.

(c) If the donee has actual notice of contrary indications by the decedent or that a gift by a member of a class is opposed by a member of the same or a prior class, the donee shall not accept the gift. The persons authorized by subsection (b) of this section may make the gift after or immediately before death.

(d) A gift of all or part of a body authorizes any examination necessary to assure medical acceptability of the gift for the purposes intended.

(e) The rights of the donee created by the gift are paramount to the rights of others except as provided by § 20-17-607(d).

§ 20-17-603. Persons who may become donees—Purposes for which anatomical gifts may be made. The following persons may become donees of gifts of bodies or parts thereof for the purposes stated:

(1) Any hospital, surgeon, or physician, for medical or dental education, research, advancement of medical or dental science, therapy, or transplantation; or

(2) Any accredited medical or dental school, college or university for education, research, advancement of medical or dental science, or therapy; or

(3) Any bank or storage facility, for medical or dental education, research, advancement of medical or dental science, therapy, or transplantation; or

(4) Any specified individual for therapy, or transplantation needed by him.

§ 20-17-604. Manner of executing anatomical gifts. (a) A gift of all or part of the body under § 20-17-602(a) may be made by will. The gift becomes effective upon the death of the testator without waiting for probate. If the will is not probated, or if it is declared invalid for testamentary purposes, the gift, to the extent that it has been acted upon in good faith, is nevertheless valid and effective.

(b) A gift of all or part of the body under § 20-17-602(a) may also be made by document other than a will. The gift becomes effective upon the death of the donor. The document, which may be a card designed to be carried on the person, must be signed by the donor in the presence of two (2) witnesses who must sign the document in his presence. If the donor cannot sign, the document may be signed for him at his direction and in his presence in the presence of two (2) witnesses who must sign the document in his presence. Delivery of the document of gift during the donor's lifetime is not necessary to make the gift valid.

(c) The gift may be made to a specified donee or without specifying a donee. If the latter, the gift may be accepted by the attending physician as donee upon or following death. If the gift is made to a specified donee who is not available at the time and place of death, the attending physician upon or following death, in the absence of any expressed indication that the donor desired otherwise, may accept the gift as donee. The physician who becomes a donee under this subsection shall not participate in the procedures for removing or transplanting a part.

(d) Notwithstanding § 20-17-607(b), the donor may designate in his will, card, or other document of gift the surgeon or physician to carry out the appropriate procedures. In the absence of a designation or if the designee is not available, the donee or other person authorized to accept the gift may employ or authorize any surgeon or physician for the purpose.

(e) Any gift by a person designated in § 20-17-602(b) shall be made by a document signed by him or made by his telegraphic, recorded telephonic, or other recorded message.

§ 20-17-605. Delivery of document of gift. If the gift is made by the donor to a specified donee, the will, card, or other document, or an executed copy thereof, may be delivered to the donee to expedite the appropriate procedures immediately after death. Delivery is not necessary to the validity of the gift. The will, card, or other document, or an executed copy thereof, may be deposited in any hospital, bank or storage facility, or registry office that accepts it for safekeeping or for facilitation of procedures after death. On request of any interested party upon or after the donor's death, the person in possession shall produce the document for examination.

§ 20-17-606. Amendment or revocation of gift. (a) If the will, card, or other document or executed copy thereof, has been delivered to a specified donee, the donor may amend or revoke the gift by:

(1) The execution and delivery to the donee of a signed statement; or

(2) An oral statement made in the presence of two (2) persons and communicated to the donee; or

(3) A statement during a terminal illness or injury addressed to an attending physician and communicated to the donee; or

(4) A signed card or document found on his person or in his effects.

(b) Any document of gift which has not been delivered to the donee may be revoked by the donor in the manner set out in subsection (a) of this section or by destruction, cancellation, or mutilation of the document and all executed copies thereof.

(c) Any gift made by a will may also be amended or revoked in the manner provided for amendment or revocation of wills or as provided in subsection (a) of this section.

§ 20-17-607. Rights and duties at death. (a) The donee may accept or reject the gift. If the donee accepts a gift of the entire body, he may, subject to the terms of the gift, authorize embalming and the use of the body in funeral services. If the gift is of a part of the body, the donee, upon the death of the donor and prior to embalming, shall cause the part to be removed without unnecessary mutilation. After removal of the part, custody of the remainder of the body vests in the surviving spouse, next of kin, or other persons under obligation to dispose of the body.

(b) The time of death shall be determined by a physician who attends the donor at his death, or, if none, the physician who certifies the death. The physician shall not participate in the procedures for removing or transplanting a part.

(c) A person who acts in good faith in accord with the terms of this subchapter or the anatomical gift laws of another state or a foreign country is not liable for damages in any civil action or subject to prosecution in any criminal proceeding for his act.

(d) The provisions of this subchapter are subject to the laws of this state prescribing powers and duties with respect to autopsies.

§ 20-17-608. Uniformity of interpretation. This subchapter shall be so construed as to effectuate its general purpose to make uniform the law of those states which enact it.

§ 20-17-609. Title. This subchapter may be cited as the "Uniform Anatomical Gift Act."

§ 20-17-610. Repeal. Acts 1949, No. 283 is hereby expressly repealed.

§ 20-17-611. Subchapter cumulative. This subchapter shall not repeal subchapter 4 of this chapter, but shall be cumulative to those sections, and in the event procedures under this subchapter and subchapter 4 of this chapter conflict, the procedures shall be regarded as alternate procedures, both of which shall be valid.

§ 20-17-612. Severability. If any provision of this subchapter or the application thereof to any person or circumstance is held invalid, the invalidity shall not affect other provisions or applications of the subchapter which can be given effect without the invalid provision or application, and to this end the provisions of this subchapter are declared severable.

§ 20-17-613. Emergency. It is hereby found and determined by the General Assembly that the present law regarding disposition of organs, fluids, and other parts of the human body after death are inadequate and cumbersome; that the rapid rate at which medical technology is advancing in the field of organ transplants makes it imperative that the law in this area be clarified and modernized immediately. Therefore, an emergency is hereby declared to exist and this subchapter being necessary for the preservation of the public peace, health, and safety shall be in effect from the date of its passage and approval.

California

§ 7150. Citation. This act may be cited as the "Uniform Anatomical Gift Act."

§ 7150.5. Definitions. As used in this chapter,

(a) "Bank or storage facility" means a facility licensed, accredited, or approved under the laws of any state for storage of human bodies or parts thereof.

(b) "Decedent" means a deceased individual, and includes a stillborn infant or fetus.

(c) "Donor" means an individual who makes a gift of all or part of his or her body.

(d) "Hospital" means a hospital licensed, accredited, or approved under the laws of any state, and includes a hospital operated by the United States government, a state, or a subdivision thereof, although not required to be licensed under state laws.

(e) "Part" means organs, tissues, the cornea, sclera, or vitreous and other segments of, or the whole, eye, bones, arteries, blood, other fluids, and any other portions of a human body.

(f) "Person" means an individual, corporation, government or governmental subdivision or agency, business trust, estate, trust, partnership, or association, or any other legal entity.

(g) "Physician" or "surgeon" means a physician or surgeon licensed or authorized to practice under the laws of any state.

§ 7151. Persons authorized to make gifts. Any individual of sound mind and 18 years of age or older may give all or any part of his body for any purpose specified in Section 7153.5, the gift to take effect upon death.

§ 7151.5. Order of priority. Any of the following persons, in order of priority stated, when persons in prior classes are not available at the time of death, and in the absence of actual notice of contrary indications by the decedent or actual notice of opposition by a member of the same or a prior class, may give all or any part of the decedent's body for any purpose specified in Section 7153.5:

(a) The spouse.

(b) An adult son or daughter.

(c) Either parent.

(d) An adult brother or sister.

(e) A guardian or conservator of the person of the decedent at the time of the decedent's death.

(f) Any other person authorized or under obligation to dispose of the body.

§ 7151.6. Determination of nonavailability of persons authorized or under obligation to dispose of the body. When all of the persons enumerated in subdivisions (a) to (e), inclusively of Section 7151.5 are determined after diligent search to be not available, then, subject to Section 7151.7, any specified parts of the decedent's body may be given to any of the donees for any of the purposes stated in Section 7153.5. Such determination of nonavailability shall be made only by a hospital which is accredited by the Joint Commission on Accreditation of Hospitals. The hospital shall certify such nonavailability and shall authorize and specify the removal and donation of such parts. Such search shall include a check of local police missing persons records, examination of personal effects, and the questioning of any persons visiting the decedent, before his or her death, in a hospital, accompanying the decedent's body, or reporting the death in order to obtain information which might lead to the location of any persons who might be authorized to consent to such donation. The search may be initiated in anticipation of death but the determination of nonavailability may not be made until such search has been underway for at least 24 hours except in the case of corneal material to be used for the purpose of human transplantation. Any such determination of nonavailability shall be made only after examination of all evidence leads to the conclusion that no relatives are available. Any such determination shall be subject to a review by such office as is designated by the board of supervisors of the county in which the death occurs.

A cemetery authority, a licensed funeral director, a physician, or any authorized assistant of a cemetery authority, licensed funeral director, or physician is not liable for performing an autopsy and donating specified body parts pursuant to such authorization unless such person or authority has actual notice that such representation of nonavailability is untrue at the time of the autopsy.

§ 7151.7. Faith healing sects; donations only by decedent. Notwithstanding any other provision of law, only the decedent shall have the authority to donate his body or any part thereof, if it is made known that the deceased at the time of his death was a member of a religion, church, sect, or denomination which relies solely upon prayer for the healing of disease or which has religious tenets that would be violated by the disposition of the human body or parts thereof for any of the purposes specified in this chapter.

§ 7152. Grounds for nonacceptance by donee; time for making gift. If the donee has actual notice of contrary indications by the decedent that a gift by a member of a class is opposed by a member of the same or a prior class, the donee shall not accept the gift. The persons authorized by Section 7151.5 may make the gift after or immediately before death.

§ 7152.5. Authority to make examination. A gift of all or part of a body authorizes any examination necessary to assure medical acceptability of the gift for the purposes intended.

§ 7153. Paramount rights of donee; exception. The rights of the donee created by the gift are paramount to the rights of others, except as provided by Section 7156.

§ 7153.5. Persons eligible to receive gifts. The following persons may become donees of gifts of bodies or parts thereof for the purposes stated:

 (a) Any hospital, surgeon, physician, or coroner, for medical or dental education, research, advancement of medical or dental science, therapy, or transplantation.

 (b) Any accredited medical or dental school, college or university for education, research, advancement of medical or dental science, therapy, or transplantation.

 (c) Any bank or storage facility, for medical or dental education, research, advancement of medical or dental science, therapy, or transplantation.

 (d) Any specified individual for therapy or transplantation needed by him.

§ 7154. Methods of making gift. (a) A gift of all or part of the body under Section 7151 may be made by will. The gift shall become effective upon the death of the testator without waiting for probate. If the will is not probated, or if it is declared invalid for testamentary purposes, the gift, to the extent that it has been acted upon in good faith, shall be nevertheless valid and effective.

 (b) A gift of all or part of the body under Section 7151 may also be made by document other than a will. The gift shall become effective upon the death of the donor. The document, which may be a card designed to be carried on the person, shall be signed by the donor. If the donor cannot sign, the document may be signed for the donor at his or her direction and in the donor's presence and in the presence of two witnesses who shall also sign the document in the donor's presence. Delivery of the document of gift during the donor's lifetime shall not be necessary to make the gift valid.

The document may also be a driver's license or identification card meeting the requirements of subdivision (b) of Section 12811 or subdivision (b) of Section 13005 of the Vehicle Code.

(c) The gift may be made to a specified donee or without specifying a donee. If no donee is specified, the gift may be accepted by the attending physician as donee upon or following death. If the gift is made to a specified donee who is not available at the time and place of death, the attending physician, upon or following the death of the donor, in the absence of any expressed indication that the donor desired otherwise, may accept the gift as donee. The physician who becomes a donee under this subdivision shall not participate in the procedures for removing or transplanting a part.

(d) Notwithstanding subdivision (b) of Section 7155.5, the donor may designate in his or her will, card, or other document of gift the surgeon or physician to carry out the appropriate procedures. In the absence of a designation, or if the designee is not available, the donee or other person authorized to accept the gift may employ or authorize any surgeon or physician for this purpose.

(e) Any gift made by a person designated in Section 7151.5 shall be made by a document signed by him or her or made by his or her telegraphic, recorded telephonic, or other recorded message.

§ 7154.5. Delivery of document of gift. If the gift is made by the donor to a specified donee, the will, card, or other document, or an executed copy thereof, may be delivered to the donee to expedite the appropriate procedures immediately after death. Delivery is not necessary to the validity of the gift. The will, card, or other document, or an executed copy thereof, may be deposited in any hospital, bank or storage facility, or registry office that accepts it for safekeeping or for facilitation of procedures after death. On request of any interested party upon or after the donor's death, the person in possession shall produce the document for examination.

§ 7155. Amendment or revocation of document of gift. (a) If the will, card, or other document, or executed copy thereof, has been delivered to a specified donee, the donor may amend or revoke the gift by any of the following:

(1) The execution and delivery to the donee of a signed statement.

(2) An oral statement made in the presence of two persons and communicated to the donee.

(3) A statement during a terminal illness or injury addressed to an attending physician and communicated to the donee.

(4) A signed card or document found on his person or in his effects.

(b) Any document of gift which has not been delivered to the donee may be revoked by the donor in the manner set out in subdivision (a), or by destruction, cancellation, or mutilation of the document and all executed copies thereof.

(c) Any gift made by a will also may be amended or revoked in the manner provided for amendment or revocation of wills, or as provided in subdivision (a).

§ 7155.5. Rights and duties of donee. (a) The donee may accept or reject a gift. If the donee accepts a gift of the entire body, the donee may, subject to the terms of the gift, authorize embalming and the use of the body in funeral services. If the gift is of a part of the body, the donee, upon the death of the donor and prior to embalming, shall cause the part to be removed without unnecessary mutilation. After removal of the part, custody of the remainder of the body vests in the surviving spouse, next of kin, or other persons specified in Section 7100.

(b) The donee, in order to receive the gift, may act through a licensed physician or trained transplant technician authorized by the donee, or through a licensed embalmer, pursuant to Section 7634 of the Business and Professions Code, who shall remove tissue from a legally dead individual for transplant, therapeutic, or scientific purposes according to an established State Department of Health Services protocol involved in removal.

(c) The time of death shall be determined by a physician who tends the donor at his or her death, or, if none, the physician or coroner who certifies the death. The physician shall not participate in the procedures for removing or transplanting a part.

(d) No county coroner or medical examiner, nor any authorized agent thereof, shall be liable for damages in any civil action as a result of his or her act of omission relative to procedures undertaken pursuant to this chapter or to anatomical gifts offered under Section 12811 of the Vehicle Code.

(e) Any person who acts in good faith with the terms of this chapter, including acts pursuant to anatomical gifts offered under Section 12811 of the Vehicle Code, shall not be liable for damages in any civil action or subject to prosecution in any criminal proceeding for his or her act.

(f) For purpose of this section, "trained transplant technician" means a person who has completed training in tissue removal for transplant, therapeutic, or scientific purposes, which the donee determines to be adequate for the purpose.

§ 7155.6. Tissue for transplantation. The use of any human tissue donated pursuant to this chapter for the purpose of transplantation in the human body shall be construed for all purposes as a rendition of a service by each person participating therein and shall not be construed as a sale of such tissue.

§ 7156. Chapter provisions subject to laws relating to autopsies. The provisions of this chapter are subject to the laws of this state prescribing powers and duties with respect to autopsies.

§ 7157. Uniformity of construction. This chapter shall be so construed as to effectuate its general purpose to make uniform the law of the states which enact it.

§ 7158. Repealed.

COLORADO

§ 12-34-101. Short title. This act shall be known and may be cited as the "Uniform Anatomical Gift Act."

§ 12-34-102. Definitions. As used in this act, unless the context otherwise requires:

(1) "Bank or storage facility" means a facility licensed, accredited, or approved under the laws of any state for storage of human bodies or parts thereof.

(2) "Decedent" means a deceased individual and includes a stillborn infant or fetus.

(3) "Donor" means an individual who makes a gift of all or part of his body.

(4) "Hospital" means a hospital licensed, accredited, or approved under the laws of any state and includes a hospital operated by the United States government, a state, or a political subdivision thereof, although not required to be licensed under state laws.

(5) "Part" includes organs, tissues, eyes, bones, arteries, blood, other fluids, and other portions of a human body.

(6) "Person" means an individual, corporation, government or political subdivision or agency thereof, business trust, estate, partnership, association, or any other legal entity.

(7) "Physician" or "surgeon" means a physician or surgeon licensed or authorized to practice under the laws of any state.

(7.5) "Procurement agency" means any agency that has been certified or recertified by the secretary of the United States department of health and human services or any agency certified by the executive director of the Colorado department of health as a qualified organ or tissue agency.

(8) "State" includes any state, district, commonwealth, territory, insular possession, and any other area subject to the legislative authority of the United States of America.

§ 12-34-103. Persons who may execute an anatomical gift. (1) Any individual of sound mind and eighteen years of age or more may give all or any part of his body, the gift to take effect upon death, for any purpose specified in Section 12-34-104.

(2) Any of the following persons, in the order of priority stated, when persons in prior classes are not available at the time of death, and in the absence of actual notice of a contrary indication as defined in Section 12-34-107, or actual notice of opposition by a member of the same or a prior class, may give all or any part of the decedent's body for any purposes specified in Section 12-34-104:

(a) The spouse;

(b) An adult son or daughter;

(c) Either parent;

(d) An adult brother or sister;

(e) A guardian of the person of the decedent at the time of his death;

(f) Any other person authorized or under obligation to dispose of the body.

(3) If the donee has actual notice of a contrary indication as defined in Section 12-34-107, or that a gift by a member of a class is opposed by a member of the same or a prior class, the donee shall not accept the gift. The persons authorized by subsection (2) of this section may make the gift after death or immediately before death.

(4) A gift of all or part of a human body authorizes any examination necessary to assure medical acceptability of the gift for the purposes intended.

(5) The rights of the donee created by the gift are paramount to the rights of others except as provided by Section 12-34-108(4).

§ 12-34-104. Persons who may become donees, and purposes for which anatomical gifts may be made. The following persons may become donees of gifts of bodies or parts thereof for the purposes stated:

(a) Any hospital, surgeon, or physician for medical or dental education, research, advancement of medical or dental science, therapy, or transplantation; or

(b) Any accredited medical or dental school, college, or university for education, research, advancement of medical or dental science, or therapy; or

(c) Any bank or storage facility, for medical or dental education, research, advancement of medical or dental science, therapy, or transplantation; or

(d) Any specified individual for therapy or transplantation needed by him.

§ 12-34-105. Manner of executing anatomical gifts. (1) A gift of all or part of a human body under Section 12-34-103(1) may be made by any of the following:

(a) By will. The gift becomes effective upon the death of the testator without waiting for probate. If the will is not probated or if it is declared invalid for testamentary purposes, the gift, to the extent that it has been acted upon in good faith, is nevertheless valid and effective.

(b) Repealed, L. 85, p. 513, Section 4, effective January 1, 1986.

(c) By document other than a will or license. The gift becomes effective upon the death of the donor. The document, which may be a card designed to be carried on the person, shall be signed by the donor in the presence of two witnesses who must then sign the document in his presence. If the donor cannot sign, the document may be signed for him at his direction and in his presence and in the presence of two witnesses who must then sign the document in his presence. Delivery of the document of gift during the donor's lifetime is not necessary to make the gift valid.

(2) The gift of all or part of a human body may be made either to a specified donee or without specifying a donee. If the latter, the gift may be accepted by the attending physician as donee upon or following death if he is not the physician determining the time and probable cause of death pursuant to Section 12-34-108(2). If the gift is made to a specified donee who is not available at the time and place of death, the attending physician upon or following death, in the absence of any expressed indication that the donor desired otherwise, may accept the gift as donee. The physician who becomes a donee under this subsection (2) shall not participate in the procedures for removing or transplanting a part.

(3) Notwithstanding the provisions of Section 12-34-108(2), the donor may designate in his will, license, card, or other document of gift the surgeon or physician to carry out the appropriate procedures. In the absence of a designation, or if the designee is not available, the donee or other person authorized to accept the gift may employ or authorize any surgeon or physician for the purpose.

(4) Any gift by a person designated in Section 12-34-103(2) shall be made by a document signed by him or by his telegraphic, recorded telephonic, or other recorded message.

(5) (a) The department of revenue shall place on the back of each driver's license, provisional driver's license, and identification card issued pursuant to article 2 of title 42, Colorado Revised Statutes, a card, as provided in paragraph (1)(c) of this section, in the form as follows:

I hereby give, at the time of my death, any of my organs and tissues designated below, that may be needed for transplantation, therapy, research, or education. I give:

                      A.___Any needed organ
                      B.___Organs listed below

Date: _____Organs: _____
Signature of Donor:_____
Witness:_____Witness:_____

(b) A gift made by a card as provided in this subsection (5) shall be deemed revoked on the expiration date of the license to which it is attached. The gift shall also be deemed revoked at any time the license is revoked or suspended.

(c) At the time the driver's license, provisional driver's license, or identification card is issued, the department of revenue, or any private organization approved by the department of revenue, may provide literature which explains the "Uniform Anatomical Gift Act" and which contains information about transplantable organs and tissues.

§ 12-34-106. **Delivery of document of gift.** If the gift is made by the donor to a specified donee, the will, card, or other document, or an executed copy thereof, may be delivered to the donee to expedite the appropriate procedures immediately after death, but delivery is not necessary to the validity of the gift. The will, card, or other document, or an executed copy thereof, may be deposited in any hospital, bank, or storage facility, or registry office that accepts the same for safekeeping or for facilitation of procedures after death. On request of any interested party upon or after the donor's death, the person in possession shall produce the document for examination.

§ 12-34-107. **Amendment or revocation of gift.** (1) If the will, card, or other document, or an executed copy thereof, has been delivered to a specified donee, the donor may amend or revoke the gift by:

(a) The execution and delivery to the donee of a signed statement; or

(b) An oral statement made in the presence of two persons and communicated to the donee; or

(c) A statement during a terminal illness or injury addressed to an attending physician and communicated to the donee; or

(d) A signed card or document found on his person or in his effects.

(2) Any document of gift which has not been delivered to the donee may be revoked by the donor in the manner set out in subsection (1) of this section or by destruction, cancellation, or mutilation of the document and all executed copes thereof.

(3) Any gift made by a will may also be amended or revoked in the manner provided for amendment or revocation of wills, or as provided in subsection (1) of this section.

(4) The donor of an anatomical gift made pursuant to Section 12-34-105(5)(a) may revoke the gift by crossing off his signature on the card.

§ 12-34-108. Rights and duties at death. (1) The donee may accept or reject the gift. If the donee accepts a gift of the entire body, he may, subject to the terms of the gift, authorize embalming and the use of the body in funeral services. If the gift is of a part of the body, the donee, upon the death of the donor and prior to embalming, shall cause the part to be removed without unnecessary mutilation. After removal of the part, custody of the remainder of the body vests in the surviving spouse, next of kin, or any other person authorized or under obligation to dispose of the body.

(2) Prior to the time the donee accepts the body, or a part thereof, the attending physician or, if none, the physician certifying death shall determine, record, and attest by his signature the time and probable cause of death in a permanent written record kept by such physician or hospital or the institution in which the death occurred, which record shall be open to the public. Such physician shall not be a donee. This physician shall not participate in the procedures for removing or transplanting a part.

(3) A person who acts in good faith in accordance with the terms of this act, or under the anatomical gift laws of another state or a foreign country, is not liable for damages in any civil action or subject to prosecution in any criminal proceeding for his act.

(4) The provisions of this act are subject to the laws of this state prescribing powers and duties with respect to autopsies.

(5) In the case of a gift of an eye as provided for in this act, a mortuary science practitioner, as defined in part 1 of article 54 of this title, who has successfully completed a course in eye enucleation and has received a certificate of competence from the department of ophthalmology of the university of Colorado school of medicine or who has successfully completed a similar course elsewhere may enuleate eyes for such gift, without charge to the estate or family of the donor, after the proper certification of death by a physician and compliance with any other requirements of this act in relation to such gift.

§ 12-34-108.5. Anatomical gift protocol required. (1) In order to ensure that donors or families of donors be informed of the option to make an anatomical gift, every hospital licensed or certified pursuant to section 25-1-107(1)(1)(I) or (1)(1)(II), C.R.S., shall develop and implement, by October 1, 1987, an organ and tissue procurement protocol for the purpose of identifying potential donors.

(2) The protocol developed pursuant to this section shall encourage discretion and sensitivity to family circumstances in all discussions regarding the making of an anatomical gift.

(3) Each hospital protocol shall:

(a) Designate individuals who shall make requests for anatomical gifts. Such individuals may be physicians, employees of the hospital, or any other persons designated by the hospital administrator.

(b) Describe the circumstances under which the request for an anatomical gift may be made.

(4) Each person designated by a hospital protocol to make requests for anatomical gifts shall be trained to make such requests by the hospital or by a procurement agency.

(5) Requests for anatomical gifts shall be of the persons listed in section 12-34-103(2) in the order of priority stated therein.

(6) The attending physician or his designee physician shall be responsible for:

  (a) The identification of all potential donors;

  (b) The notification of the individuals designated in the protocol as to when the request for the anatomical gift should be made;

  (c) The notification of the appropriate hospital personnel as to when the anatomical gift should be obtained from the donor; and

  (d) Making the appropriate entry in the medical record of the donor as to the fact that an anatomical gift was made.

(7) Each hospital, in conjunction with procurement agencies, shall establish medical criteria for determining the suitability of potential donors.

(8) No request for an anatomical gift shall be made when:

  (a) The hospital or the attending physician, or his designee physician, has actual notice of a contrary indication by the decedent or by a member of a class listed in section 12-34-103(2); or

  (b) The attending physician has notified the hospital that a donation is not suitable for medical reasons; or

  (c) Circumstances surrounding the death are such that a report to the county coroner is required pursuant to section 30-10-606, C.R.S. In such cases, however, the coroner may direct the anatomical gift protocol of the hospital to be implemented, so long as the coroner is still able to fulfill his statutory duties. Each individual designated in the hospital protocol as the person responsible for making the request for an anatomical gift may request the coroner to implement the protocol.

(9) The individual designed in the protocol to make the request for an anatomical gift shall, after being notified by the attending physician pursuant to paragraph (b) of subsection (6) of this section, make the request for an anatomical gift. Such request shall be noted in the medical record of the donor and shall indicate who made the request, the person of whom the request was made and his relationship to the donor, whether the request was granted, and, if the request was granted, the organs or tissue donated.

(10) Any hospital which determines that its resources or geographical location makes it impractical to implement a protocol covering all types of organs and tissues for anatomical gifts in a particular situation may request an exemption from the requirements of this section. When such determination is made, the governing body of the hospital shall notify the executive director of the department of health in writing as to the reasons for such determination. The executive director of the department of health, upon receipt of a request from a hospital seeking exemption, may grant or deny such request or, prior to denying or granting the request, may request additional information.

(11) All costs associated with the administration of this section shall be paid by the procurement agency requesting the anatomical gift. Payment for such costs shall be made by the procurement agency within sixty days from the date on which the agency receives the bill.

(12) It is the responsibility of all procurement agencies to:

  (a) Inform hospitals of the need for organs and tissue;

  (b) Assist hospitals and other providers in the training of personnel and the development of the protocols required by this section;

  (c) Coordinate with all other procurement agencies a central clearinghouse which is available twenty-four hours per day for the purpose of allowing hospitals to contact one source so that the procurement process is expedited.

(13) In the event there is more than one procurement agency seeking the same anatomical gift, the hospital obtaining the anatomical gift may designate which agency will receive the gift.

(14) Any person who in good faith participates in any activity required or authorized by this section, including the development or implementation of any protocol, shall be immune from any civil or criminal liability.

§ 12-34-109. Uniformity of interpretation. This part shall be so construed to effectuate its general purpose to make uniform the law of those states which enact it.

CONNECTICUT

§ 19a-272. Definitions. As used in this act:

(a) "Bank or storage facility" means a facility for storage of human bodies or parts thereof;

(b) "Decedent" means a deceased individual and includes a stillborn infant or fetus;

(c) "Donor" means an individual who makes a gift of all or part of his body;

(d) "Hospital" means a hospital licensed under sections 19a-490 to 19a-503, inclusive, or licensed, accredited or approved under the laws of any other state and includes a hospital operated by the United States government, a state, or a subdivision thereof, although not required to be licensed under state laws;

(e) "Part" includes organs, tissues, eyes, bones, arteries, blood, other fluids and other portions of a human body, and "part" includes "parts";

(f) "Person" means an individual, corporation, government or governmental subdivision or agency, business trust, estate, trust, partnership or association or any other legal entity;

(g) "Physician" or "surgeon" means a doctor of medicine licensed under chapter 370 or licensed to practice medicine under the laws of any other state;

(h) "State" includes any state, district, commonwealth, territory, insular possession, and any other area subject to the legislative authority of the United States of America.

§ 19a-273. Donation of all or part of the anatomy. (a) Any person of sound mind and eighteen years of age or older, or any person of sound mind and fourteen years of age or older but less than eighteen years of age with the consent of his parent or legal guardian, may give all or any part of his body for any of the purposes specified in section 19a-274, the gift to take effect after death. Such gifts are prohibited when death has occurred from diseases specified in section 19a-282.

(b) Any of the following persons, in the order of priority stated, in the absence of actual notice of contrary indications by the decedent, or actual notice of opposition by a member of the same or a prior class, may, after the death or immediately before the death of the decedent, give all or any part of the decedent's body for any of the purposes specified in section 19a-274:

(1) The spouse,

(2) an adult son or daughter,

(3) either parent,

(4) an adult brother or sister,

(5) a guardian of the person of the decedent at the time of his death,

(6) any other person authorized or under obligation to dispose of the body after death.

(c) If the donee or his agent or representative has actual notice of contrary indications by the decedent, or that a gift by a member of a class is opposed by a member of the same or a prior class, the donee shall not accept the gift.

(d) A gift of all or part of a body authorizes any examination necessary to assure medical acceptability of the gift for the purposes intended.

(e) The rights of the donee created by the gift are paramount to the rights of others except as provided by subsection (d) of section 19a-278.

(f) A valid gift of the whole of the donor's body shall take precedence over a gift of any part thereof under the provisions of sections 19a-271 to 19a-279, inclusive, unless the instrument of gift of such part expressly indicates to the contrary.

§ 19a-274. Eligible donees and authorized purposes of donation. The following persons, when approved by the state commissioner of health services, may become donees of gifts of bodies or parts thereof for the purposes stated:

(a) Any hospital, surgeon or physician for medical or dental education, research, advancement of medical or dental science, therapy or transplantation; or

(b) any accredited medical or dental school, college or university for education, research, advancement of medical or dental science or therapy; or

(c) any bank or storage facility for medical or dental education, research, advancement of medical or dental science, therapy or transplantation; or

(d) any specified individual for therapy or transplantation needed by him.

§ 19a-275. Methods and effective date of gifts. (a) A gift of all or part of the body under subsection (a) of section 19a-273 may be made by will. Such gift shall become effective upon the death of the testator without waiting for admission of the will to probate. If the will is not probated, or if it is declared invalid for testamentary purposes, the gift, to the extent that it has been acted upon in good faith, shall nevertheless be valid and effective.

(b) A gift of all or part of the body under said subsection (a) may also be made by document other than a will. Such gift shall become effective upon the death of the donor. The document, which may be a card designed to be carried on the person, shall be signed by the donor, in the presence of two witnesses who shall sign the document in his presence. In the case of a donor fourteen years of age or older but less than eighteen years of age, one such witness shall be his parent or guardian. If the donor cannot sign, the document shall be signed for him at his direction and in his presence, and in the presence of two witnesses who shall sign the document in his presence. Delivery of the document of gift during the donor's lifetime shall not be necessary to make the gift valid.

(c) The gift may be made to a specified donee or without specifying a donee. If no donee is specified, the gift may be accepted by the attending physician as donee upon or following death. If the gift is made to a specified donee who is not available at the time and place of death, the attending physician upon or following death, in the absence of any expressed indication that the donor desired otherwise, may accept the gift as donee.

(d) Notwithstanding subsection (b) of section 19a-278, the donor may designate in his will, card or other document of gift the surgeon or physician to carry out the appropriate procedures. In the absence of a designation, or if the designee is not available, the donee or other person authorized to accept the gift may employ or authorize any surgeon or physician for the purpose.

(e) Any gift by a person designated in subsection (b) of section 19a-273 shall be made by a document signed by him, or made by his telegraphic, recorded telephonic or other recorded message.

§ 19a-275a. Development of protocol by hospitals to identify potential donors. Each hospital included within the definition of health care facilities or institutions under section 19a-145 and licensed as a short-term general hospital shall develop a protocol for identifying potential organ or tissue donors under this chapter. The protocol shall require the health care facility or institution, upon the identification of a potential organ or tissue donor, to notify an organ or tissue procurement organization and cooperate in the procurement of the anatomical gift. The protocol shall require that the hospital determine from the next of kin of the deceased patient, or from any person authorized under subsection (b) of section 19a-273, whether such patient was an organ or tissue donor. If such patient was not an organ or tissue donor, the family of such patient shall be informed of the option to donate organs and tissues pursuant to section 19a-273. The protocol shall encourage reasonable sensitivity to the family circumstances in all discussions regarding donation of organs or tissues and shall take into account the known religious belief of the patient or family or the obvious non-suitability for organ or tissue donation.

§ 19a-276. Perfection of gift. If the gift is made by the donor to a specified donee, the will, card or other document, or an executed copy thereof, may be delivered to the donee to expedite the appropriate procedures immediately after death, but delivery is not necessary to the validity of the gift. The will, card or other document, or an executed copy thereof, may be deposited (a) with the department of health services or (b) in any hospital, bank or storage facility that accepts them, with a copy to the department of health services, for safekeeping or for facilitation of procedures after death. On request of any interested party upon or after the donor's death, the person in possession shall produce the document for examination.

§ 19a-277. Amendment and revocation of gift. (a) If the will, card or other document, or an executed copy thereof, has been delivered to a specified donee, the donor may amend or revoke the gift by:

(1) The execution and delivery to the donee of a signed statement; or

(2) an oral statement made in the presence of two persons and communicated to the donee, or

(3) a statement during a terminal illness or injury addressed to an attending physician and communicated to the donee, or

(4) a signed card or document found on his person or in his effects.

(b) Any document of gift which has not been delivered to a specified donee may be revoked by the donor in the manner set out in subsection (a) or by destruction, cancellation or mutilation of the document and all executed copies thereof.

(c) Any gift under sections 19a-272 to 19a-279, inclusive, made by a will may be amended or revoked in the manner provided for amendment or revocation of wills, or as provided in subsection (a).

§ 19a-278. Acceptance or rejection of gift. Determination of time of death. Civil and criminal liability. Approval by medical examiner. (a) The donee may accept or reject the gift. If the donee accepts a gift of the entire body, he may, except as provided in section 19a-283 and subject to the terms of the gift, authorize embalming and the use of the body in funeral services. If the gift is of a part of the body, the donee, upon the death of the donor and prior to embalming, shall cause the part to be removed without unnecessary mutilation. After removal of the part, custody of the remainder of the body shall vest in the surviving spouse, next of kin or other persons under obligation to dispose of the body.

(b) The time of death shall be determined by two physicians who attend the donor at his death, or if none, two physicians who certify death, who shall use generally recognized and accepted scientific and clinical means to determine such time of death. Without limiting any other method of determining death, a donor may be pronounced dead if two physicians determine, in accordance with the usual and customary standards of medical practice, that the donor has suffered a total and irreversible cessation of all brain function. A total and irreversible cessation of all brain function shall mean that the heart and lungs of the donor cannot function, and are not functioning, without artificial supportive measures. The physicians who so certify shall not participate in the procedures for removing or transplanting a part. No organ shall be removed for transplantation until death has been pronounced.

(c) A person who acts in good faith in accordance with the terms of sections 19a-271 to 19a-279, inclusive, shall not be liable for damages in any civil action or subject to prosecution in any criminal proceeding for his act.

(d) When the donor's death is subject to investigation by the chief medical examiner, the gift of any part or parts of the donor's body shall be contingent upon the approval of the chief medical examiner, deputy chief medical examiner, an associate medical examiner or an authorized assistant medical examiner.

§ 19a-279. Regulations. The commissioner of health services shall promulgate such regulations as may be necessary to carry out the purposes of sections 19a-272 to 19a-279, inclusive.

DELAWARE

§ 2710. Definitions. (1) "Bank or storage facility" means a facility licensed, accredited or approved under the laws of any state for storage of human bodies or parts thereof.

(2) "Decedent" means a deceased individual and includes a stillborn infant or fetus.

(3) "Donor" means an individual who makes a gift of all or part of his body.

(4) "Hospital" means a hospital licensed, accredited or approved under the laws of any state and includes a hospital operated by the United States government, a state or a subdivision thereof, although not required to be licensed under state laws.

(5) "Part" includes organs, tissues, eyes, bones, arteries, blood, other fluids and other portions of a human body, and "part" includes "parts."

(6) "Person" means an individual, corporation, government or governmental subdivision or agency, business trust, estate, trust, partnership or association or any other legal entity.

(7) "Physician or surgeon" means a physician or surgeon licensed or authorized to practice under the laws of any state.

(8) "State" includes any state, district, commonwealth, territory, insular possession and any other area subject to the legislative authority of the United States of America.

§ 2711. Persons who may execute an anatomical gift. (a) Any individual of sound mind and 18 years of age or more or an individual not of such age who has parental consent may give all or any part of his or her body for any purposes specified in Section 2712 of this act, the gift to take effect upon the donor's death. However, a married minor may make such a donation without parental consent.

(b) "Parental consent" as used in this section shall be defined as the written permission by any of the following persons in order of priority stated below when persons of prior classes are no longer living or no longer have contractual capacity and when there is no notice to a donee of an objection, written or otherwise, by a person of the same class:

(1) Either parent;
(2) A legal guardian;
(3) Any individual having legal custody.

(c) Any of the following persons in order of priority stated, when persons in prior classes are not available at the time of death and in the absence of actual notice of contrary indications by the decedent or actual notice of opposition by a member of the same or a prior class, may give all or any part of the decedent's body for any purpose specified in Section 2712 of this act:

(1) The spouse;

(2) An adult son or daughter, 18 years of age or older;

(3) Either parent;

(4) An adult brother or sister;

(5) A guardian of the person of the decedent at the time of his death;

(6) Any other person authorized or under obligation to dispose of the body.

(d) If the donee has actual notice of contrary indications by the decedent or that a gift by a member of a class is opposed by a member of the same or a prior class, the donee shall not accept the gift. The persons authorized by subsection (b) of this section may make the gift after death or immediately before death.

(e) A gift of all or part of a body authorizes any examination necessary to assure medical acceptability of the gift for the purposes intended.

(f) The rights of the donee created by the gift are paramount to the rights of others except as provided by Section 2716(e) of this act.

§ 2712. Persons who may become donees, and purposes for which anatomical gifts may be made. The following persons may become donees of gifts of bodies or parts thereof for the purposes stated:

(1) Any hospital, surgeon or physician, for medical or dental education, research, advancement of medical or dental science, therapy of transplantation; or

(2) Any accredited medical or dental school, college or university for education, research, advancement of medical or dental science or therapy; or

(3) Any bank or storage facility, for medical or dental education, research, advancement of medical or dental science, therapy or transplantation; or

(4) Any specified individual for therapy or transplantation needed by him.

§ 2713. Manner of executing anatomical gifts. (a) A gift of all or part of the body under Section 2711(a) of this act may be made by will. The gift becomes effective upon the death of the testator without waiting for probate. If the will is not probated, or if it is declared invalid for testamentary purposes, the gift, to the extent that it has been acted upon in good faith, is nevertheless valid and effective.

(b) A gift of all or part of the body under Section 2711(a) of this act may also be made by document other than a will. The gift becomes effective upon the death of the donor. The document, which may be a card designed to be carried on the person, must be signed by the donor in the presence of 2 witnesses who need not be in the presence of each other but who must sign the document in his presence. If the donor cannot sign, the document may be signed for him at his direction and in his presence and in the presence of 2 witnesses who must sign the document in his presence. Delivery of the document of gift during the donor's lifetime is not necessary to make the gift valid.

(c) The gift may be made to a specified donee or without specifying a donee. If the latter, the gift may be accepted by the attending physician as donee upon or following death. If the gift is made to a specified donee who is not available at the time and place of death, the attending physician upon or following death, in the absence of any expressed indication that the donor desired otherwise, may accept the gift as donee. The physician who becomes a donee under this subsection shall not participate in the procedures for removing or transplanting a part.

(d) Notwithstanding Section 2716(b) of this act, the donor may designate in his will, card, or other document of gift the surgeon or physician to carry out the appropriate procedures. In the absence of a designation or if the designee is not available, the donee or other person authorized to accept the gift may employ or authorize any surgeon or physician for the purpose or, in the case of a gift of eyes, he may employ or authorize an undertaker licensed by the State who has successfully completed a course in eye enucleation approved by the Medical Examiner of the State to enucleate eyes for the gift after certification of death by a physician. A qualified undertaker acting in accordance with this subsection shall be free from civil and criminal liability with respect to the eye enucleation.

(e) Any gift by a person designated in Section 2711(b) of this act shall be made by a document signed by him or made by his telegraphic, recorded telephonic or other recorded message.

(f) A person who so directs the manner in which his body or any part of his body shall be disposed of shall receive no remuneration or other thing of value for such disposition.

§ 2714. **Delivery of document of gift.** If the gift is made by the donor to a specified donee, the will, card or other document, or an executed copy thereof, may be delivered to the donee to expedite the appropriate procedures immediately after death, but delivery is not necessary to the validity of the gift. The will, card or other document, or an executed copy thereof, may be deposited in any hospital, bank or storage facility or registry office that accepts them for safekeeping or for facilitation of procedures after death. On request of any interested party upon or after the donor's death, the person in possession shall produce the document for examination.

§ 2715. **Amendment or revocation of the gift.** (a) If the will, card or other document or executed copy thereof has been delivered to a specified donee, the donor may amend or revoke the gift by:

(1) The execution and delivery to the donee of a signed statement; or

(2) An oral statement made in the presence of 2 persons and communicated to the donee; or

(3) A statement during a terminal illness or injury addressed to an attending physician and communicated to the donee; or

(b) A signed card or document which has not been delivered to the donee may be revoked by the donor in the manner set forth in subsection (a) of this section or by destruction, cancellation or mutilation of the document and all executed copies thereof.

(c) Any gift made by a will may also be amended or revoked in the manner provided for amendment or revocation of wills or as provided in subsection (a) of this section.

§ 2716. **Rights and duties at death.** (a) The donee may accept or reject the gift. If the donee accepts a gift of the entire body, he may, subject to the terms of the gift, authorize embalming and the use of the body in funeral services. If the gift is of a part of the body, the donee, upon the death of the donor and prior to embalming, shall cause the part to be removed without unnecessary mutilation. After removal of the part, custody of the remainder of the body vests in the surviving spouse, next of kin or other persons under obligation to dispose of the body. The heir of any donor, at the time the disposition of the body takes place, may submit a request in writing to the donee that the body be returned to the heir at such time as the donee either refuses the disposition of the entire body or the parts thereof or determines that he no longer has use of the remains.

(b) A surgeon, physician, funeral director or eye bank technician who is authorized to remove any part in accordance with this subchapter is also authorized to draw or secure a blood sample from the donor, in order to screen the tissue received for medical purposes.

(c) The time of death shall be determined by a physician who attends the donor at his death or, if none, the physician who certifies the death. This physician shall not participate in the procedures for removing or transplanting a part.

(d) A person who acts in good faith in accord with the terms of this subchapter or under the anatomical gift laws of another state (or a foreign country) is not liable for damages in any civil action or subject to prosecution in any criminal proceeding for his act.

(e) Where no other provision for the same exists, a body, or the remains thereof, after it is no longer needed for the purpose indicated by the donor, may be buried at pubic expense on order of the Medical Council of Delaware, but in no case shall the expense of the burial exceed $100.

(f) This subchapter is subject to the laws of this State prescribing powers and duties with respect to autopsies.

§ 2717. Uniformity of interpretation. This subchapter shall be so construed as to effectuate its general purpose to make uniform the law of those states which enact it.

§ 2718. Short title. This subchapter may be cited as the Uniform Anatomical Gift Act.

§ 2719. The following forms may be used to accomplish the purposes of this subchapter. **See Appendix A for these forms: Anatomical Gift by Next of Kin or Other Authorized Person; Anatomical Gift by Living Donor; Anatomical Gift by a Living Minor Donor.**

DISTRICT OF COLUMBIA

§ 2-1501. Definitions; short title. (a) As used in this chapter, the term:

(1) "Bank or storage facility" means a facility licensed, accredited, or approved under the laws of any state for storage of human bodies or parts thereof.

(2) "Decedent" means a deceased individual and includes a stillborn infant or fetus.

(3) "Donor" means an individual who makes a gift of all or part of his body.

(4) "Hospital" means a hospital licensed, accredited, or approved under the laws of any state and includes a hospital operated by the United States government, a state, or a subdivision thereof, although not required to be licensed under state laws.

(5) "Part" includes organs, tissues, eyes, bones, arteries, blood, other fluids, and other portions of a human body, and "part" includes "parts."

(6) "Person" means an individual, corporation, government, or governmental subdivision or agency, business trust, estate, trust, partnership, or association or any other legal entity.

(7) "Physician" or "surgeon" means a physician or surgeon licensed or authorized to practice under the laws of any State.

(8) "State" includes any state, district, commonwealth, territory, insular possession, the District of Columbia, and any other area subject to the legislative authority of the United States of America.

(b) This chapter shall be known as the "District of Columbia Anatomical Gift Act."

§ 2-1502. Persons eligible to execute gifts; nonacceptance by donee; rights of donee created by gift. (a) Any individual of sound mind and 18 years of age or more may give all or any part of his body for any purposes specified in section 2-1503, the gift to take effect upon death.

(b) Any of the following persons, in order of priority stated, when persons in prior classes are not available at the time of death, and in the absence of actual notice of contrary indications by the decedent, or actual notice of opposition by a member of the same or a prior class, may give all or any part of the decedent's body for any purposes specified in section 2-1503:

(1) The spouse;

(2) An adult son or daughter;

(3) Either parent;

(4) An adult brother or sister;

(5) A guardian of the person of the decedent at the time of his death; or

(6) Any other person authorized or under obligation to dispose of the body.

(c) If the donee has actual notice of contrary indications by the decedent, or that a gift by a member of a class is opposed by a member of the same or a prior class, the donee shall not accept the gift. The persons authorized by subsection (b) of this section may make the gift after death or immediately before death.

(d) A gift of all or part of a body authorizes any examination necessary to assure medical acceptability of the gift for the purposes intended.

(e) The rights of the donee created by the gift are paramount to the rights of others except as provided by section 2-1507(d).

§ 2-1503. Persons who may become donees; purposes for which gifts may be made. The following persons may become donees of gifts of bodies or parts thereof for the purposes stated:

(1) Any hospital, surgeon, or physician, for medical or dental education, research, advancement of medical or dental science, therapy, or transplantation; or

(2) Any accredited medical or dental school, college, or university, for education, research, advancement of medical or dental science, or therapy; or

(3) Any bank or storage facility, for medical or dental education, research, advancement of medical or dental science, therapy, or transplantation; or

(4) Any specified individual for therapy or transplantation needed by him.

§ 2-1504. Manner of executing gifts. (a) A gift of all or part of the body under section 2-1502(a) may be made by will. The gift becomes effective upon the death of the testator without waiting for probate. If the will is not probated, or if it is declared invalid for testamentary purposes, the gift, to the extent that it has been acted upon in good faith, is nevertheless valid and effective.

(b)(1) A gift of all or part of the body under section 2-1502(a) may also be made by document other than a will. The gift becomes effective upon death of the donor. The document, which may be a card designed to be carried on the person, must be signed by the donor, in the presence of 2 witnesses who must sign the document in his presence. If the donor cannot sign, the document may be signed for him at his direction and in his presence, and in the presence of 2 witnesses who must sign the document in his presence. Delivery of the document of gift during the donor's lifetime is not necessary to make the gift valid.

(2) Any such document referred to in paragraph (1) of this subsection may be in the following form and contain the following information: **See Appendix for this form (Uniform Donor Card).** This is a legal document under the District of Columbia Anatomical Gift Act or similar laws.

(c) The gift may be made to a specified donee or without specifying a donee. If the latter, the gift may be accepted by the attending physician as donee upon or following death. If the gift is made to a specified donee who is not available at the time and place of death, the attending physician upon or following death, in the absence of any expressed indication that the donor desired otherwise, may accept the gift as donee. The physician who becomes a donee under this subsection shall not participate in the procedures for removing or transplanting a part.

(d) Notwithstanding section 2-1507(b), the donor may designate in his will, card, or other document of gift the surgeon or physician to carry out the appropriate procedures. In the absence of a designation, or if the designee is not available, the donee or other person authorized to accept the gift may employ or authorize any surgeon or physician for the purpose.

(e) Any gift by a person designated in section 2-1502(b) shall be made by a document signed by him, or made by his telegraphic, recorded telephonic, or other recorded message.

§ 2-1505. Delivery of document of gift. If the gift is made by the donor to a specified donee, the will, card, or other document, or an executed copy thereof, may be delivered to the donee to expedite the appropriate procedures immediately after death, but delivery is not necessary to the validity of the gift. The will, card, or other document, or an executed copy thereof, may be deposited in any hospital, bank or storage facility, or registry office that accepts them for safekeeping or for facilitation of procedures after death. On request of any interested party upon or after the donor's death, the person in possession shall produce the document for examination.

§ 2-1506. Amendment or revocation of gift. (a) If the will, card, or other document or executed copy thereof, has been delivered to a specified donee, the donor may amend or revoke the gift by:

(1) The execution and delivery to the donee of a signed statement; or

(2) An oral statement made in the presence of two persons and communicated to the donee; or

(3) A statement during a terminal illness or injury addressed to an attending physician and communicated to the donee; or

(4) A signed card or document found on his person or in his effects.

(b) Any document of gift which has not been delivered to the donee may be revoked by the donor in the manner set out in subsection (a) of this section or by destruction, cancellation, or mutilation of the document and all executed copies thereof.

(c) Any gift made by a will may also be amended or revoked in the manner provided for amendment or revocation of wills, or as provided in subsection (a) of this section.

§ 2-1507. Duties of donee; determination of time of death; immunity. (a) The donee may accept or reject the gift. If the donee accepts a gift of the entire body, he may, subject to the terms of the gift, authorize embalming and the use of the body in funeral services. If the gift is of a part of the body, the donee, upon the death of the donor and prior to embalming, shall cause the part to be removed without unnecessary mutilation. After removal of the part, custody of the remainder of the body vests in the surviving spouse, next of kin or other persons under obligation to dispose of the body.

(b) The time of death shall be determined by a physician who attends the donor at his death, or, if none, the physician who certifies the death. This physician shall not participate in the procedures for removing or transplanting a part.

(c) A person, who acts in good faith, in accord with the terms of this chapter, or under the anatomical gift laws of another state is not liable for damages in any civil action or subject to prosecution in any criminal proceeding for his act.

(d) The provisions of this chapter are subject to the laws of the District of Columbia prescribing powers and duties with respect to autopsies.

§ 2-1508. Construction. This chapter shall be so construed as to effectuate its general purpose to make uniform the law of those states which enacted it.

§ 2-1509. Duties of hospitals and hospices. (a) As of January 1, 1988, whenever a patient of a hospital or hospice dies, is determined to be a suitable candidate for organ or tissue donation, and has not made an anatomical gift by will or uniform donor card, a representative of the hospital or hospice shall, in accordance with section 2-1502(b) and (c), request a person authorized by section 2-1502(b) to consent to an anatomical gift of all or part of the decedent's body.

(b) The request required by subsection (a) of this section shall be made only if a nonprofit organ or tissue bank or retrieval organization has notified the hospital or hospice that a donation can be properly obtained and used in a manner consistent with accepted medical standards.

(c) Upon the discovery of a properly executed uniform donor card or the receipt of a consent under subsection (a) of this section, a hospital or hospice shall immediately notify a nonprofit organ or tissue bank or retrieval organization and shall cooperate in procuring the anatomical gift.

§ 2-1510. Certificate requirement. (a) Whenever a request for consent is made pursuant to section 2-1509, the hospital or hospice representative making the request shall complete a certificate of request for an anatomical gift on a form supplied by the Mayor. The certificate shall include the following:

(1) A statement indicating that a request for an anatomical gift was made;

(2) The name and affiliation of the person making the request;

(3) An indication of whether consent was granted and, if so, what organs and tissues were donated; and

(4) The name of the person granting or refusing the request, and his or her relationship to the decedent.

(b) A copy of the certificate described in subsection (a) of this section shall be included in the decedent's medical record.

§ 2-1511. Rules. The Mayor shall, no later than August 1, 1987, and pursuant to subchapter I of Chapter 15 of Title 1, issue all rules necessary to carry out the purposes of section 2-1509 and 2-1510. These rules shall at a minimum include:

(1) Standards for the training and qualification of those hospital and hospice representatives who have been designated to make consent requests pursuant to section 2-1509;

(2) Procedures to be used when making consent requests under section 2-1509; and

(3) Procedures to facilitate effective coordination among hospitals, hospices, other health-care facilities and agencies, organ and tissue banks, and retrieval organizations.

FLORIDA

§ 732.910. Legislative declaration. Because of the rapid medical progress in the fields of tissue and organ preservation, transplantation of tissue, and tissue culture, and because it is in the public interest to aid the medical developments in these fields, the Legislature in enacting this part intends to encourage and aid the development of reconstructive medicine and surgery and the development of medical research by facilitating premortem and postmortem authorizations for donations of tissue and organs. It is the purpose of this part to regulate the gift of a body or parts of a body, the gift to be made after the death of a donor.

§ 732.911 Definitions. For the purpose of this part:

(1) "Bank" or "storage facility" means a facility licensed, accredited, or approved under the laws of any state for storage of human bodies or parts thereof.

(2) "Donor" means an individual who makes a gift of all or part of his body.

(3) "Hospital" means a hospital licensed, accredited, or approved under the laws of any state and includes a hospital operated by the United States Government or a state, or a subdivision thereof, although not required to be licensed under state laws.

(4) "Physician" or "surgeon" means a physician or surgeon licensed to practice under chapter 458 or chapter 459 or similar laws of any state. "Surgeon" includes dental or oral surgeon.

§ 732.912. Persons who may make an anatomical gift. (1) Any persons who may make a will may give all or part of his body for any purpose specified in Section 732.910, the gift to take effect upon death.

(2) In the order of priority stated and in the absence of actual notice of contrary indications by the decedent or actual notice of opposition by a member of the same or a prior class, any of the following persons may give all or any part of the decedent's body for any purpose specified in Section 732.910:

(a) The spouse of the decedent;

(b) An adult son or daughter of the decedent;

(c) Either parent of the decedent;

(d) An adult brother or sister of the decedent;

(e) A guardian of the person of the decedent at the time of his death; or

(f) A representative ad litem who shall be appointed by a court of competent jurisdiction forthwith upon a petition heard ex parte filed by any person, which representative ad litem shall ascertain that no person of higher priority exists who objects to the gift of all or any part of the decedent's body and that no evidence exists of the decedent's having made a communication expressing a desire that his body or body parts not be donated upon death;

but no gift shall be made by the spouse if any adult son or daughter objects, and provided that those of higher priority, if they are reasonably available, have been contacted and made aware of the proposed gift, and further provided that a reasonable search is made to show that there would have been no objection on religious grounds by the decedent.

(3) If the donee has actual notice of contrary indications by the decedent or objection of an adult son or daughter or actual notice that a gift by a member of a class is opposed by a member of the same or a prior class, the donee shall not accept the gift.

(4) The person authorized by subsection (2) may make the gift after the decedent's death or immediately before the decedent's death.

(5) A gift of all or part of a body authorizes any examination necessary to assure medical acceptability of the gift for the purposes intended.

(6) The rights of the donee created by the gift are paramount to the rights of others, except as provided by Section 732.917.

§ 732.913. Persons who may become donees; purposes for which anatomical gifts may be made. The following persons may become donees of gifts of bodies or parts of them for the purposes stated:

(1) Any hospital, surgeon, or physician for medical or dental education or research, advancement of medical or dental science, therapy, or transplantation.

(2) Any accredited medical or dental school, college, or university for education, research, advancement of medical or dental science, or therapy.

(3) Any bank or storage facility for medical or dental education, research, advancement of medical or dental science, therapy, or transplantation.

(4) Any specified individual for therapy or transplantation needed by him.

§ 732.914. Manner of executing anatomical gifts. (1) A gift of all or part of the body under subsection 732.912(1) may be made by will. The gift becomes effective upon the death of the testator without waiting for probate. If the will is not probated or if it is declared invalid for testamentary purposes, the gift is nevertheless valid to the extent that it has been acted upon in good faith.

(2)(a) A gift of all or part of the body under subsection 732.912(1) may also be made by a document other than a will. The gift becomes effective upon the death of the donor. The document must be signed by the donor in the presence of two witnesses who shall sign the document in his presence. If the donor cannot sign, the document may be signed for him at his direction and in his presence and the presence of two witnesses who must sign the document in his presence. Delivery of the document of gift during the donor's lifetime is not necessary to make the gift valid.

(b) The following form of written instrument shall be sufficient for any person to give all or part of his body for the purposes of this part: **See Appendix for form (Uniform Donor Card).**

(3) The gift may be made to a specified donee or without specifying a donee. In the latter case, the gift may be accepted by the attending physician as donee upon or following the donor's death. If the gift is made to a specified donee who is not available at the time and place of death, the attending physician may accept the gift as donee upon or following death in the absence of any expressed indication that the donor desired otherwise. The physician who becomes a donee under this subsection shall not participate in the procedures for removing or transplanting a part.

(4) Notwithstanding subsection 732.917(2), the donor may designate in his will or other document of gift the surgeon or physician to carry out the appropriate procedures. In the absence of a designation or if the designee is not available, the donee or other person authorized to accept the gift may employ or authorize any surgeon or physician for the purpose.

(5) Any gift by a person designated in subsection 732.719(2) shall be made by a document signed by him or made by his telegraphic, recorded telephonic, or other recorded message.

§ 732.915. Delivery of the document. (1) If a gift is made through the program established by the Department of Health and Rehabilitative Services and the Department of Highway Safety and Motor Vehicles under the authority of section 732.921, the completed donor registration card shall be delivered to the Department of Highway Safety and Motor Vehicles and placed in its file, but the delivery is not necessary to the validity of the gift. If the donor withdraws the gift, the donor registration card shall be destroyed.

(2) If a gift is not made through the program established by the Department of Health and Rehabilitative Services and the Department of Highway Safety and Motor Vehicles under the authority of section 732.921 and is made by the donor to a specified donee, the document, other than a will, may be delivered to the donee to expedite the appropriate procedures immediately after death, but delivery is not necessary to the validity of the gift. Such document may be deposited in any hospital, bank, storage facility, or registry office that accepts such documents for safekeeping or for facilitation of procedures after death.

(3) On the request of any interested party upon or after the donor's death, the person in possession shall produce the document for examination.

§ 732.916. Amendment or revocation of gift. (1) If the will or other document authorized under the provisions of section 732.915(2) has been delivered to a specified donee, the donor may amend or revoke the gift by:

(a) The execution and delivery to the donee of a signed statement.

(b) An oral statement made in the presence of two persons and communicated to the donee.

(c) A statement during a terminal illness or injury addressed to an attending physician and communicated to the donee.

(d) A signed document found on his person or in his effects.

(2) A document of gift that has not been delivered to the donee may be revoked by the donor in the manner set out in subsection (1) or by destruction, cancellation, or mutilation of the document.

(3) Any gift made by a will may also be amended or revoked in the manner provided for amendment or revocation of wills or as provided in subsection (1).

§ 732.917. Rights and duties at death. (1) The donee, as specified under the provisions of section 732.915(2), may accept or reject the gift. If the donee accepts a gift of the entire body or a part of the body to be used for scientific purposes other than a transplant, he may authorize embalming and the use of the body in funeral services, subject to the terms of the gift. If the gift is of a part of the body, the donee shall cause the part to be removed without unnecessary mutilation upon the death of the donor and before or after embalming. After removal of the part, custody of the remainder of the body vests in the surviving spouse, next of kin, or other persons under obligation to dispose of the body.

(2) The time of death shall be determined by a physician who attends the donor at his death or, if there is no such physician, the physician who certifies the death. This physician shall not participate in the procedures for removing or transplanting a part.

(3) A person who acts in good faith and without negligence in accord with the terms of this part or under the anatomical gift laws of another state or foreign country is not liable for damages in any civil action or subject to prosecution for his acts in any criminal proceeding.

(4) The provisions of this part are subject to the laws of this state prescribing powers and duties with respect to autopsies.

§ 732.918. **Eye banks.** (1) Any state, county, district, or other public hospital may purchase and provide the necessary facilities and equipment to establish and maintain an eye bank for restoration of sight purposes.

(2) The Department of Health and Rehabilitative Services may have prepared, printed, and distributed:

(a) A form document of gift for a gift of the eyes.

(b) An eye bank register consisting of the names of persons who have executed documents for the gift of their eyes.

(c) Wallet cards reciting the document of gift.

§ **732.9185. Corneal removal by medical examiners.** (1) In any case in which a patient is in need of corneal tissue for a transplant, a district medical examiner or an appropriately qualified designee with training in ophthalmologic techniques may, upon request of any eye bank authorized under section 732.918, provide the cornea of a decedent whenever all of the following conditions are met:

(a) A decedent who may provide a suitable cornea for the transplant is under the jurisdiction of the medical examiner and an autopsy is required in accordance with section 406.11.

(b) No objection by the next of kin of the decedent is known by the medical examiner.

(c) The removal of the cornea will not interfere with the subsequent course of an investigation or autopsy.

(2) Neither the district medical examiner nor his appropriately qualified designee nor any eye bank authorized under section 732.918 may be held liable in any civil or criminal action for failure to obtain consent of the next of kin.

§ 732.919. **Enucleation of eyes by licensed funeral directors.** With respect to a gift of an eye as provided for in this part, a licensed funeral director as defined in chapter 470 who has completed a course in eye enucleation and has received a certificate of competence from the Department of Ophthalmology of the University of Florida School of Medicine, the University of South Florida School of Medicine, or the University of Miami School of Medicine may enucleate eyes for gift after proper certification of death by a physician and in compliance with the intent of the gift as defined in this chapter. No properly certified funeral director acting in accordance with the terms of this part shall have any civil or criminal liability for eye enucleation.

§ 732.921. **Donations as part of driver license or identification card process.** (1) The Department of Health and Rehabilitative Services and the Department of Highway Safety and Motor Vehicles shall develop and implement a program encouraging and allowing persons to make anatomical gifts as part of the process of issuing identification cards and issuing and renewing driver licenses. The donor registration card distributed by the Department of Highway Safety and Motor

Vehicles shall include the material specified by section 732.914(2)(b) and may require such additional information, and include such additional material, as may be deemed necessary by that department. The Department of Highway Safety and Motor Vehicles shall also develop and implement a program to identify donors, which program may include notations on identification cards, driver licenses, and driver records or such other methods as the department may develop. The Department of Health and Rehabilitative Services shall provide the necessary supplies and forms through funds appropriated from general revenue or contributions from interested voluntary, nonprofit organizations. The Department of Highway Safety and Motor Vehicles shall provide the necessary recordkeeping system through funds appropriated from general revenue. The Department of Highway Safety and Motor Vehicles and the Department of Health and Rehabilitative Services shall incur no liability in connection with the performance of any acts authorized herein.

(2) The Department of Highway Safety and Motor Vehicles, after consultation with and concurrence by the Department of Health and Rehabilitative Services, shall promulgate rules and regulations to implement the provisions of this section according to the provisions of chapter 120.

(3) Funds expended by the Department of Health and Rehabilitative Services to carry out the intent of this section shall not be taken from any funds appropriated for patient care.

§ 732.9215. Education program relating to anatomical gifts. The Department of Health and Rehabilitative Services, subject to the concurrence of the Department of Highway Safety and Motor Vehicles, shall develop a continuing program to educate and inform medical professionals, law enforcement agencies and officers, and the public regarding the laws of this state relating to anatomical gifts and the need for anatomical gifts.

(1) The program shall be implemented by contract with one or more medical schools located in the state.

(2) The Legislature finds that particular difficulties exist in making members of the various minority communities within the state aware of laws relating to anatomical gifts and the need for anatomical gifts. Therefore, the program shall include, as a demonstration project, activities targeted at providing such information to the nonwhite, Hispanic, and Caribbean populations of the state.

§ 732.922. Duty of certain hospital administrators. (1) When used in this section, "hospital" means any establishment licensed under chapter 395 that is a verified trauma center or that provides emergency medical care services or acute care services.

(2) Where, based on accepted medical standards, a hospital patient is a suitable candidate for organ or tissue donation, the hospital administrator or his designee shall at or near the time of death request any of the persons specified in section 732.912, in the order of priority stated, when persons in prior classes are not available and in the absence of actual notice of contrary intentions by the decedent or actual notice of opposition by a member of any of the classes specified in section 732.912, to consent to the gift of all or any part of the decedent's body for any purpose specified in this part.

(3) Where the hospital administrator or his designee has actual notice of opposition from any of the persons specified in section 732.912, such gift of all or any part of the decedent's body shall not be requested. Except as provided in section 732.912, in the absence of actual notice of opposition, consent or refusal need only be obtained from the person or persons in the highest priority class available.

(4) A gift made pursuant to a request required by this section shall be executed pursuant to section 732.914.

(5) The Department of Health and Rehabilitative Services shall establish rules and guidelines con-

cerning the education of individuals who may be designated to perform the request and the procedures to be used in making the request. The department is authorized to adopt rules concerning the documentation of the request, where such request is made.

(6) No recovery shall be allowed nor shall civil or criminal proceedings be instituted in any court in this state against the licensed hospital or the hospital administrator or his designee when, in his best judgment, he deems such a request for organ donation to be inappropriate according to the procedures established by the Department of Health and Rehabilitative Services, or he has made every reasonable effort to comply with the provisions of this section.

GEORGIA

§ 44-5-140. **Short title.** This article may be cited as the "Georgia Anatomical Gift Act."

§ 44-5-141. **Intent; legislative purpose.** This article shall be so construed as to effectuate its general purpose to make uniform the law of those states which enact it.

§ 44-5-142. **Definitions.** As used in this article, the term:

(1) "Bank or storage facility" means a tissue bank or eye bank licensed or approved by the State of Georgia and also means an organ procurement agency or other facilities for the storage of human bodies or parts thereof in this state.

(2) "Decedent" means a deceased individual and includes a stillborn infant or fetus.

(3) "Donor" means an individual who makes a gift of all or part of his body.

(4) "Hospital" means a hospital licensed, accredited, or approved under the laws of any state, although not required to be licensed under state laws, and includes hospitals operated by the United States government or by the state or a subdivision thereof.

(4.5) "Organ procurement agency" means an organization located in the State of Georgia that is designated by the Health Care Financing Administration of the federal Department of Health and Human Services under the end stage renal disease facility regulations to perform or coordinate the performance of all of the following services:

(A) Procurement of donated kidneys;

(B) Preservation of donated kidneys;

(C) Transportation of donated kidneys; and

(D) Maintenance of a system to locate prospective recipients of procured organs.

An organ procurement agency may also perform these services for extrarenal vital organs and includes any organization certified by the federal Department of Health and Human Services as an organ procurement agency.

(5) "Part" means organs, tissues, eyes, bones, arteries, blood and other fluids, and any other portions of a human body. The term "part" also means a heart pacemaker.

(6) "Person" means an individual, corporation, government or governmental subdivision or agency, business trust, estate, trust, partnership or association, or any other legal entity.

(7) "Physician" or "surgeon" means a physician or surgeon licensed or authorized to practice under the laws of any state.

(8) "State" means any state, district, commonwealth, territory, insular possession, and any other area subject to the legislative authority of the United States of America.

§ 44-5-143. Adult decedents. (a) Any individual who is 18 years of age or older and of sound mind may give all or any part of his body for any purpose specified in Code Section 44-5-144, the gift to take effect upon death.

(b) On or before the occurrence of death in a hospital, when persons in prior classes are not available and in the absence of actual notice of contrary indications by the decedent or actual notice of opposition by a member of the same or a prior class, the person in charge of the hospital or his designated representative shall notify the applicable type of bank or storage facility which shall, if appropriate, request that any of the following persons, in order of priority stated, give all or any part of the decedent's body for any purpose specified in Code Section 44-5-144:

(1) The spouse;

(2) An adult son or daughter;

(3) Either parent;

(4) An adult brother or sister;

(5) A guardian of the person of the decedent at the time of his death other than a guardian ad litem appointed for such purpose; or

(6) Any other person authorized or under obligation to dispose of the body.

(c)(1) The person in charge of the hospital or his designated representative shall record in a book kept for this purpose a statement to the effect that the applicable type of bank or storage facility has been notified and whether, if appropriate, a request for a consent to an anatomical gift has been made and shall further indicate whether or not consent was granted, the name of the person granting the consent, and his or her relationship to the decedent.

(2) A request under subsection (b) of this Code section is appropriate only when consent would yield a donation suitable for use pursuant to medical and other criteria as defined by regulations of the Board of Human Resources.

(d) If the donee has actual notice of contrary indications by the decedent or actual notice that a gift by a member of a class is opposed by a member of the same or a prior class, the donee shall not accept the gift. The persons authorized by subsection (b) of this Code section may make the gift after or immediately before death. Upon admission of a person to any hospital, at his request, the hospital shall record in a book kept for the purpose the expression of intent of such person with regard to the disposition of his body and such expression shall be deemed to be sufficient notice under this Code section not to be contravened by opposition from persons listed in subsection (b) of this Code section.

(e) A gift of all or part of a body authorizes any examination necessary to assure medical acceptability of the gift for the purposes intended.

(f) The rights of the donee created by the gift are paramount to the rights of others except as provided by subsection (d) of Code Section 44-5-148.

(g) The Board of Human Resources shall establish regulations concerning the training of any person or persons who may be designated to perform the request and the procedures to be employed in making it. In addition, the board shall establish such regulations as are necessary to implement appropriate hospital procedures to facilitate the delivery of donations from receiving hospitals to potential recipients.

(h) The Board of Human Resources shall establish such additional rules and regulations as are necessary for the implementation of this Code section.

(i) In promulgating or amending all rules and regulations required for the proper implementation and administration of this Code section, the Board of Human Resources shall consult with and receive input from any and all affected associations, agencies, or entities including but not limited to the Medical Association of Georgia, the Atlanta Regional Organ Procurement Agency, the Atlanta Regional Tissue Bank, the Medical College of Georgia Regional Organ Procurement Program, the Georgia Lions Eye Bank, Inc., and the Georgia Hospital Association.

(j) In the absence of a specification by a decedent or a person authorized to give all or part of the decedent's body, any bank or storage facility that becomes the donee shall give preference to potential recipients of that donation who are residents of this state if:

(1) The donation is medically acceptable to the potential recipients who are residents of this state;

(2) Potential recipients who are residents of other states are not in greater need of the donation than potential recipients who are residents of this state; and

(3) The requisite medical procedure required to receive the donation will be performed in this state.

§ 44-5-143.1. Minor decedents. (a) The parents, legal guardian, or other person authorized under subsection (b) of this Code section may, unless otherwise directed by a will, give all or any part of the body of a person who is under 18 years of age for any purpose specified in Code Section 44-5-144, the gift to take effect upon death.

(b) On or before the occurrence of death in a hospital, when persons in prior classes are not available and in the absence of actual notice of contrary indications by the decedent or actual notice of opposition by a member of the same or a prior class, the person in charge of the hospital or his designated representative shall notify the applicable type of bank or storage facility which shall, if appropriate, request that any of the following persons, in order of priority stated, give all or any part of the decedent's body for any purpose specified in Code Section 44-5-144:

(1) Both parents;

(2) If both parents are not readily available and no contrary indications of the absent parent are known, one parent;

(3) If the parents are divorced or legally separated, the custodial parent;

(4) In the absence of the custodial parent, when no contrary indications of the absent parent are known, the noncustodial parent;

(5) If there are no parents, the legal guardian; or

(6) Any other person authorized or obligated to dispose of the body.

(c)(1) The person in charge of the hospital or his designated representative shall record in a book kept for this purpose a statement to the effect that the applicable type of bank or storage facility has been notified and whether, if appropriate, a request for a consent to an anatomical gift has been made and shall further indicate whether or not consent was granted, the name of the person granting the consent, and his or her relationship to the decedent.

(2) A request under subsection (b) of this Code section is appropriate only when consent would yield a donation suitable for use pursuant to medical and other criteria as defined by regulations of the Board of Human Resources.

(d) If the donee has actual notice of contrary indications by the decedent or actual notice that a gift by a member of a class is opposed by a member of the same or a prior class, the donee shall not accept the gift. The persons authorized by subsection (b) of this Code section may make the gift after or immediately before death. Upon admission of a person to any hospital, at his request, the hospital shall record in a book kept for the purpose the expression of intent of such person with regard to the disposition of his body and such expression shall be deemed to be sufficient notice under this Code section not to be contravened by opposition from persons listed in subsection (b) of this Code section.

(e) A gift of all or part of a body authorizes any examination necessary to assure medical acceptability of the gift for the purposes intended.

(f) The rights of the donee created by the gift are paramount to the rights of others except as provided by subsection (d) of Code Section 44-5-148.

(g) The Board of Human Resources shall establish regulations concerning the training of any person or persons who may be designated to perform the request and the procedures to be employed in making it. In addition, the board shall establish such regulations as are necessary to implement appropriate hospital procedures to facilitate the delivery of donations from receiving hospitals to potential recipients.

(h) The Board of Human Resources shall establish such additional rules and regulations as are necessary for the implementation of this Code section.

(i) In promulgating or amending all rules and regulations required for the proper implementation and administration of this Code section, the Board of Human Resources shall consult with and receive input from any and all affected associations, agencies, or entities including but not limited to the Medical Association of Georgia, the Atlanta Regional Organ Procurement Agency, the Atlanta Regional Tissue Bank, the Medical College of Georgia Regional Organ Procurement Program, the Georgia Lions Eye Bank, Inc., and the Georgia Hospital Association.

(j) In the absence of a specification by a decedent or a person authorized to give all or part of the decedent's body, any bank or storage facility that becomes the donee shall give preference to potential recipients of that donation who are residents of this state if:

(1) The donation is medically acceptable to the potential recipients who are residents of this state;

(2) Potential recipients who are residents of other states are not in greater need of the donation than potential recipients who are residents of this state; and

(3) The requisite medical procedure required to receive the donation will be performed in this state.

§ 44-5-144. Permissible donees and purposes of anatomical gifts. The following persons may become donees of gifts of bodies or parts thereof for the purposes stated:

(1) Any hospital, surgeon, or physician, for medical or dental education, research, advancement of medical or dental science, therapy, or transplantation;

(2) Any accredited medical or dental school, college, or university, for education, research, advancement of medical or dental science, or therapy;

(3) Any bank or storage facility, for medical or dental education, research, advancement of medical or dental science, therapy, or transplantation; or

(4) Any specified individual, for therapy or transplantation needed by him.

§ 44-5-145. Gifts made by will; donor card or other instruments; specification of donee, etc.; procedures in absence of specified donee, etc.; certain physicians not to participate in procedures; signatures or recordings.

(a) A gift of all or part of the body under subsection (a) of Code Section 44-5-143 may be made by will. The gift becomes effective upon the death of the testator without waiting for probate. If the will is not probated or if it is declared invalid for testamentary purposes, the gift, to the extent that it has been acted upon in good faith, is nevertheless valid and effective.

(b) A gift of all or part of the body under subsection (a) of Code Section 44-5-143 may also be made by a document other than a will. Unless the gift is deemed medically unsuitable, the gift becomes effective and irrevocable upon the death of the donor. The document, which may be a card designed to be carried on the person, must be signed by the donor in the presence of two witnesses who must sign the document in his presence. If the donor cannot sign, the document may be signed for him at his direction and in his presence and in the presence of two witnesses who must sign the document in his presence. Delivery of the document of gift during the donor's lifetime is not necessary to make the gift valid.

(c) The gift may be made to a specified donee or an unspecified donee. If no donee is specified, the gift may be accepted by the attending physician as donee upon or following death. If the gift is made to a specified donee who is not available at the time and place of death, the attending physician, upon or following death, may accept the gift as donee in the absence of any expressed indication that the donor desired otherwise. The physician who becomes a donee under this subsection shall not participate in the procedures for removing or transplanting a part.

(d) Notwithstanding subsection (b) of Code Section 44-5-148, the donor may designate in his will, card, or other document of gift the surgeon or physician who shall carry out the appropriate procedures. In the absence of a designation or if the designee is not available, the donee or other person authorized to accept the gift may employ or authorize any surgeon or physician for the purpose.

(e) Any gift by a person designated in subsection (b) of Code Section 44-5-143 shall be made by a document signed by him or made by his telegraphic, recorded telephonic, or other recorded message.

§ 44-5-146. Delivery of gift document to specific donee or deposit in hospital, bank, etc.; necessity for delivery. If the gift is made by the donor to a specified donee, the will, card, other document, or an executed copy thereof may be delivered to the donee to expedite the appropriate procedures immediately after death. Delivery is not necessary to the validity of the gift. The will, card, other document, or an executed copy thereof may be deposited in any hospital, bank or storage facility, or registry office that accepts it for safekeeping or for facilitation of procedures after death. Upon the request of any interested party upon or after the donor's death, the person in possession shall produce the document for examination.

§ 44-5-147. Amendment or revocation of gift. (a) If the will, card, other document, or an executed copy thereof has been delivered to a specified donee, the donor may amend or revoke the gift by:

(1) The execution and delivery to the donee of a signed statement;

(2) An oral statement made in the presence of two persons and communicated to the donee;

(3) A statement during a terminal illness or injury, which statement is addressed to an attending physician and communicated to the donee; or

(4) A signed card or document found on his person or in his effects.

(b) Any document of gift which has not been delivered to the donee may be revoked by the donor in the manner set out in subsection (a) of this Code section or by the destruction, cancellation, or mutilation of the document and all executed copies thereof.

(c) Any gift made by a will may also be amended or revoked in the manner provided for the amendment or revocation of wills or as provided in subsection (a) of this Code section.

§ 44-5-148. Acceptance by donee; embalming, removal of donated part, etc.; time of death; certain physicians not to participate; civil liability; autopsies. (a) The donee may accept or reject the gift. If the donee accepts a gift of the entire body, he may, subject to the terms of the gift, authorize embalming and using the body in funeral services. If the gift is of a part of the body, the donee, upon the death of the donor and prior to embalming, shall cause the part to be removed without unnecessary mutilation. After removal of the part, custody of the remainder of the body vests in the surviving spouse, next of kin, or other persons under obligation to dispose of the body.

(b) The time of death shall be determined by a physician who attends the donor at his death or, if there is no attending physician, by the physician who certifies the death. The physician shall not participate in the procedures for removing or transplanting a part.

(c) A person who acts in good faith in accordance with the terms of this article is not liable for damages in any civil action or subject to prosecution in any criminal proceeding for his act.

(d) This article is subject to the laws of this state prescribing powers and duties with respect to autopsies.

HAWAII

§ 327-1. Definitions. "Bank or storage facility" means a facility licensed, accredited, or approved under the laws of any state for storage of human bodies or parts thereof.

"Decedent" means a deceased individual and includes a stillborn infant or fetus.

"Donor" means an individual who makes a gift of all or part of the individual's body.

"Hospital" means a hospital licensed, accredited, or approved under the laws of any state; includes a hospital operated by the United States government, a state, or a subdivision thereof, although not required to be licensed under state laws.

"Part" means organs, tissues, eyes, bones, arteries, blood, other fluids, and any other portions of a human body.

"Person" has the meaning prescribed in section 1-19.

"Physician" or "surgeon" means a physician or surgeon licensed or authorized to practice under the laws of any state.

"State" includes any state, district, commonwealth, territory, insular possession, and any other area subject to the legislative authority of the United States of America.

§ 327-2. Persons who may execute an anatomical gift. (a) Any individual of sound mind and eighteen years of age or more may give all or any part of the individual's body for any purpose specified in section 327-3, the gift to take effect upon death.

(b) Any of the following persons, in order of priority stated, when persons in prior classes are not available at the time of death, and in the absence of actual notice of contrary indications by the decedent or actual notice of opposition by a member of the same or a prior class, may give all or any part of the decedent's body for any purpose specified in section 327-3 :

(1) The spouse,
(2) An adult son or daughter,
(3) Either parent,
(4) An adult brother or sister,
(5) A guardian of the person of the decedent at the time of the decedent's death,
(6) Any other person authorized or under obligation to dispose of the body.

(c) If the donee has actual notice of contrary indications by the decedent or that a gift by a member of a class is opposed by a member of the same or a prior class, the donee shall not accept the gift. The persons authorized by subsection (b) may make the gift after or immediately before death.

(d) A gift of all or part of a body authorizes any examination necessary to assure medical acceptability of the gift for the purposes intended.

(e) The rights of the donee created by the gift are paramount to the rights of others except as provided by subsection 327-7(d).

§ 327-3. Persons who may become donees; purposes for which anatomical gifts may be made. The following persons may become donees of gifts of bodies or parts thereof for the purposes stated:

(1) Any hospital, surgeon, or physician, for medical or dental education, research, advancement of medical or dental science, therapy, or transplantation; or

(2) Any accredited medical or dental school, college, or university for education, research, advancement of medical or dental science, or therapy; or

(3) Any bank or storage facility, for medical or dental education, research, advancement of medical or dental science, therapy, or transplantation; or

(4) Any specified individual for therapy or transplantation needed by the individual.

§ 327-4. Manner of executing anatomical gifts. (a) A gift of all or part of the body under subsection 327-2(a) may be made by will. The gift becomes effective upon the death of the testator without waiting for probate. If the will is not probated, or if it is declared invalid for testamentary purposes, the gift, to the extent that it has been acted upon in good faith, is nevertheless valid and effective.

(b) A gift of all or part of the body under subsection 327-2(a) may also be made by document other than a will. The gift becomes effective upon the death of the donor. The document, which may be a card designed to be carried on the person, must be signed by the donor in the presence of two witnesses who must sign the document in the donor's presence. If the donor cannot sign, the document may be signed for the donor at the donor's direction and in the donor's presence in the presence of two witnesses who must sign the document in the donor's presence. Delivery of the document of gift during the donor's lifetime is not necessary to make the gift valid.

(c) The gift may be made to a specified donee or without specifying a donee. If the latter, the gift may be accepted by the attending physician as donee upon or following death. If the gift is made to a specified donee who is not available at the time and place of death, the attending physician upon or following death, in the absence of any expressed indication that the donor desired otherwise, may accept the gift as donee. The physician who becomes a donee under this subsection shall not participate in the procedures for removing or transplanting a part.

(d) Notwithstanding subsection 327-7(b), the donor may designate in the donor's will, card, or other document of gift the surgeon or physician to carry out the appropriate procedures. In the absence of a designation or if the designee is not available, the donee or other person authorized to accept the gift may employ or authorize any surgeon or physician for the purpose.

(e) Any gift by a person designated in subsection 327-2(b) shall be made by a document signed by the person or made by the person's telegraphic, recorded telephonic, or other recorded message.

§ 327-5. Delivery of document of gift. If the gift is made by the donor to a specified donee, the will, card, or other document, or an executed copy thereof, may be delivered to the donee to expedite the appropriate procedures immediately after death. Delivery is not necessary to the validity of the gift. The will, card, or other document, or an executed copy thereof, may be deposited in any hospital, bank or storage facility or office of the department of health that accepts it for safekeeping or for facilitation of procedures after death. On request of any interested party upon or after the donor's death, the person in possession shall produce the document for examination.

§ 327-6. Amendment or revocation of gift. (a) If the will, card, or other document, or executed copy thereof, has been delivered to a specified donee, the donor may amend or revoke the gift by:

(1) The execution and delivery to the donee of a signed statement, or

(2) An oral statement made in the presence of two persons and communicated to the donee, or

(3) A statement during a terminal illness or injury addressed to an attending physician and communicated to the donee, or

(4) A signed card or document found on the donor's person or in the donor's effects.

(b) Any document of gift which has not been delivered to the donee may be revoked by the donor in the manner set out in subsection (a) or by destruction, cancellation, or mutilation of the document and all executed copies thereof.

(c) Any gift made by a will may also be amended or revoked in the manner provided for amendment or revocation of wills, or as provided in subsection (a).

§ 327-7. Rights and duties at death. (a) The donee may accept or reject the gift. If the donee accepts a gift of the entire body, the donee may, subject to the terms of the gift, authorize embalming and the use of the body in funeral services. If the gift is of a part of the body, the donee, upon the death of the donor and prior to embalming, shall cause the part to be removed without unnecessary mutilation. After removal of the part, custody of the remainder of the body vests in the surviving spouse, next of kin, or other persons under obligation to dispose of the body.

(b) The time of death shall be determined by a physician who tends the donor at the donor's death, or, if none, the physician who certifies the death. The physician shall not participate in the procedures for removing or transplanting a part.

(c) A person who acts in good faith in accord with the terms of this part or with the anatomical gift laws of another state or foreign country is not liable for damages in any civil action or subject to prosecution in any criminal proceeding for the person's act.

(d) The provisions of this part are subject to the laws of this State prescribing powers and duties with respect to autopsies.

(e) A technician who has successfully completed a course of training acceptable to the board of medical examiners may enucleate the eyes of a donor.

§ 327-8. Uniformity of interpretation. This part shall be so construed as to effectuate its general purpose to make uniform the law of those states which enact it.

§ 327-9. Short title. This part may be cited as the Uniform Anatomical Gift Act.

§ 327-52. Requests for anatomical gifts. Any person in charge of a hospital, or the designated representative of the person in charge of the hospital, other than a person connected with the determination of death, may request any of the persons in section 327-2(b), in the order of priority stated, to give consent to the gift of all or any part of the decedent's body to any potential donee for any purpose provided in section 327-3.

IDAHO

§ 39-3401. Definitions. (1) "Bank or storage facility" means a facility licensed, accredited, or approved under the laws of any state for storage of human bodies or parts thereof.

(2) "Decedent" means a deceased individual and includes a stillborn infant or fetus.

(3) "Donor" means an individual who makes a gift of all or part of his body.

(4) "Hospital" means a hospital licensed, accredited, or approved under the laws of any state and includes a hospital operated by the United States government, a state, or a subdivision thereof, although not required to be licensed under state laws.

(5) "Part" means organs, tissues, eyes, bones, arteries, blood, other fluids and other portions of a human body.

(6) "Person" means an individual, corporation, government or governmental subdivision or agency, business trust, estate, trust, partnership or association, or any other legal entity.

(7) "Physician" or "surgeon" means a physician or surgeon licensed or authorized to practice under the laws of any state.

(8) "State" includes any state, district, commonwealth, territory, insular possession, and any other area subject to the legislative authority of the United States of America.

§ 39-3402. Persons who may authorize gift; rights of donee. (1) Any individual of sound mind and eighteen (18) years of age or more may give all or any part of his body for any purpose specified in section 39-3403, the gift to take effect upon death.

(2) Any of the following persons, in order of priority stated, when persons in prior classes are not available at the time of death, and in the absence of actual notice of contrary indications by the decedent or actual notice of opposition by a member of the same or a prior class, may give all or any part of the decedent's body for any purpose specified in section 39-3403:

(a) The spouse,

(b) An adult son or daughter,

(c) Either parent,

(d) An adult brother or sister,

(e) A guardian of the person of the decedent at the time of his death,

(f) Any other person authorized or under obligation to dispose of the body.

(3) If the donee has actual notice of contrary indications by the decedent or that a gift by a member of a class is opposed by a member of the same or a prior class, the donee shall not accept the gift. The persons authorized by subsection (2) may make the gift after or immediately before death.

(4) A gift of all or part of a body authorizes any examination necessary to assure medical acceptability of the gift for the purposes intended.

(5) The rights of the donee created by the gift are paramount to the rights of others except as provided by section 39-3407(4).

§ 39-3403. Who may be donees. The following persons may become donees of gifts of bodies or parts thereof for the purposes stated:

(1) Any hospital, surgeon, or physician, for medical or dental education, research, advancement of medical or dental science, therapy, or transplantation; or

(2) Any accredited medical or dental school, college or university for education, research, advancement of medical or dental science, or therapy; or

(3) Any bank or storage facility, for medical or dental education, research, advancement of medical or dental science, therapy, or transplantation; or

(4) Any specified individual for therapy or transplantation needed by him.

§ 39-3404. Manner of making gift. (1) A gift of all or part of the body under section 39-3402(1), Idaho Code, may be made by will. The gift becomes effective upon the death of the testator without waiting for probate. If the will is not probated, or if it is declared invalid for testamentary purposes, the gift, to the extent that it has been acted upon in good faith, is nevertheless valid and effective.

(2) A gift of all or part of the body under section 39-3402(1), Idaho Code, may also be made by document other than a will. The gift becomes effective upon the death of the donor. The document, which may be a card designed to be carried on the person, must be signed by the donor in the presence of two (2) witnesses who must sign the document in his presence. If the donor cannot sign, the document may be signed for him at his direction and in his presence, in the presence of two (2) witnesses who must sign the document in his presence. Delivery of the document of gift during the donor's lifetime is not necessary to make the gift valid.

(3) The gift may be made to a specified donee or without specifying a donee. If the latter, the gift may be accepted by the attending physician as donee upon or following death. If the gift is made to a specified donee who is not available at the time and place of death, the attending physician upon or following death, in the absence of any expressed indication that the donor desired otherwise, may accept the gift as donee. The physician who becomes a donee under this subsection shall not participate in the procedures for removing or transplanting a part.

(4) Notwithstanding section 39-3407(2), Idaho Code, the donor may designate in his will, card, or other document of gift the surgeon or physician to carry out the appropriate procedures. In the absence of a designation or if the designee is not available, the donee or other person authorized to accept the gift may employ or authorize any surgeon or physician for the purpose.

If the part of the body that is the gift is an eye, the donee may authorize or the person authorized to accept the gift may employ or authorize a qualified embalmer licensed under chapter 11, title 54, Idaho Code, or a qualified eye bank technician to perform the appropriate procedures. The embalmer or technician must have completed a course in eye enucleation and have a certificate of competence from an agency or organization designated by the Idaho board of medicine for the purpose of providing such training.

(5) Any gift by a person designated in section 39-3402(2), Idaho Code, shall be made by a document signed by him or made by his telegraphic, recorded telephonic, or other recorded message.

§ 39-3405. Delivery of document; custodian. If the gift is made by the donor to a specified donee, the will, card, or other document, or an executed copy thereof, may be delivered to the donee to expedite the appropriate procedures immediately after death. Delivery is not necessary to the validity of the gift. The will, card, or other document, or an executed copy thereof, may be deposited in any hospital, bank or storage facility, or registry office that accepts it for safekeeping or for facilitation of procedures after death. On request of any interested party upon or after the donor's death, the person in possession shall produce the document for examination.

§ 39-3406. Amendment or revocation. (1) If the will, card, or other document or executed copy thereof, has been delivered to a specified donee, the donor may amend or revoke the gift by:

(a) The execution and delivery to the donee of a signed statement, or

(b) An oral statement made in the presence of two (2) persons and communicated to the donee, or

(c) A statement during a terminal illness or injury addressed to an attending physician and communicated to the donee, or

(d) A signed card or document found on his person or in his effects.

(2) Any document of gift which has not been delivered to the donee may be revoked by the donor in the manner set out in subsection (1) or by destruction, cancellation, or mutilation of the document and all executed copies thereof.

(3) Any gift made by a will may also be amended or revoked in the manner provided for amendment or revocation of wills or as provided in subsection (1).

§ 39-3407. Acceptance or rejection; custody of body; time of death; freedom from liability; autopsies. (1) The donee may accept or reject the gift. If the donee accepts a gift of the entire body, he may, subject to the terms of the gift, authorize embalming and the use of the body in funeral services. If the gift is of a part of the body, the donee, upon the death of the donor and prior to embalming, shall cause the part to be removed without unnecessary mutilation. After removal of the part, custody of the remainder of the body vests in the surviving spouse, next of kin, or other persons under obligation to dispose of the body.

(2) The time of death shall be determined by a physician who attends the donor at his death, or, if none, the physician who certifies the death. The physician shall not participate in the procedure for removing or transplanting a part.

(3) A person who acts in good faith in accord with the terms of this act or the anatomical gift laws of another state or a foreign country is not liable for damages in any civil action or subject to prosecution in any criminal proceeding for his act.

(4) The provisions of this act are subject to the laws of this state prescribing powers and duties with respect to autopsies.

§ 39-3408. Section 39-268 inapplicable. The provisions of section 39-268, Idaho Code, shall not apply to any gift made under this act.

§ 39-3409. Form of anatomical gift. (1) A form substantially as follows is sufficient to comply with the provisions of this act for the making of an anatomical gift by a living donor: **See Appendix for this form (Anatomical Gift by a Living Donor).** (2) A form substantially as follows is sufficient to comply with the provisions of this act for the making of an anatomical gift by next of kin or other authorized person: **See Appendix for this form (Anatomical Gift by Next of Kin or Other Authorized Person).**

§ 39-3410. Uniformity of construction. This act shall be so construed as to effectuate its general purpose to make uniform the law of those states which enact it.

§ 39-3411. Title of act. This act may be cited as the "Uniform Anatomical Act."

ILLINOIS

§ 301. Short Title. This Act may be cited as the Uniform Anatomical Gift Act.

§ 302. Definitions. (a) "Bank or storage facility" means a facility licensed, accredited, or approved under the laws of any state for storage of human bodies or parts thereof.

(b) "Death" means for the purposes of the Act, the irreversible cessation of total brain function, according to usual and customary standards of medical practice.

(c) "Decedent" means a deceased individual and includes a stillborn infant or fetus.

(d) "Donor" means an individual who makes a gift of all or parts of his body.

(e) "Hospital" means a hospital licensed, accredited or approved under the laws of any state; and includes a hospital operated by the United States government, a state, or a subdivision thereof, although not required to be licensed under state laws.

(f) "Part" means organs, tissues, eyes, bones, arteries, blood, other fluids and any other portions of a human body.

(g) "Person" means an individual, corporation, government or governmental subdivision or agency, business trust, estate, trust, partnership or association or any other legal entity.

(h) "Physician" or "surgeon" means a physician or surgeon licensed or authorized to practice medicine in all of its branches under the laws of any state.

(i) "State" includes any state, district, commonwealth, territory, insular possession, and any other area subject to the legislative authority of the United States of America.

(j) "Technician" means an individual trained and certified to remove tissue by a recognized training institution in the State of Illinois.

§ 303. **Persons who may execute an anatomical gift.** (a) Any individual of sound mind and being an adult may give all or any part of his body for any purpose specified in Section 304, the gift to take effect upon death, or if no such gift is made, then

(b) The following persons any one of whom is living at the time of the gift, in the order of priority stated, in the absence of a gift made pursuant to Section 305, may give all or any part of the decedent's body for any purpose specified in Section 304:

(1) the spouse,
(2) adult sons or daughters,
(3) either parent,
(4) adult brothers or sisters,
(5) a guardian of the person of the decedent at the time of his death.
(6) any person authorized or under obligation to dispose of the body.

(c) If the donee has actual notice of contrary indications by the decedent or actual notice that a gift by a member of a class is opposed by a member of the same or a prior class, the donee shall not accept the gift. The persons authorized by subsection (b) may make the gift after or immediately before death.

(d) A gift of all or part of a body authorizes any examination necessary to assure medical acceptability of the gift for the purposes intended.

(e) The rights of the donee created by the gift are paramount to the rights of others except as provided by Section 308(d).

§ 304. **Persons who may become donees; purposes for which anatomical gifts may be made.** The following persons may become donees of gifts of bodies or parts thereof for the purposes stated:

(1) any hospital, surgeon, or physician, for medical or dental education, research, advancement of medical or dental science, therapy, or transplantation; or

(2) any accredited medical, chiropractic, mortuary or dental school, college or university for education, research, advancement of medical or dental science, or therapy; or

(3) any bank or storage facility, for medical or dental education, research, advancement of medical or dental science, therapy, or transplantation; or

(4) any specified individual for therapy or transplantation needed by him.

§ 305. **Manner of executing anatomical gifts.** (a) A gift of all or part of the body under Section 303(a) may be made by will. The gift becomes effective upon the death of the testator without waiting for probate. If the will is not probated, or if it is declared invalid for testamentary purposes, the gift, to the extent that it has been acted upon in good faith, is nevertheless valid and effective.

(b) A gift of all or part of the body under Section 303(a) may also be made by a written, signed document other than a will. The document, which may be a card designed to be carried on the person, must be signed by the donor in the presence of 2 witnesses who must sign the document in his presence and who thereby certify that he was of sound mind and memory and free from any undue influence and knows the objects of his bounty and affection. Delivery of the document of gift during the donor's lifetime is not necessary to make the gift valid.

(c) The gift may be made to a specified donee or without specifying a donee. If the latter, the gift may be accepted by the attending physician as donee upon or following death. If the gift is made to a specified donee who is not available at the time and place of death, the attending physician upon or following death, in the absence of any expressed indication that the donor desired otherwise, may accept the gift as donee. The physician who becomes a donee under this subsection shall not participate either physically or financially in the procedures for removing or transplanting a part.

(d) Notwithstanding Section 308(b), the donor may designate in his will, card, or other document of gift the surgeon or physician to carry out the appropriate procedures. In the absence of a designation or if the designee is not available, the donee or other person authorized to accept the gift may employ or authorize any surgeon or physician for the purpose.

(e) Any gift by a person designated in Section 303(b) shall be made by a document signed by him or made by his telegraphic, recorded telephonic, or other recorded message.

§ 306. Delivery of document of gift. If the gift is made by the donor to a specified donee, the will, card, or other document, or an executed copy thereof, may be delivered to the donee to expedite the appropriate procedures immediately after death. Delivery is not necessary to the validity of the gift. The will, card, or other document, or an executed copy thereof, may be deposited in any hospital, bank or storage facility, or registry office that accepts it for safekeeping or for facilitation of procedures after death. On request of any interested party upon or after the donor's death, the person in possession shall produce the document for examination.

§ 307. Amendment or revocation of the gift. (a) If the will, card, or other document or executed copy thereof, has been delivered to a specified donee, the donee may amend or revoke the gift by:

(1) the execution and delivery to the donee of a signed statement witnessed and certified as provided in Section 305(b)

(2) a signed card or document found on his person, or in his effects, executed at a date subsequent to the date the original gift was made and witnessed and certified as provided in Section 305(b)

(b) Any document of gift which has not been delivered to the donee may be revoked by the donor in the manner set out in subsection (a).

(c) Any gift made by a will may also be amended or revoked in the manner provided for amendment or revocation of wills or as provided in subsection (a).

§ 308. Rights and duties at death. (a) The donee may accept or reject the gift. If the donee accepts a gift of the entire body, he may, subject to the terms of the gift, authorize embalming and the use of the body in funeral services, unless a person named in subsection (b) of Section 303 of this chapter has requested, prior to the final disposition by the donee, that the remains of said body be returned to his or her custody for the purpose of final disposition. Such request shall be honored by the donee if the terms of the gift are silent on how final disposition is to take place. If the gift is of a part of the body, the donee or technician designated by him upon the death of the donor and prior to embalming, shall cause the part to be removed without unnecessary mutilation and without undue delay in the release of the body for the purposes of final disposition. After removal of the part, custody of the remainder of the body vests in the surviving spouse, next of kin, or other persons under obligation to dispose of the body, in the order of priority listed in subsection (b) of Section 303 of this Act.

(b) The time of death shall be determined by a physician who attends the donor at his death, or, if none, the physician who certifies the death. The physician shall not participate in the procedures for removing or transplanting a part.

(c) A person who acts in good faith in accord with the terms of this Act or the anatomical gift laws of another state or a foreign country is not liable for damages in any civil action or subject to prosecution in any criminal proceeding for his act.

(d) This Act is subject to the provisions of "an Act to revise the law in relation to coroners", approved February 6, 1874, as now or hereafter amended (chapter 31, § 1 et seq.), to the laws of this State prescribing powers and duties with respect to autopsies, and to the statutes, rules, and regulations of this State with respect to the transportation and disposition of deceased human bodies.

§ 309. Uniformity of interpretation. This Act shall be so construed as to effectuate its general purpose to make uniform the law of those states which enact it.

§ 310. Repeal. Section 42a of the "Probate Act", approved July 24, 1939, as amended (chapter 3, § 42a), is repealed.

§ 311. Time of taking effect. This Act shall take effect October 1, 1969.

INDIANA

§ 29-2-16-1. Definitions. Except where the context clearly indicates a different meaning, the terms used in this chapter shall be construed as follows:

(a) "Bank or storage facility" means a facility licensed, accredited or approved under the laws of any state for storage of human bodies or parts thereof.

(b) "Decedent" means a deceased individual and includes a stillborn infant or fetus.

(c) "Donor" means an individual who makes a gift of all or part of his body.

(d) "Hospital" means a hospital licensed, accredited or approved under the laws of any state; includes a hospital operated by the United States government, a state or a subdivision thereof, although not required to be licensed under state laws.

(e) "Part" means organs, tissues, eyes, bones, arteries, blood, other fluids and any other portions of a human body.

(f) "Person" means an individual, corporation, government or governmental subdivision or agency, business trust, estate, trust, partnership or association, or any other legal entity.

(g) "Physician" or "surgeon" means a physician or surgeon licensed or authorized to practice under the laws of any state.

(h) "State" includes any state, district, commonwealth, territory, insular possession and any other area subject to the legislative authority of the United States of America.

§ 29-2-16-2. Persons who may give all or parts of a body—Exceptions.

(a) Any individual of sound mind and eighteen (18) years of age or more may give all or any part of his body for any purpose specified in section 29-2-16-3, the gift to take effect upon death.

(b) Any of the following persons, in order of priority stated, when persons in prior classes are not available at the time of death, and in the absence of actual notice of contrary indications by the decedent or actual notice of opposition by a member of the same or a prior class, may give all or any part of the decedent's body for any purpose specified in section 29-2-16-3 of this chapter:

(1) the spouse;

(2) a son or daughter, at least eighteen (18) years of age;

(3) either parent;

(4) a brother or sister, at least eighteen (18) years of age;

(5) a guardian of the person of the decedent at the time of his death;

(6) any other person authorized or under obligation to dispose of the body.

(c) If the donee has actual notice of contrary indications by the decedent or that a gift by a member of a class is opposed by a member of the same or a prior class, the donee shall not accept the gift. The persons authorized by subsection (b) of this section may make the gift after or immediately before death.

(d) A gift of all or part of a body authorizes any examination necessary to assure medical acceptability of the gift for the purposes intended.

(e) The rights of the donee created by the gift are paramount to the rights of others except as provided by subsection 29-2-16-7(d) of this chapter.

§ 29-2-16-3. Persons who may become donees. The following persons may become donees of gifts of bodies or parts thereof for the purposes stated:

(1) any hospital, surgeon or physician for medical or dental education, research, advancement of medical or dental science, therapy or transplantation, or

(2) any accredited medical or dental school, college or university for education, research, advancement of medical or dental science, or therapy, or

(3) any bank or storage facility, for medical or dental education, research, advancement of medical or dental science, therapy, or transplantation or

(4) any specified individual for therapy or transplantation needed by him.

§ 29-2-16-4. Method of making gifts. (a) A gift of all or part of the body under subsection 29-2-16-2(a) of this chapter may be made by will. The gift becomes effective upon the death of the testator without waiting for probate. If the will is not probated, or if it is declared invalid for testamentary purposes, the gift, to the extent that it has been acted upon in good faith, is nevertheless valid and effective.

(b) A gift of all or part of the body under subsection 29-2-16-2(a) may also be made by document other than a will. The gift becomes effective upon the death of the donor. The document, which may be a card designed to be carried on the person, must be signed by the donor in the presence of two (2) witnesses who must sign the document in his presence. If the donor cannot sign, the document may be signed for him:

(1) At his direction and in his presence; and

(2) In the presence of two (2) witnesses who must sign the document in his presence.

Delivery of the document of gift during the donor's lifetime is not necessary to make the gift valid.

(c) The gift may be made to a specified donee or without specifying a donee. If the latter, the gift may be accepted by the attending physician as donee upon or following death. If the gift is made to a specified donee who is not available at the time and place of death, the attending physician upon or following death, in the absence of any expressed indication that the donor desired otherwise, may accept the gift as donee. The gift of an eye or part of an eye made without specifying a donee, or made to a donee who is not available at the time and place of death and without an expression of a contrary desire, may be accepted by the attending physician as donee on behalf of an eye bank in Indiana. The physician who becomes a donee under this subsection shall not participate in the procedures for removing or transplanting a part.

(d) Notwithstanding subsection 29-2-16-7(b) of this chapter, the donor may designate in his will, card, or other document of gift the surgeon or physician to carry out the appropriate procedures. In the absence of a designation or if the designee is not available, the donee or other person authorized to accept the gift may employ or authorize any surgeon or physician for the purpose. With respect to an eye or part of an eye, the eye or part may be removed for the gift after proper certification of death by a physician and compliance with the intent of the gift as determined by reference to this chapter, by:

(1) A surgeon or physician;

(2) An embalmer or a funeral director who, before September 1, 1983, completed a course in eye enucleation and was certified as competent to enucleate eyes by an accredited school of medicine; or

(3) A person who is registered with the state board of health as an eye enucleator.

(e) An applicant for registration as an eye enucleator must submit evidence that he has successfully completed a training program in the enucleation of eyes approved by the state board of health. To be approved, a training program must:

(1) Be taught by one (1) or more surgeons or physicians;

(2) Include instruction and practice in anatomy and physiology of the eye, the maintenance of a sterile field during the removal of an eye, and the use of appropriate instruments and sterile procedures for removing the eye or part of the eye; and

(3) Comply with rules adopted by the state board of health under Indiana Code 4-22-2.

(f) The state board of health may revoke a person's registration as an eye enucleator upon a showing of good cause for revocation.

(g) A person who, in good faith reliance upon a will, card, or other document of gift, and without actual notice of amendment, revocation, or invalidity of the will, card, or document:

(1) Takes possession of a decedent's body, or performs, or causes to be performed surgical operations upon a decedent's body; or

(2) Removes or causes to be removed organs, tissues, or other parts from a decedent's body; is not liable in damages in any civil action brought against him for that act.

(h) Any gift by a person designated in subsection 29-2-16-2(b) of this chapter shall be made by a document signed by him or made by his telegraphic, recorded telephonic, or other recorded message.

§ 29-2-16-5. Delivery of will, card, or document. If the gift is made by the donor to a specified donee, the will, card or other document, or an executed copy thereof, may be delivered to the donee to expedite the appropriate procedures immediately after death. Delivery is not necessary to the validity of the gift. The will, card or other document, or an executed copy thereof, may be deposited in any hospital, bank or storage facility or registry office that accepts it for safekeeping or for facilitation of procedures after death. On request of any interested party upon or after the donor's death, the person in possession shall produce the document for examination.

§ 29-2-16-6. Amendment or revocation of gift by donor. (a) If the will, card or other document, or executed copy thereof, has been delivered to a specified donee, the donor may amend or revoke the gift by:

(1) the execution and delivery to the donee of a signed statement, or

(2) an oral statement made in the presence of two (2) persons and communicated to the donee, or

(3) a statement during a terminal illness or injury addressed to an attending physician and communicated to the donee, or

(4) a signed card or document found on his person or in his effects.

(b) Any document of gift which has not been delivered to the donee may be revoked by the donor in the manner set out in subsection (a), or by destruction, cancellation or mutilation of the document and all executed copies thereof.

(c) Any gift made by a will may also be amended or revoked in the manner provided for amendment or revocation of wills, or as provided in subsection (a).

§ 29-2-16-7. Acceptance or rejection of gift by donee. (a) The donee may accept or reject the gift. If the donee accepts a gift of the entire body, he may, subject to the terms of the gift, authorize embalming and the use of the body in funeral services. If the gift is of a part of the body, the donee, upon the death of the donor and prior to embalming, shall cause the part to be removed without unnecessary mutilation. After removal of the part, custody of the remainder of the body vests in the surviving spouse, next of kin, or other persons under obligation to dispose of the body.

(b) The time of death shall be determined by a physician who tends the donor at his death, or, if none, the physician who certifies the death. The physician shall not participate in the procedures for removing or transplanting a part.

(c) A person who acts in good faith in accord with the terms of this chapter or with the anatomical gift laws of another state (or a foreign country) is not liable for damages in any civil action or subject to prosecution in any criminal proceeding for his act.

(d) The provisions of this chapter are subject to the laws of this state prescribing powers and duties with respect to autopsies.

§ 29-2-16-8. Construction. This chapter shall be so construed as to effectuate its general purpose to make uniform the law of those states which enact it.

§ 29-2-16-9. Short title. This chapter may be cited as the "Uniform Anatomical Gift Act."

§ 29-2-16-10. Hospital administrator to inform representative of decedent of procedures—Surrender of driver's license upon which gift made.

(a) As used in this section:

"Administrator" means a hospital administrator or a hospital administrator's designee.

"Gift" means a gift of all or any part of the human body made under this chapter.

"Representative" means a person who is:

(1) authorized under section 2(b) [29-2-16-2(b)] of this chapter to make a gift on behalf of a decedent; and

(2) available at the time of the decedent's death when members of a prior class under section 2(b) of this chapter are unavailable.

(b) The administrator shall inform the representative of the procedures available under this chapter for making a gift whenever:

(1) an individual dies in a hospital;

(2) the hospital had not been notified that a gift has been authorized under section 2 [29-2-16-2] of this chapter; and

(3) a physician determines that the individual's body may be suitable of yielding a gift.

(c) If:

(1) An individual makes an anatomical gift on the individual driver's license under IC 9-1-4-32:5; and

(2) The individual dies;

the person in possession of the individual driver's license shall immediately produce the driver's license for examination upon request, as provided in section 5 [29-2-16-5] of this chapter.

(d) A gift made in response to information provided under this section must be documented as described under section 4(h) [29-2-16-4(h)] of this chapter.

(e) When a representative is informed under this section about the procedures available for making a gift, the fact that the representative was so informed must be noted in the decedent's medical record.

IOWA

§ 142A.1. Definitions.
1. "Bank or storage facility" means a facility licensed, accredited, or approved under the laws of any state for storage of human bodies or parts thereof.
2. "Decedent" means a deceased individual and includes a stillborn infant or fetus.
3. "Donor" means an individual who makes a gift of all or part of his body.
4. "Hospital" means a hospital licensed under the laws of this state, or licensed, accredited, or approved under the laws of any other state and includes a hospital operated by the United States government, a state, or a subdivision thereof, although not required to be licensed under state laws.
5. "Part" includes organs, tissues, eyes, bones, arteries, blood, other fluids and other portions of a human body, and "part" includes "parts."
6. "Person" means an individual, corporation, government or governmental subdivision or agency, business trust, partnership, association, or any other legal entity.
7. "Physician" or "surgeon" means a physician, surgeon, or osteopathic physician and surgeon, licensed or authorized to practice under the laws of any state.
8. "State" includes any state, district, commonwealth, territory, insular possession, and any other area subject to the legislative authority of the United States of America.

§ 142A.2. Persons who may execute an anatomical gift.
1. Any individual of sound mind and eighteen years of age or more may give all or any part of his body for any purposes specified in section 142A.3, the gift to take effect upon death.
2. Any of the following persons, in order of priority stated, when persons in prior classes are not available at the time of death, and in the absence of actual notice of contrary indications by the decedent, or actual notice of opposition by a member of the same or a prior class, may give all or any part of the decedent's body for any purposes specified in section 142A.3:
   a. The spouse.
   b. An adult son or daughter.
   c. Either parent.
   d. An adult brother or sister.
   e. A guardian of the person of the decedent at the time of his death.
   f. Any other person authorized or under obligation to dispose of the body.

The persons authorized by this subsection may make the gift after death or immediately before death.

3. If the donee has actual notice of contrary indications by the decedent, or that a gift by a member of a class is opposed by a member of the same or a prior class, the donee shall not accept the gift.
4. A gift of all or part of a body authorizes any examination necessary to assure medical acceptability of the gift for the purposes intended.
5. The rights of the donee created by the gift are paramount to the rights of others except as provided by section 142A.7, subsection 4.

§ 142A.3. Persons who may become donees, and purposes for which anatomical gifts may be made. The following persons may become donees of gifts of bodies or parts thereof for the purposes stated:

1. Any hospital, surgeon, or physician, for medical or dental education, research, advancement of medical or dental science, therapy, or transplantation.

2. Any accredited medical or dental school, college, or university, for education, research, advancement of medical or dental science, or therapy.

3. Any bank or storage facility, for medical or dental education, research, advancement of medical or dental science, therapy, or transplantation.

4. Any specified individual for therapy or transplantation needed by him.

§ 142A.4. Manner of executing anatomical gifts.

1. A gift of all or part of the body under section 142A.2, subsection 1 may be made by will. The gift becomes effective upon the death of the testator without waiting for probate. If the will is not probated, or if it is declared invalid for testamentary purposes, the gift, to the extent that it has been acted upon in good faith, is nevertheless valid and effective.

2. A gift of all or part of the body under section 142A.2, subsection 1, may also be made by a document other than a will. The gift becomes effective upon the death of the donor. The document, which may be a card designed to be carried on the person, must be signed by the donor, in the presence of two witnesses who must sign the document in his presence. If the donor cannot sign, the document may be signed for him at his direction and in his presence, and in the presence of two witnesses who must sign the document in his presence. Delivery of the document of gift during the donor's lifetime is not necessary to make the gift valid.

3. The gift may be made to a specified donee or without specifying a donee. If the latter, the gift may be accepted by the attending physician as donee upon or following death. If the gift is made to a specified donee who is not available at the time and place of death, the attending physician upon or following death, in the absence of any expressed indication that the donor desired otherwise, may accept the gift as donee. The physician who becomes a donee under this subsection shall not participate in the procedures for removing or transplanting a part, except as provided in section 142A.7, subsection 2 [said exception is the "enucleation of eyes"—ed. note].

4. Notwithstanding section 142A.7, subsection 2, the donor may designate in his will, card or other document of gift the surgeon or physician to carry out the appropriate procedures. In the absence of a designation, or if the designee is not available, the donee or other person authorized to accept the gift may employ or authorize any surgeon or physician for the purpose.

5. Any gift by a person designated in section 142A.2, subsection 2 shall be made by a document signed by him, or made by his telegraphic, recorded telephonic or other recorded message.

§ 142A.5. Delivery of document of gift. If the gift is made by the donor to a specified donee, the will, card, or other document, or an executed copy thereof, may be delivered to the donee to expedite the appropriate procedures immediately after death, but delivery is not necessary to the validity of the gift. The will, card, or other document, or an executed copy thereof, may be deposited in any hospital, bank, or storage facility, or registry office that accepts documents for safekeeping or for facilitation of procedures after death. On request of any interested party upon or after the donor's death, the person in possession shall produce the document for examination.

§ 142A.6. Amendment or revocation of the gift.

1. If the will, card, or other document, or executed copy thereof, has been delivered to a specified donee, the donor may amend or revoke the gift by:

   a. The execution and delivery to the donee of a signed statement.

b. An oral statement made in the presence of two persons and communicated to the donee.

c. A statement during a terminal illness or injury addressed to an attending physician and communicated to the donee.

d. A signed card or document found on his person or in his effects.

2. Any document of gift which has not been delivered to the donee may be revoked by the donor in the manner set out in subsection 1, or by destruction, cancellation, or mutilation of the document and all executed copies thereof.

3. Any gift made by a will may also be amended or revoked in the manner provided for amendment or revocation of wills, or as provided in subsection 1.

4. An anatomical gift is not amendable or revocable by a person other than the donor.

§ 142A.7. **Rights and duties at death.**

1. The donee may accept or reject the gift. If the donee accepts a gift of the entire body, he may, subject to the terms of the gift, authorize embalming and the use of the body in funeral services. If the gift is of a part of the body, the donee, upon the death of the donor and prior to embalming, shall cause the part to be removed without unnecessary mutilation. After removal of the part, custody of the remainder of the body vests in the surviving spouse, next of kin, or other persons under obligation to dispose of the body.

2. The time of death shall be determined by a physician who attends the donor at the donor's death, or, if none, the physician who certifies the death. This physician shall not participate in the procedures for removing or transplanting a part, the enucleation of eyes being the exception. A licensed funeral director, as defined in chapter 156, upon successfully completing a course in eye enucleation and receiving a certificate of competence from the department of ophthalmology, college of medicine, of the University of Iowa, may enucleate the eyes of a donor.

3. A person who acts in good faith in accordance with the terms of this chapter, or under the anatomical gift laws of another state, is not liable for damages in any civil action or subject to prosecution in any criminal proceeding for his act.

4. The provisions of this chapter are subject to the laws of this state prescribing powers and duties with respect to autopsies.

§ 142A.8. **Service but not a sale.** The procurement, processing, distribution or use of whole blood, plasma, blood products, blood derivatives and other human tissues such as corneas, bones or organs for the purpose of injecting, transfusing or transplanting any of them into the human body is declared to be, for all purposes, the rendition of a service by every person participating therein and, whether or not remuneration is paid therefor, is declared not to be a sale of such whole blood, plasma, blood products, blood derivatives or other tissues, for any purpose, subsequent to July 1, 1969. However, any person or entity that renders such service warrants only under this section that due care has been exercised and that acceptable professional standards of care in providing such service according to the current state of medical arts have been followed. Strict liability, in tort, shall not be applicable to the rendition of such service.

§ 142A.9. **Uniformity of interpretation.** This chapter shall be so construed as to effectuate its general purpose to make uniform the law of those states which enact it.

§ 142A.10. **Short title.** This chapter may be cited as the "Uniform Anatomical Gift Act."

KANSAS

§ 65-3209. Definitions. (a) "Bank or storage facility" means a facility licensed, accredited, or approved under the laws of any state for storage of human bodies or parts thereof.

(b) "Decedent" means a deceased individual and includes a stillborn infant or fetus.

(c) "Donor" means an individual who makes a gift of all or part of his body.

(d) "Hospital" means a hospital licensed, accredited, or approved under the laws of any state; includes a hospital operated by the United States government, a state, or a subdivision thereof, although not required to be licensed under state laws.

(e) "Part" means organs, tissues, eyes, bones, arteries, blood, other fluids and any other portions of a human body.

(f) "Person" means an individual, corporation, government or governmental subdivision or agency, business trust, estate, trust, partnership or association, or any other legal entity.

(g) "Physician" or "surgeon" means a physician or surgeon licensed or authorized to practice under the laws of any state.

(h) "State" includes any state, district, commonwealth, territory, insular possession, and any other area subject to the legislative authority of the United States of America.

§ 65-3210. Persons who may execute an anatomical gift. (a) Any individual of sound mind and eighteen (18) years of age or more may give all or any part of his body for any purpose specified in Kansas Statutes Annotated 65-3211, the gift to take effect upon death.

(b) Any of the following persons, in order of priority stated, when persons in prior classes are not available at the time of death, and in the absence of actual notice of contrary indications by the decedent or actual notice of opposition by a member of the same or a prior class, may give all or any part of the decedent's body for any purpose specified in K.S.A. 65-3211:

(1) the spouse,
(2) an adult son or daughter,
(3) either parent,
(4) an adult brother or sister,
(5) a guardian of the person of the decedent at the time of his death,
(6) any other person authorized or under obligation to dispose of the body.

(c) If the donee has actual notice of contrary indications by the decedent or that a gift by a member of a class is opposed by a member of the same or a prior class, the donee shall not accept the gift. The persons authorized by subsection (b) may make the gift after or immediately before death.

(d) A gift of all or part of a body authorizes any examination necessary to assure medical acceptability of the gift for the purposes intended.

(e) The rights of the donee created by the gift are paramount to the rights of others except as provided in K.S.A. 65-3215(d).

§ 65-3211. Persons who may become donees; purpose for which anatomical gifts may be made. The following persons may become donees of gifts of bodies or parts thereof for the purposes stated:

(1) any hospital, surgeon, or physician, for medical or dental education, research, advancement of medical or dental science, therapy, or transplantation; or

(2) any accredited medical or dental school, college or university for education, research, advancement of medical or dental science, or therapy; or

(3) any bank or storage facility, for medical or dental education, research, advancement of medi-

cal or dental science, therapy, or transplantation; or

(4) any specified individual for therapy or transplantation needed by him.

§ 65-3212. Manner of executing anatomical gifts. (a) A gift of all or part of the body under K.S.A. 65-3210(a) may be made by will. The gift becomes effective upon the death of the testator without waiting for probate. If the will is not probated, or if it is declared invalid for testamentary purposes, the gift, to the extent that it has been acted upon in good faith, is nevertheless valid and effective.

(b) A gift of all or part of the body under K.S.A. 65-3210(a) may also be made by document other than a will. The gift becomes effective upon the death of the donor. The document, which may be a card designed to be carried on the person, must be signed by the donor in the presence of two (2) witnesses who must sign the document in his presence. If the donor cannot sign, the document may be signed for him at his direction and in his presence in the presence of two (2) witnesses who must sign the document in his presence. Delivery of the document of gift during the donor's lifetime is not necessary to make the gift valid.

(c) The gift may be made to a specified donee or without specifying a donee. If the latter, the gift may be accepted by the attending physician as donee upon or following death. If the gift is made to a specified donee who is not available at the time and place of death, the attending physician upon or following death, in the absence of any expressed indication that the donor desired otherwise, may accept the gift as donee. The physician who becomes a donee under this subsection shall not participate in the procedures for removing or transplanting a part.

(d) Notwithstanding K.S.A. 65-3215(b), the donor may designate in his will, card, or other document of gift the surgeon or physician to carry out the appropriate procedures. In the absence of a designation or if the designee is not available, the donee or other person authorized to accept the gift may employ or authorize any surgeon or physician for the purpose.

(e) Any gift by a person designated in K.S.A. 65-3210(b) shall be made by a document signed by him or made by his telegraphic, recorded telephonic, or other recorded message.

§ 65-3213. Delivery of document of gift. If the gift is made by the donor to a specified donee, the will, card, or other document, or an executed copy thereof, may be delivered to the donee to expedite the appropriate procedures immediately after death. Delivery is not necessary to the validity of the gift. The will, card, or other document, or an executed copy thereof, may be deposited in any hospital, bank or storage facility, or registry office that accepts it for safekeeping or for facilitation of procedures after death. On request of any interested party upon or after the donor's death, the person in possession shall produce the document for examination.

§ 65-3214. Amendment or revocation of the gift. (a) If the will, card, or other document, or executed copy thereof, has been delivered to a specified donee, the donor may amend or revoke the gift by:

(1) the execution and delivery to the donee of a signed statement, or

(2) an oral statement made in the presence of two (2) persons and communicated to the donee, or

(3) a statement during a terminal illness or injury addressed to an attending physician and communicated to the donee, or

(4) a signed card or document found on his person or in his effects.

(b) Any document of gift which has not been delivered to the donee may be revoked by the donor in the manner set out in subsection (a) or by destruction, cancellation, or mutilation of the document and all executed copies thereof.

(c) Any gift made by a will may also be amended or revoked in the manner provided for amendment or revocation of wills or as provided in subsection (a).

§ 65-3215. Rights and duties at death. (a) The donee may accept or reject the gift. If the donee accepts a gift of the entire body, he may, subject to the terms of the gift, authorize embalming and the use of the body in funeral services. If the gift is of a part of the body, the donee, upon the death of the donor and prior to embalming, shall cause the part to be removed without unnecessary mutilation. After removal of the part, custody of the remainder of the body vests in the surviving spouse, next of kin, or other persons under obligation to dispose of the body.

(b) The time of death shall be determined by a physician who attends the donor at his death, or, if none, the physician who certifies the death. The physician shall not participate in the procedures for removing or transplanting a part.

(c) A person who acts in good faith in accord with the terms of this act or the anatomical gift laws of another state or a foreign country is not liable for damages in any civil action or subject to prosecution in any criminal proceeding for his act.

(d) The provisions of this act are subject to the laws of this state prescribing powers and duties with respect to autopsies.

§ 65-3216. Uniformity of interpretation. This act shall be so construed as to effectuate its general purpose to make uniform the law of those states which enact it.

§ 65-3217. Short title. This act may be cited as the uniform anatomical gift act.

KENTUCKY

§ 311.165. Definitions. (1) "Bank or storage facility" means a facility licensed, accredited, or approved under the laws of any state for storage of human bodies or parts thereof:

(2) "Decedent" means a deceased individual and includes a stillborn infant or fetus;

(3) "Donor" means an individual who makes a gift of all or part of his body;

(4) "Hospital" means a hospital licensed, accredited, or approved under the laws of any state; includes a hospital operated by the United States government, a state, or a subdivision thereof, although not required to be licensed under state laws;

(5) "Part" means organs, tissues, eyes, bones, arteries, blood, other fluids and any other portions of a human body;

(6) "Person" means an individual, corporation, government or governmental subdivision or agency, business trust, estate, trust, partnership or association, or any other legal entity;

(7) "Physician" or "surgeon" means a physician or surgeon licensed or authorized to practice under the laws of any state;

(8) "State" includes any state, district, commonwealth, territory, insular possession, and any other area subject to the legislative authority of the United States of America.

§ 311.175. Persons who may execute an anatomical gift. (1) Any individual of sound mind and eighteen (18) years of age or more may give all or any part of his body for any purpose specified in Kentucky Revised Statutes 311.185, the gift to take effect upon death.

(2) Any of the following persons, in order of priority stated, when persons in prior classes are not available at the time of death, and in the absence of actual notice of contrary indications by the decedent or actual notice of opposition by a member of the same or a prior class, may give all or any

part of the decedent's body for any purpose specified in KRS 311.185:
- (a) The spouse,
- (b) An adult son or daughter,
- (c) Either parent,
- (d) An adult brother or sister,
- (e) A guardian of the person of the decedent at the time of his death,
- (f) Any other person authorized or under obligation to dispose of the body.

(3) If the donee has actual notice of contrary indications by the decedent or that gift by a member of a class is opposed by a member of the same or a prior class, the donee shall not accept the gift. The persons authorized by subsection (2) of this section may make the gift after or immediately before death.

(4) A gift of all or part of a body authorizes any examination necessary to assure medical acceptability of the gift for the purposes intended.

(5) The rights of the donee created by the gift are paramount to the rights of others except as provided by subsection (4) of KRS 311.225.

§ 311.185. Persons who may become donees; purposes for which anatomical gifts may be made. The following persons may become donees of gifts of bodies or parts thereof for the purposes stated:

(1) Any hospital, surgeon, or physician, for medical or dental education, research, advancement of medical or dental science, therapy, or transplantation; or

(2) Any accredited medical or dental school, college or university for education, research, advancement of medical or dental science, or therapy; or

(3) Any bank or storage facility, for medical or dental education, research, advancement of medical or dental science, therapy, or transplantation; or

(4) Any specified individual for therapy or transplantation needed by him.

§ 311.187. Removal of cornea or corneal tissue from decedent whose death defined as a coroner's case; conditions; who may remove. (1) In any case in which a patient is in need of a cornea or corneal tissue for a transplant, the coroner, medical examiner, or his appropriately qualified designee with training in ophthalmologic techniques may, upon the request of any person authorized under KRS 311.185, provide or authorize the removal of the cornea or corneal tissue by a qualified physician under the following conditions:

(a) The decedent has been defined as a "coroner's case" as set forth by KRS 72.405(2), an autopsy has been ordered pursuant to KRS 72.410, and the cornea or corneal tissue are suitable for transplant;

(b) No objection by the next of kin is known by the coroner or medical examiner; and

(c) The removal of the cornea or corneal tissue will not interfere with the subsequent course of an investigation or autopsy or alter the post mortem facial appearance.

(2) The medical examiner, coroner, or his appropriately qualified designee or any persons authorized under KRS 311.185 shall not be held liable in any civil or criminal action for failure to obtain consent of the next of kin.

(3) An individual certified by a department of ophthalmology in an accredited school of medicine as having received competent training may remove corneas for gift after proper certification of death by a physician and in compliance with the provisions of KRS 311.175.

§ 311.195. Manner of executing anatomical gifts. (1) A gift of all or part of the body under subsection (1) of KRS 311.175 may be made by will. The gift becomes effective upon the death of the testator without waiting for probate. If the will is not probated, or if it is declared invalid for testamentary purposes, the gift, to the extent that it has been acted upon in good faith, is nevertheless valid and effective.

(2) A gift of all or part of the body under subsection (1) of KRS 311.175 may also be made by document other than a will. The gift becomes effective upon the death of the donor. The document, which may be a card designed to be carried on the person, must be signed by the donor in the presence of two (2) witnesses who must sign the document in his presence. If the donor cannot sign, the document may be signed for him at his direction and in his presence in the presence of two (2) witnesses who must sign the document in his presence. Delivery of the document of gift during the donor's lifetime is not necessary to make the gift valid.

(3) A gift of all or part of the body under KRS 186.412 may also be made by a statement provided for on all Kentucky operators' licenses. The gift becomes effective upon the death of the owner. The statement must be signed by the owner of the motor vehicle or motorcycle license in the presence of two (2) witnesses, who must sign the statement in the presence of the donor. Delivery of the license during the donor's lifetime is not necessary to make the gift valid. The gift shall become invalidated upon expiration, cancellation, revocation, or suspension of the license, and the gift must be renewed upon renewal of each license.

(4) The gift may be made to a specified donee or without specifying a donee. If the latter, the gift may be accepted by the attending physician as donee upon or following death. If the gift is made to a specified donee who is not available at the time and place of death, the attending physician upon or following death, in the absence of any expressed indication that the donor desired otherwise, may accept the gift as donee. The physician who becomes a donee under this subsection shall not participate in the procedures for removing or transplanting a part.

(5) Notwithstanding subsection (2) of KRS 311.225, the donor may designate in his will, card, or other document of gift the surgeon or physician to carry out the appropriate procedures. In the absence of a designation or if the designee is not available, the donee or other person authorized to accept the gift may employ or authorize any surgeon or physician for the purpose.

(6) Any gift by a person designated in subsection (2) of KRS 311.175 shall be made by a document signed by him or made by his telegraphic, recorded telephonic or other recorded message.

§ 311.205. Delivery of document of gift. If the gift is made by the donor to a specified donee, the will, card, or other document, or an executed copy thereof, may be delivered to the donee to expedite the appropriate procedures after death. Delivery is not necessary to the validity of the gift. The will, card, or other document, or an executed copy thereof, may be deposited in any hospital, bank or storage facility or registry office that accepts it for safekeeping or for facilitation of procedures after death. On request of any interested party upon or after the donor's death, the person in possession shall produce the document for examination.

§ 311.215. Amendment or revocation of the gift. (1) If the will, card, or other document, or executed copy thereof, has been delivered to a specified donee, the donor may amend or revoke the gift by:

(a) The execution and delivery to the donee of a signed statement, or

(b) An oral statement made in the presence of two (2) persons and communicated to the donee, or

(c) A statement during a terminal illness or injury addressed to an attending physician and communicated to the donee, or

(d) A signed card or document found on his person or in his effects.

(2) Any document of gift which has not been delivered to the donee may be revoked by the donor in the manner set out in subsection (1) of this section, or by destruction, cancellation, or mutilation

of the document and all executed copies thereof.

(3) Any gift made by a will may also be amended or revoked in the manner provided for amendment or revocation of wills, or as provided in subsection (1) of this section.

§ 311.225. Rights and duties at death. (1) The donee may accept or reject the gift. If the donee accepts a gift of the entire body, he may, subject to the terms of the gift, authorize embalming and the use of the body in funeral services. If the gift is of a part of the body, the donee, upon the death of the donor and prior to embalming, shall cause the part to be removed without unnecessary mutilation. After removal of the part, custody of the remainder of the body vests in the surviving spouse, next of kin, or other persons under obligation to dispose of the body.

(2) The time of death shall be determined by a physician who tends the donor at his death, or, if none, the physician who certifies the death. The physician shall not participate in the procedures for removing or transplanting a part.

(3) A person who acts in good faith in accord with the terms of KRS 311.165 to 311.235 or with the anatomical gift laws of another state is not liable for damages in any civil action or subject to prosecution in any criminal proceeding for his act.

(4) The provisions of KRS 311.165 to 311.235 are subject to the laws of this state prescribing powers and duties with respect to autopsies.

§ 311.235. Uniformity of interpretation. (1) KRS 311.165 to 311.235 shall be so construed as to effectuate its general purpose to make uniform the law of those states which enact it.

(2) KRS 311.165 to 311.235 may be cited as the Uniform Anatomical Gift Act.

§ 311.241. Hospitals to establish organ procurement protocol; notification to federally certified organ procurement organization of potential availability of organ and identity of potential donor. (1) Each hospital licensed under the provisions of KRS Chapter 216B shall, as a condition of licensure, establish an organ procurement for transplant protocol, in consultation with a federally certified organ procurement organization, which encourages organ donation and identifies potential organ donors.

(2) When an individual has died or has been identified by a medical hospital staff member as having a terminal condition and is further identified as a potential organ donor and meets the criteria set forth in the hospital's organ procurement for transplant protocol, the hospital administrator or his official designee shall then notify the federally certified organ procurement organization of the potential availability of the organ. The notification of the federally certified organ procurement organization as to the identity of a potential organ donor shall be documented in such patient's medical record. Any identified contraindication to organ donation shall be documented in the patient's medical record.

§ 311.243. Family of donor not financially liable for cost of evaluation of donor organ suitability or retrieval of organ. The family of any individual whose organ is donated for transplantation shall not be financially liable for any cost related to the evaluation of donor organ suitability and any cost retrieval of the organ.

§ 311.245. Duty of hospital and allied health personnel to make known patient's intent to donate organ. All hospital physicians, nurses, and other allied health personnel shall make every reasonable effort to convey to the appropriate hospital unit the intent of any hospitalized patient to make a donation of all or any part of his body, as provided in KRS 311.175, in order that necessary documents may be executed under the provisions of this chapter.

§ 311.247. Duty of law enforcement and medical personnel in accident and coroners' cases. Law enforcement and medical personnel involved with the investigation of accidents and coroners' cases shall make a reasonable effort to ascertain if the victim had elected to give all or any part of his body as provided in KRS 311.175 and shall make a reasonable effort to send that information on to the coroner, medical examiner, or hospital personnel.

LOUISIANA

§ 2351. Definitions. (1) "Bank or storage facility" means a facility licensed or approved under the laws of any state for storage of human bodies or parts thereof, for use in medical education, research, therapy, or transplantation to individuals.

(2) "Decedent" means an individual of any age and includes a stillborn infant.

(3) "Hospital" means a hospital licensed, accredited, or approved under the laws of any state and includes a hospital operated by the United States Government, a state, or a subdivision thereof, although not required to be licensed under state laws.

(4) "Part" of a body includes organs, tissues, eyes, bones, arteries, blood, other fluids and other portions of bodies, and "part" includes "parts."

(5) "Person" means an individual, corporation, government or governmental subdivision or agency, business trust, estate, trust, partnership or association, or any other legal entity.

(6) "Physician" or "surgeon" means a physician or surgeon licensed to practice under the laws of any state.

(7) "State" includes any state, district, commonwealth, territory, insular possession, and any other area subject to the legislative authority of the United States of America.

(8) "Technician" means any individual who has successfully completed a course in eye enucleation for ophthalmic medical assistants approved by the American Association of Ophthalmology and possesses documentary proof of qualifications.

§ 2352. Persons who may execute an anatomical gift.

A. Any individual who is competent to execute a will may give all or any part of his body for any of the purposes specified in Revised Statutes 17:2353, the gift to take effect after death. The rights of the donee are superior to the rights of the surviving spouse and next of kin.

B. Unless he has knowledge that contrary directions have been given by the decedent, any of the following persons, in the order of priority stated, may give all or any part of a decedent's body for any of the purposes specified in R.S. 17:2353:

(1) The spouse if one survives; if not,

(2) An adult son or daughter,

(3) Either parent,

(4) An adult brother or sister,

(5) The guardian of the person of the decedent at the time of his death,

(6) Any other person authorized or under obligation to dispose of the body.

If there is no surviving spouse, and an adult son or daughter is not immediately available at the time of death, the gift may be made by either parent; if neither an adult son or daughter nor a parent is immediately available, it may be made by any adult brother or sister; but the donee shall not accept the gift if he or his agent has received notice that there is controversy within the class of relatives enabled under the above priorities to make the gift. The persons authorized by this subsection to make the gift may execute the document of gift either after death or immediately before death during a terminal illness or injury.

C. Any gift of all or part of a body is deemed to authorize such examination as may be necessary to assure medical acceptability of gift for the purposes intended.

D. No person shall disclose, disseminate or make public the fact of the making or acceptance of a gift authorized under the provisions of this Part without the prior specific consent of the donor, or if he is unable, that of the person authorized to make gifts under the provisions of Subsection (B) hereof in the order therein prescribed, unless otherwise required by law. Any person who makes any such disclosure as contemplated herein in violation of the provisions of this subsection shall be subject to absolute liability for damages in an amount of not less than five thousand dollars nor more than ten thousand dollars in a civil action instituted pursuant hereto by the person whose authorization therefor had not been obtained.

§ 2353. Persons who may become donees; purposes for which anatomical gifts may be made.

The following persons may become donees of gifts of bodies or parts thereof for the purposes stated:

(1) Any hospital, surgeon, or physician, for medical or dental education, research, advancement of medical or dental science, therapy, or transplantation to individuals;

(2) Any accredited medical or dental school, college, or university engaged in medical or dental education or research for educational, research, or medical or dental science purposes;

(3) Any person operating a bank or storage facility;

(4) Any specific donee, for therapy or transplantation needed by him.

§ 2354. Manner of executing anatomical gifts.

A. A gift of all or part of the body under this Part may be made by will, in which case the gift becomes effective at the death of the testator without waiting for probate. If the will is not probated, or if it is declared invalid for testamentary purposes, the gift, to the extent that it has been acted upon in good faith, is nevertheless valid and effective.

B. A gift of all or part of the body under this Part may also be made by a document other than a will. The document must be signed by the donor, in the presence of two witnesses who in turn shall sign the document in his presence. If the donor cannot sign in person, the document may be signed for him at his direction and in his presence, and in the presence of two witnesses who shall sign the document in his presence. Delivery of the document of gift during the donor's lifetime is not necessary to make the gift valid. The gift becomes effective at the death of the donor.

C. The document of gift may consist of a properly executed card carried on the donor's person or in his effects. The document of gift may also be printed on the reverse side of an operator's or chauffeur's license as provided by R.S. 32:410.

D. The gift may be made either to a named donee or without the naming of a donee. If the latter, the gift may be accepted by and utilized under the direction of the attending physician at or following death. If the gift is made to a named donee who is not reasonably available at the time and place of death, and the gift is evidenced by a properly executed card or other writing carried on the donor's person or in his effects, the attending physician at or following death, in reliance upon the card or writing, and in the absence of any expressed indication that the donor desired otherwise, may accept and utilize the gift as the agent of the donee for any purpose authorized in R.S. 17:2353. The agent possesses and may exercise all of the rights and is entitled to all of the immunities of the donee under this Part.

E. Except as provided in R.S. 17:2357(B), the donor may designate in his will or other document of gift the surgeon, physician or technician to implement the appropriate procedures. In the absence of such designation, or if the designee is not reasonably available, the donee or other person authorized to accept the gift may employ or authorize any licensed surgeon, physician or technician to implement the appropriate procedures herein authorized.

F. Any gift by a person designated in Subsection (B) of R.S. 17:2352, shall be by a document signed by the person authorized by that section in the presence of two witnesses who shall sign the document in his presence.

G. Except as provided in R.S. 17:2357(B), in the situation relative to a gift of one's eye or eyes, the donor may designate in his will or other document of gift the surgeon, physician or technician to implement the enucleation of his eye or eyes. In the absence of such designation by the donor or if such designee is unavailable, the donee or other person authorized to accept the gift may employ or authorize any surgeon, physician, any state licensed funeral director, embalmer, technician, or trained medical school student; provided that the funeral director, embalmer, or trained medical school student has successfully completed an eye enucleation course in any accredited medical school in the United States.

§ 2354.1. Coroner's consent for eye enucleation.

A. A physician, technician, or other authorized person trained in eye enucleation may remove the eyes of a decedent immediately following certification of death provided:

(1) There is written authorization by a person empowered to execute an anatomical gift as provided in R.S. 17:2352(B); or

(2) There is authorization by the parish coroner; and

(3) The eyes will be donated to an authorized donee of gifts of bodies or parts thereof as defined in R.S. 17:2353 for the purposes of advancing medical science or for the replacement or rehabilitation of eyes in living persons.

B. Neither the coroner, physician, surgeon, technician, hospital, bank or storage facility, nor the donee, who acts in good faith to comply with this Section, shall be liable in any civil action to a claimant who alleges that his authorization for use of the eyes was required.

The provisions of this Subsection shall not be construed as limiting or restricting the liability of a coroner, physician, surgeon, technician, hospital, bank, storage facility or the donee as provided by R.S. 17:2357(C).

§ 2354.2. Coroner's consent for kidney removal.

A. A physician or surgeon may remove the kidneys of a decedent immediately following certification of death provided:

(1) There is written authorization by a person empowered to execute an anatomical gift as provided in R.S. 17:2352(B); or

(2) There is authorization by the parish coroner; and

(3) The kidneys will be or are intended to be donated to an authorized donee of gifts of bodies or parts thereof as defined in R.S. 17:2353 for the purpose of advancing medical science or for the replacement of kidneys in living persons.

B. Neither the coroner, physician, surgeon, technician, hospital, bank or storage facility, nor the donee, who acts in good faith to comply with this Section, shall be liable in any civil action to a claimant who alleges that his authorization for use of the kidneys was required.

The provisions of this Subsection shall not be construed as limiting or restricting the liability of a coroner, physician, surgeon, technician, hospital, bank, storage facility or the donee as provided in R.S. 17:2357(C).

§ 2354.3. Coroner's consent for heart, lungs, liver, soft tissue, or bone removal.

A. A physician or surgeon may remove the heart, lungs, liver, soft tissue, or bone of a decedent immediately following certification of death provided:

(1) There is written authorization by a person empowered to execute an anatomical gift as provided in R.S. 17:2352(B); or

(2) There is authorization by the parish coroner; and

(3) The heart, lungs, liver, soft tissue, or bone will be donated to an authorized donee of gifts of bodies or parts thereof as defined in R.S. 17:2353 for the purpose of advancing medical science or for the replacement of the heart, lungs, liver, soft tissue, or bone in living persons.

B.(1) Neither the coroner, physician, surgeon, technician, hospital, bank or storage facility, nor the donee, who acts in good faith to comply with this Section, shall be liable in any civil action to a claimant who alleges that his authorization for use of the heart, lungs, liver, soft tissue, or bone was required.

(2) The provisions of this Subsection shall not be construed as limiting or restricting the liability of a coroner, physician, surgeon, technician, hospital, bank or other storage facility, or the donee as provided by R.S. 17:2357(C).

§ 2354.4. Duties of hospital administrator; training; coordination.

A. As used in this Section:

(1) "Administrator" means the chief operating officer of a hospital.

(2) "Death" shall have the meaning provided in R.S. 9:111.

(3) "Hospital" means any institution, place, building, or agency, public or private, whether for profit or not, devoted primarily to the maintenance and operation of facilities for ten or more individuals for the diagnosis, treatment, or care of persons admitted for overnight stay or longer who are suffering from illness, injury, infirmity, or deformity or other physical condition for which obstetrical, medical, or surgical services would be available and appropriate. The term "hospital" does not include the following:

(a) Physicians' offices or clinics where patients are not regularly kept as bed patients for twenty-four hours or more;

(b) Nursing homes as defined by and regulated under the provisions of R.S. 40:2009.1 through R.S. 40:2009.12;

(c) Persons, schools, institutions, or organizations engaged in the care and treatment of mentally retarded children and which are required to be licensed by the provisions of R.S. 28:421 through R.S. 28:427;

(4) "Suitable candidate" means a patient who is certified by the attending physician, at or immediately before the time of death, to be a suitable donor for any organ or tissue donation based on accepted medical standards, and who has been released by the coroner in those instances required by law.

B. When death occurs in a hospital, to a person determined to be a suitable candidate for organ or tissue donation based on accepted medical standards, the hospital administrator or designated representative shall request the appropriate person described in Subsection H of this Section to consent to the gift of any part of the decedent's body as an anatomical gift.

C. No request shall be required, pursuant to this Section, when the requesting person has actual notice of contrary intention by the decedent or those persons described in Subsection H of this Section according to the priority stated therein, or reason to believe that an anatomical gift is contrary to the decedent's religious beliefs.

D.(1) A nonprofit organ or tissue bank or retrieval organization shall notify said hospital administrator in writing that any donation can be properly obtained and fully utilized in a manner consistent with accepted medical standards. Such notice shall provide that the nonprofit organ or tissue bank or retrieval organization will be responsible for all costs and charges of the hospital relating to obtaining the donated organ or tissue. The time within which the notice is to be effective shall be specified.

(2) Requests under this Section shall be limited to nonprofit organ or tissue banks or retrieval organizations.

E. Upon approval of the proper individual specified in Subsection H of this Section, the hospital administrator or designated representative shall notify an appropriate organ or tissue bank, or retrieval organization and cooperate in the procurement of the anatomical gift.

F. When a request is made, pursuant to Subsection B of this Section, the person making the request shall complete a certificate of request for an anatomical gift, on a form supplied by the secretary of the Department of Health and Human Resources. The certificate shall include the following:

(1) A statement indicating that a request for an anatomical gift was made.

(2) The name and affiliation of the person making the request.

(3) An indication of whether consent was granted and, if so, what organs and tissues were donated.

(4) The name of the person granting or refusing the request, and his relationship to the decedent.

G. A copy of the certificate described in Subsection F of this Section shall be included in the decedent's medical records.

H. The following persons shall be requested to consent to a gift, in the order of priority stated:

(1) The spouse if one survives; if not,

(2) An adult son or daughter,

(3) Either parent,

(4) An adult brother or sister,

(5) The curator or tutor of the person of the decedent at the time of his death,

(6) Any other person authorized or under obligation to dispose of his body.

I. When a donation is requested, consent or refusal need only be obtained from the person in the highest priority class available after best efforts have been exercised to contact those persons in a higher priority class. If there is more than one person within an above named class, then the consent to the donation shall be made by all members of that class reasonably available for consultation.

J. The secretary of the Department of Health and Human Resources shall:

(1) Establish rules concerning the procedures to be employed in making the request.

(2) Compile and disseminate a list of those nonprofit organ or tissue banks or retrieval organizations authorized to receive donations under this Section.

(3) Establish rules to implement appropriate procedures to facilitate proper coordination among hospitals, organ and tissue banks, and retrieval organizations.

K.(1) Neither the physician, administrator, surgeon, technician, hospital, organ and tissue bank, retrieval organization, nor the donee, who acts in good faith to comply with this Section, shall be liable in any civil action to a claimant who alleges that his consent for the donation was required.

(2) The provisions of R.S. 17:2354.1(B), R.S. 17:2354.2(B), R.S. 2354.3(B)(1) and R.S. 9:2797 are applicable to this Section.

§ 2355. Delivery of document of gift. If the gift is made by the donor to a named donee, the will or other document, or a copy thereof, may be delivered to him to expedite the appropriate procedures immediately after death, but such delivery is not necessary to validity of the gift. The document may also be deposited in any hospital or registry office that accepts such documents for safekeeping or for facilitation of procedures after death. Upon request of any interested party at or after the donor's death, the person in possession must produce the document for examination.

§ 2356. Revocation of the gift.

A. If the document of gift has been delivered to a named donee, it may be revoked by either:

(1) The execution and delivery to the donee or his agent of a revocation in writing signed by the

donor, or

   (2) An oral statement of revocation made in the presence of two persons, communicated to the donee or his agent, or

   (3) A statement during a terminal illness addressed to the attending physician and communicated to the donee, or

   (4) A card or writing, signed by the donor and carried on his person or in his effects, revoking the gift.

  B. Any document of gift which has not been delivered to the donee may be revoked in the manner set out in Subsection (A) of this Section or by destruction, cancellation, or mutilation of the document.

  C. Any gift made by a will may be revoked or amended in the manner provided for revocation or amendment of wills.

  D. An anatomical gift may not be amended or revoked by any person other than the donor, except that when the gift is of the entire body, the body shall be returned after removal of all the usable organs to the surviving spouse or the next of kin upon the request of either.

§ 2357. Rights and duties at death.

  A. The donee may accept or reject the gift. If the donee accepts, and if the gift is of the entire body, the donee or his agent, if he deems it desirable, may authorize embalming and funeral services. If the gift is of a part of the body, the donee or his agent, immediately after the death of the donor and prior to embalming, may cause the part included in the gift to be removed without unnecessary mutilation. After removal of the part, custody of the remainder of the body shall be transferred promptly to the surviving spouse or next of kin or other persons under obligation to dispose of the body.

  B. The time of death shall be determined by the physician who attends the donor at his death, or, if none, the physician who certifies the death. The physician shall not be a participant in the procedures for removing the part or transplanting it.

  C. The donee, agent of a donee, other person authorized to accept and utilize the gift, or any person authorized by the donor or donee to perform the surgical operation to remove parts covered by the gift is not liable for damages in any civil action or subject to prosecution in any criminal proceeding for his act if he acts in good faith and without actual knowledge of revocation of the gift and in accord with the terms of a gift under this Part, in accord with a document carried by the donor as provided in this Part, or in accord with the laws of the state in which the document of gift was executed.

  D. The provisions of this Part are subject to the laws of this state prescribing powers and duties with respect to autopsies.

§ 2358. Uniformity of interpretation. This Part shall be so construed as to effectuate its general purpose to make uniform the law of those states which enact it.

§ 2359. Short title. This Part may be cited as the Anatomical Gift Act.

MAINE

§ 2901. Definitions.

  1. Bank or storage facility. "Bank or storage facility" means a facility licensed, accredited or approved under the laws of any state for storage of human bodies or parts thereof.

2. Decedent. "Decedent" means a deceased individual and includes a stillborn infant or fetus.

3. Donor. "Donor" means an individual who makes a gift of all or part of his body.

4. Hospital. "Hospital" means a hospital licensed, accredited or approved under the laws of any state and includes a hospital operated by the United States Government, a state or a subdivision thereof, although not required to be licensed under state laws.

5. Part. "Part" includes organs, tissues, eyes, bones, arteries, blood, other fluids and other portions of a human body, and "part" includes "parts."

6. Person. "Person" means an individual, corporation, government or governmental subdivision or agency, business trust, estate, trust, partnership or association or any other legal entity.

7. Physician or surgeon. "Physician" or "surgeon" means a physician or surgeon licensed or authorized to practice under the laws of any state.

8. State. "State" includes any state, district, commonwealth, territory, insular possession, and any other area subject to the legislative authority of the United States of America.

§ 2902. Persons who may execute an anatomical gift.

1. Individuals. Any person of sound mind and of legal age may give all or any part of his body for any purposes specified in section 2903, the gift to take effect upon death.

2. Others. Any of the following persons, in order of priority stated, when persons in prior classes are not available at the time of death, and in the absence of actual notice of contrary indications by the decedent, or actual notice of opposition by a member of the same or a prior class, may give all or any part of the decedent's body for any purposes specified in section 2903:

A. The spouse;

B. An adult son or daughter;

C. Either parent;

D. An adult brother or sister;

E. A guardian of the person of the decedent at the time of his death;

F. Any other person authorized or under obligation to dispose of the body.

3. Notice to donee. If the donee has actual notice of contrary indications by the decedent, or that a gift by a member of a class is opposed by a member of the same or a prior class, the donee shall not accept the gift. The persons authorized by subsection 2 may make the gift after death or immediately before death.

4. Examination. A gift of all or part of a body authorizes any examination necessary to assure medical acceptability of the gift for the purposes intended.

5. Rights. The rights of the donee created by the gift are paramount to the rights of others, except as provided by section 2907, subsection 4.

§ 2903. Persons who may become donees, and purposes for which anatomical gifts may be made.

The following persons may become donees of gifts of bodies or parts thereof for the purposes stated:

1. Medical. Any hospital, surgeon or physician, for medical or dental education, research, advancement of medical or dental science, therapy or transplantation; or

2. School. Any accredited medical or dental school, college or university for education, research, advancement of medical or dental science or therapy; or

3. Storage facility. Any bank or storage facility, for medical or dental education, research, advancement of medical or dental science, therapy or transplantation; or

4. Specified individuals. Any specified individual for therapy or transplantation needed by him.

§ 2904. Manner of executing anatomical gifts.

1. Will. A gift of all or part of the body under section 2902, subsection 1, may be made by will. The gift becomes effective upon the death of the testator without waiting for probate. If the will is not probated, or if it is declared invalid for testamentary purposes, the gift, to the extent that it has been acted upon in good faith, is nevertheless valid and effective.

2. Other documents. A gift of any part of the body under section 2902, subsection 1, may be made by document other than a will. The gift becomes effective upon the death of the donor and upon acceptance by the donee. The document, which may be a card designed to be carried on the person, must be signed by the donor, in the presence of 2 witnesses who must sign the document in his presence. If the donor cannot sign, the document may be signed for him at his direction and in his presence, and in the presence of 2 witnesses who must sign the document in his presence. Delivery of the document of gift during the donor's lifetime is not necessary to make the gift valid.

3. Donee. The gift may be made to a specified donee or without specifying a donee. If the latter, the gift may be accepted by the attending physician as donee upon or following death. If the gift is made to a specified donee who is not available at the time and place of death, the attending physician, upon or following death in the absence of any expressed indication that the donor desired otherwise, may accept the gift as donee. The physician who becomes a donee under this subsection shall not participate in the procedures for removing or transplanting a part.

4. Designee. Notwithstanding section 2907, subsection 2, the donor may designate in his will, card, or other document of gift the surgeon or physician to carry out the appropriate procedures; provided that eye enucleations may also be performed by a person who has successfully completed a course of training either taught by an ophthalmologist, or given by the New England Eye Bank, and that the person is then examined and certified as qualified to perform eye enucleations by an ophthalmologist licensed to practice in Maine. The course shall include instruction and practice in anatomy and physiology of the eye, maintaining a sterile field during the procedure, use of the appropriate instruments and sterile procedures for removing the corneal button and preserving it in a preservation fluid. In the absence of a designation, or if the designee is not available, the donee or other person authorized to accept the gift may employ or authorize any surgeon or physician for the purpose.

5. How made. Any gift by a person designated in section 2902, subsection 2, shall be made by a document signed by him, or made by his telegraphic, recorded telephonic or other recorded message.

This subsection includes, but is not limited to, gifts made pursuant to section 2910. Any gift pursuant to section 2910, by a person designated in section 2902, subsection 2, shall be made by a document signed by him, by a telegraphic, recorded telephonic or other recorded message, or by a telephonic message witnessed by at least 2 people in which case the witnesses shall document the telephonic message in writing.

§ 2905. Delivery of document of gift.
If the gift is made by the donor to a specified donee, the will, card or other document, or an executed copy thereof, may be delivered to the donee to expedite the appropriate procedures immediately after death, but delivery is not necessary to the validity of the gift. The will, card or other document, or an executed copy thereof, may be deposited in any hospital, bank or storage facility or registry office that accepts them for safekeeping or for facilitation of procedures after death. On request of any interested party upon or after the donor's death, the person in possession shall produce the document for examination.

§ 2906. Amendment or revocation of the gift.

1. Amendment. If the will, card or other document or executed copy thereof has been delivered to a specified donee, the donor may amend or revoke the gift by:

    A. The execution and delivery to the donee of a signed statement; or

    B. An oral statement made in the presence of 2 persons and communicated to the donee; or

    C. A statement during a terminal illness or injury addressed to an attending physician and communicated to the donee; or

    D. A signed card or document found on his person or in his effects.

2. Revocation. Any document of gift which has not been delivered to the donee may be revoked by the donor in the manner set out in subsection 1 or by destruction, cancellation or mutilation of the document and all executed copies thereof.

3. Other methods. Any gift made by a will may also be amended or revoked in the manner provided for amendment or revocation of wills, or as provided in subsection 1.

§ 2907. Rights and duties at death.

1. Accepted or rejected. The donee may accept or reject the gift. If the donee accepts a gift of the entire body, he may, subject to the terms of the gift, authorize embalming and the use of the body in funeral services. If the gift is of a part of the body, the donee, upon the death of the donor and prior to embalming, shall cause the part to be removed without unnecessary mutilation. After removal of the part, custody of the remainder of the body vests in the surviving spouse, next of kin or other persons under obligation to dispose of the body.

2. Time of death. The time of death shall be determined by a physician who attends the donor at his death, or, if none, the physician who certifies the death. This physician shall not participate in the procedures for removing or transplanting a part.

3. Good faith. A person who acts in good faith in accord with the terms of this chapter, or under the anatomical gift laws of another state or a foreign country, is not liable for damages in any civil action or subject to prosecution in any criminal proceeding for his act.

4. Applicability of other laws. This chapter is subject to the laws of this State prescribing powers and duties with respect to autopsies and to the provisions of chapter 711 (section 3021 et seq. of this title), the Medical Examiner Act.

§ 2908. Uniformity of interpretation.
This chapter shall be so construed as to effectuate its general purpose to make uniform the law of those states which enact it.

§ 2909. Short title.
This chapter may be cited as the Uniform Anatomical Gift Act.

§ 2910. Request for consent required to an anatomical gift.

1. Request for consent required. When a death occurs in a hospital, a request for consent to an anatomical gift shall be made in accordance with the following provisions.

    A. Where, based upon acceptable medical standards, a decedent who has not made an anatomical gift is a suitable candidate for organ or tissue donation, the attending physician, or if he is unavailable or if he made the determination of death, the hospital administrator, or his designated representative, shall at the time of death request the person designated in section 2902, subsection 2, to consent to the gift of all or any part of the decedent's body as an anatomical gift for any or all of the purposes expressed in section 2903. This request is subject to all the provisions of this chapter.

    B. Persons who will make requests for anatomical gifts shall be given training in the appropriate procedures for making a request. A person who determined the death of the decedent may not make the request for that decedent.

2. Medical records. When a request for an anatomical gift is made pursuant to this section, the request and its disposition shall be noted in the decedent's medical record.

3. Interhospital agreements. Hospitals shall develop and implement interhospital agreements among themselves which establish protocols for the retrieval and transportation of all or any part of a body found suitable for transplantation and for the costs associated with transplantation.

4. Annual reports. Hospitals shall report annually to the commissioner the number of requests for anatomical gifts made and the number of organs retrieved pursuant to this section and the overall impact of this section. This report shall not contain any information which can identify the decedents or any person to whom a request for an anatomical gift was made.

5. Rules. The commissioner shall establish rules concerning the training of persons who will perform the request for an anatomical gift pursuant to this section and may establish other rules necessary to implement this section. The commissioner shall appoint a committee of medical and hospital representatives to make recommendations regarding rules concerning the interhospital agreements pursuant to subsection 3.

MARYLAND

§ 4-501. Definitions. (a) In this subtitle the following words have the meanings indicated.

(b) Body or part of body.—"Body" or "part of body" includes organs, tissues, bones, blood, and other body fluids.

(c) Licensed hospital.—"Licensed hospital" includes any hospital licensed by the State Department of Health and Mental Hygiene under the laws of the State, and any hospital operated by the United States government, although not required to be licensed under the laws of the State.

(d) Next of kin.—"Next of kin" includes spouse.

(e) Person.—"Person" means any individual, corporation, government or governmental agency or subdivision, estate, trust, partnership or association, or any other legal entity.

(f) Physician or surgeon.—"Physician" or "surgeon" means any physician or surgeon licensed to practice under the laws of the State.

§ 4-502. Legislative policy; purpose of subtitle.

(a) Legislative policy.—Because of the rapid medical progress in the field of tissue and organ preservation, the transplantation of tissue, and tissue culture, and because it is in the public interest to aid the development of this field of medicine, it is the policy and purpose of the General Assembly of Maryland in enacting this subtitle to encourage and aid the development of reconstructive medicine and surgery and the development of medical research by facilitating authorizations for premortem and postmortem donations of tissue and organs.

(b) Purpose of subtitle.—It is the purpose of this subtitle to regulate only the gift of a body or parts of a body to be made after the death of a donor.

§ 4-503. Execution of documents of anatomical gift.

(a) Competence of donor.—Any individual who is 18 years of age or over and who is competent to execute a will may give all or any part of his body for any one or more of the purposes specified in this subtitle. The gift takes effect after death of the donor.

(b) Persons who may make gift.—Unless he has knowledge that contrary directions have been given by the decedent, the following persons, in the order of priority stated, may give all or any part of a body of a decedent for any one or more of the purposes specified in this subtitle:

(1) The spouse, if one survives;

(2) An adult son or daughter;

(3) Either parent;
(4) An adult brother or sister;
(5) The guardian of the person of the decedent at the time of his death;
(6) Any other person or agency authorized or under obligation to dispose of the body.

If there is no surviving spouse and an adult son or daughter is not immediately available at the time of death of a decedent, the gift may be made by either parent. If a parent of decedent is not immediately available, the gift may be made by any adult brother or sister of decedent. If there is known to be a controversy within the class of persons first entitled to make the gift, the gift may not be accepted. The persons authorized by this subsection to make the gift may execute the document of gift either after death or during a terminal illness.

(c) **Method of making gift.**—If the gift is made by a person designated in section 4-503(b) of this section, it shall be by a document signed by him or by his telegraphic, recorded telephonic, or other recorded message.

(d) **Examination for medical acceptance.**—A gift of all or part of a body authorizes any examination of the body, or any other procedure, necessary to assure medical acceptability of the gift for the purposes intended.

(e) **Rights of donee.**—Except as provided in section 4-507 of this subtitle, the rights of the donee created by the gift are paramount to the rights of others.

§ 4-504. **Persons eligible to become donees of anatomical gifts.**

(a) **General.**—The persons listed in this section are eligible to receive gifts of human bodies or parts of them for the purposes stated.

(b) **Hospital, surgeon, or physician.**—Any licensed hospital, surgeon, or physician may receive a gift for medical education, research, advancement of medical science, therapy, or transplantation to individuals.

(c) **Medical school.**—An accredited medical school, college, or university engaged in medical education or research may receive a gift for therapy, educational research, or medical science purposes.

(d) **Storage of blood or human organs.**—Any licensed person operating a bank or storage facility for blood, arteries, eyes, pituitaries, or other human parts may receive a gift for use in medical education, research, therapy, or transplantation to individuals.

(e) **Specified donee.**—Any specified donee may receive a gift for therapy or transplantation needed by him.

§ 4-505. **Methods of making anatomical gifts.**

(a) **Gift by will.**—A gift of all or part of the body for purposes of this subtitle may be made by will, in which case the gift becomes effective immediately upon death of the testator without waiting for probate. If the will is not probated, or if it is declared invalid for testamentary purposes, the gift, to the extent that it has been acted upon in good faith, is nevertheless valid and effective.

(b) **Gift by document.**—A gift of all or part of the body for purposes of this subtitle also may be made by document other than a will. The document must be signed by the donor in the presence of two witnesses, who, in turn, shall sign the document in the presence of the donor. If the donor cannot sign in person, the document may be signed for him, at his direction and in his presence, and in the presence of two witnesses, who, in turn, shall sign the document in the presence of the donor. Delivery of the document of gift during the lifetime of the donor is not necessary to make the gift valid. The document may consist of a properly executed card carried on the person of the donor or in his effects. The document and card may conform substantially to the following form:

Anatomical Gift by a Living Donor

I am at least 18 years of age amd make this anatomical gift to take effect upon my death. The marks in the appropriate squares and words filled into the blanks below indicate my desires.

1. I give: [ ]my body; [ ]any needed organs or parts; [ ]the following organs or parts ....;

2. To the following person, agency, or institution: [ ]any person, tissue bank, or institution authorized by law;
[ ]the Anatomy Board of Maryland;
[ ]the following named physician, hospital, tissue bank or other medical institution..;

3. For the following purposes: [ ]any purpose authorized by law; [ ] transplantation; [ ] therapy; [ ]medical research and education.

Dated.......City and State..........
Signed by the Donor in the presence of the following who sign as witnesses:
Witness_____ Signature of Donor_____
Witness_____ Address of Donor_____

(c) **Designation of donee; acceptance of gift by attending physician.**—The gift may be made either to a named donee, or without the naming of a donee. If the latter, the gift may be accepted by and utilized at the discretion of the attending physician at or following death. If the gift is made to a named donee who is not readily available at the time and place of death, and if the gift is evidenced by a properly executed card or other document carried on the person of the donor, or in his effects, the attending physician at or following death, in reliance upon the card or other document, may accept and utilize the gift in his discretion, as the agent of the donee. The agent possesses and may exercise all rights and is entitled to all immunities of the donee under this subtitle.

(d) **Designation of surgeon to carry out procedures.**—The donor may designate in his will or other document of gift the surgeon, physician, or technician to carry out the appropriate procedures. In the event the designee is not available, or in the absence of a designation, the donee or other person authorized to accept the gift may employ or authorize any licensed surgeon, licensed physician, or technician for the purpose.

(e) **Validity of document of gift executed in another state.**—A document of gift executed in another state and in accord with the laws of that state or executed in a territory or possession of the United States under the control and dominion of the federal government exclusively, and in accord with a federal law is valid as a document of gift within the state, even if the document does not substantially conform to the requirements of section 4-505(b) of this subtitle.

§ 4-506. **Delivery of will or document of gift to donee.**

(a) **Delivery to expedite procedure.**—Immediately after death if the gift is made to a named donee, the will or other document or an attested true copy of it may be delivered to him to expedite the appropriate procedure, but delivery is not necessary to validate the gift.

(b) **Production of will.**—Upon request of the named donee or his agent after the death of the donor, the person in possession shall produce the will or other document of gift for examination.

§ 4-507. **Revocation of gift.**

(a) **Revocation of delivered document.**—Any document of gift which has been delivered to the donee may be revoked by

(1) The execution and delivery to the donee or his agent of a revocation in writing, signed by the donor,

(2) An oral statement of revocation witnessed by two persons, and communicated to the donee

or his agent,

(3) A statement during a terminal illness addressed to the attending physician and communicated to the donee, or his agent, or

(4) A card or other writing signed by the donor and carried on his person or in his effects, revoking the gift.

(b) Revocation of undelivered document.—Any document of gift which has not been delivered to the donee may be revoked in the manner set out in subsection (a) of this section, or by destruction, cancellation, or mutilation of the document.

(c) Revocation of will.—Any gift made by a will may be revoked in the manner set out in subsection (a) of this section, or in the manner provided for revocation or amendment of wills.

§ 4-508. **Rights of next of kin and donee; time of death; civil or criminal liability; autopsies.**

(a) Acceptance or rejection of gift; custody of body of decedent; determining time of death.—The donee may accept or reject the gift. If the gift is only a part of the body, promptly following the removal of the part named, custody of the remaining parts of the body shall be transferred to the next of kin or other person or agency authorized or under obligation to dispose of the body. The time of death shall be determined by the physician in attendance upon the terminal illness of the donor or certifying his death, and the physician may not be a member of the team of physicians which transplants the part to another individual.

(b) No civil or criminal liability for unknowingly violating subtitle.—A person who, in good faith and acting in reliance upon an authorization made under the provisions of this subtitle or under the anatomical gift laws of another state or foreign country and without notice of revocation, takes possession of, performs surgical operations upon, or removes tissue, substances, or parts from the human body or refuses the gift, or a person who unknowingly fails to carry out the wishes of the donor according to the provisions of this subtitle or under the anatomical gift laws of another state or foreign country, is not subject to prosecution in any criminal proceedings or liable for damages in a civil action brought against him for the act or failure to act.

(c) Effect of laws concerning autopsies.—The provisions of this subtitle are subject to the laws prescribing powers and duties with respect to autopsies and are not in contravention of them.

§ 4-509. **When Chief Medical Examiner or his deputy or assistant may provide organ for transplant.**

(a) Requirements.—In any case where a patient is in immediate need for an internal organ as a transplant, the Chief Medical Examiner, the deputy chief medical examiner, or an assistant medical examiner may provide the organ upon the request of the transplanting surgeon under the following conditions:

(1) The medical examiner has charge of a decedent who may provide a suitable organ for transplant;

(2) A reasonable, unsuccessful search has been made by the treating physician and the hospital where the patient is located to contact the next of kin;

(3) No known objection by the next of kin is foreseen by the medical examiner; and

(4) The organ for transplant will not interfere with the subsequent course of an investigation or autopsy;

(b) Liability of medical examiner.—The Chief Medical Examiner, the deputy chief medical examiner, and an assistant chief medical examiner are not liable for civil action if the next of kin is located subsequently and contends that authorization of that kin was required, if the Chief Medical Examiner has obtained a written statement from the treating physician or the hospital where the patient was located that a reasonable unsuccessful search was conducted for the next of kin prior to the removal of the tissue for transplantation.

§ 4-509.1. When Chief Medical Examiner or his deputy or assistant may provide cornea for transplant.

(a) Requirements.—In any case where a patient is in need of corneal tissue for a transplant, the Chief Medical Examiner, the deputy chief medical examiner, or an assistant medical examiner may provide the cornea upon the request of the Medical Eye Bank of Maryland, Incorporated under the following conditions:

(1) The medical examiner has charge of a decedent who may provide a suitable cornea for the transplant;

(2) An autopsy will be required;

(3) No objection by the next of kin is known by the medical examiner; and

(4) Removal of the cornea for transplant will not interfere with the subsequent course of an investigation or autopsy or alter the postmortem facial appearance.

(b) Liability of medical examiner.—The Chief Medical Examiner, the deputy chief medical examiner, an assistant medical examiner, and the Medical Eye Bank of Maryland, Incorporated are not liable for civil action if the next of kin subsequently contends that authorization of that kin was required.

§ 4-510. Gifts completed during lifetime of donor. The provisions of this subtitle do not apply to gifts of parts of the body if the gifts are made during the lifetime of the donor with the intention that the part of body is delivered to the donee during the lifetime of the donor.

§ 4-511. Validity of authority of instrument executed prior to July 1, 1968. Nothing in this subtitle invalidates any authority of instrument executed prior to July 1, 1968.

§ 4-512. Short title. This subtitle may be cited as the Maryland Anatomical Gift Act.

MASSACHUSETTS

§ 7. Definitions. In sections eight to fourteen, inclusive, unless the context otherwise requires, the following words shall have the following meanings:

"Acute hospital," any hospital licensed under section fifty-one of chapter one hundred and eleven, and the teaching hospital of the University of Massachusetts medical school, which contain a majority of medical-surgical, pediatric, obstetric, and maternity beds as defined by the department of public health.

"Bank or storage facility," a facility licensed, accredited or approved by the department of public health.

"Commissioner," the commissioner of the department of public health.

"Decedent," a deceased individual and includes a stillborn infant or fetus.

"Department," the department of public health.

"Donor," an individual who makes a gift of all or part of his body.

"Hospital," a hospital licensed, accredited or approved under the laws of any state and includes a hospital operated by the United States government, a state or a subdivision thereof, although not required to be licensed under state laws.

"Part," includes organs, tissues, skin, eyes, bones, arteries, blood, other fluids and other portions of a human body and "part" includes "parts."

"Person," an individual, corporation, government or governmental subdivision or agency, business trust, estate, trust, partnership or association or any other legal entity.

"Physician" or "surgeon," a physician or surgeon licensed or authorized to practice under the laws of any state.

"State," includes any state, district, commonwealth, territory, insular possession, and any other area subject to the legislative authority of the United States of America.

§ 8. Gifts of Human Bodies, Organs, and Tissues, Who May Make; Rights Created. (a) A person of sound mind and who is eighteen years of age or older may make a gift of all or any part of his body for any purposes specified in section nine, said gift to take effect upon his death, or in the case of a living donor at such time prior to his death as he may specify in accordance with the requirements of subsection (b) of section ten, so long as such donation does not jeopardize in any way the life and health of the donor.

(b) On or before the occurrence of death in an acute hospital, the director or other person in charge of such hospital, or his designated representative, including, but not limited to, the physician responsible for the care of the patient, shall inform any of the persons listed below in the order of priority stated, when persons in prior classes are not available, of the opportunity of authorizing a gift of all or part of the decedent's body for purposes of organ and tissue transplantation as specified in section nine; provided, however, that (1) no actual notice of contrary intentions by such persons has been received, (2) such information shall not cause undue emotional stress to the next of kin and (3) consent to such transplantation would yield an organ or tissue donation suitable for use in accordance with medical criteria as defined by physicians engaged in clinical transplantation therapy and as established by rules and regulations promulgated by the department which shall contain standards consistent with the standards set forth in the Manual of the New England Organ Bank. The order of priority of such persons shall be:

(1) the spouse,

(2) an adult son or daughter,

(3) either parent,

(4) an adult brother or sister,

(5) a guardian of the person of the decedent at the time of his death,

(6) any other person authorized or under obligation to dispose of the body.

(c) The director or person in charge of such hospital or his designated representative shall record in a book kept for such purpose (1) the names of those patients for whom consent to an anatomical gift had been granted, (2) the organs or tissues donated, (3) the name of the person granting consent, and (4) the relationship of such person to the decedent.

(d) If the donee has actual notice of contrary indications by the decedent, or that a gift authorized by a member of a class is opposed by a member of the same or a prior class, the donee shall not accept the gift. The persons authorized by subsection (b) may make the gift after death or immediately before death.

(e) A gift of all or part of a body authorizes premortem tests, and any other examination necessary to assure medical acceptability of the gift for the purposes intended by the donor.

(f) The rights of the donee created by the gift are paramount to the rights of others except as provided by subsection (d) of section thirteen.

(g) The commissioner shall issue an annual report summarizing and evaluating the data collected pursuant to subsection (c).

§ 9. Who May Become Donees of Anatomical Gifts. The following persons may become donees of gifts of bodies or parts thereof for the purposes stated:

(1) any hospital, surgeon, or physician, for medical or dental education, research, advancement of medical or dental science, therapy or transplantation; or

(2) any accredited medical or dental school, college, or university for education, research, advancement of medical or dental science or therapy; or

(3) any bank or storage facility for medical or dental education, research, advancement of medical or dental science, therapy or transplantation; or

(4) any specified individual for therapy or transplantation needed by him.

§ 10. Gift May Be Made by Will or Other Instrument; When Effective; Execution; Donee When None Specified. (a) A gift of all or part of the body under subsection (a) of section eight may be made by will. Such gift shall become effective upon the death of the testator. If the will is not probated, or if it is declared invalid for testamentary purposes, such gift, to the extent that it has been acted upon in good faith, shall be nevertheless valid and effective.

(b) A gift of all or part of the body under subsection (a) of section eight may also be made by a document other than a will. Such gift shall become effective upon the death of the donor.

In the case of a gift of a living donor intended for transplantation, the donor shall authorize such gift in a document signed by the donor and also by at least two of the physicians who are to participate in the transplantation operation and who shall have previously examined the donor in connection with his gift. In all cases other than those involving the gift of a living donor, the document may be a card designed to be carried on the person which shall be signed by the donor in the presence of two competent witnesses who shall attest to and subscribe the document in said donor's presence. If the donor cannot sign, the document may be signed for him at his direction and in his presence, and in the presence of two witnesses who must sign the document in his presence. Delivery of such document during the donor's lifetime is not necessary to make the gift valid.

(c) The gift may be made to a specified donee or without specifying a donee. If no donee is specified, the gift may be accepted by the attending physician as donee upon the death of the donor. If the gift is made to a specified donee who is available at the time and place of death, the attending physician upon the death of the donor, in the absence of any expressed indication that the donor desired otherwise, may accept the gift as donee. The physician who becomes a donee under this subsection shall not participate in the procedures for removing or transplanting a part.

(d) Notwithstanding subsection (b) of section thirteen, the donor may designate in his will, card or other document of gift the surgeon or physician to carry out the appropriate procedures; provided, however, that eye enucleations may be performed also by a technician who has successfully completed a course of training acceptable to the Eye Bank of the Massachusetts Eye and Ear Infirmary. In the absence of a designation, or if the designee is not available, the donee or other person authorized to accept the gift may employ or authorize any surgeon or physician for said purpose.

(e) Any gift by a person designated in subsection (b) of section eight shall be made by a document signed by him, or made by his telegraphic, recorded telephonic or other recorded message.

§ 11. Gift Instrument May Be Delivered to Donee or Deposited for Safekeeping; Production on or after Donor's Death. If the gift is made by the donor to a specified donee, the will, card, or other document, or an executed copy thereof, may be delivered to the donee to expedite the appropriate procedures immediately after death, but delivery is not necessary to the validity of the gift. The will, card or other document, or an executed copy thereof, may be deposited in any hospital, bank or storage facility or registry office that accepts them for safekeeping or for facilitation of procedures after death. On request of any interested party upon or after the donor's death, the person in possession shall produce the document for examination.

§ 12. Amendment or Revocation of Gift. (a) If the will, card or other document or executed copy thereof has been delivered to a specified donee, the donor may amend or revoke the gift by:

(1) the execution and delivery to the donee of a signed statement, or

(2) an oral statement made in the presence of two persons and communicated to the donee, or

(3) a statement during a terminal illness or injury addressed to an attending physician and communicated to the donee, or

(4) a signed card or document found on his person or in his effects.

(b) Any document of gift which has not been delivered to the donee may be revoked by the donor in the manner set out in subsection (a) or by destruction, cancellation, or mutilation of the document and all executed copies thereof.

(c) Any gift made by a will may also be amended or revoked in the manner provided for amendment or revocation of wills, or as provided in subsection (a).

§ 13. Donee May Accept or Reject Gift; Procedure upon Acceptance; Who Shall Determine Time of Death; Persons Acting in Good Faith Shall Not Be Liable, etc. (a) The donee may accept or reject the gift. If the donee accepts a gift of the entire body, he may, subject to the terms of the gift, authorize embalming and the use of the body in funeral services. If the gift is of a part of the body, the donee, upon the death of the donor and prior to embalming, shall cause the part to be removed without unnecessary mutilation. After removal of the part, custody of the remainder of the body vests in the surviving spouse, next of kin or other persons under obligation to dispose of the body. If the donee is responsible for the disposition of the body, he shall dispose of it in accordance with the terms specified by the donor, or if no such terms are specified, he shall have said body decently buried or cremated.

(b) The time of death shall be determined by a physician who attends the donor at his death, or, if none, the physician who certifies the death. This physician shall not participate in the procedures for removing or transplanting a part.

(c) A person who acts in good faith in accordance with the terms of sections seven to thirteen, inclusive, or under the anatomical gift laws of another state or a foreign country shall not be liable for damages in any civil action or be subject to prosecution in any criminal proceeding for his act.

(d) The provisions of sections seven to thirteen, inclusive, shall be subject to the laws of the commonwealth relative to autopsies.

§ 14. Cornea; Removal for Transplant Purposes; Procedure; Penalty for Violation. Upon request of the New England Eye Bank, an unincorporated nonprofit association registered with the attorney general, located at the Massachusetts Eye and Ear Infirmary, a medical examiner or a physician acting under his direction may provide the cornea of a decedent to said New England Eye Bank under the following conditions: (a) the body of the decedent is under the jurisdiction of the medical examiner authorizing the removal of the cornea and an autopsy is required in accordance with the provisions of chapter thirty-eight; (b) a period of one hour has elapsed after the medical examiner or physician acting under his direction has notified said eye bank and said eye bank has received such notification that the cornea of the decedent is available for transplant, and during such period said eye bank has made a good faith effort to notify decedent's spouse or next of kin that such transplant is proposed; (c) no objections to the donation have been made known by the decedent prior to his death or by the decedent's spouse or next of kin to said medical examiner or physician; (d) the removal of the cornea for transplant will not interfere with a subsequent investigation or autopsy; and (e) the removal of the cornea will not alter the decedent's facial appearance.

The time of such notification by said medical examiner or physician acting under his direction to said eye bank, shall be entered into a log kept specifically for such purpose and such log shall be available for inspection upon request during regular business hours, by a spouse or next of kin of a decedent whose cornea has been removed.

No medical examiner, physician or said eye bank, acting under the provisions of this section, shall be liable in any criminal or civil action brought as a result of a removal of a decedent's cornea if such good faith effort to notify decedent's spouse or next of kin of such transplant has been made.

MICHIGAN

§ 333.10101. Definitions. As used in this part:

(a) "Bank or storage facility" means a facility licensed, accredited, or approved under the laws of any state for storage of human bodies or physical parts thereof.

(b) "Decedent" means a deceased individual and includes a stillborn infant or fetus.

(c) "Donor" means an individual who makes a gift of all or a physical part of his or her body.

(d) "Hospital" means a hospital licensed, accredited, or approved under the laws of any state. It includes a hospital operated by the United States government, a state or a subdivision thereof, although not required to be licensed under state laws.

(e) "Person" means an individual, corporation, government or governmental subdivision or agency, business trust, estate, trust, partnership or association, or any other legal entity.

(f) "Physical part" means organs, tissues, eyes, bones, arteries, blood, other fluids, and any other portions of a human body.

(g) "Physician" or "surgeon" means a physician or surgeon licensed or authorized to practice under the laws of any state.

(h) "State medical school" means the university of Michigan school of medicine, the Michigan state university college of human medicine, the Michigan state university college of osteopathic medicine, or the Wayne state university school of medicine.

§ 333.10102. Gift of all or part of body; right to make gift. (1) An individual of sound mind and 18 years of age or more may give all or any physical part of the individual's body for any purpose specified in section 10103, the gift to take effect upon death.

Permission to give all or portion of decedent's body, priorities. (2) Any of the following persons, in order of priority stated, when persons in prior classes are not available at the time of death, and in the absence of actual notice of contrary indications by the decedent or actual notice of opposition by a member of the same or a prior class, may give all or any physical part of the decedent's body for any purpose specified in section 10103:

(a) The spouse.

(b) An adult son or daughter.

(c) Either parent.

(d) An adult brother or sister.

(e) A guardian of the person of the decedent at the time of the death.

(f) Any other person authorized or under obligation to dispose of the body.

Notice of opposition to gift; acceptance; time for making gift. (3) If the donee has actual notice of contrary indications by the decedent or that a gift by a member of a class is opposed by a member of the same or a prior class, the donee shall not accept the gift. The persons authorized by subsection (2) may make the gift after or immediately before death.

Gift; authorization of examination. (4) A gift of all or a physical part of a body authorizes any examination necessary to assure medical acceptability of the gift for the purposes intended.

Rights of donee. (5) The rights of the donee created by the gift are paramount to the rights of others except as provided by section 10108(4).

§ 333.10102a. Request for consent for donation. (1) Subject to section 10102(3) and subsections (2) to (7), the person designated pursuant to subsection (7) shall, at or near the death of a patient whose body, according to accepted medical standards, is suitable for donation or for the donation of physical parts, request 1 of the persons listed in section 10102(2), in the order of priority stated, to consent to the gift of all or any physical part of the decedent's body.

Conditions preventing request for consent for donation. (2) The person designated pursuant to subsection (7) shall not make a request for consent pursuant to subsection (1) if 1 or more of the following conditions exist:

(a) The person designated pursuant to subsection (7) has actual notice of contrary indications by the patient or decedent.

(b) The person designated pursuant to subsection (7) has actual notice of opposition by a person listed in section 10102(2) unless a person in a prior class under that section is available for a request to be made.

(c) The person designated pursuant to subsection (7) has knowledge that the gift of all or a physical part of a body is contrary to the religious beliefs of the decedent.

Hospital's duty to maintain organ donation log; contents. (3) Each hospital shall maintain a hospital organ donation log sheet on a form provided by the department. The organ donation log sheet shall include all of the following information:

(a) The name and age of the patient or decedent for whom a request is made pursuant to this section.

(b) A list of patients or decedents for whom a request was not made pursuant to this section and the reason for not making the request, as set forth in subsection (2).

(c) An indication that a request for consent to a gift of all or a physical part of a body has been made.

(d) An indication of whether or not consent was granted.

(e) If consent was granted, an indication of which physical parts of the body were donated, or whether the entire body was donated.

(f) The name and signature of the person making the request.

Completion of organ donation log. (4) After making a request for a gift pursuant to subsection (1), the person designated pursuant to subsection (7) shall complete the hospital's organ donation log sheet.

Donation log summary; contents; transmittal to department of health. (5) A summary of the information contained in the organ donation log sheets annually shall be transmitted by each hospital to the department. The summary shall include all of the following:

(a) The number of deaths.

(b) The number of requests made.

(c) The number of consents granted.

(d) The number of bodies or physical parts donated in each category as specified on the organ donation log sheet.

Execution of donation. (6) A gift made pursuant to a request required by this section shall be executed pursuant to this part.

Requirements for development and implementation of hospital policy. (7) The chief executive officer of each hospital shall develop and implement a policy regarding requests made pursuant to this section. The policy shall provide, at a minimum, for all of the following:

(a) The designation of persons who shall make requests under this section.

(b) That if a patient's religious preference is known, a clergy of that denomination shall, if possible, be made available upon request to the persons to whom a request under this section is made.

(c) The development of a support system which facilitates the making of requests under this section.

(d) The maintenance of the organ donation log sheet required by subsection (3).

Promulgation of rules; training standards; donation log sheet revision. (8) The director may promulgate rules to establish minimum training standards for persons required to make requests pursuant to this section and to revise the organ donation log sheet required by subsection (3).

Prohibition against withdrawal or withholding of medical care. (9) This section shall not be construed to authorize the withdrawal or withholding of medical care for a patient who is a possible donor and who is near death.

§ 333.10103. **Lawful donees.** The following persons may become donees of gifts of bodies or physical parts thereof for the purposes stated:

(a) Any hospital, surgeon, or physician for medical or dental education, research, advancement of medical or dental science, therapy, or transplantation.

(b) Any accredited medical or dental school, college, or university for education, research, advancement of medical or dental science, or therapy.

(c) Any bank or storage facility for medical or dental education, research, advancement of medical or dental science, therapy, or transplantation.

(d) Any specified individual for therapy or transplantation needed by that individual.

(e) Any approved or accredited school of optometry, nursing, or veterinary medicine.

§ 333.10104. **Testamentary gift; effective gift; validity.** (1) A gift of all or a physical part of the body under section 10102(1) may be made by will. The gift becomes effective upon the death of the testator without waiting for probate. If the will is not probated, or if it is declared invalid for testamentary purposes, the gift, to the extent that it has been acted upon in good faith, is nevertheless valid and effective.

Nontestamentary gift; effective date; signature; witnesses; delivery; document. (2) A gift of all or a physical part of the body under section 10102(1) may also be made by document other than a will. The gift becomes effective upon the death of the donor. The document, which may be a card designed to be carried on the person, shall be signed by the donor in the presence of 2 witnesses who shall sign the document in the donor's presence. If the donor cannot sign, the document may be signed for the donor at his or her direction and in his or her presence in the presence of 2 witnesses who shall sign the document in the donor's presence. Delivery of the document of gift during the donor's lifetime is not necessary to make the gift valid. A document which conforms substantially to the following form is sufficient for the purposes of this subsection. **See Appendix for this form (Uniform Donor Card).**

Specification of donee; acceptance; physician donee, participation in removal, transplant. (3) The gift may be made to a specified donee or without specifying a donee. If the latter, the gift may be accepted by the attending physician as donee upon or following death. If the gift is made to a specified donee who is not available at the time and place of death, the attending physician upon or following death, in the absence of any expressed indication that the donor desired otherwise, may accept the gift as donee. The physician who becomes a donee under this subsection shall not participate in the procedures for removing or transplanting a physical part.

Designation of surgeon or physician; failure, effect. (4) Notwithstanding section 10108(4), the donor may designate in his or her will, card, or other document of gift the surgeon or physician to carry out the appropriate procedures. In the absence of a designation or if the designee is not available, the donee or other person authorized to accept the gift may employ or authorize any surgeon or physician for the purpose.

Same; method. (5) Any gift by a person designated in section 10102(2) shall be made by a document signed by the person or made by the person's telegraphic, recorded telephonic, or other recorded message.

Document executed in foreign state or country; validity. (6) A document of gift executed in another state or foreign country and in accord with the laws of that state or country is valid as a document of gift in this state, although the document does not conform substantially to the form set forth in subsection (2).

§ 333.10105. Eye removal; persons qualified; certifications; conditions. In the absence of designation of a physician or surgeon by either the donor or the donee of an eye or a physical part thereof of a decedent, or because the physician or surgeon is not readily available to excise the eye or physical part thereof as specified in a donor card or will, a licensed physician or a person who is certified by a state medical school may perform the operation and arrange for placement of the gift in the nearest eye bank. A state medical school may certify a person as qualified to perform the operation required for the removal of an eye or a physical part thereof only after successfully completing a comprehensive course in eye enucleation organized and conducted by the state medical school or who has successfully completed a similar course offered by a nationally accredited medical school located outside this state.

§ 333.10106. Specified donee; delivery of document; necessity; safekeeping; production of document. If the gift is made by the donor to a specified donee, the will, card, or other document, or an executed copy thereof, may be delivered to the donee to expedite the appropriate procedures immediately after death. Delivery is not necessary to the validity of the gift. The will, card, or other document, or an executed copy thereof, may be deposited in any hospital, bank or storage facility, or registry office that accepts it for safekeeping or for facilitation of procedures after death. On request of any interested party upon or after the donor's death, the person in possession shall produce the document for examination.

§ 333.10107. Amendment, revocation of delivered document. (1) If the will, card, or other document or executed copy thereof, has been delivered to a specified donee, the donor may amend or revoke the gift by any of the following methods:

(a) The execution and delivery to the donee of a signed statement.

(b) An oral statement made in the presence of 2 persons and communicated to the donee.

(c) A statement during a terminal illness or injury addressed to an attending physician and communicated to the donee.

(d) A signed card or document found on the donor's person or in the donor's effects.

Revocation of nondelivered gift. (2) Any document of gift which has not been delivered to the donee may be revoked by the donor in the manner set out in subsection (1), or by destruction, cancellation, or mutilation of the document and all executed copies thereof.

Testamentary gift; amendment or revocation. (3) Any gift made by a will may also be amended or revoked in the manner provided for amendment or revocation of wills, or as provided in subsection (1).

§ 333.10108. Acceptance or rejection; disposition of body; custody; liability of mortuary science practitioners. (1) The donee may accept or reject the gift. If the donee accepts a gift of the entire body, the surviving spouse, next of kin, or other persons having authority to direct and arrange for the funeral and burial or other disposition of the body, subject to the terms of the gift, may authorize embalming and the use of the body in funeral services. If the gift is a physical part of the body, the donee, upon the death of the donor and prior to embalming, shall cause the physical part to be removed without unnecessary mutilation. After removal of the physical part, custody of the remainder of the body vests in the surviving spouse, next of kin, or such other persons having authority to direct and arrange for the funeral and burial or other disposition of the remainder of the body. The holder of a license for the practice of mortuary science under article 18 of the occupational code, Act No. 299 of the Public Acts of 1980, being sections 339.1801 to 339.1812 of the Michigan Compiled Laws, who acts pursuant to the directions of persons alleging to have authority to direct and arrange for the funeral and burial or other disposition of the remainder of the body, is relieved of any liability for the funeral and for the burial or other disposition of the remainder of the body. A holder of a license for the practice of mortuary science under that act may rely on the instructions and directions of any person alleging to be either a donee or a person authorized under this part to donate a body or any physical part thereof. A holder of a license for the practice of mortuary science under that act is not liable for removal of any physical part of a body donated under this part.

Time of death; determination. (2) The time of death shall be determined by a physician who attends the donor at the death, or, if none, the physician who certifies the death. The attending or certifying physician shall not participate in the procedures for removing or transplanting a physical part.

Good faith action; civil liability. (3) A person, including a hospital, who acts in good faith in accord with the terms of this part or with the anatomical gift laws of another state or a foreign country is not liable for damages in any civil action or subject to prosecution in any criminal proceeding for the act.

Autopsies. (4) This part is subject to the laws of this state prescribing powers and duties with respect to autopsies.

§ 333.10109. Construction. This part shall be so construed as to effectuate its general purpose to make uniform the law of those states which enact it.

MINNESOTA

§ 525.921. Definitions. Subdivision 1. For the purposes of sections 525.921 to 525.93 the terms defined in this section have the meanings given them.

Subd. 2. "Bank or storage facility" means a facility licensed, accredited, or approved under the laws of any state for storage of human bodies or parts thereof.

Subd. 3. "Decedent" means a deceased individual and includes a stillborn infant or fetus.

Subd. 4. "Donor" means an individual who makes a gift of all or part of his body.

Subd. 5. "Hospital" means a hospital licensed, accredited, or approved under the laws of any state; includes a hospital operated by the United States government, a state, or a subdivision thereof, although not required to be licensed under state laws.

Subd. 6. "Part" means organs, tissues, eyes, bones, arteries, blood, other fluids and any other portions of a human body.

Subd. 7. "Person" means an individual, corporation, government or governmental subdivision or agency, business trust, estate, trust, partnership or association, or any other legal entity.

Subd. 8. "Physician" or "surgeon" means a physician or surgeon licensed or authorized to practice medicine under the laws of any state.

Subd. 9. "State" includes any state, district, commonwealth, territory, insular possession, and any other area subject to the legislative authority of the United States of America.

§ 525.922. Persons who may execute an anatomical gift. Subdivision 1. Any individual of sound mind and 18 years of age or more, or any minor, with written consent of both parents, a legal guardian, or the parent or parents with legal custody may give all or any part of the individual's body for any purpose specified in section 525.923, the gift to take effect upon death.

Subd. 2. Any of the following persons, in order of priority stated, when persons in prior classes are not available at the time of death, and in the absence of actual notice of contrary indications by the decedent or actual notice of opposition by a member of the same or a prior class, may give all or any part of the decedent's body for any purpose specified in section 525.923:

(a) the spouse,

(b) an adult son or daughter,

(c) either parent,

(d) an adult brother or sister,

(e) a guardian of the person of the decedent at the time of his death,

(f) any other person authorized or under obligation to dispose of the body.

Subd. 3. If the donee has actual notice of contrary indications by the decedent or that a gift by a member of a class is opposed by a member of the same or a prior class, the donee shall not accept the gift. The persons authorized by subdivision 2 may make the gift after or immediately before death.

Subd. 4. A gift of all or part of a body authorizes any examination necessary to assure medical acceptability of the gift for the purposes intended.

Subd. 5. The rights of the donee created by the gift are paramount to the rights of others except as provided by Minnesota Statutes 1967, Section 390.11.

§ 525.923. Persons who may become donees; purposes for which anatomical gifts may be made. The following persons may become donees of gifts of bodies or parts thereof for the purposes stated:

(1) any hospital, surgeon, or physician, for medical or dental education, research, advancement of medical or dental science, therapy, or transplantation; or

(2) any accredited medical or dental school, college or university for education, research, advancement of medical or dental science, therapy, or transplantation; or

(3) any bank or storage facility for medical or dental education, research, advancement of medical or dental science, therapy, or transplantation; or

(4) any specified individual for therapy or transplantation needed by the individual; or

(5) any approved chiropractic college for education, research or advancement of chiropractic science.

§ 525.924. Manner of executing anatomical gifts. Subdivision 1. A gift of all or part of the body under section 525.922, subdivision 1, may be made by will. The gift becomes effective upon the death of the testator without waiting for probate. If the will is not probated, or if it is declared invalid for testamentary purposes, the gift, to the extent that it has been acted upon in good faith, is nevertheless valid and effective.

Subdivision 2. A gift of all or part of the body under section 525.922, subdivision 1, may also be made by document other than a will. The gift becomes effective upon the death of the donor. The document, which may be a card designed to be carried on the person, must be signed by the donor in the presence of two witnesses who must sign the document in the donor's presence. If the donor cannot sign, the document may be signed for the donor at the donor's direction and in the donor's presence in the presence of two witnesses who must sign the document in the donor's presence. Delivery of the document of gift during the donor's lifetime is not necessary to make the gift valid.

Subd. 2a. A gift of all or part of the body under section 525.922, subdivision 1, may be made by a minor, in a document other than a will. The gift becomes effective upon the death of the donor. The document, which may be a card designed to be carried on the person, must: (1) be signed by the minor donor and both of the minor donor's parents, a legal guardian, or the parent or parents with legal custody; (2) give the minor donor's date of birth; (3) give the address of the minor donor; and (4) contain the following words: "In hope that I may help others to live, I hereby make this anatomical gift, if medically acceptable, to take effect upon my death. I give (organ name) for the purpose of transplantation." If the minor cannot sign, the card may not be signed for the minor. Delivery of the gift document during the minor donor's lifetime is not necessary to make the gift valid.

Subd 3. The gift may be made to a specified donee or without specifying a donee. If the latter, the gift may be accepted by the attending physician as donee upon or following death. If the gift is made to a specified donee who is not available at the time and place of death, the attending physician upon or following death, in the absence of any expressed indication that the donor desired otherwise, may accept the gift as donee. The physician who becomes a donee under this subdivision shall not participate in the procedures for removing or transplanting a part.

Subd. 4. Notwithstanding section 525.927, subdivision 2, the donor may designate in a will, card, or other document of gift the surgeon or physician to carry out the appropriate procedures. In the absence of a designation or if the designee is not available, the donee or other person authorized to accept the gift may employ or authorize any surgeon or physician for the purpose.

Subd. 5. Any gift by a person designated in section 525.922, subdivision 2, shall be made by a document signed by the person or made by telegraphic, recorded telephonic, or other recorded message.

Subd. 6. In respect to a gift of an eye, a person licensed to practice mortuary science under chapter 149, or any other person who has completed a course in eye enucleation conducted and certified by the department of ophthalmology of any accredited college of medicine, and holds a valid certificate of competence for completing the course, may enucleate eyes for a gift after pronouncement of death by a physician. A written release authorizing the enucleation must be obtained prior to the performance of the procedure. The release shall be obtained from a relative or other person in the order of priority stated in section 525.922, subdivision 2. A mortician or other person acting in accordance with the provisions of this subdivision shall not have any liability, civil or criminal, for the eye enucleation.

Subd. 7. The designation "donor" on the front side of a donor's driver's license or nonqualification certificate, pursuant to the provisions of section 171.07, subdivision 5, shall constitute sufficient legal authority for the removal of all body organs or parts, upon the death of the donor for the purpose of transplantation.

§ 525.925. Delivery of document of gift. Subdivision 1. If the gift is made by the donor to a specified donee, the will, card, or other document, or an executed copy thereof, may be delivered to the donee to expedite the appropriate procedures immediately after death. Delivery is not necessary to the validity of the gift. The will, card, or other document, or an executed copy thereof, may be deposited in any hospital, bank or storage facility, or registry office that accepts it for safekeeping or for facilitation of procedures after death. On request of any interested party upon or after the donor's death, the person in possession shall produce the document for examination.

Subd. 2. A card, or other document, or an executed copy thereof, may be filed with the local registrar of vital statistics in the city or county of the donor's residence. The local registrar upon filing or recording the same shall transmit to the state registrar of vital statistics on or before the tenth of each month a copy thereof. The applicable provisions of the uniform vital statistics act shall apply to the filing and recording of the instrument referred to in this subdivision.

§ 525.926. Amendment or revocation of gift. Subdivision 1. If the will, card, or other document or executed copy thereof, has been delivered to a specified donee, the donor may amend or revoke the gift by:

(a) the execution and delivery to the donee of a signed statement, or

(b) an oral statement made in the presence of two persons and communicated to the donee, or

(c) a statement during a terminal illness or injury addressed to an attending physician and communicated to the donee, or

(d) a signed card or document found on his person or in his effects.

Subd. 2. Any document of gift which has not been delivered to the donee may be revoked by the donor in the manner set out in subdivision 1 or by destruction, cancellation, or mutilation of the document and all executed copies thereof.

Subd. 3. Any gift made by a will may also be amended or revoked in the manner provided for amendment or revocation of wills or as provided in subdivision 1. If an amendment or revocation of the gift is made in conformity with subdivision 1, such amendment or revocation shall not affect any other part of the will.

§ 525.927. Rights and duties at death. Subdivision 1. The donee may accept or reject the gift. If the donee accepts a gift of the entire body, he may, subject to the terms of the gift, authorize embalming and the use of the body in funeral services. If the gift is of a part of the body, the donee, upon the death of the donor and prior to embalming, shall cause the part to be removed without unnecessary mutilation. After removal of the part, custody of the remainder of the body vests in the surviving spouse, next of kin, or other persons under obligation to dispose of the body.

Subd. 2. The time of death shall be determined by a physician who attends the donor at his death, or, if none, the physician who certifies the death. The physician shall not participate in the procedures for removing or transplanting a part.

Subd. 3. A person who acts in good faith in accord with the terms of sections 525.921 to 525.93, sections 171.07, subdivision 5, 171.12, subdivision 5 or the anatomical gift laws of another state or foreign country is not liable for damages in any civil action or subject to prosecution in any criminal proceeding for his act.

§ 525.928. Parts for transplantation. The use of any part of a body for the purpose of transplantation in the human body shall be construed, for all purposes whatsoever, as a rendition of a service by each and every person participating therein and shall not be construed as a sale of such part for any purpose whatsoever.

§ 525. 929. Uniformity of interpretation. Sections 525.921 to 525.93 shall be so construed as to effectuate its general purpose to make uniform the law of those states which enact it.

§ 525.93. Short title. Sections 525.921 to 525.93 may be cited as the Uniform Anatomical Gift Act.

§ 525.94. Establishment of protocol to obtain organs for transplantation. Subdivision 1. Requirement to establish organ procurement protocol. A hospital licensed under sections 144.50 to 144.58 must establish written protocols for the identification of potential organ donors for transplantation to:

(1) assure that families of potential organ donors are made aware of the option of organ and tissue donation and their option to decline;

(2) require that an organ procurement agency be notified of potential organ donors; and

(3) establish medical criteria and practical considerations concerning the suitability and feasibility of organ donation for transplantations.

For purposes of this subdivision, the term "organ" or "tissue" includes but is not limited to a human kidney, liver, heart, lung, pancreas, skin, bone, ligament, tendon, eye, and cornea.

Subd. 2. Notification requirement. If an individual dies in a hospital or is identified by an appropriate hospital staff member as having a terminal condition and is further identified as a suitable candidate for organ or tissue donation based on medical criteria established in the written protocol, in accordance with the hospital's protocol, the hospital administrator or the administrator's designated representative shall notify any of the following persons listed below in order of priority, of the option of organ or tissue donation and their option to decline:

(1) the spouse;

(2) an adult child;

(3) either parent;

(4) an adult brother or sister; or

(5) a guardian of the decedent's person at the time of death.

The hospital administrator or the designated representative shall attempt to locate the person's driver's license, organ donation card, or other documentation of the person's desire to be an organ donor. If documentation of the person's desire to be a donor is located, it constitutes consent if there is no objection from the relative or guardian in clauses (1) to (5) or if no relative or guardian can be located.

If a person listed in clauses (1) to (5) wishes to consent to the gift of all or part of the decedent's body for transplantation, consent may be obtained by either the hospital administrator's representative or the organ procurement agency's representative. Consent or refusal must be obtained only from the available person highest on the list in clauses (1) to (5).

Subd. 3. Documentation. Notification under subdivision 1, as well as any identified contradiction to organ donation, must be documented in the patient's medical record, which must include the name of the person notified and the person's relationship to the decedent.

Subd. 4. Financial liability. The family of an individual whose organ is donated for transplantation is not financially liable for costs related to the evaluation of donor organ suitability or retrieval of the organ.

Subd. 5. Compliance with uniform anatomical gift act. A gift made pursuant to the request required under this section must be executed according to the uniform anatomical gift act.

Sub. 6. Training. The commissioner of health shall work with hospital representatives and other interested persons to develop guidelines for training hospital employees who may notify persons of the option to make an anatomical gift and the procedure to be used in executing the gift and ensuring that each tissue or organ is tested for possible disease before being made available for transplantation.

MISSISSIPPI

§ 41-39-11. Certified licensed embalmers may enucleate eyes which are subject of gift. (1) In respect to a gift of an eye as provided for in this chapter, a person licensed for the practice of funeral service under the provisions of sections 73-11-41 et seq., who has successfully completed a course in eye enucleation and has received a certificate of competence from the state board of health may enucleate eyes for such gift after the proper certification of death by a physician and compliance with the extent of such gift as defined within sections 41-39-31 through 41-39-53. No such properly certified funeral service licensee acting in accordance with the terms of this chapter shall have any liability, civil or criminal, for such eye enucleation.

(2) The state board of health shall promulgate such rules as are necessary to provide for the proper certification of such funeral service licensees for the implementation of this section.

§ 41-39-31. Title. Sections 41-39-31 to 41-39-51 may be cited as "the Anatomical Gift Law."

§ 41-39-33. Definitions. As used in section 41-39-31 to 41-39-51, the following terms shall have the meaning indicated:

(a) "Person" means individual, corporation, government or governmental agency or subdivision, estate, trust, partnership or association, or any other legal entity.

(b) "Body or part of body" includes organs, tissues, bones, blood and other body fluids, and "part" includes "parts."

(c) "Licensed hospital" includes any hospital licensed by the state board of health under the laws of this state and any hospital operated by the United States Government although not required to be licensed under the laws of the state of Mississippi.

(d) "Licensed physician or surgeon" means any physician or surgeon licensed to practice under the laws of this state.

(e) "Technician" means an individual other than a physician or surgeon who is certified by the state board of health as being qualified to remove and preserve parts of a body pursuant to this chapter.

(f) "Accredited school of mortuary science" means a mortuary science program in a state junior college approved by the state junior college commission and the vocational technical division of the Mississippi Department of Education.

§ 41-39-35. Persons authorized to make donations. (a) Any individual who is eighteen (18) years of age or over and who is competent to execute a will may give all or any part of his body for any one or more of the purposes specified in sections 41-39-31 to 41-39-51, the gift to take effect after death.

(b) Unless he has knowledge that contrary directions have been given by the decedent, the following persons, in the order of priority stated, may give all or any part of a decedent's body for any one or more of the purposes specified in sections 41-39-31 to 41-39-51:

(1) The spouse, if one survives.
(2) An adult son or daughter.
(3) Either parent.
(4) An adult brother or sister.
(5) The guardian of the person of the decedent at the time of his death.
(6) Any other person or agency authorized or under obligation to dispose of the body.

If there is no surviving spouse and an adult son or daughter is not immediately available at the time of death of a decedent, the gift may be made by either parent.

If a parent of decedent is not immediately available, the gift may be made by an adult brother or sister of decedent. If there is known to be a controversy within the class of persons first entitled to make the gift, the gift will not be accepted. The persons authorized herein to make the gift may execute the document of gift either after death or during a terminal illness. The decedent may be a minor or a stillborn infant.

If the gift is made by a person designated above, it shall be by written or telegraphic consent.

§ 41-39-37. Persons eligible to receive donations. The following persons are eligible to receive gifts of human bodies or parts thereof for the purposes stated:

(1) Any licensed hospital, surgeon or physician, for medical education, research, advancement of medical science, therapy or transplantation to individuals.

(2) Any accredited medical school, college or university engaged in medical education or research, for therapy, educational research or medical science purposes.

(3) Any persons operating a bank or storage facility for blood, arteries, eyes, pituitaries, or other human parts, for use in medical education, research, therapy or transplantation to individuals.

(4) Any specified donee, for therapy or transplantation needed by him.

(5) Any accredited school of mortuary science.

§ 41-39-39. Manner of effecting donation. (1) A gift of all or part of the body for purposes of sections 41-39-31 to 41-39-51 may be made by will, in which case the gift becomes effective immediately upon death of the testator without waiting for probate. If the will is not probated, or if it is declared invalid for testamentary purposes, the gift, to the extent that it has been acted upon in good faith, is nevertheless valid and effective.

(2) A gift of all or part of the body for purposes of sections 41-39-31 to 41-39-51 may also be made by document other than a will. The document must be signed by the donor in the presence of two (2) witnesses who, in turn, shall sign the document in the donor's presence. If the donor cannot sign in person, the document may be signed for him, at his direction and in his presence, and in the presence of two (2) witnesses who, in turn, shall sign the document in the donor's presence. The gift becomes effective immediately upon death of donor.

Delivery of the document of gift during the donor's lifetime is not necessary to make the gift valid. The document may consist of a properly executed card carried on the donor's person or in his effects. The document and/or card shall conform substantially to the following form:

Certificate of Authorization for Post-Mortem Study and Examination or Removal of Tissues or Organs

I, the undersigned, this____day of _____, 19___, desiring that my _____ be made available after my demise for:

(1) Any licensed hospital, surgeon or physician, for medical education, research, advancement of medical science, therapy or transplantation to individuals;

(2) Any accredited medical school, college or university engaged in medical education or research, for therapy, educational research or medical science purposes or any accredited school of mortuary science;

(3) Any person operating a bank or storage facility for blood, arteries, eyes, pituitaries, or other human parts, for use in medical education, research, therapy or transplantation to individuals;

(4) The donee specified below, for therapy or transplantation needed by him or her, do hereby donate my _____ for said purpose to _____(Name) at _____ (Address).

I hereby authorize a licensed physician, surgeon or certified technician or the state anatomy board to remove and preserve for use my _____ for said purpose.

Witnessed this ____day of _____, 19___.

_____   _____
(Name and Address)   (Donor)

_____   _____
(Name and Address)   (Address)

                                 _____
                                  (Telephone)

(3) The gift may be made either to a named donee or without the naming of a donee. If the latter, the gift may be accepted by and utilized at the discretion of the attending physician at or following death.

If the gift is made to a named donee who is not readily available at the time and place of death, and if the gift is evidenced by a properly executed card or other document carried on the donor's person or in his effects, the attending physician at or following death may, in reliance upon the card or other document, accept and utilize the gift in his discretion as the agent of the donee. The agent possesses and may exercise all of the rights and is entitled to all of the immunities of the donee under sections 41-39-31 to 41-39-51.

If the gift is made to a named donee, the will or other document or an attested true copy thereof may be delivered to him to expedite the appropriate procedure immediately after death, but such delivery is not necessary to validity of the gift. Upon request of the named donee or his agent on or after the donor's death, the person in possession shall produce for examination the will or other document of gift.

(4) The donor may designate in his will or other document of gift the surgeon, physician or technician to carry out the appropriate procedures. In the event of the nonavailability of such designee, or in the absence of a designation, the donee or other person authorized to accept the gift may employ or authorize any licensed physician, licensed surgeon or technician for the purpose.

(5) A document of gift executed in another state and in accord with the laws of that state thereunto pertaining, or executed in a territory or possession of the United States under the control and dominion of the federal government exclusively and in accord with a federal law thereunto pertaining, shall be deemed valid as a document of gift within the state of Mississippi, notwithstanding that said document does not substantially conform to the requirements of this section.

§ 41-39-41. **Revocation.** (a) Any document of gift which has been delivered to the donee may be revoked by either:

(1) the execution and delivery to the donee or his agent of a revocation in writing, signed by the donor, or

(2) an oral statement of revocation witnessed by two persons, and communicated to the donee or his agent, or

(3) a statement during a terminal illness addressed to the attending physician and communicated to the donee or his agent, or

(4) a card or other writing signed by the donor and carried on his person or in his effects revoking the gift.

(b) Any document of gift which has not been delivered to the donee may be revoked in the manner set out above or by destruction, cancellation or mutilation of the document.

(c) Any gift made by a will may be revoked in the manner set out in subsection (a) above or in the manner provided for revocation or amendment of wills.

§ 41-39-43. **Acceptance or rejection of gift; determination of time of death.** The donee may accept or reject the gift. When the gift is only a part of the body, promptly following the removal of the part named, custody of the remaining parts of the body shall be transferred to the next of kin or other person or agency authorized or under obligation to dispose of the body. The time of death shall be determined by the physician in attendance upon the donor's terminal illness or certifying his death. Said physician shall not be a member of the team of physicians which transplants the part to another individual.

§ 41-39-45. Civil liability. Any person who, in good faith and acting in reliance upon and authorization made under the provisions of sections 41-39-31 to 41-39-51 and without notice of revocation thereof, takes possession of, performs surgical operations upon, removes tissue, substances or parts from the human body, or refuses such a gift, and any person who unknowingly fails to carry out the wishes of the donor according to the provisions of said sections shall not be liable for damages in a civil action brought against him for such act.

§ 41-39-47. Effect of laws respecting autopsies. The provisions of sections 41-39-31 to 41-39-51 are subject to the laws of this state prescribing powers and duties with respect to autopsies, and are not in contravention thereof.

§ 41-39-49. Application to gifts intended to be made during donor's lifetime. The provisions of sections 41-39-31 to 41-39-51 shall not apply to gifts of parts of the body when said gifts are made during the lifetime of the donor with the intention that said part of the body be delivered to the donee during the lifetime of the donor.

§ 41-39-51. Effect of prior authority or instrument. Nothing in sections 41-39-31 to 41-39-51 shall invalidate any authority or instrument executed prior to April 6, 1970.

§ 41-39-53. Identification of donors on driver's license; duties of public safety commissioner. (1) The commissioner of public safety is hereby directed to adopt and implement a program whereby anatomical organ donors may be so identified by an appropriate decal, sticker or other marking to be affixed to the driver's license of such person.

(2) The commissioner shall provide space on every application for a driver's license or renewal thereof in which the applicant may indicate his desire to have such marking on his driver's license. In addition, any person whose license has not expired or who has already obtained a license may have such marking affixed by the commissioner upon request.

(3) The commissioner shall publish the existence of such program along with information regarding the procedures for having such marking affixed to a license.

(4) The commissioner shall notify his counterparts in each of the other states as to the existence of the program and the significance of the marking.

(5) No provision of this section shall be construed to modify or repeal any provisions of the Anatomical Gift Law. Sections 41-39-31 et seq., and the actual donation of such anatomical organ shall be in conformity with and subject to all provisions of the Anatomical Gift Law.

MISSOURI

§ 194.210. Definitions. As used in sections 194.210 to 194.290, the following words and terms mean:

(1) **"Bank or storage facility,"** a facility licensed, accredited, or approved under the laws of any state for storage of human bodies or parts thereof;

(2) **"Decedent,"** a deceased individual and includes a stillborn infant or fetus;

(3) **"Donor,"** an individual who makes a gift of all or part of his body;

(4) **"Hospital,"** a hospital licensed, accredited, or approved under the laws of any state and includes a hospital operated by the United States government, a state, or a subdivision thereof, although not required to be licensed under state laws;

(5) **"Part,"** organs, tissues, eyes, bones, arteries, blood, other fluids and any other portions of a human body;

(6) **"Person,"** an individual, corporation, government or governmental subdivision or agency, business trust, estate, trust, partnership or association, or any other legal entity;

(7) **"Physician"** or **"surgeon,"** a physician or surgeon licensed or authorized to practice under the laws of any state;

(8) **"State"** includes any state, district, commonwealth, territory, insular possession, and any other area subject to the legislative authority of the United States of America.

§ 194.220. Persons who may execute an anatomical gift.

1. Any individual of sound mind who is at least eighteen years of age may give all or any part of his body for any purpose specified in section 194.230, the gift to take effect upon death.

2. Any of the following persons, in order of priority stated, when persons in prior classes are not available at the time of death, and in the absence of actual notice of contrary indications by the decedent or actual notice of opposition by a member of the same or a prior class, may give all or any part of the decedent's body for any purpose specified in section 194.230:

(1) The spouse,

(2) An adult son or daughter,

(3) Either parent,

(4) An adult brother or sister,

(5) A guardian of the person of the decedent at the time of his death,

(6) Any other person authorized or under obligation to dispose of the body.

3. If the donee has actual notice of contrary indications by the decedent or that a gift by a member of a class is opposed by a member of the same or a prior class, the donee shall not accept the gift. The persons authorized by subsection 2 may make the gift after or immediately before death.

4. A gift of all or part of a body authorizes any examination necessary to assure medical acceptability of the gift for the purposes intended.

5. The rights of the donee created by the gift are paramount to the rights of others except as provided by subsection 4 of section 194.270.

§ 194.230. Persons who may become donees—purposes for which anatomical gifts may be made. The following persons may become donees of gifts of bodies or parts thereof for the purposes stated:

(1) Any hospital, surgeon, or physician, for medical or dental education, research, advancement of medical or dental science, therapy, or transplantation; or

(2) Any accredited medical or dental school, college or university or the state anatomical board for education, research, advancement of medical or dental science, or therapy; or

(3) Any bank or storage facility, for medical or dental education, research, advancement of medical or dental science, therapy, or transplantation; or

(4) Any specified individual for therapy or transplantation needed by him.

§ 194.233. Anatomical gifts—hospital to make request, to whom, when—verification in patient's record—hospital not liable for cost of retrieval.

1. The chief executive officer of each hospital in this state shall designate one or more trained persons to request anatomical gifts, which persons shall not be connected with determination of death.

The hospital official may designate a representative of an organ or tissue procurement organization to request consent.

2. Where there is a patient who is a suitable candidate for organ or tissue donation based on hospital accepted criteria the designee shall request consent to a donation from the persons authorized to give consent as specified in subdivision (1), (2), (3), or (4) of subsection 2 of section 194.220. The request shall be made in the order of priority stated in subsection 2 of section 194.220.

3. No request shall be required if the hospital designee has actual notice of contrary indications by the decedent or by a member of a prior class specified in subsection 2 of section 194.220.

4. Consent shall be obtained by the methods specified in section 194.240.

5. Where a donation is requested, the designee shall verify such request in the patient's medical record. Such verification of request for organ donation shall include a statement to the effect that a request for consent to an anatomical gift has been made, and shall further indicate thereupon whether or not consent was granted, the name of the person granting or refusing the consent, and his or her relationship to the decedent.

6. Upon the approval of the designated next of kin or other individual, as set forth in subsection 2 of section 194.220, the hospital shall then notify an organ or tissue procurement organization and cooperate in the procurement of the anatomical gift or gifts pursuant to applicable provisions of sections 194.210 to 194.290.

7. No hospital shall have an obligation to retrieve the organ or tissue donated pursuant to this section.

§ 194.240. Methods of executing anatomical gifts—person to carry out procedure.

1. A gift of all or part of the body under subsection 1 of section 194.220 may be made by will. The gift becomes effective upon the death of the testator without waiting for probate. If the will is not probated, or if it is declared invalid for testamentary purposes, the gift, to the extent that it has been acted upon in good faith, is nevertheless valid and effective.

2. A gift of all or part of the body under subsection 1 of section 194.220 may also be made by document other than a will. The gift becomes effective upon the death of the donor. The document, which may be a card designed to be carried on the person, must be signed by the donor in the presence of two witnesses who must sign the document in his presence or before a notary or other official authorized to administer oaths generally. If the donor cannot sign, the document may be signed for him at his direction and in his presence in the presence of two witnesses who must sign the document in his presence. Delivery of the document of gift during the donor's lifetime is not necessary to make the gift valid.

3. The gift may be made to a specified donee or without specifying a donee. If the latter, the gift may be accepted by the attending physician as donee upon or following death. If the gift is made to a specified donee who is not available at the time and place of death, the attending physician upon or following death, in the absence of any expressed indication that the donor desired otherwise, may accept the gift as donee. The physician who becomes a donee under this subsection shall not participate in the procedures for removing or transplanting a part.

4. Notwithstanding the provisions of subsection 2 of section 194.270, the donor may designate in his will, card, or other document of gift the surgeon or physician to carry out the appropriate procedures. In the absence of a designation or if the designee is not available, the donee or other person authorized to accept the gift may employ or authorize any surgeon or physician to carry out the appropriate procedures. For the purpose of removing an eye or part thereof, any medical technician employed by a hospital, physician or eye bank and acting under supervision may perform the appropriate procedures. Any medical technician authorized to perform such procedure shall success-

fully complete the course prescribed in section 194.295 for embalmers.

5. Any gift by a person designated in subsection 2 of section 194.220 shall be made by a document signed by him or made by his telegraphic, recorded telephonic, or other recorded message.

6. A gift of part of the body under subsection 1 of section 194.220 may also be made by a statement on a form which shall be provided on the reverse side of all Missouri motor vehicle operators' and chauffeurs' licenses. The statement to be effective shall be signed by the owner of the operator's or chauffeur's license in the presence of two witnesses, who shall sign the statement in the presence of the donor. Delivery of the license during the donor's lifetime is not necessary to make the gift valid. The gift shall become invalidated upon expiration, cancellation, revocation, or suspension of the license, and the gift must be renewed upon renewal of each license. Pertinent medical information which may affect the quality of the gift may be included in the statement of gift.

§ 194.250. Delivery of document of gift. If the gift is made by the donor to a specified donee, the will, card, or other document, or an executed copy thereof, may be delivered to the donee to expedite the appropriate procedures immediately after death. Delivery is not necessary to the validity of the gift. The will, card, or other document, or an executed copy thereof, may be deposited in any hospital, bank or storage facility or registry office that accepts it for safekeeping or for facilitation of procedures after death. On request of any interested party upon or after the donor's death, the person in possession shall produce the document for examination.

§ 194. 260. Amendment or revocation of the gift.

1. If the will, card, or other document or executed copy thereof, has been delivered to a specified donee, the donor may amend or revoke the gift by:

(1) The execution and delivery to the donee of a signed statement, or

(2) An oral statement made in the presence of two persons and communicated to the donee, or

(3) A statement during a terminal illness or injury addressed to an attending physician and communicated to the donee, or

(4) A signed card or document found on his person or in his effects.

2. Any document of gift which has not been delivered to the donee may be revoked by the donor in the manner set out in subsection 1, or by destruction, cancellation, or mutilation of the document and all executed copies thereof.

3. Any gift made by a will may also be amended or revoked in the manner provided for amendment or revocation of wills, or as provided in subsection 1.

§ 194.270. Rights and duties at death.

1. The donee may accept or reject the gift. If the donee accepts a gift of the entire body, he may, subject to the terms of the gift, authorize embalming and the use of the body in funeral services. If the gift is of a part of the body, the donee, upon the death of the donor and prior to embalming, shall cause the part to be removed without unnecessary mutilation. After removal of the part, custody of the remainder of the body vests in the surviving spouse, next of kin, or other persons under obligation to dispose of the body.

2. The time of death shall be determined by a physician who tends the donor at his death, or, if none, the physician who certifies the death. The physician shall not participate, directly or indirectly, in the procedures for removing or transplanting a part or be a relative within the fourth degree of consanguinity of any donee of a body or part thereof which is removed or transplanted.

3. A person who acts without negligence and in good faith in accord with the terms of this act or with the anatomical gift laws of another state or a foreign country is not liable for damages in any civil action or subject to prosecution in any criminal proceeding for his act.

4. The provisions of this act are subject to the laws of this state prescribing powers and duties with respect to autopsies.

§ 194.280. Uniformity of interpretation. Sections 194.210 to 194.290 shall be so construed as to effectuate its general purpose to make uniform the law of those states which enact it.

§ 194.290. Short title. Sections 194.210 to 194.290 may be cited as the "Uniform Anatomical Gift Act."

§ 194.295. Embalmers authorized to enucleate eyes, when. Any embalmer, licensed under the provisions of chapter 333, Revised Statutes of Missouri, who has successfully completed a course in eye enucleation conducted or certified by the department of ophthalmology of a college of medicine offering said course, and who holds a valid certificate of competence for completing the course, may enucleate eyes when the eyes have been donated as a gift as provided by the Missouri uniform anatomical gift act. No embalmer is subject to any civil or criminal liability for performing any act necessary to enucleate eyes as provided by this section.

MONTANA

Part 1: General Provisions

§ 72-17-101. Short title. This chapter may be cited as the "Uniform Anatomical Gift Act."

§ 72-17-102. Definitions. (1) "Bank or storage facility" means a facility for storage of human bodies or parts thereof, operated by or under the supervision of a person who qualifies as a donee under subsection (1)(a) or (1)(b) of 72-17-202.

(2) "Decedent" means a deceased individual and includes a stillborn infant or fetus.

(3) "Department" means the department of health and environmental sciences provided for in Title 2, chapter 15, part 21.

(4) "Donor" means an individual who makes a gift of all or part of his body.

(5) "Eyebank association of America" means the organization nationally recognized by that name, with headquarters in Houston, Texas, that surveys banks or storage facilities for the storage of eye tissue upon their requests and grants membership and certification status to any such bank or storage facility that it finds meets its standards and requirements.

(6) "Hospital" means a hospital licensed, accredited, or approved under the laws of any state; includes a hospital operated by the United States government, a state, or a subdivision thereof, although not required to be licensed under state laws.

(7) "Ophthalmologist" means a licensed physician or surgeon who specializes in the treatment or correction of diseases of the eye.

(8) "Parts" means organs, tissues, eyes, bones, arteries, blood or other fluids, and any other portions of a human body.

(9) "Person" means an individual, corporation, government, or governmental subdivision or agency, business trust, estate, trust, partnership, or association or any other legal entity.

(10) "Physician" or "surgeon" means a physician or surgeon licensed or authorized to practice under the laws of any state.

(11) "State" includes any state, district, commonwealth, territory, insular possession, and any other area subject to the legislative authority of the United States of America.

(12) "Technician trained in eye enucleation" means an individual who has satisfactorily completed a course in eye enucleation taught by an ophthalmologist.

§ 72-17-103. Uniformity of interpretation. This chapter shall be so construed as to effectuate its general purpose to make uniform the law of those states which enact it.

§ 72-17-104. Chapter subject to autopsy laws. The provisions of this chapter are subject to the laws of this state prescribing powers and duties with respect to autopsies.

Part 2: Execution and Operation of Anatomical Gift

§ 72-17-201. Persons who may make gift—priorities—donee not to accept over objection of prior right. (1) Any individual of sound mind and 18 years of age or more may give all or any part of his body for any purpose specified in 72-17-202, the gift to take effect upon death.

(2) Any of the following persons, in order of priority stated, when persons in prior classes are not available at the time of death and in the absence of actual notice of contrary indications by the decedent or actual notice of opposition by a member of the same or a prior class, may give all or any part of the decedent's body for any purpose specified in 72-17-202:

(a) the spouse;

(b) an adult son or daughter;

(c) either parent;

(d) an adult brother or sister;

(e) a guardian of the person of the decedent at the time of his death.

(3) The persons authorized by subsection (2) may make the gift after or immediately before death.

(4) If the donee has actual notice of contrary indications by the decedent or that a gift by a member of a class is opposed by a member of the same or a prior class, the donee shall not accept the gift.

§ 72-17-202. Persons who may become donees—permissible purposes of gift—nonliability. (1) The following persons may become donees of gifts of bodies or parts thereof for the purposes stated:

(a) any hospital, surgeon, or physician for medical or dental education, research, advancement of medical or dental science, therapy, or transplantation;

(b) any accredited medical or dental school, college, or university for education, research, advancement of medical or dental science, or therapy;

(c) any bank or storage facility licensed, accredited, or approved under the laws of any state for medical or dental education, research, advancement of medical or dental science, therapy, or transplantation;

(d) any specified individual for therapy or transplantation needed by him.

(2) A physician, surgeon, technician trained in eye enucleation, hospital, bank or storage facility, or donee acting in good faith compliance with the provisions of this chapter is not liable in a civil action to any claimant who alleges that the claimant's authorization for use of the body or part was required.

§ 72-17-203. Rights of donee paramount. The rights of the donee created by the gift are paramount to the rights of others, except as provided in 72-17-104.

§ 72-17-204. Manner of executing gift—effectiveness. (1) A gift of all or part of the body under 72-17-201(1) may be made by will. The gift becomes effective upon the death of the testator without waiting for probate. If the will is not probated or if it is declared invalid for testamentary purposes, the gift, to the extent that it has been acted upon in good faith, is nevertheless valid and effective.

(2) (a) A gift of all or part of the body under 72-17-201(1) may also be made by document other than a will. The gift becomes effective upon the death of the donor.

(b) The document may be a card designed to be carried on the person and must be signed by the donor in the presence of two witnesses who must sign the document in his presence. If the donor cannot sign, the document may be signed for him at his direction and in his presence in the presence of two witnesses who must sign the document in his presence. Delivery of the document of gift during the donor's lifetime is not necessary to make the gift valid.

(c) The document may be a statement attached to the reverse side of the person's Montana motor vehicle driver's license. The statement must be signed by the owner of the driver's license in the presence of two witnesses who must sign the statement in the presence of the donor.

(3) Any gift by a person designated in 72-17-201(2) shall be made by a document signed by him or made by his telegraphic, recorded telephonic, or other recorded message.

§ 72-17-205. Specified or unspecified donee—powers and duties of physician. (1) The gift may be made to a specified donee or without specifying a donee. If the latter, the gift may be accepted by the attending physician as donee upon or following death. If the gift is made to a specified donee who is not available at the time and place of death, the attending physician upon or following death, in the absence of any expressed indication that the donor desired otherwise, may accept the gift as donee.

(2) The physician who becomes a donee under this section shall not participate in the procedures for removing or transplanting a part.

§ 72-17-206. Designation of physician by donor—absence of designation. The donor may designate in his will, card, or other document of gift the surgeon or physician to carry out the appropriate procedures, except as provided in 72-17-205 and 72-17-310(2). In the absence of a designation or if the designee is not available, the donee or other person authorized to accept the gift may employ or authorize any surgeon or physician for the purpose, except as provided in 72-17-205 and 72-17-301(2).

§ 72-17-207. Gift authorizes examination. A gift of all or part of a body authorizes any examination necessary to assure medical acceptability of the gift for the purposes intended.

§ 72-17-208. Delivery of document to expedite procedures—delivery not necessary to validity. (1) If the gift is made by the donor to a specified donee, the will, card, or other document or an executed copy thereof may be delivered to the donee to expedite the appropriate procedures immediately after death. Delivery is not necessary to the validity of the gift.

(2) The will, card, or other document or an executed copy thereof may be deposited in any hospital, bank or storage facility, or registry office that accepts it for safekeeping or for facilitation of procedures after death.

(3) On request of any interested party upon or after the donor's death, the person in possession shall produce the document for examination.

§ 72-17-209. Amendment or revocation of gift. (1) If the will, card, or other document or executed copy thereof has been delivered to a specified donee, the donor may amend or revoke the gift by:

(a) the execution and delivery to the donee of a signed statement;

(b) an oral statement made in the presence of two persons and communicated to the donee;

(c) a statement during a terminal illness or injury addressed to an attending physician and communicated to the donee; or

(d) a signed card or document found on his person or in his effects.

(2) Any document of gift which has not been delivered to the donee may be revoked by the donor in the manner set out in subsection (1) or by destruction, cancellation, or mutilation of the document and all executed copies thereof.

(3) Any gift made by a will may also be amended or revoked in the manner provided for amendment or revocation of wills or as provided in subsection (1).

§ 72-17-210. Renumbered 72-17-301 by Code Commissioner, 1983.

§ 72-17-211. When organ donation may be requested. (1) When, based on generally accepted medical standards, a hospital patient is a suitable candidate for organ or tissue donation and has not made an anatomical gift as provided in this part, the hospital administrator, or his designated representative shall request the person authorized in 72-17-201 to donate all or any part of the decedent's body as an anatomical gift. Requests shall be made in order of priority stated in 72-17-201 when persons in prior classes are not available at the time of death.

(2) Donation of all or part of the decedent's body may not be requested:

(a) if the hospital administrator or his designated representative:

(i) has actual notice of opposition to the gift by the decedent or a person in the class authorized to make a gift under 72-17-201; or

(ii) has reason to believe that an anatomical gift is contrary to the decedent's religious beliefs; or

(b) if there are medical or emotional conditions under which the request would contribute to severe emotional distress.

(3) When a request is made pursuant to this section, the request and its disposition must be noted in the patient's medical record and documented as provided in 72-17-204(3).

§ 72-17-212. Immunity from liability. A person who acts in good faith in accordance with the terms of 72-17-211 is not liable for damages in any civil proceeding or subject to prosecution in any criminal proceeding that might result from this action.

Part 3: Regulation—Qualifications

§ 72-17-301. Rights and duties at death. (1) The donee may accept or reject the gift. If the donee accepts a gift of the entire body, he may, subject to the terms of the gift, authorize embalming and the use of the body in funeral services. If the gift is of a part of the body, the donee, upon the death of the donor and prior to embalming, shall cause the part to be removed without unnecessary mutilation. After removal of the part, custody of the remainder of the body vests in the surviving spouse, next of kin, or other persons under obligation to dispose of the body.

(2) The time of death shall be determined by a physician who tends the donor at his death or, if none, the physician who certifies the death. The physician who tends the donor at his death or, if none, the physician who certifies the death shall not participate in the procedures for removing or transplanting a part.

§ 72-17-302 through 72-17-310 reserved.

§ 72-17-311. Eye enucleations—technicians—qualifications. (1) Eye enucleations for purposes of anatomical gifts may be performed:

(a) by a licensed physician or surgeon; or

(b) by a technician trained in eye enucleation;

(2) An acceptable course in eye enucleation must include the anatomy and physiology of the eye, instruction in maintaining a sterile field during the enucleation procedure, and use of appropriate

instruments and sterile procedures for removal and preservation of corneal tissue.

(3) Certification of satisfactory completion of a course in eye enucleation must be provided by the ophthalmologist who teaches the course. This certification qualifies a technician to perform eye enucleations for a period of 3 years from the date of completion of the course.

§ 72-17-312. Approval of eye banks. Any bank or storage facility that furnishes to the department written evidence of its membership and certification and reports and recommendations for future compliance, granted by the eyebank association of America, is approved for receipt and storage of eye tissue for the term of such membership and certification and is eligible during such term to be a donee of eye tissue pursuant to 72-17-202(1)(c).

NEBRASKA

§ 71-4801. Terms, defined. As used in sections 71-4801 to 71-4812, unless the context otherwise requires:

(1) Bank or storage facility means a facility licensed, accredited or approved under the laws of any state for storage of human bodies or parts thereof;

(2) Decedent means a deceased individual and includes a stillborn infant or fetus;

(3) Donor means an individual who makes a gift of all or part of his body;

(4) Hospital means a hospital licensed, accredited or approved under the laws of any state and includes a hospital operated by the United States government, a state, or a subdivision thereof, although not required to be licensed under state laws;

(5) Part includes organs, tissues, eyes, bones, arteries, blood, other fluids and other portions of a human body, and part includes parts;

(6) Person means an individual, corporation, government or governmental subdivision or agency, business trust, estate, trust, partnership or association or any other legal entity;

(7) Physician or surgeon means a physician or surgeon licensed or authorized to practice under the laws of any state; and

(8) State includes any state, district, commonwealth, territory, insular possession, and any other area subject to the legislative authority of the United States of America.

§ 71-4802. Persons who may execute anatomical gift; when. (1) Any individual of sound mind and nineteen years of age or more may give all or any part of his body for any purposes specified in section 71-4803, the gift to take effect upon death.

(2) Any of the following persons, in order of priority stated, when persons in prior classes are not available at the time of death, and in the absence of actual notice of contrary indications by the decedent, or actual notice of opposition by a member of the same or a prior class, may give all or any part of the decedent's body for any purposes specified in section 71-4803:

(a) The spouse,

(b) An adult son or daughter,

(c) Either parent,

(d) An adult brother or sister,

(e) A guardian of the person of the decedent at the time of his death, and

(f) Any other person authorized or under obligation to dispose of the body.

The persons authorized by this subsection may make the gift after death or immediately before death.

(3) If the donee has actual notice of contrary indications by the decedent, or that a gift by a member of a class is opposed by a member of the same or a prior class, the donee shall not accept the gift.

(4) A gift of all or part of a body authorizes any examination necessary to assure medical acceptability of the gift for the purposes intended.

(5) The rights of the donee created by the gift are paramount to the rights of others except as provided by subdivision (4) of section 71-4807.

§ 71-4803. Persons who may become donees; purposes for which anatomical gifts may be made. The following persons may become donees of gifts of bodies or parts thereof for the purposes stated:

(1) Any hospital, surgeon, or physician, for medical or dental education, research, advancement of medical or dental science, therapy or transplantation;

(2) Any accredited medical or dental school, college or university for education, research, advancement of medical or dental science or therapy;

(3) The State Anatomical Board, any bank or storage facility, for medical or dental education, research, advancement of medical or dental science, therapy or transplantation; or

(4) Any specified individual for therapy or transplantation needed by him.

§ 71-4804. Manner of executing anatomical gifts. (1) A gift of all or part of the body under subdivision (1) of section 71-4802 may be made by will. The gift becomes effective upon the death of the testator without waiting for probate. If the will is not probated, or if it is declared invalid for testamentary purposes, the gift, to the extent that it has been acted upon in good faith, is nevertheless valid and effective.

(2) A gift of all or part of the body under subdivision (1) of section 71-4802 may also be made by document other than a will. The gift becomes effective upon the death of the donor. The document, which may be a card designed to be carried on the person, must be signed by the donor, in the presence of two witnesses who must sign the document in his presence. If the donor cannot sign, the document may be signed for him at his direction and in his presence, and in the presence of two witnesses who must sign the document in his presence. Delivery of the document of gift during the donor's lifetime is not necessary to make the gift valid.

(3) A gift of all or part of the body under subdivision (1) of section 71-4802 may also be made by an indication on a motor vehicle operator's license pursuant to sections 60-406.01 to 60-406.03. The gift shall become effective upon the death of the owner.

(4) The gift may be made to a specified donee or without specifying a donee. If the latter, the gift may be accepted by the attending physician as donee upon or following death. If the gift is made to a specified donee who is not available at the time and place of death, the attending physician upon or following death, in the absence of any expressed indication that the donor desired otherwise, may accept the gift as donee. Any physician who becomes a donee under this subsection shall not participate in the procedures for removing or transplanting any part of the body, except as provided in subsection (2) of section 71-4807.

(5) Notwithstanding subdivision (2) of section 71-4807, the donor may designate in his will, card, or other document of gift the surgeon or physician to carry out the appropriate procedures. In the absence of a designation, or if the designee is not available, the donee or other person authorized to accept the gift may employ or authorize any surgeon or physician for the purpose.

(6) Any gift by a person designated in subdivision (2) of section 71-4802 shall be made by a document signed by him, or made by his telegraphic, recorded telephonic or other recorded message.

§ 71-4805. Document of gift; delivery. If the gift is made by the donor to a specified donee, the will, card or other document, or an executed copy thereof, may be delivered to the donee to expedite the appropriate procedures immediately after death, but delivery is not necessary to the validity of the gift. The will, card or other document, or an executed copy thereof, may be deposited in any hospital, medical or dental school, State Anatomical Board, bank or storage facility or registry office that accepts them for safekeeping or for facilitation of procedures after death. On request of any interested party upon or after the donor's death, the person in possession shall produce the document for examination.

§ 71-4806. Gifts; amendment; revocation. (1) If the will, card or other document or executed copy thereof, has been delivered to a specified donee, the donor may amend or revoke the gift by:

(a) The execution and delivery to the donee of a signed statement;

(b) An oral statement made in the presence of two persons and communicated to the donee;

(c) A statement during a terminal illness or injury addressed to an attending physician and communicated to the donee; or

(d) A signed card or document found on his person or in his effects.

(2) Any document of gift which has not been delivered to the donee may be revoked by the donor in the manner set out in subsection (1) of this section or by destruction, cancellation, or mutilation of the document and all executed copies thereof.

(3) Any gift made by a will may also be amended or revoked in the manner provided for amendment or revocation of wills, or as provided in subsection (1) of this section.

§ 71-4807. Rights and duties at death. (1) The donee may accept or reject the gift. If the donee accepts a gift of the entire body, he may, subject to the terms of the gift, authorize embalming and the use of the body in funeral services. If the gift is of a part of the body, the donee, upon the death of the donor and prior to embalming, shall cause the part to be removed without unnecessary mutilation. After removal of the part, custody of the remainder of the body vests in the surviving spouse, next of kin or other persons under obligation to dispose of the body.

(2) The time of death shall be determined by a physician who attends the donor at his death, or, if none, the physician who certifies the death. This physician shall not participate in the procedures for removing or transplanting a part, except the enucleation of eyes. A licensed funeral director or mortician, as defined in section 71-1325, upon (a) successfully completing a course in eye enucleation and (b) receiving a certificate of competence from the Department of Ophthalmology, College of Medicine of the University of Nebraska, may enucleate the eyes of the donor.

(3) A person who acts in good faith in accord with the terms of sections 71-4801 to 71-4812, or under the anatomical gift laws of another state is not liable for damages in any civil action or subject to prosecution in any criminal proceeding for his act.

(4) The provisions of sections 71-4801 to 71-4812 are subject to the laws of this state prescribing powers and duties with respect to autopsies.

§ 71-4808. Blood and human tissues; who may consent to donate. Any individual of sound mind and seventeen years of age or more may consent to donate whole blood and any individual of sound mind and nineteen years of age or more may consent to donate other human tissues such as corneas, bones, or organs, for the purpose of injecting, transfusing, or transplanting such blood or other human tissues in the human body. No person seventeen or eighteen years of age shall receive compensation for any donation of whole blood without parental permission or authorization.

§ 71-4809. Legal liability; policy of state. The availability of scientific knowledge, skills and materials for the transplantation, injection, transfusion or transfer of human tissue, organs, blood and components thereof is important to the health and welfare of the people of this state. The imposition of legal liability without fault upon the persons and organizations engaged in such scientific procedures inhibits the exercise of sound medical judgment and restricts the availability of important scientific knowledge, skills and materials. It is therefore the public policy of this state to promote the health and welfare of the people by limiting the legal liability arising out of such scientific procedures to the instances of negligence or willful misconduct.

§ 71-4810. Legal liability; exemption; exceptions. No physician, surgeon, hospital, blood bank, tissue bank, licensed funeral director or mortician, or other person or entity who donates, obtains, prepares, transplants, injects, transfuses or otherwise transfers, or who assists or participates in obtaining, preparing, transplanting, injecting, transfusing or transferring any tissue, organ, blood or component thereof from one or more human beings, living or dead, to another human being, shall be liable in damages as a result of any such activity, save and except that each such person or entity shall remain liable in damages for his or its own negligence or willful misconduct.

§ 71-4811. Act, how construed. Sections 71-4801 to 71-4812 shall be construed as to effectuate its general purpose to make uniform the law of those states which enact it.

§ 71-4812. Act, how cited. Sections 71-4801 to 71-4812 may be cited as the Uniform Anatomical Gift Act.

§ 71-4813. Eye tissue; pituitary gland; removal; when authorized. When an autopsy is performed by the physician authorized by the county coroner to perform such autopsy, the physician or an appropriately qualified designee with training in ophthalmologic techniques, as provided for in subsection (2) of section 71-4807, may remove eye tissue of the decedent for the purpose of transplantation. The physician may also remove the pituitary gland for the purpose of research and treatment of hypopituitary dwarfism and of other growth disorders. Removal of the eye tissue or the pituitary gland shall only take place if:

(1) Autopsy was authorized by the county coroner;

(2) County coroner receives permission from the person having control of the disposition of the decedent's remains pursuant to section 71-1339; and

(3) Removal of eye tissue or pituitary gland will not interfere with the course of any subsequent investigation or alter the decedent's post mortem facial appearance.

The removed eye tissue or pituitary gland shall be transported to the Director of Health or any desired institution or health facility as prescribed by section 71-1341.

NEVADA

§ 451.500. Short title. Nevada Revised Statutes 451.500 to 451.585, inclusive, may be cited as the Uniform Anatomical Gift Act.

§ 451.505. Uniformity of interpretation. NRS 451.500 to 451.585, inclusive, shall be so construed as to effectuate their general purpose to make uniform the law of those states which enact them.

§ 451.510. Definitions. Unless the context otherwise requires, as used in NRS 451.500 to 451.590, inclusive, the words and terms defined in NRS 451.515 to 451.550, inclusive, have the meanings ascribed to them in those sections.

§ 451.515. "Bank or storage facility" defined. "Bank or storage facility" means a facility licensed, accredited or approved under the laws of the State of Nevada for storage of human bodies or parts thereof.

§ 451.520. "Decedent" defined. "Decedent" means a deceased individual and includes a stillborn infant or fetus.

§ 451.525. "Donor" defined. "Donor" means an individual who makes a gift of all or part of his body.

§ 451.530. "Hospital" defined. "Hospital" means a hospital licensed, accredited or approved under the laws of the State of Nevada, but includes a hospital operated by the United States Government, the state or a subdivision thereof, although not required to be licensed under state laws.

§ 451.535. "Part" defined. "Part" means organs, tissues, eyes, bones, arteries, blood, other fluids and any other portions of a human body.

§ 451.540. "Person" defined. "Person" includes a government, a governmental agency and a political subdivision of a government.

§ 451.545. "Physician" defined. "Physician" means a person authorized to practice as a physician or surgeon under the laws of any state.

§ 451.550. "State" defined. "State" includes any state, district, commonwealth, territory, insular possession and any other area subject to the legislative authority of the United States of America.

§ 451.555. Person may make anatomical gift.

1. Any individual of sound mind and 18 years of age or more may give all or any part of his body for any purpose specified in NRS 451.560, the gift to take effect upon death.

2. Any of the following persons, in order of priority stated, when persons in prior classes are not available at the time of death, and in the absence of actual notice of contrary indications by the decedent or actual notice of opposition by a member of the same or a prior class, may give all or any part of the decedent's body for any purpose specified in NRS 451.560:

   (a) The spouse.
   (b) An adult son or daughter.
   (c) Either parent.
   (d) An adult brother or sister.
   (e) A guardian of the person of the decedent at the time of his death.
   (f) Any other person authorized or under obligation to dispose of the body. The legal procedure for authorization shall be defined and established by the committee on anatomical dissection established by the University of Nevada System.

3. If the donee has actual notice of contrary indications by the decedent or that a gift by a member of a class is opposed by a member of the same or a prior class, the donee shall not accept the gift. The persons authorized under subsection 2 may make the gift after or immediately before death.

4. A gift of all or part of a body authorizes any examination necessary to assure medical acceptability of the gift for the purposes intended.

5. The rights of the donee created by the gift are paramount to the rights of others except as provided by NRS 451.585.

§ 451.560. Qualifications of donee; purpose for which gifts may be made. The following persons may become donees of gifts of bodies or parts thereof for the purposes stated:

1. Any hospital, physician or dentist, for medical or dental education, research, advancement of medical or dental science, therapy or transplantation.

2. Any accredited medical or dental school, college or university, for education, research, advancement of medical or dental science or therapy.

3. Any bank or storage facility, for medical or dental education, research, advancement of medical or dental science, therapy or transplantation.

4. Any specified person, for therapy or transplantation needed by him.

§ 451.565. Manner of making anatomical gift.

1. A gift of all or part of the body under subsection 1 of NRS 451.555 may be made by will. The gift becomes effective upon the death of the testator without waiting for probate. If the will is not probated, or if it is declared invalid for testamentary purposes, the gift, to the extent that it has been acted upon in good faith is nevertheless valid and effective.

2. A gift of all or part of the body under subsection 1 of NRS 451.555 may also be made by document other than a will. The gift becomes effective upon the death of the donor. The document, which may be a card designed to be carried on the person, must be signed by the donor in the presence of two witnesses, who must sign the document in his presence. If the donor cannot sign, the document may be signed for him at his direction and in his presence in the presence of two witnesses, who must sign the document in his presence. Delivery of the document of gift during the donor's lifetime is not necessary to make the gift valid.

3. The gift may be made to a specified donee or without specifying a donee. If the latter, the gift may be accepted by the attending physician as donee upon or following death. If the gift is made to a specified donee who is not available at the time and place of death, the attending physician upon or following death, in the absence of any expressed indication that the donor desired otherwise, may accept the gift as donee. The physician who becomes a donee under this subsection shall not participate in the procedures for removing or transplanting a part.

4. Notwithstanding subsection 3 of this section and subsection 2 of NRS 451.580, the donor may designate in his will, card or other document of gift the physician to carry out the appropriate procedures. In the absence of a designation or if the designee is not available, the donee or other person authorized to accept the gift may employ or authorize any physician for the purpose.

5. Any gift by a person designated in subsection 2 of NRS 451.555 shall be made by a document signed by him or made by his telegraphic, recorded telephonic, or other recorded message.

§ 451.570. Delivery of document of gift. If the gift is made by the donor to a specified donee, the will, card or other document, or an executed copy thereof, may be delivered to the donee to expedite the appropriate procedures immediately after death. Delivery is not necessary to the validity of the gift. The will, card or other document, or an executed copy thereof, may be deposited in any hospital, bank or storage facility or registry office that accepts it for safekeeping or for facilitation of procedures after death. On request of any interested party upon or after the donor's death, the person in possession shall produce the document for examination.

§ 451.573. Permission of donor may be attached to driver's license or identification card; immunity of department and representatives from damages or criminal prosecution.

1. A person who makes a gift of all or part of his body may attach written permission for a physician to carry out the appropriate procedures on a driver's license or an identification card issued by the department of motor vehicles and public safety.

2. The department and its representatives are not liable for damages in a civil action or subject to prosecution in any criminal proceeding on account of any entry on or document attached to a driver's license or an identification card issued by the department.

§ 451.575. Amendment or revocation of gift.

1. If the will, card or other document or executed copy thereof has been delivered to a specified donee, the donor may amend or revoke the gift by:

(a) The execution and delivery to the donee of a signed statement;

(b) An oral statement made in the presence of two persons and communicated to the donee;

(c) A statement during a terminal illness or injury addressed to an attending physician and communicated to the donee; or

(d) A signed card or document found on his person or in his effects.

2. Any document of gift which has not been delivered to the donee may be revoked by the donor in the manner set out in subsection 1, or by destruction, cancellation or mutilation of the document and all executed copies thereof.

3. Any gift made by a will may also be amended or revoked in the manner provided for amendment or revocation of wills, or as provided in subsection 1.

§ 451.580. Rights and duties at death.

1. The donee may accept or reject the gift. If the donee accepts a gift of the entire body, he may, subject to the terms of the gift, authorize embalming and the use of the body in funeral services. If the gift is of a part of the body, the donee, upon the death of the donor and before embalming, shall cause the part to be removed without unnecessary mutilation. After removal of the part, custody of the remainder of the body vests in the surviving spouse, next of kin, or other persons under obligation to dispose of the body.

2. The time of death must be determined by a physician who tends the donor at his death, or, if none, the physician who certifies the death. The physician shall not participate in the procedures for removing or transplanting a part.

3. A person who acts or fails to act in good faith in accord with the terms of NRS 451.500 to 451.590, inclusive, or with any other laws of the State of Nevada relating to anatomical gifts is not liable for damages in any civil action or subject to prosecution in any criminal proceeding for his act.

§ 451.583. Enucleation of eyes.
A licensed funeral director, a licensed embalmer, a medical technician or a licensed nurse may enucleate an eye of a dead person in order to carry out a gift made pursuant to the Uniform Anatomical Gift Act if the director, embalmer, technician or nurse has successfully completed a course, approved by the board of medical examiners, in the procedure for enucleation of eyes.

§ 451.585. Applicability of provisions governing autopsies.
The provisions of NRS 451.500 to 451.590, inclusive, are subject to the laws of this state prescribing powers and duties with respect to autopsies.

§ 451.590. Hospitals to establish procedures to identify potential donors.
Every hospital shall establish policies and procedures to identify potential donors. The policies and procedures must require the administrator of the hospital or his representative:

1. To determine whether a person is a donor.

2. If the person is not a donor, to determine if the person is a potential donor including the consideration of:

(a) His religious and cultural beliefs;

(b) The suitability of his organs and tissues for donation.

3. At or near the time of death of a person identified as a potential donor, to request the person designated in subsection 2 of NRS 451.555, in the stated order of priority if persons in a prior class are not available, to consent to the gift of all or any part of the decedent's body as an anatomical gift.

4. If he has actual knowledge of a contrary intent of the decedent or opposition by a person in the same class as or a prior class than a person who has consented to an anatomical gift, not to procure an anatomical gift.

5. If an anatomical gift is made, to notify an organization which procures organs and tissues and cooperate in the procurement of the anatomical gift.

NEW HAMPSHIRE

§ 291-A:1. Definitions. As used in this chapter the following words shall have the following meanings:

I. "Bank or storage facility" means a facility licensed, accredited, or approved under the laws of any state for storage of human bodies or parts thereof.

II. "Decedent" means a deceased individual and includes a stillborn infant or fetus.

III. "Donor" means an individual who makes a gift of all or part of his body.

IV. "Hospital" means a hospital licensed, accredited, or approved under the laws of any state, and includes a hospital operated by the United States Government although not required to be licensed under state law.

V. "Part" means organs, tissues, eyes, bones, arteries, blood, other fluids and any other portions of a human body.

VI. "Person" means an individual, corporation, government or governmental subdivision or agency, business trust, estate, trust, partnership or association, or any other legal entity.

VII. "Physician" or "surgeon" means a physician or surgeon licensed or authorized to practice under the laws of any state.

§ 291-A:2. Persons Who May Execute Gift.

I. Any individual of sound mind and 18 years of age or more may give all or any part of his body for any purpose specified in RSA 291-A:3, the gift to take effect upon death.

II. Any of the following persons, in order of priority stated, when persons in prior classes are not available at the time of death, and in the absence of actual notice of contrary indications by the decedent or actual notice of opposition by a member of the same or a prior class, may give all or any part of the decedent's body for any purpose specified in RSA 291-A:3:

(a) The spouse, an adult son or daughter.
(b) Either parent.
(c) An adult brother or sister.
(d) A guardian of the person of the decedent at the time of his death.
(e) Any other person authorized or under obligation to dispose of the body.

III. If the donee has actual notice of contrary indications by the decedent or that a gift by a member of a class is opposed by a member of the same or a prior class, the donee shall not accept the gift. The persons authorized by paragraph II may make the gift after or immediately before death.

IV. A gift of all or part of a body authorizes any examination necessary to assure medical acceptability of the gift for the purposes intended.

V. The rights of the donee created by the gift are paramount to the rights of others except as provided by RSA 291-A:7, IV.

§ 291-A:2-a. Request for Consent to an Anatomical Gift.

I. When, based on accepted medical standards, a patient in a hospital is a suitable candidate to donate an anatomical gift, any hospital licensed under RSA 151 shall request the gift of all or any part of the decedent's body for any purpose specified in RSA 291-A:3.

II. Each hospital licensed under RSA 151 shall develop a plan to be followed in requesting an anatomical gift. Such plan shall be filed with the director, division of public health services, department of health and human services, and shall be available for inspection by other hospitals during regular business hours.

§ 291-A:3. Persons Who May Become Donees; Purposes for Which Gifts May Be Made. The following persons may become donees of gifts of bodies or parts thereof for the purposes stated:

I. Any hospital, surgeon, or physician, for medical or dental education, research, advancement of medical or dental science, therapy, or transplantation; or

II. Any accredited medical or dental school, college or university for education, research, advancement of medical or dental science, or therapy; or

III. Any bank or storage facility, for medical or dental education, research, advancement of medical or dental science, therapy, or transplantation; or

IV. Any specified individual for therapy or transplantation needed by him.

§ 291-A:4. Manner of Executing Gifts.

I. A gift of all or part of the body under RSA 291-A:2 may be made by will. The gift becomes effective upon the death of the testator without waiting for probate. If the will is not probated, or if it is declared invalid for testamentary purposes, the gift, to the extent that it has been acted upon in good faith, is nevertheless valid and effective.

II. A gift of all or part of the body under RSA 291-A:2, I may also be made by document other than a will. The gift becomes effective upon the death of the donor. The document, which may be a card designed to be carried on the person, must be signed by the donor in the presence of 2 witnesses who must sign the document in his presence. If the donor cannot sign, the document may be signed for him at his direction and in his presence in the presence of 2 witnesses who must sign the document in his presence. Delivery of the document of gift during the donor's lifetime is not necessary to make the gift valid.

III. The gift may be made to a specified donee or without specifying a donee. If the latter, the gift may be accepted by the attending physician as donee upon or following death. If the gift is made to a specified donee who is not available at the time and place of death, the attending physician upon or following death, in the absence of any expressed indication that the donor desired otherwise, may accept the gift as donee.

IV. Notwithstanding RSA 291-A:7, II, the donor may designate in his will, card, or other document of gift, the surgeon or physician to carry out the appropriate procedures. In the absence of a designation or if the designee is not available, the donee or other person authorized to accept the gift may employ or authorize any surgeon or physician for the purpose. Eye enucleations may also be performed by persons who have successfully completed a course of training acceptable to the eye bank of Massachusetts eye and ear infirmary and who have been licensed to perform such eye enucleations by the board of registration of funeral directors and embalmers.

V. Any gift by a person designated in RSA 291-A:2, II shall be made by a document signed by him or made by his telegraphic, recorded telephonic, or other recorded message.

§ 291-A:5. Delivery of Document of Gift. If the gift is made by the donor to a specified donee, the will, card, or other document, or an executed copy thereof, may be delivered to the donee to expedite the appropriate procedures immediately after death. Delivery is not necessary to the validity of the gift. The will, card, or other document, or an executed copy thereof, may be deposited in any hospital, bank or storage facility, or registry office that accepts it for safekeeping or for facilitation of procedures after death. On request of any interested party upon or after the donor's death, the person in possession shall produce the document for examination.

§ 291-A:6. Amendment or Revocation of Gift.

I. If the will, card, or other document or executed copy thereof, has been delivered to a specified donee, the donor may amend or revoke the gift by:

(a) The execution and delivery to the donee of a signed statement, or

(b) An oral statement made in the presence of 2 witnesses and communicated to the donee, or

(c) A statement during a terminal illness or injury addressed to an attending physician or communicated to the donee, or

(d) A signed card or document found on his person or in his effects.

II. Any document of gift which has not been delivered to the donee may be revoked by the donor in the manner set out in paragraph I, or by destruction, cancellation, or mutilation of the document and all executed copies thereof.

III. Any gift made by a will may be revoked in the manner provided for in RSA 551:13 for revocation of will, or as provided in paragraph I.

§ 291-A:7. Rights and Duties at Death.

I. The donee may accept or reject the gift. If the donee accepts a gift of the entire body, he may, subject to the terms of the gift, authorize embalming and the use of the body in funeral services. If the gift is of a part of the body, the donee, upon the death of the donor and prior to embalming, shall cause the part to be removed without unnecessary mutilation. After removal of the part, custody of the remainder of the body vests in the surviving spouse, next of kin, or other persons under obligation to dispose of the body.

II. The time of death shall be determined by a physician who attends the donor at his death, or, if none, the physician who certifies the death. The physician shall not participate in the procedures for removing or transplanting a part.

III. A person who acts in good faith in accord with the terms of this chapter is not liable for damages in any civil action or subject to prosecution in any criminal proceeding for his act.

IV. The provisions of this chapter are subject to RSA 611:10 through 611:15 prescribing powers and duties with respect to autopsies.

§ 291-A:8. Uniformity of Interpretation. This chapter shall be so construed as to effectuate its general purpose to make uniform the law of those states which enact it.

§ 291-A:9. Short title. This chapter may be cited as the Uniform Anatomical Gift Act.

NEW JERSEY

§ 26:6-57. Definitions. As used in this act:

(a) "Bank or storage facility" means a facility licensed, accredited, or approved under the laws of any State for storage of human bodies or parts thereof.

(b) "Decedent" means a deceased individual and includes a stillborn infant or fetus.

(c) "Donor" means an individual who makes a gift of all or part of his body.

(d) "Hospital" means a hospital licensed, accredited, or approved under the laws of any State; includes a hospital operated by the United States Government, a State, or a subdivision thereof, although not required to be licensed under State laws.

(e) "Part" means organs, tissues, eyes, bones, arteries, blood, other fluids and any other portions of a human body.

(f) "Person" means an individual, corporation, government or governmental subdivision or agency, business trust, estate, trust, partnership or association, or any other legal entity.

(g) "Physician" or "surgeon" means a physician or surgeon licensed or authorized to practice under the laws of any State.

(h) "State" includes any State, district, commonwealth, territory, insular possession, and any other area subject to the legislative authority of the United States of America.

§ 26:6-58. Gift of all or part of body; consent; examination; rights of donee.

(a) Any individual of sound mind and 18 years of age or more may give all or any part of his body for any purpose specified in section 26:6-59, the gift to take effect upon death.

(b) Any of the following persons, in order of priority stated, when persons in prior classes are not available at the time of death, and in the absence of actual notice of contrary indications by the decedent or actual notice of opposition by a member of the same or a prior class, may give all or any part of the decedent's body for any purpose specified in section 26:6-59:

(1) The spouse,
(2) An adult son or daughter,
(3) Either parent,
(4) An adult brother or sister,
(5) A guardian of the person of the decedent at the time of his death.
(6) Any other person authorized or under obligation to dispose of the body.

(c) If the donee has actual notice of contrary indications by the decedent or that a gift by a member of a class is opposed by a member of the same or a prior class, the donee shall not accept the gift. The persons authorized by subsection (b) may make the gift after or immediately before death.

(d) A gift of all or part of a body authorizes any examination necessary to assure medical acceptability of the gift for the purposes intended.

(e) The rights of the donee created by the gift are paramount to the rights of others except as provided by section 26:6-63(d).

§ 26:6-59. Donees; purposes. The following persons may become donees of gifts of bodies or parts thereof for the purposes stated:

(1) Any hospital, surgeon, or physician, for medical or dental education, research, advancement of medical or dental science, therapy, or transplantation; or

(2) Any accredited medical or dental school, college or university for education, research, advancement of medical or dental science, or therapy; or

(3) Any bank or storage facility, for medical or dental education, research, advancement of medical or dental science, therapy, or transplantation; or

(4) Any specified individual for therapy or transplantation needed by him.

§ 26:6-60. Gift by will or other document or recorded message.

(a) A gift of all or part of the body under section 26:6-58(a) may be made by will. The gift becomes effective upon the death of the testator without waiting for probate. If the will is not probated, or if it is declared invalid for testamentary purposes, the gift, to the extent that it has been acted upon in good faith, is nevertheless valid and effective.

(b) A gift of all or part of the body under section 26:6-58(a) may also be made by document other than a will. The gift becomes effective upon the death of the donor. The document, which may be a card designed to be carried on the person, must be signed by the donor in the presence of two witnesses who must sign the document in his presence. If the donor cannot sign, the document may be signed for him at his direction and in his presence in the presence of two witnesses who must sign the document in his presence. Delivery of the document of gift during the donor's lifetime is not necessary to make the gift valid.

(c) The gift may be made to a specified donee or without specifying a donee. If the latter, the gift may be accepted by the attending physician as donee upon or following death. If the gift is made to a specified donee who is not available at the time and place of death, the attending physician upon or following death, in the absence of any expressed indication that the donor desired otherwise, may accept the gift as donee. The physician who becomes a donee under this subsection shall not participate in the procedures for removing or transplanting a part.

(d) Notwithstanding section 26:6-63(b), the donor may designate in his will, card, or other document of gift the surgeon or physician to carry out the appropriate procedures. In the absence of a designation or if the designee is not available, the donee or other person authorized to accept the gift may employ or authorize any surgeon or physician for the purpose or, in the case of a gift of eyes, he may employ or authorize a practitioner of mortuary science licensed by the State Board of Mortuary Science of New Jersey who has successfully completed a course in eye enucleation approved by the State Board of Medical Examiners to enucleate eyes for the gift after certification of death by a physician. A practitioner of mortuary science acting in accordance with the provisions of this subsection shall not have any liability, civil or criminal, for the eye enucleation.

(e) Any gift by a person designated in section 26:6-58(b) shall be made by a document signed by him or made by his telegraphic, recorded telephonic, or other recorded message.

§ 26:6-60.1. Anatomical gifts by hospital patients; ascertainment of existence of gift and identification of donee. A hospital shall, if possible, ascertain from a patient upon admission whether or not the patient has made a gift of all or part of the patient's body pursuant to section 4 of P.L.1969, c. 161 (C 26:6-60), and the donee, if any, to whom the gift has been made.

§ 26:6-60.2. Anatomical gift records; contacting donee upon death of hospital patient donor. A hospital shall maintain, as part of a patient's permanent record, the information required under this act and any other pertinent information concerning the anatomical gift which will facilitate the discharge of the patient's wishes in the event of the patient's death. Upon the death of a patient who has made an anatomical gift, a hospital shall make every good faith effort to contact, without delay, the donee, if any, to whom the gift has been made.

§ 26:6-61. Delivery of will, card, or other document to donee. If the gift is made by the donor to a specified donee, the will, card, or other document, or an executed copy thereof, may be delivered to the donee to expedite the appropriate procedures immediately after death. Delivery is not necessary to the validity of the gift. The will, card, or other document, or an executed copy thereof, may be deposited in any hospital, bank, or storage facility, or registry office that accepts it for safekeeping or for facilitation of procedures after death. On request of any interested party upon or after the donor's death, the person in possession shall produce the document for examination.

§ 26:6-62. Amendment or revocation of gift by donor.

(a) If the will, card, or other document or executed copy thereof, has been delivered to a specified donee, the donor may amend or revoke the gift by:

(1) The execution and delivery to the donee of a signed statement, or

(2) An oral statement made in the presence of 2 persons and communicated to the donee, or

(3) A statement during a terminal illness or injury addressed to an attending physician and communicated to the donee, or

(4) A signed card of document found on his person or in his effects.

(b) Any document of gift which has not been delivered to the donee may be revoked by the donor in the manner set out in subsection (a) or by destruction, cancellation, or mutilation of the document and all executed copies thereof.

(c) Any gift made by a will may also be amended or revoked in the manner provided for amendment or revocation of wills or as provided in subsection (a).

§ 26:6-63. Acceptance or rejection of gift; determination of time of death; civil liability; application of autopsy laws.

(a) The donee may accept or reject the gift. If the donee accepts a gift of the entire body, he may, subject to the terms of the gift, authorize embalming and the use of the body in funeral services, and after it has served its scientific purposes, provide for its disposal by burial or cremation. If the gift is of a part of the body, the donee, upon the death of the donor and prior to embalming, shall cause the part to be removed without unnecessary mutilation. After removal of the part, custody of the remainder of the body vests in the surviving spouse, next of kin, or other persons under obligation to dispose of the body.

(b) The time of death shall be determined by a physician who attends the donor at his death, or, if none, the physician who certifies the death. The physician shall not participate in the procedures for removing or transplanting a part.

(c) A person who acts in good faith in accord with the terms of this act or the anatomical gift laws of another State or foreign country is not liable for damages in any civil action or subject to prosecution in any criminal proceeding for his act.

(d) The provisions of this act are subject to the laws of this State prescribing powers and duties with respect to autopsies.

§ 26:6-64. Construction of act. This act shall be so construed as to effectuate its general purpose to make uniform the laws of those States which enact it.

§ 26:6-65. Short title. This act may be cited as the "Uniform Anatomical Gift Act."

NEW MEXICO

§ 24-6-1. Definitions. As used in the Uniform Anatomical Gift Act:

A. "bank or storage facility" means a facility licensed, accredited or approved under the laws of any state for storage of human bodies or parts thereof;

B. "decedent" means a deceased individual and includes a stillborn infant or fetus;

C. "donor" means an individual who makes a gift of all or part of his body;

D. "eye bank" means any nonprofit agency which is organized to procure eye tissue for the purpose of transplantation or research and which meets the medical standards set by the eye bank association of America;

E. "hospital" means a hospital licensed, accredited or approved under the laws of any state and includes a hospital operated by the United States government, a state or a subdivision thereof, although not required to be licensed under state laws;

F. "organ procurement agency" means any nonprofit agency designated by the health care financing administration to procure and place human organs and tissues for transplantation, therapy or research;

G. "part" includes organs, tissues, eyes, bones, arteries, blood, other fluids and other portions of a human body, and includes parts;

H. "person" means an individual, corporation, government or governmental subdivision or agency, business trust, estate, trust, partnership or association or any other legal entity;

I. "physician" or "surgeon" means a physician or surgeon licensed or authorized to practice under the laws of any state; and

J. "state" includes any state, district, commonwealth, territory, insular possession and any other area subject to the legislative authority of the United States of America.

§ 24-6-2. Persons who may execute an anatomical gift.

A. Any individual of sound mind and eighteen years of age or more may give all or any part of his body for any purposes specified in Section 24-6-3 New Mexico Statutes Annotated 1978, the gift to take effect upon death.

B. Any of the following persons in order of priority stated, when persons in prior classes are not available at the time of death and in the absence of actual notice of contrary indications by the decedent, may give all or any part of the decedent's body for any purposes specified in Section 24-6-3 NMSA 1978:

(1) the spouse;
(2) an adult son or daughter;
(3) either parent;
(4) an adult brother or sister;
(5) a guardian of the person of the decedent at the time of his death; or
(6) any other person authorized or under obligation to dispose of the body.

C. If the donee has actual notice of contrary indications by the decedent, the donee shall not accept the gift. The persons authorized in Subsection B of this section may make the gift after death or immediately before death.

D. A gift of all or part of a body authorizes any examination necessary to assure medical acceptability of the gift for the purposes intended.

E. The rights of the donee created by the gift are paramount to the rights of others except as provided by Subsection D of Section 24-6-7 NMSA 1978.

F. If a decedent is a donor who has executed an anatomical gift as provided in Section 24-6-4 NMSA 1978 and has not revoked that gift as provided in Section 24-6-6 NMSA 1978, his gift of all or a part of his body, as amended if applicable, shall be valid and effective and shall not be revoked by any other person listed in Paragraphs (1) through (6) of Subsection B of this section.

§ 24-6-4. Manner of executing anatomical gifts.

A. A gift of all or part of the body under Subsection A of Section 24-6-2 NMSA 1978 may be made by will. The gift becomes effective upon the death of the testator without waiting for probate. If the will is not probated or if it is declared invalid for testamentary purposes, the gift to the extent that it has been acted upon in good faith, is nevertheless valid and effective.

B. A gift of all or part of the body under Subsection A of Section 24-6-2 NMSA 1978 may also be made by a document other than a will. The gift becomes effective upon the death of the donor. The document, which may be a card designed to be carried on the person, must be signed by the donor in the presence of two witnesses who must sign the document in his presence, unless the document is a driver's license application or renewal form or a driver's license, in which case, the presence and signature of only one witness is necessary. If the donor cannot sign, the document must be signed for him at his direction and in his presence and in the presence of two witnesses who must sign the document in his presence. Delivery of the document of gift during the donor's lifetime is not necessary to make the gift valid.

C. The gift may be made to a specified donee or without specifying a donee. If the latter, the gift may be accepted by the attending physician as donee upon or following death. If the gift is made to a specified donee who is not available at the time and place of death, the attending physician upon or following death, in the absence of any expressed indication that the donor desired otherwise, may accept the gift as donee. The physician who becomes a donee under this subsection shall not participate in the procedures for removing or transplanting a part.

D. Notwithstanding Subsection B of Section 24-6-7 NMSA 1978, the donor may designate in his will, card or other document of gift the surgeon or physician to carry out the appropriate procedures. In the absence of a designation or if the designee is not available, the donee or other person authorized to accept the gift may employ or authorize any surgeon or physician for the purpose.

E. Any gift by a person designated in Subsection B of Section 24-6-2 NMSA 1978 shall be made by a document signed by him or made by his telegraphic, recorded telephonic or other recorded message.

§ 24-6-5. Delivery of document of gift. If the gift is made by the donor to a specified donee, the will, card or other document or an executed copy thereof may be delivered to the donee to expedite the appropriate procedures immediately after death, but delivery is not necessary to the validity of the gift. The will, card or other document or an executed copy thereof may be deposited in any hospital, bank or storage facility or registry office that accepts them for safekeeping or for facilitation of procedures after death. On request of any interested party upon or after the donor's death, the person in possession shall produce the document for examination. If the document is executed pursuant to a driver's license application or renewal, it shall be microfilmed and filed in the statewide organ and tissue donor registry provided pursuant to Section 66-5-10 NMSA 1978. Upon request of authorized hospital and/or organ and tissue donor program personnel, immediately prior to or after the donor's death, the New Mexico state police shall verify the donor information on the microfilmed document. The motor vehicle division of the transportation department shall produce a copy of the document upon request to authorized personnel or any other interested party immediately prior to or after the donor's death.

§ 24-6-6. Amendment or revocation of the gift.

A. If the will, card or other document or executed copy thereof has been delivered to a specified donee, the donor may amend or revoke the gift by:

(1) the execution and delivery to the donee of a signed statement;

(2) an oral statement made in the presence of two persons and communicated to the donee;

(3) a statement during a terminal illness or injury addressed to an attending physician and communicated to the donee; or

(4) a signed card or document found on his person or in his effects.

B. Any document of gift which has not been delivered to the donee may be revoked by the donor in the manner set out in Subsection A of this section, by destruction, cancellation or mutilation of the document and all executed copies thereof or in the case of a driver's license and the document executed pursuant to application for or renewal of such driver's license, by written notice to the motor vehicle division of the transportation department revoking the gift or by signing a donor revocation statement in person at any motor vehicle field office in the presence and with the signature of one witness.

C. Any gift made by a will may also be amended or revoked in the manner provided for amendment or revocation of wills or as provided in Subsection A of this section.

§ 24-6-10. Organ and tissue donation policy and procedure; duties; immunity from liability.

A. Every hospital in New Mexico shall adopt and implement an organ and tissue donation policy and procedure to assist the medical, surgical and nursing staff in identifying and evaluating potential organ or tissue donors.

B. The organ and tissue donation policy and procedure shall contain information on acceptable donor criteria, methods for routine education of the hospital staff about the policy and procedure, the name and telephone number of the local organ procurement agency and eye bank which will provide a standard organ and tissue donation consent form, mechanisms for informing the next of kin of a potential donor about organ and tissue donation options and provisions for the maintenance and procurement of donated organs and tissues.

C. Every hospital's written policy and procedure for identification of potential organ and tissue donors shall:

(1) assure that families of potential organ or tissue donors are made aware of the option of organ or tissue donation and the option to decline;

(2) encourage discretion and sensitivity with respect to the circumstance, views and beliefs of those families; and

(3) require that the appropriate organ procurement agency or eye bank be notified when a potential organ or tissue donor is identified.

D. All physicians and hospital personnel shall make every reasonable effort to carry out the organ and tissue donation policy and procedure adopted by the hospital so that the wishes of a donor may be conveyed to an appropriate local organ procurement agency or eye bank and the necessary donation documents may be properly executed.

E. Every hospital shall develop and implement a policy and procedure for the determination of brain death pursuant to Section 12-2-4 NMSA 1978.

F. The health and environment department shall issue an annual report summarizing the data pertaining to the implementation of this section and its impact on organ and tissue procurement activity.

G. Laws pertaining to notification of the office of the medical investigator should be complied with in all cases of reportable deaths.

H. Failure to comply with any provision of this section shall not subject any physician, hospital, hospital employee or other person to civil or criminal liability for such failure.

I. As used in this section, "hospital" means any general acute care hospital in New Mexico.

§ 24-6-11. **Human organ or tissue transfers; prohibited actions; penalty.**

A. No person may acquire, receive or otherwise transfer for valuable consideration any human organ or tissue.

B. All costs which are incurred at the request of an organ procurement agency or eye bank and which are related to the evaluation of a potential organ or tissue donor, maintenance of organ or tissue viability following brain death declaration or removal of donated organs and tissues shall be paid by the receiving organ procurement agency or eye bank. The next of kin or the estate of the donor shall not be responsible for payment of any of these costs.

C. Any person who violates any provision of this section is guilty of a misdemeanor and upon conviction shall be punished in accordance with the provisions of Section 31-19-1 NMSA 1978.

NEW YORK

§ 4300. **Definitions.** As used in this section, the following terms shall have the following meanings:

(1) "Bank or storage facility" means a hospital, laboratory or other facility licensed or approved under the laws of any state for storage of human bodies or parts thereof, for use in medical education, research, therapy, or transplantation to individuals.

(2) "Decedent" means a deceased individual of any age and includes a stillborn infant or fetus.

(3) "Donor" means an individual who makes a gift of all or part of his body.

(4) "Hospital" means a hospital licensed, accredited, or approved under the laws of any state and includes a hospital operated by the United States Government, a state, or a subdivision thereof, al-

though not required to be licensed under state laws.

(5) "Part" of a body includes organs, tissues, eyes, bones, arteries, blood, other fluids and other portions of a human body, and "part" includes "parts".

(6) "Person" means an individual, corporation, government or governmental subdivision or agency, business trust, estate, trust, partnership or association, or any other legal entity.

(7) "Physician" or "surgeon" means a physician or surgeon licensed or authorized to practice under the laws of any state.

(8) "State" includes any state, district, commonwealth, territory, insular possession, and any other area subject to the legislative authority of the United States of America.

§ 4301. Persons who may execute an anatomical gift. (1) Any individual of sound mind and eighteen years of age or more may give all or any part of his body for any purpose specified in Section 4302 of this article, the gift to take effect upon death.

(2) Any of the following persons, in the order of priority stated, may, when persons in prior classes are not available at the time of death, and in the absence of actual notice of contrary indications by the decedent, or actual notice of opposition by a member of any of the classes specified in paragraph (a), (b), (c), (d) or (e), or other reasons to believe that an anatomical gift is contrary to the decedent's religious or moral beliefs, give all or any part of the decedent's body for any purpose specified in Section 4302 of this article:

(a) the spouse,

(b) a son or daughter twenty-one years of age or older,

(c) either parent,

(d) a brother or sister twenty-one years of age or older,

(e) a guardian of the person of the decedent at the time of his death,

(f) any other person authorized or under obligation to dispose of the body.

(3) If the donee has actual notice of contrary indication by the decedent or that the gift is opposed by a member of any of the classes specified in paragraph (a), (b), (c), (d) or (e), or other reasons to believe that an anatomical gift is contrary to the decedent's religious or moral beliefs, the donee shall not accept the gift.

(4) A gift of all or part of a body authorizes any examination necessary to assure medical acceptability of gift for the purposes intended.

(5) The rights of the donee created by the gift are paramount to the rights of others except as provided by Section 4307 of this article.

§ 4302. Persons who may become donees and purposes for which anatomical gifts may be made. The following persons may become donees of gifts of bodies or parts thereof for the purposes stated:

(1) Any hospital, surgeon, physician, for medical or dental education, research, advancement of medical or dental science, therapy, or transplantation;

(2) any accredited medical or dental school, college or university for education, research, advancement of medical or dental science, or therapy;

(3) any bank or storage facility, for medical or dental education, research, advancement of medical or dental science, therapy or transplantation;

(4) any specific donee, for therapy or transplantation needed by him.

§ 4303. Manner of executing anatomical gifts. (1) A gift of all or part of the body under this article may be made by will. The gift becomes effective upon the death of the testator without waiting for probate. If the will is not probated, or if it is declared invalid for testamentary purposes, the gift, to the extent that it has been acted upon in good faith, is nevertheless valid and effective.

(2) A gift of all or part of the body under this article may also be made by document other than a will. The gift becomes effective upon the death of the donor. The document, which may be a card designed to be carried on the person, must be signed by the donor in the presence of two witnesses who must sign the document in the donor's presence. Delivery of the document of gift during the donor's lifetime is not necessary to make the gift valid.

(3) The gift may be made either to a specified donee or without specifying a donee. If the latter, the gift may be accepted by and utilized under the direction of the attending physician upon or following death. If the gift is made to a specified donee who is not available at the time and place of death, the attending physician upon or following death, in the absence of any expressed indication that the donor desired otherwise, may accept the gift as donee. The physician who becomes a donee under this subdivision shall not participate in the procedures for removing or transplanting a part.

(4) Subject to the prohibitions in subdivision two of Section 4306, the donor may designate in his will, card or other document of gift the surgeon or physician to carry out the appropriate procedures. In the absence of a designation, or if the designee is not available, the donee or other person authorized to accept the gift may employ or authorize any surgeon or physician for the purpose.

(5) Any gift by a person designated in subdivision two of Section 4301 of this article shall be by a document signed by him or made by his telegraphic, recorded telephonic, or other recorded message.

FORMS

Form 1—Anatomical gift—general form
Form 2—Anatomical gift—By next of kin or other authorized person

Form 1

Anatomical gift—General form

For the purposes of transplantation, therapy, medical or dental research or education, I give_____[specify: any needed organs or parts or only the following organs or parts_____or my entire body] if medically acceptable, to _____[name of donee] located at _____[address], City of_____, County of _____, State of New York, or if the designated donee is unavailable at my death, to the attending physician at my death.
_____[indicate special wishes or limitations, if any].

Form 2

Anatomical gift—By next of kin or other authorized person

ANATOMICAL GIFT BY _____ [next of kin or authorized person]
  I, _____ , of _____ [address], City of _____,
County of _____, State of New York, make this anatomical gift from the body of _____ [name of decedent], who died on _____, 19____, in the City of _____, County of _____, State of New York.

   The marks in the appropriate squares and the words filled into the blanks below indicate my relationship to the decedent according to the following order of priority as presented by the New York Uniform Anatomical Gifts Act, and indicate my desires respecting the gift.

   1. I am the surviving: [ ]spouse; [ ]adult son or daughter; [ ]parent; [ ]adult brother or sister; [ ]guardian of decedent at the time of his death; or [ ]any other person authorized or under obligation to dispose of body _____ [specify].

   2. I give: [ ]any needed organs or parts; [ ]the following organs or parts _____ [specify];

   3. To the following _____ [person or institution]: _____ [insert name of physician, hospital, research or educational institution, storage bank, or individual];

   4. For the following purpose: [ ]any purpose authorized by law; [ ]transplantation; [ ]therapy; [ ]medical research and education.

   Dated ____, 19___, in the City of _____, County of _____, State of New York.

                    _____ Signature of survivor]
                    _____ [Address of survivor]

§ 4304. Delivery of document of gift. If the gift is made by the donor to a specified donee, the will, card or other document or an executed copy thereof, may be delivered to him to expedite the appropriate procedures immediately after death; delivery is not necessary to validity of the gift. The will, card or other document, or an executed copy thereof, may be deposited in any hospital, bank, storage facility or registry office that accepts it for safekeeping or for facilitation of procedures after death. On request of an interested party upon or after the donor's death, the person in possession shall produce the documentation for examination.

FORMS: DONOR CARD

Donor Card of

                    _____ [name of donor]
  I, _____, of _____ [address], County of _____, New York, with the desire that I may help others, do hereby make this anatomical gift, to take effect at my death, under the New York Anatomical Gifts Act.
   _____ [If donor wishes to make gift to specific donee, add: I desire to make the gift to _____ (name of physician, hospital, educational institution,

storage facility, research foundation, or individual), located at _____(address), County of _____, New York, or if the designated donee is unavailable at my death, to the attending physician at my death] _____[If donee has no specific donee in mind, add: I do not wish to specify a donee, but make this gift to the attending physician at my death.]

For the purposes of transplantation, therapy, medical or dental research or education, I give _____[specify: any needed organs or parts or only the following organs or parts _____or my entire body] if medically acceptable.

_____[Indicate special wishes or limitations, if any.]

Signed by the donor and the following two witnesses in the presence of each other

_____[witness]   _____[signature of donor]
_____[dated]   _____[dated]
_____[witness]   _____[date of birth of donor]
_____[dated]

§ 4305. Revocation of the gift. (1) If the will, card, or other document or executed copy thereof has been delivered to a specified donee, the donor may amend or revoke the gift by:

(a) the execution and delivery to the donee of a signed statement, or

(b) an oral statement of revocation made in the presence of two persons, communicated to the donee, or

(c) a statement during a terminal illness or injury addressed to an attending physician and communicated to the donee, or

(d) a signed card or document, found on his person or in his effects.

(2) Any document of gift which has not been delivered to the donee may be revoked in the manner set out in subdivision one of this section or by destruction, cancellation, or mutilation of the document and all executed copies thereof.

(3) Any gift made by will may be revoked or amended in the manner provided for revocation or amendment of wills or as provided in subdivision one of this section.

§ 4306. Rights and duties at death. (1) The donee may accept or reject the gift. If the donee accepts a gift of the entire body, he may, subject to the terms of the gift, authorize embalming and the use of the body in funeral services. If the gift is of a part of the body, the donee, upon the death of the donor and prior to embalming, may cause the part to be removed without unnecessary mutilation. After removal of the part, custody of the remainder of the body vests in the surviving spouse, next of kin, or other persons under obligation to dispose of the body.

(2) The time of death shall be certified by the physician who attends the donor at his death and one other physician, neither of whom shall participate in the procedure for removing or transplanting the part.

(3) A person who acts in good faith in accord with the terms of this article or with the anatomical gift laws of another state is not liable for damages in any civil action or subject to prosecution in any criminal proceeding for his act.

§ 4307. Prohibition of sales and purchases of human organs. It shall be unlawful for any person to knowingly acquire, receive, or otherwise transfer for valuable consideration any human organ for use in human transplantation. The term human organ means the human kidney, liver, heart, lung, bone marrow, and any other human organ or tissue as may be designated by the commissioner but shall exclude blood. The term "valuable consideration" does not include the reasonable payments associated with the removal, transportation, implantation, processing, preservation, quality control, and storage of a human organ or the expenses of travel, housing, and lost wages incurred by the donor of a human organ in connection with the donation of the organ. Any person who violates this section shall be guilty of a misdemeanor.

§ 4308. Application. The provisions of this article shall not be deemed to supersede or affect the provisions of the public health law relating to the functions, powers and duties of coroners, coroner's physicians or medical examiners.

§ 4351. Duties of hospital administrator.

1. Where, based on accepted medical standards, a patient is a suitable candidate for organ or tissue donation, the person in charge of such hospital, or his designated representative, other than a person connected with the determination of death, shall at the time of death request any of the following persons, in the order of priority stated, when persons in prior classes are not available and in the absence of (1) actual notice of contrary intentions by the decedent, or (2) actual notice of opposition by a member of any of the classes specified in paragraph (a), (b), (c), (d), or (e) hereof or (3) other reason to believe that an anatomical gift is contrary to the decedent's religious beliefs, to consent to the gift of all or any part of the decedent's body for any purpose specified in article forty-three of this chapter:

   (a) the spouse;
   (b) a son or daughter twenty-one years of age or older;
   (c) either parent;
   (d) a brother or sister twenty-one years of age or older;
   (e) a guardian of the person of the decedent at the time of his death.

Where said hospital administrator or his designee shall have received actual notice of opposition from any of the persons named in this subdivision or where there is otherwise reason to believe that an anatomical gift is contrary to the decedent's religious beliefs, such gift of all or any part of the decedent's body shall not be requested. Where a donation is requested, consent or refusal need only be obtained from the person or persons in the highest priority class available.

2. Where a donation is requested, such person in charge of such hospital or his designated representative shall complete a certificate of request for an anatomical gift, on a form supplied by the commissioner. Said certificate shall include a statement to the effect that a request for consent to an anatomical gift has been made, and shall further indicate thereupon whether or not consent was granted, the name of the person granting or refusing the consent, and his or her relationship to the decedent. Upon completion of the certificate, said person shall attach the certificate of request for an anatomical gift to the death certificate required by this chapter or, in the city of New York, to the death certificate required by the administrative code of the city of New York.

3. A gift made pursuant to the request required by this section shall be executed pursuant to applicable provision of article forty-three of this chapter.

4. The commissioner shall establish regulations concerning the training of hospital employees who may be designated to perform the request, and the procedures to be employed in making it.

5. The commissioner shall establish such additional regulations as are necessary for the implementation of this section.

NORTH CAROLINA

§ 130A-402. Short title. This Part may be cited as the Uniform Anatomical Gift Act.

§ 130A-403. Definitions. The following definitions shall apply throughout this Part:

(1) "Bank or storage facility" means a facility licensed, accredited or approved under the laws of

any state for storage or distribution of a human body or its parts.

(2) "Decedent" means a deceased individual and includes a stillborn infant or fetus.

(3) "Donor" means an individual who makes a gift of all or part of the individual's body.

(4) "Hospital" means a hospital licensed, accredited or approved under the laws of any state and a hospital operated by the United States government, a state or its subdivision, although not required to be licensed under state laws.

(5) "Part" means organs, tissues, eyes, bones, arteries, blood, other fluids and any other portions of a human body.

(6) "Physician" or "surgeon" means a physician or surgeon licensed to practice medicine under the laws of any state.

(7) "State" includes any state, district, commonwealth, territory, insular possession and any other area subject to the legislative authority of the United States of America.

(8) "Qualified individual" means any of the following individuals who has completed a course in eye enucleation and has been certified as competent to enucleate eyes by an accredited school of medicine in this State:

  a. An embalmer licensed to practice in this State;

  b. A physician's assistant approved by the Board of Medical Examiners pursuant to General Statutes 90-18(13);

  c. A registered or a licensed practical nurse licensed by the Board of Nursing pursuant to Article 9 of Chapter 90 of the General Statutes;

  d. A student who is enrolled in an accredited school of medicine operating within this State and who has completed two or more years of a course of study leading to the awarding of a degree of doctor of medicine;

  e. A technician who has successfully completed a written examination by the North Carolina Eye and Human Tissue Bank, Inc., certified by the Eye Bank Association of America.

§ 130A-404. Persons who may make an anatomical gift. (a) An individual of sound mind and 18 years of age or more may give all or any part of that individual's body for any purpose specified in G.S. 130A-405. The gift shall take effect upon death.

(b) Any of the following persons, in order of priority stated, when persons in prior classes are not available at the time of death, and in the absence of actual notice of contrary indications by the decedent or actual notice of opposition by a member of the same or a prior class, may give all or any part of the decedent's body for any purpose specified in G.S. 130A-405.

(1) The spouse;

(2) An adult child;

(3) Either parent;

(4) An adult sibling;

(5) A guardian of the person of the decedent at the time of decedent's death;

(6) Any other person authorized or under obligation to dispose of the body.

(c) The persons authorized by subsection (b) may make the gift after or immediately before death. However, the guardian of the person of a ward may make the gift at any time during the guardianship and the gift shall become effective upon the death of the ward unless the guardianship is terminated before death.

(d) If the donee has actual notice of contrary indications by the decedent or that a gift by a member of a class is opposed by a member of the same or a prior class, the donee shall not accept the gift.

(e) A gift of all or part of a body authorizes any examination necessary to assure medical acceptability of the gift for the purposes intended.

(f) The rights of the donee created by the gift are paramount to the rights of others except as provided by G.S. 130A-409(d).

§ 130A-405. Persons who may become donees; purposes for which anatomical gifts may be made. The following persons may become donees of gifts of a human body or its parts for the purposes stated:

(1) A hospital, surgeon or physician for medical or dental education, research, advancement of medical or dental science, therapy or transplantation;

(2) An accredited medical or dental school, college or university for education, research, advancement of medical or dental science or therapy;

(3) A bank or storage facility, for medical or dental education, research, advancement of medical or dental science, therapy or transplantation;

(4) A specified individual for therapy or transplantation needed by that individual; or

(5) The Commission of Anatomy for the distribution of a human body or its parts for the purpose of promoting the study of anatomy in this State.

§ 130A-406. Manner of making anatomical gifts. (a) A gift of all or part of the body under G.S. 130A-404(a) may be made by will. The gift becomes effective upon the death of the testator without waiting for probate. If the will is not probated, or if it is declared invalid for testamentary purposes, the gift, to the extent that it has been acted upon in good faith, is valid and effective.

(b) A gift of all or part of the body under G.S. 130A-404(a) may also be made by a document other than a will. The gift becomes effective upon the death of the donor. The document, which may be a card designed to be carried on the individual, must be signed by the donor in the presence of two witnesses who must sign the document in the donor's presence. If the donor cannot sign, the document may be signed for the donor at the direction and in the presence of the donor and in the presence of two witnesses who must sign the document in the donor's presence. Delivery of the document of gift during the donor's lifetime is not necessary to make the gift valid.

(c) The gift may be made to a specified donee or without specifying a donee. If the latter, the gift may be accepted by the attending physician as donee upon or following death. If the gift is made to a specified donee who is not available at the time and place of death, the attending physician upon or following death, in the absence of any expressed indication that the donor desired otherwise, may accept the gift as donee.

(d) The donor may designate by will, card, or other document of gift the surgeon or physician to carry out the appropriate procedures, subject to the provisions of G.S. 130A-409(b). In the absence of a designation or if the designee is not available, the donee or other persons authorized to accept the gift may employ or authorize any surgeon or physician for that purpose.

(e) In respect to a gift of an eye, a qualified individual may enucleate eyes for the gift after proper certification of death by a physician and upon the express direction of a physician other than the one who certified the death of the donor.

(f) A gift by a person designated in G.S. 130A-404(b) shall be made by a document signed by the donor or made by the donor's telegraphic, recorded telephonic, or other recorded message. However, a guardian of the person of a ward who makes a gift of all or any part of the ward's body prior to the ward's death shall make the gift by a document signed by the guardian and filed with the clerk of court having jurisdiction over the guardian.

(g) The making of a gift shall be deemed to include an authorization to the donee to review any medical records of the donor after the death of the donor.

§ 130A-407. Delivery of document of gift. If the gift is made by the donor or the guardian to a specified donee, the will, card or other document or executed copy may be delivered to the donee at any time to expedite the appropriate procedures immediately after death. Delivery is not necessary to the validity of the gift. The will, card or other document or executed copy may be deposited in a hospital, bank or storage facility, or registry office that accepts it for safekeeping or for facilitation of procedures after death. On request of any interested party upon or after the donor's or ward's death, the person in possession shall produce the document for examination.

§ 130A-408. Amendment or revocation of gift. (a) If the will, card or other document or executed copy has been delivered to a specified donee, the donor may amend or revoke the gift by:

(1) The execution and delivery to the donee of a signed statement;

(2) An oral statement made in the presence of two persons and communicated to the donee;

(3) A statement during a terminal illness or injury addressed to an attending physician and communicated to the donee; or

(4) A signed card or document found on the individual or in the individual's effects, and made known to the donee.

(b) A guardian may amend or revoke the gift by the execution and delivery to the donee of a signed statement.

(c) Any document of gift which has not been delivered to the donee may be revoked by the donor or guardian in the manner set out in subsection (a) or by destruction, cancellation or mutilation of the document and all executed copies.

(d) Any gift made by a will may also be amended or revoked in the manner provided for amendment or revocation of wills or as provided in subsection (a).

§ 130A-409. Rights and duties at death. (a) The donee may accept or reject the gift. If the donee accepts a gift of the entire body, the donee, shall, subject to the terms of the gift, authorize embalming and the use of the body in funeral services, upon request of the surviving spouse or other person listed in the order stated in G.S. 130A-404(b). If the gift is of a part of the body, the donee, upon the death of the donor or ward and prior to embalming, shall, within 24 hours, cause the part to be removed without unnecessary mutilation. After removal of the part, custody of the remainder of the body vests in the surviving spouse, next-of-kin or other persons under obligation to dispose of the body.

(b) The time of death shall be determined by a physician who attends the donor or ward at death, or, if none, the physician who certifies the death. The physician shall not participate in the procedures for removing or transplanting a part.

(c) A person who acts with due care in accord with the terms of this Part or the anatomical gift laws of another state is not liable for damages in any civil action or subject to prosecution in any criminal proceeding for the act.

(d) The provisions of this Part are subject to the laws of this State prescribing powers and duties with respect to autopsies.

§ 130A-410. Use of tissue declared a service; standard of care; burden of proof. The procurement, processing, distribution or use of whole blood, plasma, blood products, blood derivatives and other human tissues such as corneas, bones or organs for the purpose of injecting, transfusing or transplanting any of them into the human body is declared to be, for all purposes, the rendition of a service by every participating person or institution. Whether or not any remuneration is paid, the service is declared not to be a sale of whole blood, plasma, blood products, blood derivatives or other human tissues, for any purpose. No person or institution shall be liable in warranty, express or implied, for the procurement, processing, distribution or use of these items but nothing in this section shall alter or restrict the liability of a person or institution in negligence or tort in consequence of these services.

§ 130A-411. Giving of blood by persons 17 years of age or more. A person who is 17 years of age or more may give or donate blood to an individual, hospital, blood bank or blood collection center without the consent of the parent or parents or guardian of the donor. It shall be unlawful for a person under the age of 18 years to sell blood.

§ 130A-412. Uniformity of interpretation. This Part shall be so construed to effectuate its general purpose to make uniform the law of those states which enact it.

§ 130A-412.1. Duty of hospitals to establish organ procurement protocols. (a) In order to facilitate the goals of this Part, each hospital shall be required to establish written protocols for the identification of potential organ and tissue donors that:

(1) Assure that the families of potential organ and tissue donors are made aware of the option of organ or tissue donation and their option to decline;

(2) Encourage discretion and sensitivity with respect to the circumstances, views and beliefs of such families;

(3) Require that an organ procurement agency be notified of potential organ and tissue donors; and

(4) Assure that procedures are established for identifying and consulting with holders of properly executed donor cards.

(b) The family of any person whose organ or tissue is donated for transplantation shall not be financially liable for any costs related to the evaluation of the suitability of the donor's organ or tissue for transplantation or any costs of retrieval of the organ or tissue.

(c) The requirements of this section, or any hospital organ procurement protocols established pursuant to this section, shall not exceed those provided for by the hospital organ protocol provisions of Title XI of the Social Security Act, except for the purposes of this section the term "organ and tissue donors" shall include cornea and tissue donors for transplantation.

NORTH DAKOTA

§ 23-06.1-01. Definitions.—For purposes of this chapter:

1. "Bank or storage facility" means a facility licensed, accredited, or approved under the laws of any state for storage of human bodies or parts thereof.

2. "Decedent" means a deceased individual and includes a stillborn infant or fetus.

3. "Donor" means an individual who makes a gift of all or part of his body.

4. "Hospital" means a hospital licensed, accredited, or approved under the laws of any state and includes a hospital operated by the United States government, a state, or a subdivision thereof, although not required to be licensed under state laws.

5. "Part" means organs, tissues, eyes, bones, arteries, blood, other fluids and other portions of a human body, and "part" includes "parts."

6. "Person" means an individual, corporation, government or governmental subdivision or agency, business trust, estate, trust, partnership, association, or any other legal entity.

7. "Physician" or "surgeon" means a physician or surgeon licensed or authorized to practice under the laws of any state.

8. "State" includes any state, district, commonwealth, territory, insular possession, and any other area subject to the legislative authority of the United States of America.

§ 23-06.1-02. Persons who may execute an anatomical gift.—

1. Every person of sound mind and eighteen years of age or more and every person under the age of eighteen with the written consent of one parent or guardian may direct the manner in which his body shall be disposed of after his death and may give all or any part of his body for any purposes specified in section 23-06.1-03, the gift to take effect upon death or upon separation of a part from his body during his lifetime.

2. Any of the following persons, in order of priority stated, when persons in prior classes are not available at the time of death, and in the absence of actual notice of contrary indications by the decedent or actual notice of opposition by a member of the same or a prior class, may give all or any part of the decedent's body for any purposes specified in section 23-06.1-03:

   a. The spouse.
   b. An adult son or daughter.
   c. Either parent.
   d. An adult brother or sister.
   e. A guardian of the person of the decedent at the time of his death.
   f. Any other person authorized or under obligation to dispose of the body.

3. If the donee has actual notice of contrary indications by the decedent, or that a gift by a member of a class is opposed by a member of the same or a prior class, the donee shall not accept the gift. The persons authorized by subsection 2 may make the gift after death or immediately before death.

4. A gift of all or part of a body authorizes any examination necessary to assure medical acceptability of the gift for the purposes intended.

5. The rights of the donee created by the gift are paramount to the rights of others except as provided by subsection 4 of section 23-06.1-07.

6. The person described in subsection 1 may direct the manner of disposition of any part of his body which becomes separated therefrom during his lifetime.

§ 23-06.1-03. Donees—Purposes for which anatomical gifts may be made.—The following persons may become donees of gifts of bodies or parts thereof for the purposes stated:

1. Any hospital, surgeon, or physician, for medical or dental education, research, advancement of medical or dental science, therapy, or transplantation.

2. Any accredited medical or dental school, college or university for education, research, advancement of medical or dental science, or therapy.

3. Any bank or storage facility, for medical or dental education, research, advancement of medical or dental science, therapy, or transplantation.

4. Any specified individual for therapy or transplantation needed by him.

§ 23-06.1-04. Manner of executing anatomical gifts.—

1. A gift of all or part of the body under subsection 1 of section 23-06.1-02 may be made by will. The gift becomes effective upon the death of the testator without waiting for probate. If the will is not probated, or if it is declared invalid for testamentary purposes, the gift, to the extent that it has been acted upon in good faith, is nevertheless valid and effective.

2. A gift of all or part of the body under subsection 1 of section 23-06.1-02 may also be made by document other than a will. The gift becomes effective upon the death of the donor or upon separation of a part from his body during his lifetime. The document which may be a card designed to be carried on the person, must be signed by the donor, in the presence of two witnesses who must sign the document in his presence. If the donor cannot sign, the document may be signed for him at his direction and in his presence, and in the presence of two witnesses who must sign the document in

his presence. Delivery of the document of gift during the donor's lifetime is not necessary to make the gift valid.

3. The gift may be made to a specified donee or without specifying a donee. If no donee is specified, the gift may be accepted by the attending physician as donee upon or following death. If the gift is made to a specified donee who is not available at the time and place of death, the attending physician upon or following death, in the absence of any expressed indication that the donor desired otherwise, may accept the gift as donee. The physician who becomes a donee under this subsection shall not participate in the procedures for removing or transplanting a part.

4. Notwithstanding subsection 2 of section 23-06.1-07, the donor may designate in his will, card, or other document of gift the surgeon or physician to carry out the appropriate procedures. In the absence of a designation, or if the designee is not available, the donee or other person authorized to accept the gift may employ or authorize any surgeon or physician for the purpose or, in the case of a gift of eyes, he may employ or authorize an embalmer licensed by the state board of embalmers who has successfully completed a course in eye enucleation conducted by the department of ophthalmology of any accredited college of medicine, which college has been approved by the state board of medical examiners, who may enucleate eyes for the gift after certification of death by a physician. The gift may be made by a relative or other person in the order of priority stated in subsection 2 of section 23-06.1-02. A licensed embalmer acting in accordance with the provisions of this subsection shall have no liability, civil or criminal, for the eye enucleation.

5. Any gift by a person designated in subsection 2 of section 23-06.1-02 shall be made by a document signed by him or made by his telegraphic, recorded telephonic, or other recorded message.

§ 23-06.1-05. Delivery of document of gift.—If the gift is made by the donor to a specified donee, the will, card, or other document, or an executed copy thereof, may be delivered to the donee to expedite the appropriate procedures immediately after death, but delivery is not necessary to the validity of the gift. The will, card, or other document, or an executed copy thereof, may be deposited in any hospital, bank or storage facility, or registry office that accepts them for safekeeping or for facilitation of procedures after death. On request of any interested party upon or after the donor's death, the person in possession shall produce the document for examination.

§ 23-06.1-06. Amendment or revocation of the gift.—

1. If the will, card, or other document, or executed copy thereof, has been delivered to a specified donee, the donor may amend or revoke the gift by any of the following:

   a. The execution and delivery to the donee of a signed statement.

   b. An oral statement made in the presence of two persons and communicated to the donee.

   c. A statement during a terminal illness or injury addressed to an attending physician and communicated to the donee.

   d. A signed card or document found on his person or in his effects.

2. Any document of gift which has not been delivered to the donee may be revoked by the donor in the manner set out in subsection 1 or by destruction, cancellation, or mutilation of the document and all executed copies thereof.

3. Any gift made by a will may also be amended or revoked in the manner provided for amendment or revocation of wills, or as provided in subsection 1.

§ 23-06.1-06.1. Request for consent to an anatomical gift—Protocol—Exceptions. When death occurs, or is deemed to be imminent, in a hospital to a patient who has not made an anatomical gift, the hospital administrator or a designated representative, other than a person connected with the determination of death, shall request the person described in subsection 2 of section 23-06.1-02, in the order of priority stated, when persons in prior classes are not available at the time of death, and in the absence of actual notice of contrary indication by the decedent or one in a prior class, to consent to the gift of organs of the decedent's body as an anatomical gift. The hospital must develop a protocol to include the training of employees or other persons designated to make the request, the procedure to be followed in making it, and a form of record identifying the person making the request, and the response and relationship to the decedent. The protocol must encourage reasonable discretion and sensitivity to the family circumstances in all discussions regarding anatomical gifts.

If, based upon medical criteria, a request would not yield an anatomical gift which would be suitable for use, there is an authorized exception to the request required by this section.

If, based upon the attending physician's special and peculiar knowledge of the decedent or the circumstances surrounding the death of the patient, the attending physician determines that a request will not be made for an anatomical gift, that determination must be noted in the patient's medical record. Such a determination is an exception to the request required by this section.

§ 23-06.1-07. Rights and duties at death.—

1. The donee may accept or reject the gift. If the donee accepts a gift of the entire body, he may, subject to the terms of the gift, authorize embalming and the use of the body in funeral services. If the gift is of a part of the body, the donee, upon the death of the donor and prior to embalming, shall cause the part to be removed without unnecessary mutilation. After removal of the part, custody of the remainder of the body vests in the surviving spouse, next of kin, or other persons under obligation to dispose of the body.

2. The time of death shall be determined by a physician who attends the donor at his death, or, if none, the physician who certifies the death. Such physician shall not participate in the procedures for removing or transplanting a part.

3. A person who acts in good faith in accordance with the terms of this chapter or under the anatomical gift laws of another state or a foreign country is not liable for damages in any civil action or subject to prosecution in any criminal proceeding for his act.

4. The provisions of this chapter are subject to the laws of this state prescribing powers and duties with respect to autopsies.

§ 23-06.1-08. Uniformity of interpretation.—Repealed.

§ 23-06.1-09. Short title.—This chapter may be cited as the Uniform Anatomical Gift Act.

OHIO

§ 2108.01. Definitions. As used in sections 2108.01 to 2108.10, inclusive, of the Revised Code:

(A) "Bank or storage facility" means a facility licensed, accredited, or approved under the laws of any state for storage of human bodies or parts thereof.

(B) "Decedent" means a deceased individual and includes a stillborn infant or fetus.

(C) "Donor" means an individual who makes a gift of all or part of his body.

(D) "Hospital" means any hospital operated in this state which is accredited by the joint commission on accreditation of hospitals of the American hospital association, the American medical association, the American college of physicians, and the American college of surgeons. "Hospital" also means a hospital licensed, accredited, registered, or approved under the laws of any state, and includes a hospital operated by the United States government, a state, or a subdivision thereof, although not required to be licensed under state laws.

(E) "Part" means organs, tissues, eyes, bones, arteries, blood or other fluids, and any other portions of a human body.

(F) "Person" means an individual, corporation, government or governmental subdivision or agency, business trust, estate, trust, partnership or association, or any other legal entity.

(G) "Physician" or "surgeon" means a physician or surgeon licensed or authorized to practice under the laws of any state.

(H) "State" means any state, district, commonwealth, territory, insular possession, and any other area subject to the legislative authority of the United States of America.

§ 2108.02. Rights of donor; donee.

(A) Any individual of sound mind and eighteen years of age or more may give all or any part of his body for any purpose specified in section 2108.03 of the Revised Code, the gift to take effect upon his death.

(B) Any of the following persons, in the order of priority stated, when persons in prior classes are not available at the time of death, and in the absence of actual notice of contrary indications by the decedent or actual notice of opposition by a member of the same or a prior class, may give any part of the decedent's body for any purpose specified in section 2108.03 of the Revised Code:

(1) The spouse;

(2) An adult son or daughter;

(3) Either parent;

(4) An adult brother or sister;

(5) A guardian of the person of the decedent at the time of his death;

(6) Any other person authorized or under obligation to dispose of the body.

(C) The donee shall not accept the gift if he has actual notice of contrary indications by the decedent or that a gift by a member of a class is opposed by a member of the same or a prior class. The persons authorized in division (B) of this section may make the gift after or immediately before death.

(D) A gift of all or part of a body authorizes any examination necessary to assure medical acceptability of the gift for the purpose intended.

(E) The rights of the donee created by the gift are paramount to the rights of others except that a coroner, or in his absence, a deputy coroner, who has, under section 313.13 of the Revised Code, taken charge of the decedent's dead body and decided that an autopsy is necessary, has a right to the dead body and any part that is paramount to the rights of the donee. The coroner, or in his absence, the deputy coroner, may waive this paramount right and permit the donee to take a donated part if the donated part is or will be unnecessary for successful completion of the autopsy or for evidence. If the coroner or deputy coroner does not waive his paramount right and later determines, while performing the autopsy, that the donated part is unnecessary for successful completion of the autopsy or for evidence, he may thereupon waive his paramount right and permit the donee to take the donated part, either during the autopsy or after it is completed.

§ 2108.02.1. Hospital to develop procurement protocol; request for gift; guidelines.

(A) As used in this section, "Certified organ and tissue procurement organization" means a nonprofit organ or tissue procurement organization that has its principal place of business in this state and is certified under Title XVIII of the "Social Security Act," 49 Stat. 620 (1935), 42 U.S.C. 301, as amended, or by the eye bank association of America.

(B) Every hospital shall develop an organ and tissue procurement protocol in consultation with a certified organ and tissue procurement organization. The protocol shall encourage reasonable discretion and sensitivity to the family circumstances in all discussions regarding donations of tissue or organs. The protocol shall identify the appropriate circumstances under which a request for organ or tissue donations is made or not made and shall require that families of potential organ donors be informed of the option to donate tissue or organs. Such notification shall be the responsibility of the certified organ and tissue procurement organization unless otherwise designated. In any case in which a hospital patient is suitable as an organ or tissue donor based on the hospital's protocol, the certified organ and tissue procurement organization, the hospital administrator, or his designated representative shall request one or more of the persons described in division (B) of section 2108.02 of the Revised Code to make a gift of appropriate parts of the patient's body, except that the certified organ and tissue procurement organization, the hospital administrator, or his designated representative shall not make such a request if he has actual notice of contrary intentions by the patient, actual notice of opposition by any of the persons described in division (B) of section 2108.02 of the Revised Code, or reason to believe that a gift for purpose described in section 2108.03 of the Revised Code is contrary to the patient's religious beliefs.

When a gift is requested under this section, the certified procurement organization, the hospital administrator, or his designated representative shall complete a certificate of request for an anatomical gift, on a form prescribed by the director of health. The certificate shall state whether or not a request for an anatomical gift was made, shall state the name of the person or persons to whom the request was made and his or their relationship to the patient, and shall state whether or not the gift was granted. Upon completion of the certificate, the certified organ and tissue procurement organization, the hospital administrator, or his designated representative shall retain the certificate in a central location for no less than three years after the date of the patient's death. Upon the request of the director of health, the certified organ and tissue organization, hospital administrator, or his designated representative shall permit the director or his authorized representative to inspect or copy the certificates or shall provide a summary of the information contained in the certificates to the director on a form prescribed by the director. All copies of such certificates or summaries in the possession of the director, except for any patient-identifying information contained in them, are public records as defined in section 149.43 of the Revised Code.

(C) The director of health shall issue guidelines establishing:

(1) Recommendations for the training of persons representing certified organ and tissue procurement organizations, hospital administrators, and representatives designated to make requests for anatomical gifts under this section;

(2) Communication and coordination procedures to improve the efficiency of making donated organs available. The guidelines shall include procedures for communicating with the appropriate certified organ and tissue procurement organization.

§ 2108.03. Who may become donees. Any of the following persons may become donees of gifts of bodies or parts thereof for the purposes stated:

(A) A hospital, surgeon, or physician, for medical or dental education, research, advancement of medical or dental science, therapy, or transplantation;

(B) An accredited medical or dental school, college, or university, for education, research, advancement of medical or dental science, or therapy;

(C) A bank or storage facility, for medical or dental education, research, advancement of medical or dental science, therapy, or transplantation;

(D) A specified individual for therapy or transplantation needed by him.

§ 2108.04. Gift made effective upon death.

(A) A gift of all or part of the body under division (A) of section 2108.02 of the Revised Code may be made by will. The gift becomes effective upon the death of the testator without waiting for probate. If the will is not probated or if it is declared invalid for testamentary purposes, the gift, to the extent that it has been acted upon in good faith, is nevertheless valid and effective.

(B) A gift of all or part of the body under division (A) of section 2108.02 of the Revised Code may also be made by any document other than a will. The gift becomes effective upon the death of the donor. The document, which may be a card designed to be carried on the person, shall be signed by the donor in the presence of two witnesses who shall sign the document in his presence. If the donor cannot sign, the document may be signed for him at his direction and in the presence of two witnesses, having no affiliation with the donee, who shall sign the document in his presence. Delivery of the document of gift during the donor's lifetime is not necessary to make the gift valid.

(C) A gift of parts of the body under division (A) of section 2108.02 of the Revised Code, may also be made by a statement to be provided for on all Ohio operator's or chauffeur's licenses or motorcycle operator's licenses, or endorsements, and on all identification cards. The gift becomes effective upon the death of the donor. The statement must be signed by the holder of the operator's or chauffeur's license or endorsement, or by the holder of the identification card, in the presence of two witnesses, who must sign the statement in the presence of the donor. Delivery of the license or identification card during the donor's lifetime is not necessary to make the gift valid. The gift shall become invalidated upon expiration or cancellation of the license or endorsement, or identification card. Revocation or suspension of the license or endorsement will not invalidate the gift. The gift must be renewed upon renewal of each license, endorsement, or identification card. If the statement is ambiguous as to whether a general or specific gift is intended by the donor, the statement shall be construed as evidencing the specific gift only. As used in this division, "identification card" means an identification card issued under section 4507.50 of the Revised Code.

(D) The gift may be made to a specified donee or without specifying a donee. If the latter, the gift may be accepted by the attending physician as donee upon or following death. If the gift is made to a specified donee who is not available at the time and place of death, the attending physician may accept the gift as donee upon or following death, in the absence of any expressed indication that the donor desired otherwise. The physician who accepts the gift as donee under this division shall not participate in the procedures for removing or transplanting a part.

(E) Notwithstanding division (B) of section 2108.07 of the Revised Code, the donor may designate in his will, card, or other document of gift the surgeon or physician to carry out the appropriate procedures. In the absence of a designation or if the designee is not available, the donee or other person authorized to accept the gift may employ or authorize any surgeon or physician to carry out the appropriate procedures.

(F) Any gift by a person specified in division (B) of section 2108.02 of the Revised Code shall be made by a document signed by him or made by his telegraphic, recorded telephonic, or other recorded message.

§ 2108.05. Safekeeping of document.

If the gift is made by the donor to a specified donee, the will, card, or other document, or an executed copy thereof, may be delivered to the donee to expedite the appropriate procedures immediately after death. Delivery is not necessary to the validity of the gift. The will, card, or other document, or an executed copy thereof, may be deposited in any hospital, bank or storage facility, or registry office that accepts it for safekeeping or for facilitation of procedures after death. On request of any interested party upon or after the donor's death, the person in possession shall produce the document for examination.

§ 2108.06. Gift revocation.

(A) If the will, card, or other document, or an executed copy thereof, has been delivered to a specified donee, the donor may amend or revoke the gift by any of the following means:

(1) The execution and delivery to the donee of a signed statement;

(2) An oral statement made in the presence of two persons and communicated to the donee;

(3) A statement during a terminal illness or injury addressed to an attending physician and communicated to the donee;

(4) A signed card or document found on his person or in his effects.

(B) The donor may revoke any document of gift which has not been delivered to the donee, in any manner specified in division (A) of this section or by destruction, cancellation, or mutilation of the document and all executed copies thereof.

(C) Any gift made by a will may also be amended or revoked in the manner provided for amendment or revocation of wills or as provided in division (A) of this section.

§ 2108.07. Removal of part; transplant restrictions.

(A) The donee may accept or reject the gift. If the donee accepts a gift of the entire body, the surviving spouse or next of kin may, subject to the terms of the gift, authorize embalming and the use of the body in funeral services. If the gift is of a part of the body, the donee, upon the death of the donor and prior to embalming, shall cause the part to be removed without unnecessary mutilation. After removal of the part, custody of the remainder of the body vests in the surviving spouse, next of kin, or other persons under obligation to dispose of the body.

(B) The attending physician or a physician selected by the donor shall determine the time of death. If it is not possible for such physician to attend the donor at his death or to certify the death within a period of time which would make it possible to carry out the terms of the gift, the time of death shall be determined by two physicians having no affiliation with the donee. The physician or physicians determining the time of death or certifying the death shall not participate in the procedures for removing or transplanting a part.

§ 2108.07.1. Eye enucleation by embalmer.

(A) With respect to the gift of an eye, an embalmer licensed pursuant to Chapter 4717 of the Revised Code who has completed a course in eye enucleation and has received a certificate of competency to that effect from a school of medicine recognized by the state medical board may enucleate eyes for the gift after proper certification of death by a physician and compliance with the intent of the gift as defined by section 2108.01 to 2108.10 of the Revised Code.

(B) As used in this section, "eye enucleation" means the removal of the eyeball in such a way that it comes out clean and whole.

§ 2108.08. Liability for damages. A person who acts in good faith in accordance with sections 2108.01 to 2108.10, inclusive, of the Revised Code, or the anatomical gift laws of another state, is not liable for damages in any civil action or subject to prosecution in any criminal proceeding for his act.

§ 2108.09. Uniform act. Sections 2108.01 to 2108.09, inclusive, of the Revised Code, are enacted to adopt the Uniform Anatomical Gift Act (1968), national conference of commissioners on uniform state laws, and shall be construed so as to effectuate its general purpose to make uniform the law of those states which enact it.

§ 2108.10. The document of gift provided for in section 2108.04 of the Revised Code shall conform substantially to the following forms. See Appendix for forms (**Uniform Donor Card and Anatomical Gift by Next of Kin or Other Authorized Person**).

OKLAHOMA

§ 2201. Citation. This act shall be known and may be cited as the Uniform Anatomical Gift Act.

§ 2202. Definitions.

(a) "Bank or storage facility" means a facility licensed, accredited, or approved under the laws of any state for storage of human bodies or parts thereof.

(b) "Decedent" means a deceased individual and includes a stillborn infant or fetus.

(c) "Donor" means an individual who makes a gift of all or part of his body.

(d) "Hospital" means a hospital licensed, accredited, or approved under the laws of any state; including a hospital operated by the United States government, a state, or a subdivision thereof, although not required to be licensed under state laws.

(e) "Part" means organs, tissues, eyes, bones, arteries, blood, other fluids and any other portions of a human body.

(f) "Person" means an individual, corporation, government or governmental subdivision or agency, business trust, estate, trust, partnership or association, or any other legal entity.

(g) "Physician" or "surgeon" means a physician or surgeon licensed or authorized to practice under the laws of any state.

(h) "State" includes any state, district, commonwealth, territory, insular possession, and any other area subject to the legislative authority of the United States of America.

§ 2203. Persons who may execute an anatomical gift.

1. Any adult of sound mind may give all or any part of his body for any purpose specified in Section 2204 of this title, the gift to take effect upon death.

2. Any of the following persons, in order of priority stated, when persons in prior classes are not available at the time of death, and in the absence of actual notice of contrary indications by the decedent or actual notice of opposition by a member of the same or a prior class, may give all or any part of the decedent's body for any purpose specified in Section 2204 of this title:

   a. the spouse,

   b. an adult son or daughter,

   c. either parent,

   d. an adult brother or sister,

   e. a guardian of the person of the decedent at the time of his death, or

   f. any other person authorized or under obligation to dispose of the body.

3. If the donee has actual notice of contrary indications by the decedent or that a gift by a member of a class is opposed by a member of the same or a prior class, the donee shall not accept the gift. The persons authorized by subsection 2 may make the gift after or immediately before the decedent's death.

4. A gift of all or part of a body authorizes any examination necessary to assure medical acceptability of the gift for the purposes intended.

5. The rights of the donee created by the gift are paramount to the rights of others except as provided by Section 2208(d) of this title.

§ 2204. Persons who may become donees—Purposes for which anatomical gifts may be made.
The following persons may become donees of gifts of bodies or parts thereof for the purposes stated:

1. Any hospital, surgeon, or physician, for medical or dental education, research, advancement of medical or dental science, therapy, or transplantation;

2. Any accredited medical or dental school, college or university for education, research, advan-

cement of medical or dental science, or therapy;

3. Any bank or storage facility, for medical or dental education, research, advancement of medical or dental science, therapy, or transplantation;

4. Any specified individual for therapy or transplantation needed by him; or

5. The Anatomical Board of the State of Oklahoma.

§ 2205. Manner of executing anatomical gifts.

(a) A gift of all or part of the body under Section 2203(a) of this title may be made by will. The gift becomes effective upon the death of the testator without waiting for probate. If the will is not probated, or if it is declared invalid for testamentary purposes, the gift, to the extent that it has been acted upon in good faith, is nevertheless valid and effective.

(b) A gift of all or part of the body under Section 2203(a) may also be made by document other than a will. The gift becomes effective upon the death of the donor. The document, which may be a card designed to be carried on the person, must be signed by the donor in the presence of two witnesses who must sign the document in his presence. If the donor cannot sign, the document may be signed for him at his direction and in his presence in the presence of two witnesses who must sign the document in his presence. Delivery of the document of gift during the donor's lifetime is not necessary to make the gift valid.

(c) The gift may be made to a specified donee or without specifying a donee. If the latter, the gift may be accepted by the attending physician as donee upon or following death. If the gift is made to a specified donee who is not available at the time and place of death, the attending physician upon or following death, in the absence of any expressed indication that the donor desired otherwise, may accept the gift as donee. The physician who becomes a donor under this subsection shall not participate in the procedures for removing or transplanting a part.

(d) Notwithstanding Section 2208(b), the donor may designate in his will, card, or other document of gift the surgeon or physician to carry out the appropriate procedures. In the absence of a designation or if the designee is not available, the donee or other person authorized to accept the gift may employ or authorize any surgeon or physician for the purpose.

(e) Any gift by a person designated in Section 2203(b) shall be made by a document signed by him or made by his telegraphic, recorded telephonic, or other recorded message.

§ 2206. Delivery of document of gift.

If the gift is made by the donor to a specified donee, the will, card, or other document, or an executed copy thereof, may be delivered to the donee to expedite the appropriate procedures immediately after death. Delivery is not necessary to the validity of the gift. The will, card, or other document, or an executed copy thereof, may be deposited in any hospital, bank or storage facility, or registry office that accepts it for safekeeping or for facilitation of procedures after death. On request of any interested party upon or after the donor's death, the person in possession shall produce the document for examination.

§ 2207. Revocation or amendment of gift.

(a) If the will, card, or other document, or executed copy thereof, has been delivered to a specified donee, the donor may amend or revoke the gift by:

  (1) the execution and delivery to the donee of a signed statement,

  (2) an oral statement made in the presence of two persons and communicated to the donee,

  (3) a statement during a terminal illness or injury addressed to an attending physician and communicated to the donee, or

  (4) a signed card or document found on his person or in his effects.

(b) Any document of gift which has not been delivered to the donee may be revoked by the donor in the manner set out in subsection (a) or by destruction, cancellation, or mutilation of the original document.

(c) Any gift made by a will may also be amended or revoked in the manner provided for amendment or revocation of wills, or as provided in subsection (a).

§ 2208. Rights and duties at death.

(a) The donee may accept or reject the gift. If the donee accepts a gift of the entire body, he may, subject to the terms of the gift, authorize embalming and the use of the body in funeral services. If the gift is of a part of the body, the donee, upon the death of the decedent and prior to embalming, shall cause the part to be removed without unnecessary mutilation. After removal of the part, custody of the remainder of the body vests in the surviving spouse, next of kin, or other persons under obligation to dispose of the body.

(b) The time of death shall be determined by a physician who attends the donor at his death, or, if none, the physician who certifies the death. The physician shall not participate in the procedures for removing or transplanting a part.

(c) A person who acts in good faith in accord with the terms of this act or the anatomical gift laws of another state or of a foreign country is not liable for damages in any civil action or subject to prosecution in any criminal proceeding for his act.

(d) The provisions of this act are subject to the laws of this state prescribing powers and duties with respect to autopsies.

§ 2209. Uniformity of interpretation. This act shall be so construed as to effectuate its general purpose to make uniform the law of those states which enact it.

§ 2210. Eye enucleation. In respect to a gift of an eye as provided for in this chapter, a licensed embalmer, as defined by Sections 396 et seq. of Title 59 of the Oklahoma Statutes, or other persons who have successfully completed a course in eye enucleation in the State of Oklahoma or elsewhere and have received a certificate of competence from the Department of Ophthalmology of the University of Oklahoma School of Medicine, may enucleate eyes for such gift after proper certification of death by a physician and compliance with the extent of such gift as defined by Sections 2201 et seq. of this title. No such properly-certified embalmer or other person acting in accordance with the terms of this chapter shall have any liability, civil or criminal, for such eye enucleation.

§ 2211. Donor cards.

A. In order to provide an expeditious procedure for a person to make a gift of all or part of his body pursuant to the provisions of the Uniform Anatomical Gift Act (Section 2201 et seq. of this title), the Department of Public Safety and all motor license agents shall make space available on the reverse side of the driver's license for an organ donor card to be signed by the donor and two witnesses. The donor card shall state that the person, upon death, is a donor of specified body organs or of his entire body or parts of said body for the purposes of transplantation, therapy, medical research or education pursuant to the provisions of the Uniform Anatomical Gift Act.

B. Said signed donor card shall constitute sufficient legal authority for the removal of the designated organs or parts of the body upon death of said person in accordance with the provisions of the Uniform Anatomical Gift Act. Except as provided by law, every surgeon, physician, hospital, or person or entity acting pursuant to the provisions of the Uniform Anatomical Gift Act may rely upon said donor card as sufficient legal authority to remove, process, store, and use the organs or parts of the body as designated on said card in accordance with accepted medical practice.

C. The carrying of said card on the persons shall be prima facie evidence that the person carrying the card is the donor named on said card. No surgeon, physician, hospital, or person or entity acting pursuant to the provisions of this section or the Uniform Anatomical Gift Act shall be held civilly or criminally liable for relying in good faith upon said donor card or its contents, or for presuming that the person carrying the card is the donor named on said card.

D. The donor card authorized and issued pursuant to the provisions of this section shall be personal to the donor, who shall be solely responsible for the accuracy of its contents. It shall be unlawful and a misdemeanor for any person to carry said signed donor card except the donor named on said card. Upon the death of the donor, the donor card may be removed and retained in the files of any surgeon, physician, hospital, or person or entity participating pursuant to the provisions of the Uniform Anatomical Gift Act and copies of said card may be made for the record or file of any other participant.

E. The gift designated may be revoked by the donor at any time by destroying the donor card, and the following shall be printed above the donor's signature line on the donor card form:
"I declare that I am at least eighteen (18) years of age and hereby make a gift of my body, organs, or body parts as designated on this card. I understand that this donor card shall constitute sufficient legal authority for donation and acceptance of such designated gift pursuant to the provisions of the Uniform Anatomical Gift Act and that I may revoke such gift at any time only by destroying this donor card."

F. The donor card shall contain other information in a format to be prescribed by the Commissioner of Public Safety, which shall be approved by the Attorney General prior to issuance to the public.

G. Upon revocation of the gift and destruction of the organ donor card, the person shall be required to make application for a renewal or duplicate of the driver's license of said person.

§ 2212. Removal of organs—Consent. In any death that the Office of the Chief Medical Examiner of the State of Oklahoma is required by law to investigate, a medical examiner may remove organs from the deceased for donation to a suitable donee pursuant to the provisions of the Uniform Anatomical Gift Act (Section 2201 et seq. of this title), if the next of kin of the deceased has been consulted and consents to said removal. In such cases where the deceased has an organ donor card the consent from next of kin shall not be required.

§ 2213. Accidental deaths, homicides and suicides—Organ donors. Law enforcement and medical personnel involved with the investigation of accidental deaths, homicides, and suicides shall make reasonable efforts to ascertain if the victims are organ donors and, if so, to pass that information on to the proper officials. Said law enforcement and medical personnel shall not be subject to criminal or civil liability for complying with the provisions of this section.

OREGON

§ 97.250. Short title for ORS 97.250 to 97.290. ORS 97.250 to 97.290 may be cited as the Uniform Anatomical Gift Act.

§ 97.255. Definitions for ORS 97.250 to 97.290. As used in ORS 97.250 to 97.290, unless the context requires otherwise:

(1) "Bank or storage facility" means a facility licensed, accredited or approved under the laws of any state for storage of human bodies or parts thereof.

(2) "Decedent" includes a deceased individual, stillborn infant or fetus.

(3) "Donor" means an individual who makes a gift of all or part of his body.

(4) "Hospital" includes a hospital licensed, accredited or approved under the laws of any state or a hospital operated by the United States Government, a state or a subdivision thereof, although not required to be licensed under state laws.

(5) "Part" means organs, tissues, eyes, bones, arteries, blood, other fluids and any other portions of a human body.

(6) "Person" includes an individual, corporation, government or governmental subdivision or agency, business trust, estate, trust, partnership or association or any other legal entity.

(7) "Physician" or "surgeon" includes a physician or surgeon licensed or authorized to practice under the laws of any state.

(8) "State" includes any state, district, commonwealth, territory, insular possession and any other area subject to the legislative authority of the United States of America.

§ 97.260. Construction. ORS 97.250 to 97.290 shall be so construed as to effectuate their general purpose to make uniform the law of those states which enact the Uniform Anatomical Gift Act.

§ 97.265. Authority to make anatomical gifts; rights of donee.

(1) Any individual of sound mind and 18 years of age or older may give all or any part of his body for any purpose specified in ORS 97.270, the gift to take effect upon death.

(2) Any of the following persons, in order of priority stated, when persons in prior classes are not available at the time of death, and in the absence of actual notice of contrary indications by the decedent or actual notice of opposition by a member of the same or a prior class, may give all or any part of a decedent's body for any purpose specified in ORS 97.270:

(a) The spouse.

(b) A son or daughter 18 years of age or older.

(c) Either parent.

(d) A brother or sister 18 years of age or older.

(e) A guardian of the decedent at the time of his death.

(f) Any other person authorized or under obligation to dispose of the body.

(3) If the donee has actual notice of contrary indications by the decedent or that a gift by a member of a class is opposed by a member of the same or a prior class, the donee shall not accept the gift. The persons authorized by subsection (2) of this section may make the gift after or immediately before death.

(4) A gift of all or part of a body authorizes any examination necessary to assure medical acceptability of the gift for the purposes intended.

(5) The rights of the donee created by the gift are paramount to the rights of others except as provided by ORS 146.117.

§ 97.270. Who may be donee of anatomical gift. The following persons may become donees of organs, tissues or parts of bodies for the purposes stated:

(1) Any hospital, surgeon or physician, for medical or dental education, research, advancement of medical or dental science, therapy or transplantation; or

(2) Any accredited medical or dental school, college or university for education, research, advancement of medical or dental science or therapy; or

(3) Any bank or storage facility, for medical or dental education, research, advancement of medical or dental science, therapy or transplantation; or

(4) Any specified individual for therapy or transplantation needed by him.

§ 97.275. Manner of executing anatomical gifts.

(1) A gift of all or part of the body under ORS 97.265(1) may be made by will. The gift becomes effective upon the death of the testator without waiting for probate. If the will is not probated, or if it is declared invalid for testamentary purposes, the gift, to the extent that it has been acted upon in good faith, is nevertheless valid and effective.

(2) A gift of all or part of the body under ORS 97.265(1) may also be made by document other

than a will. The gift becomes effective upon the death of the donor. The document, which may be a card designed to be carried on the person, must be signed by the donor in the presence of two witnesses who must sign the document in his presence. If the donor cannot sign, the document may be signed for him at his direction and in his presence in the presence of two witnesses who must sign the document in his presence. Delivery of the document of gift during the donor's lifetime is not necessary to make the gift valid.

(3) The gift may be made to a specified donee or without specifying a donee. If the latter, the gift may be accepted by the attending physician as donee upon or following death. If the gift is made to a specified donee who is not available at the time and place of death, the attending physician upon or following death, in the absence of any expressed indication that the donor desired otherwise, may accept the gift as donee. The physician who becomes a donee under this subsection shall not participate in the procedures for removing or transplanting a part.

(4) Notwithstanding ORS 97.290(2), the donor may designate in his will, card, or other document of gift the surgeon or physician to carry out the appropriate procedures. In the absence of a designation or if the designee is not available, the donee or other person authorized to accept the gift may employ or authorize any surgeon or physician for the purpose. If the part of the body that is the gift is an eye, the donee may authorize or the person authorized to accept the gift may employ or authorize a qualified embalmer licensed under ORS chapter 692 or a qualified eye bank technician to perform the appropriate procedures. The embalmer or technician must have completed a course in eye enucleation and have a certificate of competence from an agency or organization designated by the Board of Medical Examiners for the State of Oregon for the purpose of providing such training.

(5) Any gift by a person designated in ORS 97.265(2) shall be made by a document signed by him or made by his telegraphic, recorded telephonic, or other recorded message.

§ 97.280. Delivery, deposit and examination of document of anatomical gift. If the gift is made by the donor to a specified donee, the will, card, or other document, or an executed copy thereof, may be delivered to the donee to expedite the appropriate procedures immediately after death. Delivery is not necessary to the validity of the gift. The will, card, or other document, or an executed copy thereof, may be deposited in any hospital, bank or storage facility, or county clerk's office that accepts it for safekeeping or for facilitation of procedures after death. On request of any interested party upon or after the donor's death, the person in possession shall produce the document for examination.

§ 97.285. Amendment or revocation of anatomical gift.

(1) If the will, card, or other document or executed copy thereof, has been delivered to a specific donee, the donor may amend or revoke the gift by:

(a) The execution and delivery to the donee of a signed statement; or

(b) An oral statement made in the presence of two persons and communicated to the donee; or

(c) A statement during a terminal illness or injury addressed to an attending physician and communicated to the donee; or

(d) A signed card or document found on his person or in his effects.

(2) Any document of gift which has not been delivered to the donee may be revoked by the donor in the manner set out in subsection (1) of this section or by destruction, cancellation, or mutilation of the document and all executed copies thereof.

(3) Any gift made by a will may also be amended or revoked in the manner provided for amendment or revocation of wills or as provided in subsection (1) of this section.

§ 97.290. Authority of donee who accepts gift; time of death; liability of one acting with probable cause; autopsies.

(1) The donee may accept or reject the gift. If the donee accepts a gift of the entire body, he may, subject to the terms of the gift, authorize embalming and the use of the body in funeral services. If the gift is of a part of the body, the donee, upon the death of the donor and prior to embalming, shall cause the part to be removed without unnecessary mutilation. After removal of the part, custody of the remainder of the body vests in the surviving spouse, next of kin, or other person under obligation to dispose of the body.

(2) The time of death shall be determined by a physician who attends the donor at his death, or, if none, the physician who certifies the death. The physician shall not participate in the procedures for removing or transplanting a part.

(3) A person who acts with probable cause in accord with the terms of ORS 97.250 to 97.290 or the anatomical gift laws of another state or a foreign country is not liable for damages in any civil action or subject to prosecution in any criminal proceeding for his act.

(4) The provisions of ORS 97.250 to 97.290 are subject to the laws of this state prescribing powers and duties with respect to autopsies.

§ 97.295. Liability of executor who carries out anatomical gift. A person named executor who carries out the gift of the testator made under the provisions of ORS 97.250 to 97.290 before issuance of letters testamentary or under a will which is not admitted to probate shall not be liable to the surviving spouse or next of kin for performing acts necessary to carry out the gift of the testator.

§ 97.300. Transplants not covered by implied warranty.

(1) The procuring, processing, furnishing, distributing, administering or using of any part of a human body for the purpose of injecting, transfusing or transplanting that part into a human body is not a sales transaction covered by an implied warranty under the Uniform Commercial Code or otherwise.

(2) As used in this section, "part" means organs, tissues, eyes, bones, arteries, blood, other fluids and any other portions of a human body.

PENNSYLVANIA

§ 8601. Definitions. As used in this chapter:

"Bank or storage facility." Means a facility licensed, accredited, or approved under the laws of any state for storage of human bodies or parts thereof.

"Decedent." Means a deceased individual and includes a stillborn infant or fetus.

"Donor." Means an individual who makes a gift of all or part of his body.

"Hospital." Means a hospital licensed, accredited, or approved under the laws of any state; includes a hospital operated by the United States Government, a state, or a subdivision thereof, although not required to be licensed under state laws.

"Part." Means organs, tissues, eyes, bones, arteries, blood, other fluids and any other portions of a human body.

"Person." Means an individual, corporation, government or governmental subdivision or agency, business trust, estate, trust, partnership or association, or any other legal entity.

"Physician" or "surgeon." Means a physician or surgeon licensed or authorized to practice under the laws of any state.

"State." Includes any state, district, commonwealth, territory, insular possession, and any other area subject to the legislative authority of the United States of America.

"**Board.**" Means the Humanity Gifts Registry.

§ 8602. Persons who may execute an anatomical gift.

(a) **General Rule.**—Any individual of sound mind and 18 years of age or more may give all or any part of his body for any purpose specified in section 8603 of this code (relating to persons who may become donees; purposes for which anatomical gifts may be made), the gift to take effect upon death. A gift of the whole body shall be invalid unless made in writing at least 15 days prior to the date of death.

(b) **Others entitled to donate anatomy of decedent.**—Any of the following persons, in order of priority stated, when persons in prior classes are not available at the time of death, and in the absence of actual notice of contrary indications by the decedent or actual notice of opposition by a member of the same or a prior class, may give all or any part of the decedent's body for any purpose specified in section 8603 of this code:

(1) the spouse;
(2) an adult son or daughter;
(3) either parent;
(4) an adult brother or sister;
(5) a guardian of the person of the decedent at the time of his death; and
(6) any other person authorized or under obligation to dispose of the body.

(c) **Donee not to accept in certain cases.**—If the donee has actual notice of contrary indications by the decedent or that a gift by a member of a class is opposed by a member of the same or a prior class, the donee shall not accept the gift. The persons authorized by subsection (b) of this section may make the gift after or immediately before death.

(d) **Examinations.**—A gift of all or part of a body authorizes any examination necessary to assure medical acceptability of the gift for the purposes intended.

(e) **Rights of donee paramount.**—The rights of the donee created by the gift are paramount to the rights of others except as provided by section 8607(d) of this code (relating to rights and duties at death).

§ 8603. Persons who may become donees; purposes for which anatomical gifts may be made.

The following persons may become donees of gifts of bodies or parts thereof for the purposes stated:

(1) any hospital, surgeon, or physician, for medical or dental education, research, advancement of medical or dental science, therapy, or transplantation; or

(2) any accredited medical or dental school, college or university for education, research, advancement of medical or dental science, or therapy; or

(3) any bank or storage facility, for medical or dental education, research, advancement of medical or dental science, therapy, or transplantation; or

(4) any specified individual for therapy or transplantation needed by him; or

(5) the board.

§ 8604. Manner of executing anatomical gifts.

(a) **Gifts by will.**—A gift of all or part of the body under section 8602(a) (relating to persons who may execute an anatomical gift) may be made by will. The gift becomes effective upon the death of the testator without waiting for probate. If the will is not probated, or if it is declared invalid for testamentary purposes, the gift, to the extent that it has been acted upon in good faith, is nevertheless valid and effective.

(b) **Gifts by other documents.**—A gift of all or part of the body under section 8602(a) may also be made by document other than a will. The gift becomes effective upon the death of the donor.

The document, which may be a card designed to be carried on the person, must be signed by the donor in the presence of two witnesses who must sign the document in his presence. If the donor is mentally competent to signify his desire to sign the document but is physically unable to do so, the document may be signed for him by another at his direction and in his presence in the presence of two witnesses who must sign the document in his presence. Delivery of the document of gift during the donor's lifetime is not necessary to make the gift valid.

   (c) Specified and unspecified donees.—The gift may be made to a specified donee or without specifying a donee. If the latter, the gift may be accepted by the attending physician as donee upon or following death. If the gift is made to a specified donee who is not available at the time and place of death, the attending physician upon or following death, in the absence of any expressed indication that the donor desired otherwise, may accept the gift as donee. The physician who becomes a donee under this subsection shall not participate in the procedures for removing or transplanting a part.

   (d) Designation of person to carry our procedures.—Notwithstanding section 8607(b) (relating to rights and duties at death), the donor may designate in his will, card, or other document of gift the surgeon or physician to carry out the appropriate procedures. In the absence of a designation or if the designee is not available, the donee or other person authorized to accept the gift may employ or authorize any surgeon or physician for the purpose or, in the case of a gift of eyes, he may employ or authorize a person who is a funeral director licensed by the State Board of Funeral Directors, an eye bank technician or medical student, if said person has successfully completed a course in eye enucleation approved by the State Board of Medical Education and Licensure, or an eye bank technician or medical student trained under a program in the sterile technique for eye enucleation approved by the State Board of Medical Education and Licensure to enucleate eyes for an eye bank for the gift after certification of death by a physician. A qualified funeral director, eye bank technician or medical student acting in accordance with the terms of this subsection shall not have any liability, civil or criminal, for the eye enucleation.

   (d.1) Consent not necessary.—Where a donor card evidencing a gift of the donor's eyes has been validly executed, consent of any person designated in section 8602(b) at the time of the donor's death or immediately thereafter is not necessary to render the gift valid and effective.

   (e) Documentation of gifts by others.—Any gift by a person designated in section 8602(b) (relating to persons who may execute an anatomical gift) shall be made by a document signed by him or made by his telegraphic, recorded telephonic, or other recorded message.

§ 8605. Delivery of document of gift. If the gift is made by the donor to a specified donee, the will, card, or other document, or an executed copy thereof, may be delivered to the donee to expedite the appropriate procedures immediately after death. Delivery is not necessary to the validity of the gift. The will, card, or other document, or an executed thereof, may be deposited in any hospital, bank or storage facility or registry office that accepts it for safekeeping or for facilitation of procedures after death. On request of any interested party upon or after the donor's death the person in possession shall produce the document for examination.

§ 8606. Amendment or revocation of the gift.

   (a) Document delivered to donee.—If the will, card, or other document or executed copy thereof, has been delivered to a specified donee, the donor may amend or revoke the gift by:

   (1) the execution and delivery to the donee of a signed statement; or

   (2) an oral statement made in the presence of two persons and communicated to the donee; or

   (3) a statement during a terminal illness or injury addressed to an attending physician and communicated to the donee; or

(4) a signed card or document found on his person or in his effects.

(b) Document not delivered to donee.—Any document of gift which has not been delivered to the donee may be revoked by the donor in the manner set out in subsection (a) of this section, or by destruction, cancellation, or mutilation of the document and all executed copies thereof.

(c) Gifts by will.—Any gift made by a will may also be amended or revoked in the manner provided for amendment or revocation of wills, or as provided in subsection (a) of this section.

§ 8607. Rights and duties at death.

(a) Donees and relatives.—The donee may accept or reject the gift. If the donee accepts a gift of the entire body, he shall, subject to the terms of the gift, authorize embalming and the use of the body in funeral services if the surviving spouse or next of kin as determined in section 8602(b) of this code (relating to persons who may execute an anatomical gift) requests embalming and use of the body for funeral services. If the gift is of a part of the body, the donee, upon the death of the donor and prior to embalming, shall cause the part to be removed without unnecessary mutilation. After removal of the part, custody of the remainder of the body vests in the surviving spouse, next of kin, or other persons under obligation to dispose of the body.

(b) Physicians.—The time of death shall be determined by a physician who tends the donor at his death, or, if none, the physician who certifies the death. The physician who certifies death or any of his professional partners or associates shall not participate in the procedures for removing or transplanting a part.

(c) Certain liability limited.—A person who acts in good faith in accord with the terms of this chapter or with the anatomical gift laws of another state or a foreign country is not liable for damages in any civil action or subject to prosecution in any criminal proceeding for his act.

(d) Law on autopsies applicable.—The provisions of this chapter are subject to the laws of this State prescribing powers and duties with respect to autopsies.

§ 8608. Requests for anatomical gifts.

(a) Procedure.—On or before the occurrence of death in an acute care general hospital, the hospital shall request consent to a gift of all or any part of the decedent's body for any purpose specified under this chapter. The request and its disposition shall be noted in the patient's medical record. Whenever medical criteria establishes that a body or body part donation would not be suitable for use, a request need not be made.

(b) Limitation.—Where the hospital administrator, or his designee, has received actual notice of opposition from any of the persons named in section 8602(b) (relating to persons who may execute an anatomical gift) and the decedent was not in possession of a validly executed donor card, the gift of all or any part of the decedent's body shall not be requested.

(c) Donor card.—Notwithstanding any provision of law to the contrary, the intent of a decedent to participate in an organ donor program as evidenced by the possession of a validly executed donor card shall not be revoked by any member of any of the classes specified in section 8602(b).

(d) Identification of potential donors.—Each acute care general hospital shall develop, with the concurrence of the hospital medical staff, a protocol for identifying potential organ and tissue donors. It shall require that, at or near the time of notification of death, persons designated under section 8602(a) and (b) be asked whether the deceased was an organ donor or if the family is a donor family. If not, such persons shall be informed of the option to donate organs and tissues. Pursuant to this chapter, the hospital shall then notify an organ and tissue procurement organization and cooperate in the procurement of the anatomical gift or gifts. The protocol shall encourage discretion and sensitivity to family circumstances in all discussions regarding donations of tissue or organs. The protocol shall take into account the deceased individual's religious beliefs or nonsuitability for organ and tissue donation. In the event an organ and tissue procurement organization does not exist in a region, the hospital shall contact an organ or a tissue procurement organization in an alternative region.

(e) Exemption.—The Department of Health is authorized to issue exemptions to any acute care general hospital it deems unable to comply with this section.

(f) Guidelines.—The Department of Health shall establish guidelines regarding efficient procedures facilitating the delivery of anatomical gift donations from receiving hospitals to potential recipients and appropriate training concerning the manner and conduct of employees making requests for anatomical gift donations.

RHODE ISLAND

§ 23-18.5-1. Definitions.—(a) "Bank or storage facility" means a facility licensed, accredited, or approved under the laws of any state for storage of human bodies or parts thereof.

(b) "Decedent" means a deceased individual and includes a stillborn infant or fetus.

(c) "Donor" means an individual who makes a gift of all or part of his body.

(d) "Hospital" means a hospital licensed, accredited, or approved under the laws of any state; includes a hospital operated by the United States government, a state, or a subdivision thereof, although not required to be licensed under state laws.

(e) "Part" means organs, tissues, eyes, bones, arteries, blood, other fluids and any other portions of a human body.

(f) "Person" means an individual, corporation, government or governmental subdivision or agency, business trust, estate, trust, partnership or association, or any other legal entity.

(g) "Physician" or "surgeon" means a physician or surgeon licensed or authorized to practice under the laws of any state.

(h) "State" includes any state, district, commonwealth, territory, insular possession, and any other area subject to the legislative authority of the United States of America.

§ 23-18.5-2. Persons who may execute an anatomical gift.—(a) Any individual of sound mind and eighteen (18) years of age or more may give all or any part of his body for any purpose specified in § 23-18.5-3, the gift to take effect upon death.

(b) Only the decedent shall have the authority to donate his body or any part thereof, if it is made known that the deceased at the time of his death was a member of a religion, church, sect or denomination which relies solely upon prayer for the healing of disease or which holds or professes the belief that it is wrong to mutilate a human body either before or after death has occurred or that it is wrong to surgically transplant any part of a human body into another human body.

(c) Unless he is prohibited by subsection (b) of this section, any of the following persons, in order of priority stated, when persons in prior classes are not available at the time of death, and in the absence of actual notice of contrary indications by the decedent or actual notice of opposition by a member of the same or a prior class, may give all or any part of the decedent's body for any purpose specified in § 23-18.5-3:

(1) The spouse;
(2) An adult son or daughter;
(3) Either parent;

(4) An adult brother or sister;

(5) A guardian of the person of the decedent at the time of his death;

(6) Any other person authorized or under obligation to dispose of the body.

(d) If the donee has actual notice of contrary indications by the decedent or that a gift by a member of a class is opposed by a member of the same or a prior class, the donee shall not accept the gift. The persons authorized by subsection (c) may make the gift after or immediately before death.

(e) A gift of all or part of a body authorizes any examination necessary to assure medical acceptability of the gift for the purposes intended.

(f) The rights of the donee created by the gift are paramount to the rights of other except as provided by § 23-18.5-7(d).

§ 23-18.5-2.1. Identifying potential organ and tissue donors—Protocol.—Each hospital shall develop a protocol for addressing the issue of organ and tissue donation whenever a death occurs in a hospital and the intention of the deceased is unknown. The protocol shall require that any deceased individual's next of kin or other individual, as specified in § 23-18.5-2(c), shall be informed of the option to donate organs and tissue pursuant to chapter 18.5 for any purpose specified in § 23-18.5-3. The protocol shall encourage reasonable discretion and sensitivity to the family circumstances in all discussions regarding donations of tissue or organs and may take into account the deceased individual's religious beliefs or obvious nonsuitability for organ and tissue donation in determining whether or not to make the request.

The protocol shall require documentation of the request in the decedent's medical record and, if no request has been made, of the reasons therefor. Whether or not consent is granted, the statement shall indicate the name of the person granting or refusing the consent, and his or her relationship to the decedent.

Each hospital shall submit a copy of the protocol to the department of health.

§ 23-18.5-3. Persons who may become donees—Purposes for which anatomical gifts may be made.—The following persons may become donees of gifts of bodies or parts thereof for the purposes stated:

(1) Any hospital, surgeon, or physician, for medical or dental education, research, advancement of medical or dental science, therapy, or transplantation; or

(2) Any accredited medical or dental school, college or university for education, research, advancement of medical or dental science, or therapy; or

(3) Any non-profit bank or storage facility, for medical or dental education, research, advancement of medical or dental science, therapy, or transplantation; or

(4) Any specified individual for therapy or transplantation needed by him.

§ 23-18.5-4. Manner of executing anatomical gifts.—(a) A gift of all or part of the body under § 23-18.5-2(a) may be made by will. The gift becomes effective upon the death of the testator without waiting for probate. If the will is not probated, or if it is declared invalid for testamentary purposes, the gift, to the extent that it has been acted upon in good faith, is nevertheless valid and effective.

(b) A gift of all or part of the body under § 23-18.5-2(a) may also be made by document other than a will. The gift becomes effective upon the death of the donor. The document, which may be a card, driver's license, or other document of gift designed to be carried on the person, must be signed by the donor in the presence of two (2) witnesses who must sign the document in his presence. If the donor cannot sign, the document may be signed for him at his direction and in his presence in the presence of two (2) witnesses who must sign the document in his presence. Delivery of the document of gift during the donor's lifetime is not necessary to make the gift valid.

(c) The gift may be made to a specified donee or without specifying a donee. If the latter, the gift may be accepted by the attending physician as donee upon or following death. If the gift is made to a specified donee who is not available at the time and place of death, the attending physician upon or following death, in the absence of any expressed indication that the donor desired otherwise, may accept the gift as donee. The physician who becomes a donee under this subsection shall not participate in the procedures for removing or transplanting a part.

(d) Notwithstanding § 23-18.5-7(b), the donor may designate in his will, card, driver's license or other document of gift the surgeon or physician to carry out the appropriate procedures. In the absence of a designation or if the designee is not available, the donee or other person authorized to accept the gift may employ or authorize any surgeon or physician for the purpose; provided however that eye enucleation may be performed also by a person or technician who has successfully completed a course of training acceptable to the New England Eye Bank at the Massachusetts Eye and Ear Infirmary.

(e) Any gift by a person designated in § 23-18.5-2(c) shall be made by a document signed by him or made by his telegraphic, recorded telephonic, or other recorded message.

§ 23-18.5-5. Delivery of document of gift.—If the gift is made by the donor to a specified donee, the will, card, driver's license, or other document, or an executed copy thereof, may be delivered to the donee to expedite the appropriate procedures immediately after death. Delivery is not necessary to the validity of the gift. The will, card, driver's license, or other document, or an executed copy thereof, may be deposited in any hospital, bank, or storage facility, or registry office that accepts it for safekeeping or for facilitation of procedures after death. On request of any interested party upon or after the donor's death, the person in possession shall produce the document for examination.

§ 23-18.5-6. Amendments or revocation of the gift.—(a) If any document other than a will or an executed copy of such document has been delivered to a specified donee and the said document or executed copy thereof purports to create a gift pursuant to the provisions of this chapter, the donor may amend or revoke the gift by:

(1) The execution and delivery to the donee of a signed statement; or

(2) An oral communication made in the presence of two (2) persons and communicated to the donee; or

(3) A statement during a terminal illness or injury addressed to an attending physician and communicated to the donee; or

(4) A signed card or document found on his person or in his effects.

(b) Any document of gift which has not been delivered to the donee may be revoked by the donor in the manner set out in subsection (a) if it is not a will or by destruction, cancellation, or mutilation of the document and all executed copies thereof.

(c) Any gift made by a will may only be amended or revoked in the manner provided for amendment or revocation of wills.

§ 23-18.5-7. Rights and duties at death.—(a)(1) The donee may accept or reject the gift. If the donee accepts a gift of the entire body, he must do so subject to the right of the surviving spouse or next of kin to authorize embalming and to have the use of the body for funeral services within one (1) week of death after which the donee shall be entitled to the return of the said body.

(2) If the gift is of a part of the body, the donee, upon the death of the donor and prior to embalming, shall cause the part to be removed without unnecessary mutilation. After removal of the part, custody of the remainder of the body vests in the surviving spouse, next of kin, or other persons under obligation to dispose of the body.

(b) The time of death shall be determined by a physician who attends the donor at his death, or, if none, the physician who certifies the death. The physician shall not participate in the procedures for removing or transplanting a part.

(c) A person who acts in good faith in accord with the terms of this chapter or the anatomical gift laws of another state (or a foreign country) is not liable for damages in any civil action or subject to prosecution in any criminal proceeding for his act.

(d) The provisions of this chapter are subject to and inferior to the laws of this state prescribing powers and duties with respect to the state and county medical examiners.

§ 23-18.5-8. Acquired immune deficiency syndrome testing.—Prior to any organ, tissue or part of a human body being transplanted in any human being, the donor shall be tested for the presence of antibodies to the probable causative agent for acquired immune deficiency syndrome (AIDS), provided that this condition shall not apply if there is a bona fide documentable medical emergency which endangers the life of any person. If the test for the presence of the antibodies is positive, the organ, tissue or body part shall not be used.

SOUTH CAROLINA

§ 44-43-310. Short title. This article may be cited as the Uniform Anatomical Gift Act.

§ 44-43-320. Definitions.

(a) *"Bank or storage facility"* means a facility licensed, accredited or approved under the laws of any state for storage of human bodies or parts thereof.

(b) *"Decedent"* means a deceased individual and includes a stillborn infant or fetus.

(c) *"Donor"* means an individual who makes a gift of all or part of his body.

(d) *"Hospital"* means a hospital licensed, accredited or approved under the laws of any state and includes a hospital operated by the United States Government, a state, or a subdivision thereof, although not required to be licensed under State laws.

(e) *"Part"* includes organs, tissues, eyes, bones, arteries, blood, other fluids and other portions of a human body, and *"part"* includes "parts."

(f) *"Person"* means an individual, corporation, government or governmental subdivision or agency, business trust, estate, trust, partnership or association or any other legal entity.

(g) *"Physician"* or *"surgeon"* means a physician or surgeon licensed or authorized to practice under the laws of any state.

(h) *"State"* includes any state, district, commonwealth, territory, insular possession, and any other area subject to the legislative authority of the United States of America.

§ 44-43-330. Persons who may make gift; situation in which donee may not accept; examination to determine medical acceptability; rights of donee shall be paramount.

(a) Any individual of sound mind and eighteen years of age or more may give all or any part of his body for any purposes specified in § 44-43-340, the gift to take effect upon death.

(b) Any of the following persons, in order of priority stated, when persons in prior classes are not available at the time of death, and in the absence of actual notice of contrary indications by the decedent, or actual notice of opposition by a member of the same or a prior class, may give all or any part of the decedent's body for any purposes specified in § 44-43-340:

(1) The spouse,

(2) An adult son or daughter,
(3) Either parent,
(4) An adult brother or sister,
(5) A guardian of the person of the decedent at the time of his death,
(6) Any other person authorized or under obligation to dispose of the body.

(c) If the donee has actual notice of contrary indications by the decedent, or that a gift by a member of a class is opposed by a member of the same or a prior class, the donee shall not accept the gift. The persons authorized by this subsection may make the gift after death or immediately before death.

(d) A gift of all or part of a body authorizes any examination necessary to assure medical acceptability of the gift for the purposes intended.

(e) The rights of the donee created by the gift are paramount to the rights of others except as provided by § 44-43-380(d).

§ 44-43-340. Persons who may become donee. The following persons may become donees of gifts of bodies or parts thereof for the purposes stated:

(1) Any hospital, surgeon, or physician, for medical or dental education, research, advancement of medical or dental science, therapy or transplantation; or

(2) Any accredited medical or dental school, college or university for education, research, advancement of medical or dental science or therapy; or

(3) Any bank or storage facility for medical or dental education, research, advancement of medical or dental science, therapy or transplantation; or

(4) Any specified individual for therapy or transplantation needed by him.

§ 44-43-350. Manner in which gift may be made.

(a) A gift of all or part of the body under § 44-43-330(a) may be made by will. The gift becomes effective upon the death of the testator without waiting for probate. If the will is not probated, or if it is declared invalid for testamentary purposes, the gift, to the extent that it has been acted upon in good faith, is nevertheless valid and effective.

(b) A gift of all or part of the body under § 44-43-330(a) may also be made by document other than a will. The gift becomes effective upon the death of the donor. The document, which may be a card designed to be carried on the person, must be signed by the donor, in the presence of two witnesses who must sign the document in his presence. If the donor cannot sign, the document may be signed for him at his direction and in his presence, and in the presence of two witnesses who must sign the document in his presence. Delivery of the document of gift during the donor's lifetime is not necessary to make the gift valid.

(c) The gift may be made to a specified donee or without specifying a donee. If the latter, the gift may be accepted by the attending physician as donee upon or following death. If the gift is made to a specified donee who is not available at the time and place of death, the attending physician upon or following death, in the absence of any expressed indication that the donor desired otherwise, may accept the gift as donee. The physician who becomes a donee under this subsection shall not participate in the procedures for removing or transplanting a part.

(d) Notwithstanding § 44-43-380(b), the donor may designate in his will, card or other document of gift the surgeon or physician to carry out the appropriate procedures. In the absence of a designation, or if the designee is not available, the donee or other person authorized to accept the gift may employ or authorize any surgeon or physician for the purpose.

(e) Any gift by a person designated in § 44-43-330(b) shall be made by a document signed by him, or made by his telegraphic, recorded telephonic or other recorded message.

§ 44-43-360. Delivery or deposit of document of gift or copy thereof. If the gift is made by the donor to a specified donee, the will, card or other document, or an executed copy thereof, may be delivered to the donee to expedite the appropriate procedures immediately after death, but delivery is not necessary to the validity of the gift. The will, card or other document, or an executed copy thereof, may be deposited in any hospital, bank or storage facility or registry office that accepts them for safekeeping or for facilitation of procedures after death. On request of any interested party upon or after the donor's death, the person in possession shall produce the document for examination.

§ 44-43-370. Amendment or revocation of gift.

(a) If the will, card or other document or executed copy thereof, has been delivered to a specified donee, the donor may amend or revoke the gift by:

(1) The execution and delivery to the donee of a signed statement, or

(2) An oral statement made in the presence of two persons and communicated to the donee, or

(3) A statement during a terminal illness or injury addressed to an attending physician and communicated to the donee, or

(4) A signed card or document found on his person or in his effects.

(b) Any document of gift which has not been delivered to the donee may be revoked by the donor in the manner set out in subsection (a) or by destruction, cancellation, or mutilation of the document and all executed copies thereof.

(c) Any gift made by a will may also be amended or revoked in the manner provided for amendment or revocation of wills, or as provided in subsection (a).

§ 44-43-380. Acceptance or rejection of gift; disposition of remainder of body; determination of time of death; immunity from liability; article subject to laws with respect to autopsies.

(a) The donee may accept or reject the gift. If the donee accepts a gift of the entire body, he may, subject to the terms of the gift, authorize embalming and the use of the body in funeral services. If the gift is of a part of the body, the donee, upon the death of the donor and prior to embalming, shall cause the part to be removed without unnecessary mutilation. After removal of the part, custody of the remainder of the body vests in the surviving spouse, next of kin or other persons under obligation to dispose of the body.

(b) The time of death shall be determined by a physician who attends the donor at his death, or, if none, the physician who certifies the death. This physician shall not participate in the procedures for removing or transplanting a part.

(c) A person who acts in good faith in accord with the terms of this article, or under the anatomical gift laws of another state is not liable for damages in any civil action or subject to prosecution in any criminal proceeding for his act. *Provided, however,* that such immunity from civil liability shall not extend to cases of provable malpractice on the part of any physician, surgeon or other medical attendant.

(d) The provisions of this article are subject to the laws of this State prescribing powers and duties with respect to autopsies.

§ 44-43-390. This article supplemental to Article 3 of this chapter. The provisions of this article are supplementary to Article 3 of this chapter, relating to the donation of eyes for the restoration of sight, and shall not be construed to in any manner repeal or replace that article. The restriction against a physician donee participating in removal or transplant of a body part in subsection (c) of § 44-43-350 shall not apply in the case of eyes or parts thereof.

§ 44-43-400. Construction. This article shall be so construed as to effectuate its general purpose to make uniform the law of those states which enact it.

SOUTH DAKOTA

§ 34-26-20. Anatomical gifts—Definition of terms. Terms used in §§ 34-26-20 to 34-26-41, inclusive, mean:

(1) "Bank" or "storage facility," a facility licensed, accredited, or approved under the laws of any state for storage of human bodies or parts thereof.

(2) "Decedent," a deceased individual and includes a stillborn infant or fetus.

(3) "Donor," an individual who makes a gift of all or part of his body.

(4) "Hospital," a hospital licensed, accredited, or approved under the laws of any state, and includes a hospital operated by the United States government, a state, or a subdivision thereof, although not required to be licensed under state laws.

(5) "Part," organs, tissues, eyes, bones, arteries, blood, other fluids and any other portions of a human body.

(6) "Person," an individual, corporation, government or governmental subdivision or agency, business trust, estate, trust, partnership or association, or any other legal entity.

(7) "Physician" or "surgeon," a physician or surgeon licensed or authorized to practice under the laws of any state.

(8) "State" includes any state, district, commonwealth, territory, insular possession, and any other area subject to the legislative authority of the United States of America.

§ 34-26-21. Eligibility to make gifts of own body. Any individual of sound mind and eighteen years of age or more may give all or any part of his body for any purpose specified in § 34-26-27, the gift to take effect upon death.

§ 34-26-22. Anatomical gift by will. A gift of all or part of the body under § 34-26-21 may be made by will. The gift becomes effective upon the death of the testator without waiting for probate. If the will is not probated, or if it is declared invalid for testamentary purposes, the gift, to the extent that it has been acted upon in good faith, is nevertheless valid and effective.

§ 34-26-23. Anatomical gift by document other than will—Execution and effectiveness of document. A gift of all or part of the body under § 34-26-21 may also be made by document other than a will. The gift becomes effective upon the death of the donor. The document, which may be a card designed to be carried on the person, must be signed by the donor in the presence of two witnesses who must sign the document in his presence. If the donor cannot sign, the document may be signed for him at his direction and in his presence in the presence of two witnesses who must sign the document in his presence. Delivery of the document of gift during the donor's lifetime is not necessary to make the gift valid.

§ 34-26-24. Anatomical gifts by spouse, kin, guardian, or authorized person—Priority of authority to make gift—Time of gift. Any of the following persons, in order of priority stated, when persons in prior classes are not available at the time of death, and in the absence of actual notice of contrary indications by the decedent or actual notice of opposition by a member of the same or a prior class, may give all or any part of the decedent's body for any purpose specified in § 34-26-27:

(1) The spouse,

(2) An adult son or daughter,

(3) Either parent,
(4) An adult brother or sister,
(5) A guardian of the person of the decedent at the time of his death,
(6) Any other person authorized or under obligation to dispose of the body.

The persons authorized may make the gift after or immediately before death.

§ 34-26-25. Execution of anatomical gift by spouse, kin, guardian or authorized person. Any gift by a person designated in § 34-26-24 shall be made by a document signed by him or made by his telegraphic, recorded telephonic, or other recorded message.

§ 34-26-26. Donee not to accept unauthorized anatomical gift. If the donee has actual notice of contrary indications by the decedent or that a gift by a member of a class is opposed by a member of the same or a prior class, the donee shall not accept the gift.

§ 34-26-27. Authorized donees of anatomical gifts—Authorized purposes. The following persons may become donees of gifts of bodies or parts thereof for the purposes stated:

(1) Any hospital, surgeon, or physician, for medical or dental education, research, advancement of medical or dental science, therapy or transplantation; or

(2) Any accredited medical or dental school, college or university for education, research, advancement of medical or dental science, or therapy; or

(3) Any bank or storage facility, for medical or dental education, research, advancement of medical or dental science, therapy, or transplantation; or

(4) Any specified individual for therapy or transplantation needed by him.

§ 34-26-28. Anatomical gift to specified donee or without specifying donee—Acceptance of gift by attending physician. The gift may be made to a specified donee or without specifying a donee. If the latter, the gift may be accepted by the attending physician as donee upon or following death. If the gift is made to a specified donee who is not available at the time and place of death, the attending physician upon or following death, in the absence of any expressed indication that the donor desired otherwise, may accept the gift as donee. The physician who becomes a donee under this section shall not participate in the procedures for removing or transplanting a part.

§ 34-26-29. Designation of surgeon or physician to carry out purposes of anatomical gift. Notwithstanding § 34-26-34, the donor may designate in his will, card, or other document of gift the surgeon or physician to carry out the appropriate procedures. In the absence of a designation or if the designee is not available, the donee or other person authorized to accept the gift may employ or authorize any surgeon or physician for the purpose.

§ 34-26-29.1. Enucleation of eye by properly certified person—Immunity from liability. In respect to a gift of an eye as provided for in § 34-26-21, a licensed funeral director, as defined in § 36-19-14, or any other person who has completed a course in eye enucleation and has received a certificate of competence from a university medical school, a university medical school of ophthalmology, or a training unit approved by a university medical school or university medical school of ophthalmology, may, at the direction of a physician, enucleate eyes for such gift after proper certification of death by a physician and compliance with the intent of such gift as defined in this chapter. No such properly certified funeral director or other person acting in accordance with the terms of this chapter may be liable, civilly or criminally, for such eye enucleation.

§ 34-26-30. Delivery of document of anatomical gift. If the gift is made by the donor to a specified donee, the will, card, or other document, or an executed copy thereof, may be delivered to the donee to expedite the appropriate procedures immediately after death. Delivery is not necessary to the validity of the gift. The will, card, or other document, or an executed copy thereof, may be deposited in any hospital, bank or storage facility, or registry office that accepts it for safekeeping or for facilitation of procedures after death. On request of any interested party upon or after the donor's death, the person in possession shall produce the document for examination.

§ 34-26-31. Amendment or revocation of anatomical gift delivered to specified donee. If the will, card, or other document or executed copy thereof, has been delivered to a specified donee, the donor may amend or revoke the gift by:

(1) The execution and delivery to the donee of a signed statement, or

(2) An oral statement made in the presence of two persons and communicated to the donee, or

(3) A statement during a terminal illness or injury addressed to an attending physician and communicated to the donee, or

(4) A signed card or document found on his person or in his effects.

§ 34-26-32. Revocation of undelivered document of anatomical gift. Any document of gift which has not been delivered to the donee may be revoked by the donor in the manner set out in § 34-26-31 or by destruction, cancellation, or mutilation of the document and all executed copies thereof.

§ 34-26-33. Amendment or revocation of anatomical gift by will. Any gift made by a will may also be amended or revoked in the manner provided for amendment or revocation of wills or as provided in § 34-26-31.

§ 34-26-34. Determination of time of death of donor of anatomical gift—Attending physician not to participate in removal or transplant of part. The time of death shall be determined by a physician who attends the donor at his death or, if none, the physician who certifies the death. The physician shall not participate in the procedures for removing or transplanting a part.

§ 34-26-35. Rights of donee paramount—Exception. The rights of the donee created by the gift are paramount to the rights of others except as provided by § 34-26-38.

§ 34-26-36. Examination for medical acceptability authorized by anatomical gift. A gift of all or part of a body authorizes any examination necessary to assure medical acceptability of the gift for the purposes intended.

§ 34-26-37. Acceptance or rejection of anatomical gift by donee—Removal of part of body. The donee may accept or reject the gift. If the donee accepts a gift of the entire body, he may, subject to the terms of the gift, authorize embalming and the use of the body in funeral services. If the gift is of a part of the body, the donee, upon the death of the donor and prior to embalming, shall cause the part to be removed without unnecessary mutilation. After removal of the part, custody of the remainder of the body vests in the surviving spouse, next of kin, or other persons under obligation to dispose of the body.

§ 34-26-38. Anatomical gift provisions subject to autopsy laws. The provisions of §§ 34-26-20 to 34-26-41, inclusive, are subject to the laws of this state prescribing powers and duties with respect to autopsies.

§ 34-26-39. Exemption from civil or criminal liability for good faith actions under anatomical gift laws. A person who acts in good faith in accord with the terms of §§ 34-26-20 to 34-26-41, inclusive, or the anatomical gift laws of another state or a foreign country is not liable for damages in any civil action or subject to prosecution in any criminal proceeding for his act.

§ 34-26-40. Uniformity of interpretation of anatomical gift provisions. Sections 34-26-20 to 34-26-41, inclusive, shall be so construed as to effectuate their general purpose to make uniform the law of those states which enact them.

§ 34-26-41. Citation of anatomical gift provisions. Sections 34-26-20 to 34-26-41, inclusive, may be cited as the Uniform Anatomical Gift Act.

TENNESSEE

§ 68-30-101. Title. This part may be cited as the "Uniform Anatomical Gift Act."

§ 68-30-102. Definitions. As used in this part:

(1) "Bank or storage facility" means a facility licensed, accredited, or approved under the laws of any state for storage of human bodies or parts thereof;

(2) "Decedent" means a deceased individual and includes a stillborn infant or fetus;

(3) "Donor" means an individual who makes a gift of all or part of his body.

(4) "Eye bank" means any not-for-profit agency certified by the Eye Bank Association of America to procure eye tissue for the purpose of transplantation or research;

(5) "Hospital" means a hospital licensed, accredited, or approved under the laws of any state; the term includes a hospital operated by the United States government, a state, or a subdivision thereof, although not required to be licensed under state laws;

(6) "Organ procurement agency" means any not-for-profit agency approved by the health care financing administration to procure and place human organs for transplantation, therapy, or research;

(7) "Part" means organs, tissues, eyes, bones, arteries, blood, other fluids and any other portions of a human body;

(8) "Person" means an individual, corporation, government or governmental subdivision or agency, business trust, estate, trust, partnership or association, or any other legal entity;

(9) "Physician" or "surgeon" means a physician or surgeon licensed or authorized to practice under the laws of any state;

(10) "State" includes any state, district, commonwealth, territory, insular possession, and any other area subject to the legislative authority of the United States of America; and

(11) "Terminal patient" means any human being afflicted with any disease, illness, injury, or condition from which there is no reasonable medical expectation of recovery and which disease, injury, illness or condition will, as a medical probability, result in the death of such human being within a short period of time regardless of the use or discontinuance of medical treatment implemented for the purpose of sustaining life, or the life processes.

§ 68-30-103. Persons who may execute an anatomical gift. (a) Any individual of sound mind and eighteen (18) years of age or more may give all or any part of his body for any purpose specified in § 68-30-104, the gift to take effect upon death.

(b) Any of the following persons, in order of priority stated, when persons in prior classes are not available at the time of death, and in the absence of actual notice of contrary indications by the decedent or actual notice of opposition by a member of the same or a prior class, may give all or any part of the decedent's body for any purpose specified in § 68-30-104:

(1) The spouse;

(2) An adult son or daughter;

(3) Either parent;

(4) An adult brother or sister;

(5) A guardian of the person of the decedent at the time of his death; or

(6) Any other person authorized or under obligation to dispose of the body.

(c) If the donee has actual notice of contrary indications by the decedent or actual notice that a gift by a member of a class is opposed by a member of the same or a prior class, the donee shall not

176 Life from Death

accept the gift. The persons authorized by subsection (b) may make the gift after or immediately before death.

(d) A gift of all or part of a body authorizes any examination necessary to assure medical acceptability of the gift for the purposes intended.

(e) The rights of the donee created by the gift are paramount to the rights of others except as provided by § 68-30-108(d).

§ 68-30-104. Persons who may become donees—Purposes for which anatomical gifts may be made. The following persons may become donees of gifts of bodies or parts thereof for the purposes stated:

(1) Any hospital, surgeon, or physician, for medical or dental education, research, advancement of medical or dental science, therapy, or transplantation;

(2) Any accredited medical or dental school, college or university for education, research, advancement of medical or dental science, or therapy;

(3) Any bank or storage facility, for medical or dental education, research, advancement of medical or dental science, therapy, or transplantation; or

(4) Any specified individual for therapy or transplantation needed by him.

§ 68-30-105. Method of executing anatomical gifts. (a) A gift of all or part of the body under § 68-30-103(a) may be made by will. The gift becomes effective upon the death of the testator without waiting for probate. If the will is not probated, or if it is declared invalid for testamentary purposes, the gift, to the extent that it has been acted upon in good faith, is nevertheless valid and effective.

(b) A gift of all or part of the body under § 68-30-103(a) may also be made by document other than a will. The gift becomes effective upon the death of the donor. The document, which may be a card designed to be carried on the person, must be signed by the donor in the presence of two (2) witnesses who must sign the document in his presence. If the donor cannot sign, the document may be signed for him at his direction and in his presence in the presence of two (2) witnesses who must sign the document in his presence. Delivery of the document of gift during the donor's lifetime is not necessary to make the gift valid.

(c) The gift may be made to a specified donee or without specifying a donee. If the latter, the gift may be accepted by the attending physician as donee upon or following death. If the gift is made to a specified donee who is not available at the time and place of death, the attending physician upon or following death, in the absence of any expressed indication that the donor desired otherwise, may accept the gift as donee. The physician who becomes a donee under this subsection shall not participate in the procedure for removing or transplanting a part.

(d) Notwithstanding § 68-30-108(b), the donor may designate in his will, card, or other document of gift the surgeon or physician to carry out the appropriate procedures. In the absence of a designation or if the designee is not available, the donee or other person authorized to accept the gift may employ or authorize any surgeon or physician for the purpose. In the case of a gift of eyes, in the absence of a designation by the donor or if such designee is not available, the donee or other person authorized to accept the gift may employ or authorize an ophthalmic technician trained in eye enucleation.

(e) Any gift by a person designated in § 68-30-103(b) shall be made by a document signed by him or made by his telegraphic, recorded telephonic, or other recorded message.

(f) A gift of all or part of the body under § 68-30-103(a) may also be made by a statement provided for on the reverse side of all Tennessee operators' and chauffeurs' licenses. The gift becomes effective upon the death of the donor. The statement must be signed by the owner of the operator's or chauffeur's license in the presence of two (2) witnesses, who must sign the statement in the presence of the donor. Delivery of the license during the donor's lifetime is not necessary to make the gift valid. The gift shall become invalidated upon expiration, cancellation, revocation, or suspension of the license, and the gift must be renewed upon renewal of each license. Any hospital, hospital personnel, physician, surgeon, undertaker, law enforcement officer, or other person may rely upon such statement when signed by the owner of such license and two (2) witnesses as a properly executed legal document, and shall be immune from civil or criminal liability when acting in good faith upon the anatomical gift made pursuant thereto.

§ 68-30-106. Delivery of document of gift. If the gift is made by the donor to a specified donee, the will, card, or other document, or an executed copy thereof, may be delivered to the donee to expedite the appropriate procedures immediately after death. Delivery is not necessary to the validity of the gift. The will, card, or other document, or an executed copy thereof, may be deposited in any hospital, bank or storage facility or registry office that accepts it for safekeeping or for facilitation of procedures after death. On request of any interested party upon or after the donor's death, the person in possession shall produce the document for examination.

§ 68-30-107. Amendment or revocation of the gift. (a) If the will, card, or other document or executed copy thereof, has been delivered to a specified donee, the donor may amend or revoke the gift by:

(1) The execution and delivery to the donee of a signed statement;

(2) An oral statement made in the presence of two (2) persons and communicated to the donee;

(3) A statement during a terminal illness or injury addressed to an attending physician and communicated to the donee; or

(4) A signed card or document found on his person or in his effects.

(b) Any document of gift which has not been delivered to the donee may be revoked by the donor in the manner set out in subsection (a), or by destruction, cancellation, or mutilation of the document and all executed copies thereof.

(c) Any gift made by a will may also be amended or revoked in the manner provided for amendment or revocation of wills, or as provided in subsection (a).

§ 68-30-108. Rights and duties at death—Embalming—Disposition of body. (a) The donee may accept or reject the gift. If the donee accepts a gift of the entire body, he may, subject to the terms of the gift, authorize embalming and the use of the body in funeral services. If the gift is of a part of the body, the donee, upon the death of the donor and prior to embalming, shall cause the part to be removed without unnecessary mutilation. After removal of the part, custody of the remainder of the body vests in the surviving spouse, next of kin, or other persons under obligation to dispose of the body.

(b) The time of death shall be determined by a physician who tends the donor at his death, or, if none, the physician who certifies the death. The physician shall not participate in the procedures for removing or transplanting a part.

(c) A person who acts in good faith in accordance with the terms of this part or with the anatomical gift laws of another state (or a foreign country) is not liable for damages in any civil action or subject to prosecution in any criminal proceeding for his act.

(d) The provisions of this part are subject to the laws of this state prescribing powers and duties with respect to autopsies.

§ 68-30-109. Uniformity of interpretation. This part shall be so construed as to effectuate its general purpose to make uniform the laws of those states which enact it.

§ 68-30-110. Conveyance of patient's wishes—Acute care hospitals—Organ and tissue donation policies and procedures. (a) All physicians, surgeons, or hospital personnel shall make every reasonable effort to convey to the appropriate hospital department the wishes of a hospitalized patient to make an anatomical donation of his body or part thereof, in order that the necessary documents are properly executed in accordance with this part.

(b) Failure to comply with the provisions of this section shall not subject any hospital, hospital personnel, physician, surgeon, or other person to civil or criminal liability for any such failure.

(c) Every acute care hospital in the state of Tennessee will establish a committee to develop and implement an organ and tissue donation policy and procedure to assist the physicians in identifying and evaluating terminal patients who may be suitable organ or tissue donors. The committee will include members of the administrative, medical, and nursing staffs and will appoint a member to act as a liaison between the hospital and the local organ procurement agency and eye bank.

(d) The organ and tissue donation policy and procedure will contain information on acceptable donor criteria, the name and number of the local organ procurement agency and eye bank, a standard organ and tissue donation consent form, mechanisms for informing the next of kin of the potential donor about organ and tissue donation options, provisions for the maintenance and procurement of donated organs and tissues, and methods for routine education of the hospital staff about the policy and procedure.

(e) Each hospital organ and tissue donation policy and procedure will include provisions for the identification of every terminal patient who, in the opinion of the attending physician, meets the criteria established in the policy and the subsequent notification to the local organ procurement agency and/or eye bank for evaluation of the suitability of the organs or tissues. Notification concerning patients who are eligible for a declaration of death based on irreversible cessation of brain function according to § 68-3-501(b)(2), upon recommendation of the attending physician, shall be made to the local organ procurement agency for evaluation prior to a declaration of death or termination of medical treatment. Notification concerning patients who are eligible for a declaration of death based on irreversible cessation of cardiorespiratory function according to § 68-3-501(b)(1), upon recommendation of the attending physician, shall be made to the local organ procurement agency for evaluation, if possible, prior to the declaration of death. In the event that death is sudden and unpredictable, such notification to the eye bank will be accomplished immediately following declaration of death.

(f) Every acute care hospital will develop and implement a protocol for the determination of death pursuant to § 68-3-501.

(g) All physicians, surgeons, and hospital personnel will make every reasonable effort to identify terminal patients who satisfy the donor criteria and to notify the appropriate agency regarding the potential donor.

(h) The commissioner of health and environment shall prepare and issue an annual report summarizing existing data pertaining to organ donation and transplantation activity in Tennessee hospitals.

§ 68-30-111. Source of body parts for transplantation—Confidentiality. It is the intent and purpose of the legislature that for the public welfare, the general public be encouraged to donate body parts for the purpose of transplantation. To this end all records containing the source of body parts for transplantation or any information concerning persons donating body parts for transplantation shall be made confidential under § 10-7-504(a).

TEXAS

Art. 4590-2. Anatomical Gift Act.
Section 1. Short title. This Act may be cited as the Texas Anatomical Gift Act.
Sec. 2. Definitions. (a) "Bank or storage facility" means a facility licensed, accredited or approved under the laws of any state for storage of human bodies or parts thereof.

(b) "Decedent" means a deceased individual and includes a stillborn infant or fetus.

(c) "Donor" means an individual who makes a gift of all or part of his body.

(d) "Hospital" means a hospital licensed, accredited or approved under the laws of any state and includes a hospital operated by the United States government, a state, or a subdivision thereof, although not required to be licensed under state laws.

(e) "Part" includes organs, tissues, eyes, bones, arteries, blood, other fluids and other portions of a human body, and "part" includes "parts."

(f) "Person" means an individual, corporation, government or governmental subdivision or agency, business trust, estate, trust, partnership or association or any other legal entity.

(g) "Physician" or "surgeon" means a physician or surgeon licensed or authorized to practice under the laws of any state.

(h) "State" includes any state, district, commonwealth, territory, insular possession, and any other area subject to the legislative authority of the United States of America.

(i) "Eye bank" means a nonprofit corporation, chartered under the laws of Texas, to obtain, store, and distribute donor eyes to be used by ophthalmologists for corneal transplants, for research, or for other medical purposes.

Sec. 3. Persons who may execute an anatomical gift. (a) Any individual who has testamentary capacity under the Texas Probate Code may give all or any part of his body for any purpose specified in Section 4, the gift to take effect upon death.

(b) Any of the following persons, in order of priority stated, when persons in prior classes are not available at the time of death, and in the absence of actual notice of contrary indications by the decedent, or actual notice of opposition by a member of the same or a prior class, may give all or any part of the decedent's body for any purposes specified in Section 4:

(1) the spouse,
(2) an adult son or daughter,
(3) either parent,
(4) an adult brother or sister,
(5) a guardian of the person of the decedent at the time of his death,
(6) any other person authorized or under obligation to dispose of the body.

(c) If the donee, or the physician of a donee, has actual notice of contrary indications by the decedent, or that a gift by a member of a class is opposed by a member of the same or a prior class, the donee shall not accept the gift. The persons authorized by subsection (b) may make the gift after death or immediately before death.

(d) A gift of all or part of a body authorizes any examination necessary to assure medical acceptability of the gift for the purposes intended.

(e) The rights of the donee created by the gift are paramount to the rights of others except as provided by Section 8(d).

Sec. 4. Persons who may become donees, and purposes for which anatomical gifts may be made. The following persons may become donees of gifts of bodies or parts thereof for the purposes stated:

(1) any hospital, surgeon, or physician, for medical or dental education, research, advancement of medical or dental science, therapy or transplantation;

(2) any accredited medical, chiropractic, or dental school, college or university for education, research, advancement of medical or dental science or therapy;

(3) any bank or storage facility, for medical or dental education, research, advancement of medical or dental science, therapy or transplantation;

(4) any individual specified by a licensed physician for therapy or transplantation needed by him;

(5) any eye bank whose medical activities are directed by a licensed physician or surgeon; or

(6) the Anatomical Board of the State of Texas.

Sec. 5. Manner of executing anatomical gifts. (a) A gift of all or part of the body under Section 3(a) may be made by will. The gift becomes effective upon the death of the testator without waiting for probate. If the will is not probated, or if it is declared invalid for testamentary purposes, the gift, to the extent that it has been acted upon in good faith, is nevertheless valid and effective.

(b) A gift of all or part of the body under Section 3(a) may also be made by document other than a will. The gift becomes effective upon the death of the donor. The document, which may be a card designed to be carried on the person, must be signed by the donor, in the presence of 2 witnesses who must sign the document in his presence. If the donor cannot sign, the document may be signed for him at his direction and in his presence, and in the presence of 2 witnesses who must sign the document in his presence. Delivery of the document of gift during the donor's lifetime is not necessary to make the gift valid.

(c) The gift may be made to a specified donee or without specifying a donee. If the latter, the gift may be accepted by the attending physician as donee upon or following death. If the gift is made to a specified donee who is not available at the time and place of death, the attending physician upon or following death, in the absence of any expressed indication that the donor desired otherwise, may accept the gift as donee. The physician who becomes a donee under this subsection shall not participate in the procedures for removing or transplanting a part.

(d) Notwithstanding Section 8(d), the donor may designate in his will, card or other document of gift the surgeon or physician to carry out the appropriate procedures. In the absence of a designation, or if the designee is not available, the donee or other person authorized to accept the gift may employ or authorize any surgeon or physician for the purpose.

(e) Any gift by a person designated in Section 3(b) shall be made by a document signed by him, or made by his telegraphic, recorded telephonic or other recorded message.

Sec. 6. Delivery of document of gift. If the gift is made by the donor to a specified donee, the will, card or other document, or an executed copy thereof, may be delivered to the donee to expedite the appropriate procedures immediately after death, but delivery is not necessary to the validity of the gift. The will, card or other document, or an executed copy thereof, may be deposited in any hospital, bank or storage facility or registry office that accepts them for safekeeping or for facilitation of procedures after death. On request of any interested party upon or after the donor's death, the person in possession shall produce the document for examination.

Sec. 7. Amendment or revocation of the gift. (a) If the will, card or other document or executed copy thereof, has been delivered to a specified donee, the donor may amend or revoke the gift by:

(1) the execution and delivery to the donee of a signed statement, or

(2) an oral statement made in the presence of 2 persons and communicated to the donee, or

(3) a statement addressed to an attending physician and communicated to the donee, or

(4) a signed card or document found on his person or in his effects.

(b) Any document of gift which has not been delivered to the donee may be revoked by the donor in the manner set out in subsection (a) or by destruction, cancellation, or mutilation of the document and all executed copies thereof.

(c) Any gift made by a will may also be amended or revoked in the manner provided for amendment or revocation of wills, or as provided in subsection (a).

Sec. 8. Rights and duties at death. (a) The donee may accept or reject the gift. If the donee accepts a gift of the entire body, the surviving spouse or any other person authorized to give all or any part of the decedent's body may authorize embalming and have the use of the body for funeral services, subject to the terms of the gift. If the gift is of a part of the body, the donee, upon the death of the donor and prior to embalming, shall cause the part to be removed without unnecessary mutilation. After removal of the part, custody of the remainder of the body vests in the surviving spouse, next of kin or other persons under obligation to dispose of the body.

(b) The time of death shall be determined by a physician who attends the donor at his death, or, if none, the physician who certifies the death. This physician shall not participate in the procedures for removing or transplanting a part.

(c) A person who acts in good faith in accordance with the terms of this Act, is not liable for damages in any civil action or subject to prosecution in any criminal proceeding for his act, so long as the prerequisites for an anatomical gift have been met under the laws applicable at the time and place of the making of the anatomical gift.

(d) The provisions of this Act are subject to the laws of this state prescribing powers and duties with respect to autopsies.

UTAH

§ 26-28-1. Gifts of parts of the body—Eligibility to make—Procedure. Any person 18 years of age or older, or less than 18 years if legally married with the consent in writing of the parent or parents or guardian of such person, may make a gift of any part of his body, or of any organ or tissue thereof, effective upon his death, by a written or printed statement of gift signed by him or his legally appointed representative in the presence of at least one attesting witness. The gift shall be deemed effective without delivery or notification to, or acceptance by, the donee and may be revoked by the donor at any time by a written revocation statement executed in like manner, subject to the provisions of Sections 26-28-5 and 26-28-6.

§ 26-28-2. Eligible donees—Failure to designate or incapacity of donee—Eye enucleation by qualified funeral service practitioner.

(1) A gift made under this chapter may designate as donee:

(a) a licensed physician or surgeon;

(b) a hospital;

(c) a medical school, college, or university engaged in medical education and research;

(d) a blood bank, artery bank, eye bank, or other storage facility for human parts or tissues to be used for transplantation or therapy; or

(e) any licensed physician or surgeon claiming the body, not naming him.

(2) If a statement of gift fails to designate a donee, or the donee designated is incapable of accepting the gift upon the donor's death, the statement of gift shall be deemed to designate any licensed physician or surgeon claiming the body as an alternate solely for the purpose of carrying out the purposes of the gift.

(3) If the part of the body that is the gift is eye tissue, the donee or the person authorized to accept the gift may employ or authorize a certified individual, licensed in the practice of funeral service under Chapter 9, Title 58, to enucleate the eye.

§ 26-28-3. Purpose of gift—Donor may designate.

(1) A gift made under this chapter may designate and limit the purpose for which the gift is made to any one or more of the following:

(a) for transplantation to replace diseased, deteriorated, or malfunctioning parts of living persons;

(b) for use or aid in therapy or in the production of therapeutic substances; or

(c) for medical education or scientific research in medicine.

(2) A statement of gift which fails to designate a purpose, or which states that the gift is for any lawful purpose, shall be so construed as a gift for all of the purposes stated in this section.

§ 26-28-4. Necessary surgery and temporary custody of body authorized. A gift made under this chapter, in addition to the authorizations contained in the statement of gift, authorizes the donee or his agent to perform any surgical procedure necessary to make the gift effective, and authorizes the donee or his agent to take and maintain custody of the donor's body immediately after death for a reasonable period of time, not exceeding 24 hours, for the purpose of performing necessary surgical procedures. Immediately following the removal of the parts of the body, or organs or tissues, designated in the statement of gift, custody of the donor's remains shall be transferred to the next of kin or his agent.

§ 26-28-5. Rights of donee—Immunity from liability. (1) The rights of a donee or his agent with respect to a gift made under this chapter are superior to those of any person claiming as spouse, relative, guardian, or in any other relationship.

(2) A person who, in good-faith reliance upon a statement of gift or upon prima facie evidence of a gift as defined in Section 26-28-7, and without actual notice of revocation thereof, takes possession of, performs or causes to be performed surgical operations upon, or removes or causes to be removed organs, tissues, or parts from a human body shall not be liable in damages in any suit brought against him for such act.

(3) Any donee who refuses such gift or in good faith fails to carry out the wishes of the donor as designated in the statement of gift, shall not be liable in damages on account thereof.

§ 26-28-6. Registration of gift—Information available without charge—Regulation by department. Registration of a statement of gift shall remain effective for all purposes until a duly executed statement of revocation of the same gift is filed with the registration service. All information in the registry shall be of public record and available for inspection on request by any member of the public. No fees shall be charged or collected for registering or revoking a statement of gift, nor shall any fees be assessed for providing information or data in the registry to any licensed physician or surgeon, or representative of any hospital, medical school organ or tissue bank, or other person or institution authorized to be designated as a donee under this chapter. The department may establish a registration and indexing service to provide for the preservation and identification of statements of gift and may adopt, amend or rescind rules necessary to effectuate the registration provisions of this chapter.

§ 26-28-7. Prima facie evidence of gift. Prima facie evidence that a valid and effective gift has been made consists of:

(1) an instrument or statement of gift in substantial conformity with Section 26-28-1, found on the person or among the personal effects of the donor at the time of his death;

(2) an instrument or statement of gift in substantial conformity with Section 26-28-1 found in the

possession of the donee or his agent at the time of the donor's death; or

(3) an unrevoked registration of a statement of gift in the records of an authorized state or local registration service.

§ 26-28-8. Act to be liberally construed—Gifts made in other states. This chapter shall be liberally construed and applied in order to carry out the purpose of providing legal procedures and safeguards by which effective gifts of parts of the human body may be made effective at death for medical, humanitarian, and scientific purposes. A gift within the purview of this chapter, made by any donor who dies within the state, shall be deemed valid and effective if valid under the law of this state or under the laws of the place where the instrument of gift was executed, and this chapter shall be fully applicable thereto.

VERMONT

§ 5231. Definitions.

(a) "Bank or storage facility" means a facility licensed, accredited, or approved under the laws of any state for storage of human bodies or parts thereof.

(b) "Decedent" means a deceased individual and includes a stillborn infant or fetus.

(c) "Donor" means an individual who makes a gift of all or part of his body.

(d) "Hospital" means a hospital licensed, accredited, or approved under the laws of any state, or a hospital operated by the United States government, a state, or a subdivision thereof, although not required to be licensed under state laws.

(e) "Part" means organs, tissues, eyes, bones, arteries, blood, other fluids and any other portions of a human body.

(f) "Person" means an individual, corporation, government or governmental subdivision or agency, business trust, estate, trust, partnership or association, or any other legal entity.

(g) "Physician" or "surgeon" means a physician or surgeon licensed or authorized to practice under the laws of any state.

(h) "State" means any state, district, commonwealth, territory, insular possession, and any other area subject to the legislative authority of the United States of America.

§ 5232. Persons who may execute an anatomical gift.

(a) Any individual of sound mind and who has attained the age of majority may give all or any part of his body for any purpose specified in section 5233 of this title, the gift to take effect upon death.

(b) Any of the following persons, in order of priority stated, when persons in prior classes are not available at the time of death, and in the absence of actual notice of contrary indications by the decedent or actual notice of opposition by a member of the same or a prior class, may give all or any part of the decedent's body for any purpose specified in section 5233 of this title:

(1) The spouse;

(2) An adult son or daughter;

(3) Either parent;

(4) An adult brother or sister;

(5) A guardian of the person of the decedent at the time of his death;

(6) Any other person authorized or under obligation to dispose of the body.

(c) If the donee has actual notice of contrary indications by the decedent or that a gift by a member of a class is opposed by a member of the same or a prior class, the donee shall not accept the gift. The persons authorized by subsection (b) of this section may make the gift after or immediately before death.

(d) A gift of all or part of a body authorizes any examination necessary to assure medical acceptability of the gift for the purposes intended.

(e) The rights of the donee created by the gift are paramount to the rights of others except as provided by section 5237(d) of this title.

§ 5233. Persons who may become donees; purposes for which anatomical gifts may be made. The following persons may become donees of gifts of bodies or parts thereof for the purposes stated:

(1) Any hospital, surgeon, or physician, for medical or dental education, research, advancement of medical or dental science, therapy, or transplantation; or

(2) Any accredited medical or dental school, college or university for education, research, advancement of medical or dental science, or therapy; or

(3) Any bank or storage facility, for medical or dental education, research, advancement of medical or dental science, therapy or transplantation; or

(4) Any specified individual for therapy or transplantation needed by him.

§ 5234. Manner of executing anatomical gifts.

(a) A gift of all or part of the body under section 5232(a) of this title may be made by will. The gift becomes effective upon the death of the testator without waiting for probate. If the will is not probated, or if it is declared invalid for testamentary purposes, the gift, to the extent that it has been acted upon in good faith, is nevertheless valid and effective.

(b) A gift of all or part of the body under section 5232(a) of this title may also be made by document other than a will. The gift becomes effective upon the death of the donor. The document, which may be a card designed to be carried on the person, must be signed by the donor in the presence of two witnesses who must sign the document in his presence. If the donor cannot sign, the document may be signed for him at his direction and in his presence in the presence of two witnesses who must sign the document in his presence. Delivery of the document of gift during the donor's lifetime is not necessary to make the gift valid.

(c) The gift may be made to a specified donee or without specifying a donee. If the latter, the gift may be accepted by the attending physician as donee upon or following death. If the gift is made to a specified donee who is not available at the time and place of death, the attending physician upon or following death, in the absence of any expressed indication that the donor desired otherwise, may accept the gift as donee. The physician who becomes a donee under this subsection shall not participate in the procedures for removing or transplanting a part.

(d) Notwithstanding section 5237(b) of this title, the donor may designate in his will, card, or other document of gift the surgeon or physician to carry out the appropriate procedures; provided, however, that eye enucleations may also be performed by a person who has successfully completed a course of training acceptable to the New England Eye Bank at the Massachusetts Eye and Ear Infirmary. In the absence of a designation or if the designee is not available, the donee or other person authorized to accept the gift may employ or authorize any surgeon or physician for the purpose.

(e) Any gift by a person designated in section 5232(b) of this title shall be made by a document signed by him or made by his telegraphic, recorded telephonic, or other recorded message.

(f) A statement may be made by the holder of an operator's license that he is, by separate instrument, an anatomical gift donor.

§ 5235. Delivery of document of gift. If the gift is made by the donor to a specified donee, the will, card, or other document, or an executed copy thereof, may be delivered to the donee to expedite the appropriate procedures immediately after death. Delivery is not necessary to the validity of the gift. The will, card, or other document, or an executed copy thereof, may be deposited in any hospital bank or storage facility or registry office that accepts it for safekeeping or for facilitation of procedures after death. On request of any interested party upon or after the donor's death, the person in possession shall produce the document for examination.

§ 5236. Amendment or revocation of gift.

(a) If the will, card, or other document or executed copy thereof, has been delivered to a specified donee, the donor may amend or revoke the gift by:

(1) The execution and delivery to the donee of a signed statement, or

(2) An oral statement made in the presence of two persons and communicated to the donee, or

(3) A statement during a terminal illness or injury addressed to an attending physician and communicated to the donee, or

(4) A signed card or document found on his person or in his effects.

(b) Any document of gift which has not been delivered to the donee may be revoked by the donor in the manner set out in subsection (a) of this section, or by destruction or cancellation of the document and all executed copies thereof.

(c) Any gift made by a will may also be amended or revoked in the manner provided for amendment or revocation of wills, or as provided in subsection (a) of this section.

§ 5237. Rights and duties at death.

(a) The donee may accept or reject the gift. If the donee accepts a gift of the entire body, he may, subject to the terms of the gift, authorize embalming and the use of the body in funeral services. If the gift is of a part of the body, the donee, upon the death of the donor and prior to embalming, shall cause the part to be removed without unnecessary mutilation. After removal of the part, custody of the remainder of the body vests in the surviving spouse, next of kin, or other persons under obligation to dispose of the body.

(b) The time of death shall be determined by a physician who tends the donor at his death, or, if none, the physician who certifies the death. The physician shall not participate in the procedures for removing or transplanting a part.

(c) A person who acts in good faith in accord with the terms of this chapter or with the anatomical gift laws of another state or foreign country is not liable for damages in any civil action or subject to prosecution in any criminal proceeding for his act.

(d) The provisions of this chapter are subject to the laws of this state prescribing powers and duties with respect to autopsies.

VIRGINIA

§ 32.1-289. Definitions.—As used in this article:

1. *"Bank or storage facility"* means a facility licensed, accredited or approved under the laws of any state for storage of human bodies or parts thereof.

2. *"Decedent"* means a deceased individual and includes a stillborn infant or fetus.

3. *"Donor"* means an individual who makes a gift of all or part of his body.

4. *"Hospital"* means a hospital licensed, accredited or approved under the laws of any state and a hospital operated by the United States government, a state, or a subdivision thereof which is not required to be licensed under state laws.

5. *"Part"* includes organs, tissues, eyes, bones, glands, arteries, blood, other fluids and other portions of a human body, and "part" includes "parts."

6. *"Person"* includes, in addition to the entities enumerated in paragraph 4 of § 32.1-3, a government and a governmental subdivision or agency.

7. *"Physician"* or *"surgeon"* means a physician or surgeon licensed or authorized to practice under the laws of any state.

8. *"State"* includes any state, district, commonwealth, territory, insular possession, and any other area subject to the legislative authority of the United States of America.

§ 32.1-289.1. Sale of body parts prohibited; exceptions; penalty.—With the exception of hair, blood and other self-replicating body fluids, it shall be unlawful for any person to sell, to offer to sell, to buy, to offer to buy or to procure through purchase any natural body part for any reason, including, but not limited to, medical and scientific uses such as transplantation, implantation, infusion or injection. Nothing in this section shall prohibit the reimbursement of expenses associated with the removal and preservation of any natural body parts for medical and scientific purposes. This section shall not apply to any transaction pursuant to Article 3 (§ 32.1-298 et seq.), Chapter 8 of this title [pertaining to the use of dead bodies for scientific study].

Any person engaging in any of these prohibited activities shall be guilty of a Class 6 felony.

§ 32.1-290. Persons who may execute anatomical gift; when gift may be executed; examination of body authorized; rights of donee paramount.—A. Any individual of sound mind and eighteen years of age or more may give all or any part of his body for any purposes specified in § 32.1-291, the gift to take effect upon death.

B. Any of the following persons, in order of priority stated, when persons in prior classes are not available at the time of death and there is no actual notice of contrary indications by the decedent and no actual notice of opposition by a member of the same or a prior class, may give all or any part of the decedent's body for any purposes specified in § 32.1-291:

1. The spouse,
2. An adult son or daughter,
3. Either parent,
4. An adult brother or sister,
5. A guardian of the person of the decedent at the time of his death, or
6. Any other person authorized or under obligation to dispose of the body.

C. If the donee has actual notice of contrary indications by the decedent or that a gift by a member of a class is opposed by a member of the same or a prior class, the donee shall not accept the gift. The persons authorized by subsection B may make the gift after death or immediately before death.

D. A gift of all or part of a body authorizes any examination necessary to assure medical acceptability of the gift for the purposes intended.

E. The rights of the donee created by the gift are paramount to the rights of others except as provided by subsection E of § 32.1-295.

§ 32.1-291. Persons who may become donees; purposes for which anatomical gifts may be made.—The following persons may become donees of gifts of bodies or parts thereof for the purposes stated:

1. Any hospital, surgeon or physician, for medical or dental education, research, advancement of medical or dental science, therapy or transplantation; or

2. Any accredited medical or dental school, college or university, for education, research, advancement of medical or dental science or therapy; or

3. Any bank or storage facility, for medical or dental education, research, advancement of medi-

cal or dental science, therapy or transplantation; or

4. Any specified individual for therapy or transplantation needed by him.

§ 32.1-292. Manner of executing anatomical gifts.—A. A gift of all or part of the body under subsection A of § 32.1-290 may be made by will. The gift becomes effective upon the death of the testator without waiting for probate. If the will is not probated or if it is declared invalid for testamentary purposes, the gift, to the extent that it has been acted upon in good faith, is nevertheless valid and effective.

B. A gift of all or part of the body under subsection A of § 32.1-290 may also be made by document other than a will. The gift becomes effective upon the death of the donor. The document, which may be a card designed to be carried on the person, must be signed by the donor in the presence of two witnesses who must sign the document in his presence. If the donor cannot sign, the document may be signed for him at his direction and in his presence and in the presence of two witnesses who must sign the document in his presence. Delivery of the document of gift during the donor's lifetime is not necessary to make the gift valid.

C. The gift may be made to a specified donee or without specifying a donee. If the latter, the gift may be accepted by the attending physician as donee upon or following death. If the gift is made to a specified donee who is not available at the time and place of death, the attending physician upon or following death, in the absence of any expressed indication that the donor desired otherwise, may accept the gift as donee. Any physician who becomes a donee under this subsection shall not participate in the determination of death.

D. Except as provided in subsection C of this section and subsection C of § 32.1-295, the donor may designate in his will, card, or other document of gift the surgeon or physician to carry out the appropriate procedures. In the absence of a designation, or if the designee is not available, the donee or other person authorized to accept the gift may employ or authorize any surgeon or physician for the purpose. In the case of a gift of eyes, in the absence of a designation by the donor or if such designee is not available, the donee or other person authorized to accept the gift may employ or authorize:

1. Any surgeon or physician; or

2. Any funeral service licensee or embalmer licensed in this Commonwealth who has successfully completed a course in eye enucleation in any accredited medical school in the United States; or

3. Any technicians who can document the successful completion of a course for ophthalmic medical assistants, provided by the American Association of Ophthalmology, and in addition has proof of successful completion of a course in eye enucleation as outlined in subdivision D 2 above, to enucleate eyes for such purpose.

In the case of a gift of skin, temporal bone or other bone, in the absence of a designation by the donor or if such designee is not available, the donee or other person authorized to accept the gift may employ or authorize to perform the appropriate procedures: (i) any physician or surgeon or in the case of temporal bone, any otolaryngologist or otorhinolaryngologist; (ii) any technician approved by the University of Virginia Skin Bank as qualified to perform the act of skin harvesting; (iii) any technician approved by the Virginia Tissue Bank as qualified to perform the act of skin or bone harvesting; or (iv) any funeral director or embalmer licensed in this Commonwealth who has completed a course for harvesting temporal bones as provided by the University of Virginia Hospital.

In the case of a gift of the brain to be used for confirmation of diagnosis and research into the etiology of any organic brain disease, the donee or other person authorized to receive the organ may employ or authorize a laboratory technician trained by a licensed neuropathologist to recover the brain.

Any person authorized by this section to perform eye enucleation, or recovery of skin, temporal bone and other bone or tissue or vascular organs may draw blood from the donor and order such tests as may be appropriate to protect his health and the health of the potential recipients of the tissues or organs.

E. A surgeon, physician, otolaryngologist, otorhinolaryngologist, funeral service licensee, embalmer, technician or ophthalmic assistant acting in accordance with the terms of this section shall not have any liability, civil or criminal, for the eye enucleation, recovery of the brain or other organ or harvesting of skin or bones.

§ 32.1-293. **Delivery of document of gift.**—If the gift is made by the donor to a specified donee, the will, card or other document, or an executed copy thereof, may be delivered to the donee to expedite the appropriate procedures immediately after death, but delivery is not necessary to the validity of the gift. The will, card or other document, or an executed copy thereof, may be deposited in any hospital, bank or storage facility or registry office that accepts them for safekeeping or for facilitation of procedures after death. On request of any interested party upon or after the donor's death, the person in possession shall produce the document for examination.

§ 32.1-294. **Amendment or revocation of gift.**—A. If the will, card or other document or executed copy thereof, has been delivered to a specified donee, the donor may amend or revoke the gift by:

1. The execution and delivery to the donee of a signed statement, or
2. An oral statement made in the presence of two persons and communicated to the donee, or
3. A statement during a terminal illness or injury addressed to an attending physician and communicated to the donee, or
4. A signed card or document found on his person or in his effects.

B. Any document of gift which has not been delivered to the donee may be revoked by the donor in the manner set out in subsection A or by destruction, cancellation, or mutilation of the document and all executed copies thereof.

C. Any gift made by a will may also be amended or revoked in the manner provided for amendment or revocation of wills or as provided in subsection A.

§ 32.1-295. **Rights and duties at death.**—A. The donee may accept or reject the gift. If the donee accepts a gift of the entire body, he may, subject to the terms of the gift, authorize embalming and the use of the body in funeral services. If the gift is of a part of the body, the donee, upon the death of the donor and prior to embalming, shall cause the part to be removed without unnecessary mutilation. After removal of the part, custody of the remainder of the body shall vest in the surviving spouse, next of kin or other persons under obligation to dispose of the body.

B. The provisions of Article 3 (§ 32.1-298 et seq.) of this chapter shall be applicable whenever a gift is made of a body for the purpose of medical or dental education, scientific study, research or advancement of medical or dental science and (i) no donee is specified or (ii) the donee requests the Commissioner to accept the body for distribution as provided in such article and the Commissioner accepts the body.

C. The time of death shall be determined by a physician who attends the donor at his death or, if none, the physician who certifies the death. This physician shall not participate in the procedures for removing or transplanting a part.

D. A person who acts in good faith in accord with the terms of this article, or under the anatomical gift laws of another state or a foreign country is not liable for damages in any civil action or subject to prosecution in any criminal proceeding for his act.

E. The provisions of this article are subject to the provisions of § 32.1-285.

§ 32.1-296. Determination of death.—The provisions of § 54-325.7 shall be applicable for the purposes of this article.

§ 32.1-297. Action for implied warranty in connection with transfer of blood or human tissue.—No action for implied warranty shall lie for the procurement, processing, distribution or use of whole blood, plasma, blood products, blood derivatives and other human tissue such as corneas, bones, or organs for the purpose of injecting, transfusing or transplanting any of them into the human body except where any defects or impurities in the said whole blood, plasma, blood products, blood derivatives and other human tissues such as corneas, bones, or organs are detectable by the use of established medical and technological procedures employed pursuant to the standards of local medical practice.

§ 32.1-297.1. (Effective July 1, 1986) The Virginia Transplant Council.—For the purpose of conducting educational and informational activities and coordinating such activities as they relate to organ and tissue procurement and transplantation efforts in the Commonwealth, there is hereby established the Virginia Transplant Council. The membership of the Council shall initially consist of the following organizations, each of whom have one vote: the University of Virginia Medical Center, the Medical College of Virginia, the Virginia Organ Procurement Agency, the Eastern Virginia Renal Transplant Program, the Eastern Virginia Tissue Bank, the Old Dominion Eye Bank, the Lion's Eye and Research Center of Eastern Virginia, the Eye Bank and Research Foundation of Virginia and the South-Eastern Organ Procurement Foundation. In order to provide flexibility, viable coordination and prevent duplication of efforts, the member organizations may agree to include as members of the Council other organizations directly involved in organ or tissue procurement or transplantation as they deem appropriate.

The Board of Health shall be designated as budgetary administrator of the Council and shall receive such funds as may be provided by the General Assembly in the appropriations act. The Board shall provide technical oversight for the Commonwealth of the activities of the Council and shall require such fiscal and substantive reports of the Council as it deems necessary. The Board shall report to the 1988 and 1991 Session of the General Assembly on the activities of the Council.

The Council shall conduct its activities in consultation and coordination with other organizations whose goals are related to organ or tissue procurement or transplantation including, but not limited to the End State Renal Disease Network of the Virginias, the North American Transplant Coordinators' Organization, the National Kidney Foundation of Virginia, the American Liver Foundation, the United Network for Organ Sharing and the Virginia Heart Association. To achieve its purpose efficiently and effectively, the Council may conduct its activities through its member organizations or may contract for services with appropriate parties.

WASHINGTON

§ 68.50.340. Definitions.

(1) "Bank or storage facility" means a facility licensed, accredited, or approved under the laws of any state for storage of human bodies or parts thereof including pacemakers.

(2) "Decedent" means a deceased individual and includes a stillborn infant or fetus.

(3) "Donor" means an individual who makes a gift of all or part of his body.

(4) "Hospital" means a hospital licensed, accredited, or approved under the laws of any state; in-

cludes a hospital operated by the United States government, a state, or a subdivision thereof, although not required to be licensed under state laws.

(5) "Part" means pacemakers, organs, tissues, eyes, bones, arteries, blood, other fluids and any other portions of a human body including artificial parts.

(6) "Person" means an individual, corporation, government or governmental subdivision or agency, business trust, estate, trust, partnership or association, or any other legal entity.

(7) "Physician" or "surgeon" means a physician or surgeon licensed or authorized to practice under the laws of any state.

(8) "State" includes any state, district, commonwealth, territory, insular possession, and any other area subject to the legislative authority of the United States of America.

§ 68.50.350. Gift of any part of body to take effect upon death authorized—Who may make—Priorities—Examination—Rights of donee paramount.

(1) Any individual of sound mind and eighteen years of age or more may give all or any part of his body for any purpose specified in RCW 68.50.360, the gift to take effect upon death.

(2) Any of the following persons, in order of priority stated, when persons in prior classes are not available at the time of death, and in the absence of actual notice of contrary indications by the decedent or actual notice of opposition by a member of the same or a prior class, may give all or any part of the decedent's body for any purpose specified in RCW 68.50.360:

(a) the spouse,

(b) an adult son or daughter,

(c) either parent,

(d) an adult brother or sister,

(e) a guardian of the person of the decedent at the time of his death,

(f) any other person authorized or under obligation to dispose of the body.

(3) If the donee has actual notice of contrary indications by the decedent or that a gift by a member of a class is opposed by a member of the same or a prior class, the donee shall not accept the gift. The persons authorized by subsection (2) may make the gift after death or during the terminal illness.

(4) A gift of all or part of a body authorizes any examination necessary to assure medical acceptability of the gift for the purposes intended.

(5) The rights of the donee created by the gift are paramount to the rights of others except as provided by RCW 68.50.400(4).

§ 68.50.360. Eligible donees—Eye removal by embalmers.

(1) The following persons may become donees of gifts of bodies or parts thereof for the purposes stated:

(a) Any hospital, surgeon, physician, or other entity which has a physician or surgeon as a regular full-time employee, for medical or dental education, research, advancement of medical or dental science, therapy, or transplantation;

(b) Any accredited medical or dental school, college or university for education, research, advancement of medical or dental science, or therapy;

(c) Any bank or storage facility, for medical or dental education, research, advancement of medical or dental science, therapy, or transplantation; or

(d) Any specified individual for therapy or transplantation needed by him.

(2) If the part of the body that is the gift is an eye, the donee or the person authorized to accept the gift may employ or authorize a qualified embalmer, licensed under chapter 18.39 RCW, to remove the eye.

§ 68.50.370. Gift by will, card, document, or driver's license—Procedures.

(1) A gift of all or part of the body under RCW 68.50.350(1) may be made by will. The gift becomes effective upon the death of the testator without waiting for probate. If the will is not probated, or if it is declared invalid for testamentary purposes, the gift, to the extent that it has been acted upon in good faith, is nevertheless valid and effective.

(2) A gift of all or part of the body under RCW 68.50.350(1), may also be made by document other than a will. The gift becomes effective upon the death of the donor. The document, which may be a card designed to be carried on the person, must be signed by the donor in the presence of two witnesses who must sign the document in his presence. If the donor cannot sign, the document may be signed for him at his direction and in his presence in the presence of two witnesses who must sign the document in his presence. Delivery of the document of gift during the donor's lifetime is not necessary to make the gift valid.

(3) A gift of all or part of the body under RCW 68.50.350(1) may also be made by a statement provided for on Washington state driver's licenses. The gift becomes effective upon the death of the licensee. The statement must be signed by the licensee in the presence of two witnesses, who must sign the statement in the presence of the donor. Delivery of the license during the donor's lifetime is not necessary to make the gift valid. The gift shall become invalidated upon expiration, cancellation, revocation, or suspension of the license, and the gift must be renewed upon renewal of each license: *Provided,* That the statement of gift herein provided for shall contain a provision, including a clear instruction to the donor, providing for a means by which the donor may at his will revoke such gift: *Provided further,* That nothing in this chapter shall be construed to invalidate a donor card located elsewhere.

§ 68.50.380. Delivery of will, card or other document to specified donee.
If the gift is made by the donor to a specified donee, the will, card, or other document, or an executed copy thereof, may be delivered to the donee to expedite the appropriate procedures immediately after death. Delivery is not necessary to the validity of the gift. The will, card, or other document, or an executed copy thereof, may be deposited in any hospital, bank or storage facility or registry office that accepts it for safekeeping or for facilitation of procedures after death. On request of any interested party upon or after the donor's death, the person in possession shall produce the document for examination.

§ 68.50.390. Amendment or revocation of gift.

(1) If the will, card, or other document or executed copy thereof, has been delivered to a specified donee, the donor may amend or revoke the gift by:

   (a) the execution and delivery to the donee of a signed statement;

   (b) an oral statement made in the presence of two persons and communicated to the donee;

   (c) a statement during a terminal illness or injury addressed to an attending physician and communicated to the donee;

   (d) a signed card or document found on his person or in his effects.

(2) Any document of gift which has not been delivered to the donee may be revoked by the donor in the manner set out in subsection (1) above, or by destruction, cancellation, or mutilation of the document and all executed copies thereof.

(3) Any gift made by a will may also be amended or revoked in the manner provided for amendment or revocation of wills, or as provided in subsection (1) above.

§ 68.50.400. Acceptance or rejection of gift—Time of death—Liability for damages.

(1) The donee may accept or reject the gift. If the donee accepts a gift of the entire body, he may, subject to the terms of the gift, authorize embalming and the use of the body in funeral services. If the gift is of a part of the body, the donee, upon the death of the donor and prior to embalming, shall

cause the part to be removed without unnecessary mutilation. After removal of the part, custody of the remainder of the body vests in the surviving spouse, next of kin, or other persons under obligation to dispose of the body.

(2) The time of death shall be determined by a physician who tends the donor at his death, or, if none, the physician who certifies the death. The physician shall not participate in the procedures for removing or transplanting a part.

(3) A person who acts in good faith in accord with the terms of RCW 68.50.340 through 68.50.510 or with the anatomical gift laws of another state (or a foreign country) is not liable for damages in any civil action or subject to prosecution in any criminal proceeding for his act.

(4) The provisions of RCW 68.50.340 through 68.50.510 are subject to the laws of this state prescribing powers and duties with respect to autopsies.

§ 68.50.410. Uniformity. RCW 68.50.340 through 68.50.510 shall be so construed as to effectuate its general purpose to make uniform the law of those states which enact it.

§ 68.50.420. Short title. RCW 68.50.340 through 68.50.510 may be cited as the "Uniform Anatomical Gift Act."

§ 68.50.500. Identification of potential donors—Hospital procedures. Each hospital shall develop procedures for identifying potential organ and tissue donors. The procedures shall require that any deceased individual's next of kin or other individual, as set forth in RCW 68.50.350, at or near the time of notification of death be asked whether the deceased was an organ donor. If not, the family shall be informed of the option to donate organs and tissues pursuant to the uniform anatomical gift act. With the approval of the designated next of kin or other individual, as set forth in RCW 68.50.350, the hospital shall then notify an established eye bank, tissue bank, or organ procurement agency including those organ procurement agencies associated with a national organ procurement transportation network or other eligible donee, as specified in RCW 68.50.360, and cooperate in the procurement of the anatomical gift or gifts. The procedures shall encourage reasonable discretion and sensitivity to the family circumstances in all discussions regarding donations of tissue or organs. The procedures may take into account the deceased individual's religious beliefs or obvious nonsuitability for organ and tissue donation. Laws pertaining to the jurisdiction of the coroner shall be complied with in all cases of reportable deaths pursuant to RCW 68.08.010.

§ 68.50.510. Good faith compliance with RCW 68.08.650—Hospital liability. No act or omission of a hospital in developing or implementing the provisions of RCW 68.50.500, when performed in good faith, shall be a basis for the imposition of any liability upon the hospital.

This section shall not apply to any act or omission of the hospital that constitutes gross negligence or wilful and wanton conduct.

WEST VIRGINIA

§ 16-19-1. Definitions.

(a) "Bank or storage facility" means a facility licensed, accredited, or approved under the laws of any state for storage or distribution of human bodies or parts thereof.

(b) "Certification of death" means a written pronouncement of death by the attending physician. Such certification shall be required before the attending physician shall allow removal of any bodily organs of the decedent for transplant purposes.

(c) "Death" means that a person will be considered dead if in the announced opinion of the attending physician, made in accordance with reasonable medical standards, the patient has sustained irreversible cessation of all functioning of the brain.

(d) "Decedent" means a deceased individual and includes a stillborn infant or fetus.

(e) "Donor" means an individual who makes a gift of all or part of his body.

(f) "Hospital" means a hospital licensed, accredited, or approved under the laws of any state; includes a hospital operated by the United States government, a state, or a subdivision thereof, although not required to be licensed under state laws.

(g) "Part" means organs, tissues, eyes, bones, arteries, blood, other fluids and any other portions of a human body.

(h) "Person" means an individual, corporation, government or governmental subdivision or agency, business trust, estate trust, partnership or association, or any other legal entity.

(i) "Physician" or "surgeon" means a physician or surgeon licensed or authorized to practice under the laws of any state.

(j) "State" includes any state, district, commonwealth, territory, insular possession, and any other area subject to the legislative authority of the United States of America.

§ 16-19-2. Persons who may execute an anatomical gift.

(a) Any individual of sound mind and eighteen years of age or more may give all or any part of his body for any purpose specified in section three [§ 16-19-3] of this article, the gift to take effect upon certification of death.

(b) Any of the following persons, in order of priority stated, when persons in prior classes are not available at the time of certification of death, and in the absence of actual notice of contrary indications by the decedent or actual notice of opposition by a member of the same or a prior class, may give all or any part of the decedent's body for any purpose specified in section three [§ 16-19-3] of this article:

(1) The spouse;

(2) An adult son or daughter;

(3) Either parent;

(4) An adult brother or sister;

(5) A guardian of the person of the decedent at the time of the certification of his death;

(6) Any other person authorized or under obligation to dispose of the body.

(c) If the donee has actual notice of contrary indications by the decedent or that a gift by a member of a class is opposed by a member of the same or a prior class, the donee shall not accept the gift. The persons authorized by subsection (b) of this section may make the gift after or immediately before certification of death.

(d) A gift of all or part of a body authorizes any examination necessary to assure medical acceptability of the gift for the purposes intended.

(e) The rights of the donee created by the gift are paramount to the rights of others except as provided by section seven [§ 16-19-7], subsection (d) of this article.

§ 16-19-3. Persons who may become donees; purposes for which anatomical gifts may be made; compliance with rules and regulations of board.

The following persons may become donees of gifts of bodies or parts thereof for the purposes stated:

(1) The West Virginia board of regents for the scientific purposes of educational institutions for which it may receive or requisition dead bodies; or

(2) Any hospital, surgeon or physician, for medical or dental education, research, advancement of medical or dental science, therapy or transplantation; or

(3) Any accredited medical or dental school, college or university for education, research, advancement of medical or dental science or therapy; or

(4) Any person operating a bank or storage facility for blood, arteries, eyes, pituitaries, or other human parts, for use in medical or dental education, advancement of medical or dental science, research, therapy or transplantation to individuals; or

(5) Any specified individual for therapy or transplantation needed by him.

The use, disposition and control of any such donated bodies or parts thereof by any such donee shall be in accordance with rules and regulations prescribed by the West Virginia board of regents.

§ 16-19-3a. Recovery of corneas; conditions; liability of medical examiner.

(a) In any case where a patient is in need of corneal tissue for a transplant, the chief medical examiner, assistant medical examiner, regional pathologist or any other person designated to perform an autopsy in accordance with article twelve [§ 61-12-1 et seq.], chapter sixty-one of this Code, may provide a cornea for transplant, under rules, regulations and procedures established by the chief medical examiner, upon the request of the medical eye bank of West Virginia, incorporated, under the following conditions:

(1) The body of the decedent having a suitable cornea for the transplant is under the jurisdiction of the chief medical examiner and an autopsy is required, in accordance with article twelve [§ 61-12-1 et seq.], chapter sixty-one of this Code;

(2) The decedent's next of kin makes no objections; and

(3) Transplanting of the cornea will not interfere with the course of any subsequent investigation or autopsy or alter the postmortem facial appearance.

(b) Neither the chief medical examiner, any assistant medical examiner, regional pathologist nor any other person designated to perform an autopsy in accordance with section ten [§ 61-12-10], article twelve, chapter sixty-one of this Code and who provides a cornea in accordance with the provisions of this section, nor the medical eye bank of West Virginia, incorporated, shall be liable for any civil damages if the decedent's next of kin subsequently contends that his authorization was required.

§ 16-19-4. Manner of executing anatomical gifts.

(a) A gift of all or part of the body under subsection (a), section two [§ 16-19-2(a)] of this article may be made by will. The gift becomes effective upon certification of death of the testator without waiting for probate. If the will is not probated, or if it is declared invalid for testamentary purposes, the gift, to the extent that it has been acted upon in good faith, is nevertheless valid and effective.

(b) A gift of all or part of the body under subsection (a), section two [§ 16-19-2(a)] of this article may also be made by document other than a will. The gift becomes effective upon certification of death of the donor. The document, which may be a card designed to be carried on the person, must be signed by the donor in the presence of two witnesses who must sign the document in his presence. If the donor cannot sign, the document may be signed for him at his direction and in his presence in the presence of two witnesses who must sign the document in his presence. Delivery of the document of gift during the donor's lifetime is not necessary to make the gift valid.

(c) The gift may be made to a specified donee or without specifying a donee. If the latter, the West Virginia board of regents will be considered to be the donee unless it declines to accept the gift, or unless there is urgent immediate need for a part of the body for transplant or other purposes in which case the gift may be accepted by the attending physician as donee upon or following certification of death. In case the board of regents is considered the donee it shall be the duty of the person who has charge or control of the body, if he or she has knowledge of the gift, to give notice thereof to the board of regents within twenty-four hours after the sending of such notice. If the board of regents makes a requisition for the body within the twenty-four-hour period, it shall be delivered, pursuant to the order of the board, to the board or its authorized agent for transportation to an educational institution which the board deems in bona fide need thereof and able to adequately control, use and dispose of the body. If the board of regents shall not so act within the twenty-four-hour period, the gift may be accepted by the attending physician as donee upon or following certification of death. If the gift is made to a specified donee who is not available at the time and place of death, the attending physician upon or following certification of death, in the absence of any expressed indication that the donor desired otherwise, may accept the gift as donee. The physician who becomes a donee under this subsection shall not participate in the procedures for removing or transplanting a part, except that this prohibition shall not apply to the removing or transplanting of an eye or eyes.

(d) Notwithstanding subsection (b), section seven [§ 16-19-7(b)] of this article, the donor may designate in his will, card or other document of gift, the surgeon or physician to carry out the appropriate procedures, or in the case of a gift of an eye or eyes, the surgeon or physician or the technician properly trained in the surgical removal of eyes to carry out the appropriate procedures. In the event of the nonavailability of such designee, or in the absence of a designation, the donee or other person authorized to accept the gift may employ or authorize for the purpose any surgeon or physician or in the case of a gift of an eye or eyes, any surgeon or physician or technician properly trained in the surgical removal of eyes or also in case of a gift of an eye or eyes, the donee or other person authorized to accept the gift may employ or authorize a licensed funeral director or embalmer licensed pursuant to article six [§§ 30-6-1 et seq.], chapter thirty of this Code who has successfully completed a course in enucleation approved by the medical licensing board of West Virginia to enucleate the eye or eyes for the gift after certification of death by a physician. The qualified funeral director or embalmer shall properly care for the enucleated eye or eyes and promptly deliver the eye or eyes to the donee or other person authorized to accept the gift. A qualified funeral director or embalmer acting in accordance with the terms of this subsection shall not be liable, civilly or criminally, for the eye enucleation.

(e) Any gift by a person designated in subsection (b) [§ 16-19-2(b)], section two of this article shall be made by a document signed by him or made by his telegraphic, recorded telephonic or other recorded message.

(f) No particular words shall be necessary for donation of all or part of a body, but the following words, in substance, properly signed and witnessed, shall be legally valid for donations made pursuant to subsection (b) of this section: **See Appendix for recommended form (Uniform Donor Card).**

§ 16-19-4a. Request for consent to an anatomical gift.

(a) Where, based on accepted medical standards, a patient is a suitable candidate for organ or tissue donation, the person in charge of a hospital, or his or her designated representative other than a person connected with the determination of death, shall at the time of death request persons listed in this section for consent to an anatomical gift. In the order of priority stated and in the absence of actual notice of contrary indications by the decedent or actual notice of opposition by a member of the same or a prior class, any of the following persons may give all or any part of the decedent's body for any purpose specified in this article:

(1) The spouse;

(2) An adult son or daughter;

(3) Either parent;

(4) An adult brother or sister;

(5) A guardian of the person of the decedent at the time of his death.

Where the person in charge of a hospital or his or her designee has received actual notice of opposition from any of the persons named in this subsection or where there is otherwise reason to believe that an anatomical gift is contrary to the decedent's religious beliefs, such gift of all or any part of the decedent's body shall not be requested. Where a donation is requested, consent or refusal need only be obtained from the person or persons in the highest priority class available.

(b) Where a donation is requested, the person in charge of a hospital or his designated representative shall complete a certificate of request for an anatomical gift, on a form supplied by the hospital. Said certificate shall include a statement to the effect that a request for consent to an anatomical gift has been made, and shall further indicate thereupon whether or not consent was granted, the name of the person granting or refusing the consent, and his or her relationship to the decedent. Upon completion of the certificate, said person shall attach the certificate of request for an anatomical gift to the death certificate.

(c) A gift made pursuant to the request required by this section shall be executed pursuant to applicable provisions of article nineteen [§ 16-19-1 et seq.] of this chapter.

(d) The director of health shall establish regulations concerning the training of hospital employees who may be designated to perform the request, and the procedures to be employed in making it.

(e) The director of health shall establish such additional regulations as are necessary for the implementation of this section.

(f) No hospital or person in charge of a hospital or his or her designated representatives shall be liable for damages for any action taken in good faith in the administering of the provisions of the article.

§ 16-19-5. Delivery of document of gift.
If the gift is made by the donor to a specified donee, the will, card, or other document, or an executed copy thereof, may be delivered to the donee to expedite the appropriate procedures immediately after death. Delivery is not necessary to the validity of the gift. The will, card, or other document, or an executed copy thereof, may be deposited in any hospital, bank or storage facility or registry office that accepts it for safekeeping or for facilitation of procedures after death. On request of any interested party upon or after the donor's death, the person in possession shall produce the document for examination.

§ 16-19-6. Amendment or revocation of the gift.
(a) If the will, card, or other document or executed copy thereof, has been delivered to a specified donee, the donor may amend or revoke the gift by:

(1) The execution and delivery to the donee of a signed statement; or

(2) An oral statement made in the presence of two persons and communicated to the donee; or

(3) A statement during a terminal illness or injury addressed to an attending physician and communicated to the donee; or

(4) A signed card or document found on his person or in his effects.

(b) Any document of gift which has not been delivered to the donee may be revoked by the donor in the manner set out in subsection (a) of this section or by destruction, cancellation, or mutilation of the document and all executed copies thereof.

(c) Any gift made by a will may also be amended or revoked in the manner provided for amendment or revocation of wills, or as provided in subsection (a) of this section.

§ 16-19-7. Rights and duties at death.
(a) The donee may accept or reject the gift. If the donee accepts a gift of the entire body, he may, subject to the terms of the gift, authorize embalming and the use of the body in funeral services. If the gift is of a part of the body, the donee, upon the death of the donor and prior to embalming, shall cause the part to be removed without unnecessary mutilation. After removal of the part, custody of the remainder of the body vests in the surviving spouse, next of kin, or other persons under obligation to dispose of the body.

(b) The time of death shall be determined by a physician who tends the donor at his death, or, if none, the physician who certifies the death. Such physician shall not participate in the procedures for removing or transplanting a part.

(c) A person who acts in good faith in accord with the terms of this article or with the anatomical gift laws of another state or a foreign country is not liable for damages in any civil action or subject to prosecution in any criminal proceeding for his act.

(d) The provisions of this article are subject to the laws of this State prescribing powers and duties with respect to autopsies.

§ 16-19-7a. Prohibition of sales and purchases of human organs; penalties. It shall be unlawful for any person to knowingly acquire, receive, or otherwise transfer for valuable consideration any human organ for use in human transplantation. The term human organ means the human kidney, liver, heart, lung, bone marrow, and any other human organ or tissue as may be designated by the director of health but shall exclude blood. The term "valuable consideration" does not include reasonable payments associated with the removal, transportation, implantation, processing, preservation, quality control, and storage of a human organ or the expenses of travel, housing, lost wages incurred by the donor of a human organ in connection with the donation of the organ, or expenses incurred by nonprofit agencies or corporations to recover expenses incurred while offering services related to the location, maintenance and distribution of said human organs. Any person who violates this section is guilty of a misdemeanor, and upon conviction thereof, shall be fined not less than five hundred nor more than one thousand dollars.

§ 16-19-8. Uniformity of interpretation. This article shall be so construed as to effectuate its general purpose to make uniform the law of those states which enact it.

§ 16-19-9. Short title. This article may be cited as the "Uniform Anatomical Gift Act."

WISCONSIN

§ 157.06. Uniform anatomical gift act.

(1) Definitions. (a) "Anatomical research" means a gift of the entire body to a medical or dental school anatomy department for purposes of dissection or other like purpose.

(am) "Bank or storage facility" means a facility licensed, accredited or approved under the laws of any state for storage of human bodies or parts thereof.

(b) "Decedent" means a deceased individual and includes a stillborn infant or fetus.

(c) "Donor" means an individual who makes a gift of all or part of his body.

(d) "Hospital" means a hospital licensed, accredited or approved under the laws of any state and includes a hospital operated by the U.S. government, a state, or a subdivision thereof, although not required to be licensed under state laws.

(e) "Part" means organs, tissues, eyes, bones, arteries, blood, other fluids and any other portions of a human body.

(f) "Physician" or "surgeon" means a physician or surgeon licensed or authorized to practice under the laws of any state.

(2) Persons who may execute an anatomical gift. (a) Except as provided in this paragraph, any individual of sound mind may give all or any part of his or her body for any purpose specified in sub. (3), the gift to take effect upon death. If a decedent has given his or her entire body to any donee for the purpose of anatomical research, a parent of an unmarried decedent under 18 years of age may revoke the gift. If a decedent has given his or her entire body to any donee for the purpose of anatomical research, unless the surviving spouse gave consent to the donation in writing prior to the donor's death, the surviving spouse of the decedent may revoke the gift.

(b) Any of the following persons, in order of priority stated, when persons in prior classes are not available at the time of death, and in the absence of actual notice of contrary indications by the decedent or actual notice of opposition by a member of the same or a prior class, may give all or any part of the decedent's body for any purpose specified in sub. (3):

1. The spouse.
2. An adult son or daughter.
3. Either parent.
4. An adult brother or sister.
5. A guardian of the person of the decedent at the time of his death.
6. Any other person authorized or under obligation to dispose of the body.

(c) If the donee has actual notice of contrary indications by the decedent or that a gift by a member of a class is opposed by a member of the same or a prior class, the donee shall not accept the gift. The persons authorized by par. (b) may make the gift after or immediately before death.

(d) A gift of all or part of a body authorizes any examination necessary to assure medical acceptability of the gift for the purposes intended.

(e) The rights of the donee created by the gift are paramount to the rights of others except as provided by subs. (2)(a) and (7)(d).

(2m) Hospital policy. (a) Each hospital shall have a policy based on accepted medical standards that requires, except as provided in par. (b), when a patient who is a suitable candidate for the gift of all or part of his or her body dies in the hospital, that the persons specified in sub. (2)(b) in the order and according to the procedure stated in sub. (2)(b) be requested to consider consenting to the gift of all or any part of the decedent's body, which has not already been given under sub. (2), for the purposes specified in sub. (3).

(b) The policy required under par. (a) does not have to require a request to consider consenting to a gift if the hospital has actual notice of contrary indications by the decedent or actual notice that a gift by a member of a class is opposed by a member of the same or a prior class under sub. (2)(b).

(c) If a gift is requested under par. (a), the hospital shall include in the decedent's medical records a statement that a request to consider consent to an anatomical gift has been made and the name of the person of whom the request is made, the person's relationship to the decedent and whether the person consented to or refused the request.

(3) Persons who may become donees; purposes for which anatomical gifts may be made. The following persons may become donees of gifts of bodies or parts thereof for the purposes stated:

(a) Any hospital, surgeon or physician, for medical or dental education, research, advancement of medical or dental science, therapy or transplantation; or

(b) Any accredited medical or dental school, college or university, for education, research, advancement of medical or dental science or therapy; or

(c) Any bank or storage facility, for medical or dental education, research, advancement of medical or dental science, therapy or transplantation; or

(d) Any specified individual for therapy or transplantation needed by him.

(4) Manner of executing anatomical gifts. (a) A gift of all or part of the body under sub. (2)(a) may be made by will. The gift becomes effective upon the death of the testator without waiting for probate. If the will is not probated, or if it is declared invalid for testamentary purposes, the gift, to the extent that it has been acted upon in good faith, is nevertheless valid and effective.

(b) A gift of all or part of the body under sub. (2)(a) may also be made by document other than a will. The gift becomes effective upon the death of the donor. The document, which may be a card designed to be carried on the person, must be signed by the donor in the presence of 2 witnesses who must sign the document in his presence. If the donor cannot sign, the document may be signed for him at his direction and in his presence in the presence of 2 witnesses who must sign the document in his presence. Delivery of the document of gift during the donor's lifetime is not necessary to make the gift valid.

(c) The gift may be made to a specified donee or without specifying a donee. If the latter, the gift may be accepted by the attending physician as donee upon or following death. If the gift is made to a specified donee who is not available at the time and place of death, the attending physician upon or following death, in the absence of any expressed indication that the donor desired otherwise, may accept the gift as donee. The physician who becomes a donee under this subsection shall not participate in the procedures for removing or transplanting a part.

(d) Notwithstanding sub. (7)(b), the donor may designate in his will, card or other document of gift the surgeon or physician to carry out the appropriate procedures. In the absence of a designation or if the designee is not available, the donee or other person authorized to accept the gift may employ or authorize any surgeon or physician for the purpose.

(e) Any gift by a person designated in sub. (2)(b) shall be made by a document signed by him or made by his telegraphic, recorded telephonic or other recorded message.

(5) Delivery of document of gift. If the gift is made by the donor to a specified donee, the will, card or other document, or an executed copy thereof, may be delivered to the donee to expedite the appropriate procedures immediately after death. Delivery is not necessary to the validity of the gift. The will, card or other document, or an executed copy thereof, may be deposited in any hospital, bank or storage facility or registry office that accepts it for safekeeping or for facilitation of procedures after death. On request of any interested party upon or after the donor's death, the person in possession shall produce the document for examination.

(6) Amendment or revocation of the gift. (a) If the will, card or other document, or executed copy thereof, has been delivered to a specified donee, the donor may amend or revoke the gift by:

1. The execution and delivery to the donee of a signed statement; or
2. An oral statement made in the presence of 2 persons and communicated to the donee; or
3. A statement during a terminal illness or injury addressed to an attending physician and communicated to the donee; or
4. A signed card or document found on his or her person or in his or her effects; or
5. Crossing our the donor authorization in the space provided on the driver's license as prescribed in s. 343.17(1)(c).

(b) Any document of gift which has not been delivered to the donee may be revoked by the donor in the manner set out in par. (a), or by destruction, cancellation or mutilation of the document and all executed copies of the document or by crossing out the authorization in the space provided on the license as prescribed in s. 343.17(1)(c).

(c) Any gift made by a will may also be amended or revoked in the manner provided for amendment or revocation of wills, or as provided in par. (a).

(7) Rights and duties at death. (a) The donee may accept or reject the gift. If the entire body is given for the purpose of anatomical research, it shall not be delivered to the donee or his agent if the surviving spouse or other person who assumes custody of the body requests a funeral service or other last rites for the deceased. If such a request is made, the body shall not be delivered until after the rites have been conducted. If the entire body is given for any purpose other than anatomical research or if the gift is of a part of the body, the donee, upon the death of the donor and prior to embalming, shall cause any parts given which it intends to remove to be removed without unnecessary mutilation. After removal of any such parts, custody of the remainder of the body vests in the surviving spouse, next of kin or other persons under obligation to dispose of the body.

(b) The medical certification of death under s. 69.18(2) shall be determined by a physician who tends the donor at his or her death or, if none, the physician who certifies the death. The physician shall not participate in the procedures for removing or transplanting a part.

(c) A person who acts in good faith in accord with the terms of this section or with the anatomical gift laws of another state (or a foreign country) is not liable for damages in any civil action or subject to prosecution in any criminal proceeding for his act.

(d) This section is subject to the laws of this state prescribing powers and duties of the coroner, medical examiner and other physicians licensed to perform autopsies with respect to autopsies and the reporting of certain deaths under ch. 979.

(e) Except as expressly provided in this section, nothing in this section affects rights or obligations of next of kin of a decedent.

(7m) Removal of eyes by funeral directors and persons acting under direction of physician. In addition to any physician licensed to practice medicine and surgery under ch. 448, any person acting under the direction of a physician or any funeral director licensed under ch. 445, who has completed a course in eye enucleation and holds a valid certificate of competence from a medical college approved by the medical examining board under s. 448.05(2) may enucleate the eyes of a deceased donor under this section. A certificate of competence shall be valid for 3 years. No licensed funeral director so certified and no funeral establishment with which such a funeral director is affiliated shall be liable for damages resulting from such enucleation.

(8) Uniformity of interpretation. This section shall be so construed as to effectuate its general purpose to make uniform the law of those states which enact it.

(9) Short title. This act may be cited as the uniform anatomical gift act.

WYOMING

§ 35-5-101. Definitions.

(a) "Bank or storage facility" means a facility licensed, accredited, or approved under the laws of any state for storage of human bodies or parts thereof.

(b) "Decedent" means a deceased individual and includes a stillborn infant or fetus.

(c) "Donor" means an individual who makes a gift of all or part of his body.

(d) "Hospital" means a hospital licensed, accredited, or approved under the laws of any state; includes a hospital operated by the United States government, a state, or a subdivision thereof although not required to be licensed under state laws.

(e) "Part" means organs, tissues, eyes, bones, arteries, blood, other fluids and any other portions of a human body.

(f) "Person" means an individual, corporation, government or governmental subdivision or agency, business trust, estate, trust, partnership or association, or any other legal entity.

(g) "Physician" or "surgeon" means a physician or surgeon licensed or authorized to practice under the laws of any state.

(h) "State" includes any state, district, commonwealth, territory, insular possession, and any other area subject to the legislative authority of the United States of America.

§ 35-5-102. Donors generally; when donee not to accept gift; when gift to be made; examination of body; rights of donee.

(a) Any individual of sound mind and eighteen (18) years of age or more may give all or any part of his body for any purpose specified in section 3 [§ 35-5-103], the gift to take effect upon death.

(b) Any of the following persons, in order of priority stated, when persons in prior classes are not available at the time of death, and in the absence of actual notice of contrary indications by the decedent or actual notice of opposition by a member of the same or a prior class, may give all or part of the decedent's body for any purpose specified in section 3 [§ 35-5-103]:

(i) The spouse;
(ii) An adult son or daughter;
(iii) Either parent;
(iv) An adult brother or sister;
(v) A guardian of the person of the decedent at the time of his death;
(vi) Any other person authorized or under obligation to dispose of the body.

(c) If the donee has actual notice of contrary indications by the decedent or that a gift by a member of a class is opposed by a member of the same or a prior class, the donee shall not accept the gift. The persons authorized by subsection (b) may make the gift after or immediately before death.

(d) A gift of all or part of a body authorizes any examination necessary to assure medical acceptability of the gift for the purposes intended.

(e) The rights of the donee created by the gift are paramount to the rights of others except as provided by section 7(d) [§ 35-5-107(d)].

§ 35-5-103. Donees generally.

(a) The following persons may become donees of gifts of bodies or parts thereof for the purposes stated:

(i) Any hospital, surgeon, or physician, for medical or dental education, research, advancement of medical or dental science, therapy, or transplantation; or

(ii) Any accredited medical or dental school, college or university for education, research, advancement of medical or dental science, or therapy; or

(iii) Any bank or storage facility, for medical or dental education, research, advancement of medical or dental science, therapy, or transplantation; or

(iv) Any specified individual for therapy or transplantation needed by him.

§ 35-5-104. Gift may be made by will or document; when gift effective; attending physician as donee; designation of surgeon or physician to carry out appropriate procedures.

(a) A gift of all or part of the body under section 2(a) [§ 35-5-102(a)] may be made by will. The gift becomes effective upon the death of the testator without waiting for probate. If the will is not probated, or if it is declared invalid for testamentary purposes, the gift, to the extent that it has been acted upon in good faith, is nevertheless valid and effective.

(b) A gift of all or part of the body under section 2(a) [§ 35-5-102(a)] may also be made by document other than a will. The gift becomes effective upon the death of the donor. The document, which may be a card designed to be carried on the person, must be signed by the donor in the presence of two (2) witnesses who must sign the document in his presence. If the donor cannot sign, the document may be signed for him at his direction and in his presence in the presence of two (2) witnesses who must sign the document in his presence. Delivery of the document of gift during the donor's lifetime is not necessary to make the gift valid.

(c) The gift may be made to a specified donee or without specifying a donee. If the latter, the gift may be accepted by the attending physician as donee upon or following death. If the gift is made to a specified donee who is not available at the time and place of death, the attending physician upon or following death, in the absence of any expressed indication that the donor desired otherwise, may accept the gift as donee. The physician who becomes a donee under this subsection shall not participate in the procedures for removing or transplanting a part.

(d) Notwithstanding section 7(b) [§ 35-5-107(b)], the donor may designate in his will, card, or other document of gift the surgeon or physician to carry out the appropriate procedures. In the absence of a designation or if the designee is not available, the donee or other person authorized to accept the gift may employ or authorize any surgeon or physician for the purpose.

(e) Any gift by a person designated in section 2(b) [§ 35-5-102(b)] shall be made by a document signed by him or made by his telegraphic, recorded telephonic, or other recorded message.

§ 35-5-105. Delivery of will or other document to specified donee; deposit for safekeeping; examination of document by interested party. If the gift is made by the donor to a specified donee, the will, card, or other document, or an executed copy thereof, may be delivered to the donee to expedite the appropriate procedures immediately after death. Delivery is not necessary to the validity of the gift. The will, card, or other document, or an executed copy thereof, may be deposited in any hospital, bank or storage facility or registry office that accepts it for safekeeping or for facilitation of procedures after death. On request of any interested party upon or after the donor's death, the person in possession shall produce the document for examination.

§ 35-5-106. Amendment or revocation of gift.

(a) If the will, card, or other document or executed copy thereof, has been delivered to a specified donee, the donor may amend or revoke the gift by:

(i) The execution and delivery to the donee of a signed statement; or

(ii) An oral statement made in the presence of two (2) persons and communicated to the donee; or

(iii) A statement during a terminal illness or injury addressed to an attending physician and communicated to the donee; or

(iv) A signed card or document found on his person or in his effects.

(b) Any document of gift which has not been delivered to the donee may be revoked by the donor in the manner set out in subsection (a), or by destruction, cancellation, or mutilation of the document and all executed copies thereof.

(c) Any gift made by a will may also be amended or revoked in the manner provided for amendment or revocation of wills, or as provided in subsection (a).

§ 35-5-107. Donee may accept or reject gift; embalming and use of body in funeral services; removal of part of body; custody of remains; by whom time of death determined; liability; act subject to state law respecting autopsies.

(a) The donee may accept or reject the gift. If the donee accepts a gift of the entire body, he may, subject to the terms of the gift, authorize embalming and the use of the body in funeral services. If the gift is of a part of the body, the donee, upon the death of the donor and prior to embalming, shall cause the part to be removed without unnecessary mutilation. After removal of the part, custody of the remainder of the body vests in the surviving spouse, next of kin, or other person under obligation to dispose of the body.

(b) The time of death shall be determined by a physician who tends the donor at his death, or, if none, the physician who certifies the death.

(c) A person who acts in good faith in accord with the terms of this act [§§ 35-5-101 to 35-5-109] or with the anatomical gift laws of another state is not liable for damages in any civil action or subject to prosecution in any criminal proceeding for his act.

(d) The provisions of this act are subject to the laws of this state prescribing powers and duties with respect to autopsies.

§ 35-5-108. Construction. This act [§§ 35-5-101 to 35-5-109] shall be so construed as to effectuate its general purpose to make uniform the law of those states which enact it.

§ 35-5-109. Citation. This act [§§ 35-5-101 to 35-5-109] may be cited as the Uniform Anatomical Gift Act.

§ 35-5-110. Transplantation of tissues, organs or components; exemption from liability; exceptions. A physician, surgeon, hospital, blood bank, tissue bank, or other person or entity who donates, obtains, prepares, transplants, injects, transfuses or otherwise transfers, or who assists or participates in obtaining, preparing, transplanting, injecting, transfusing or transferring any tissue, organ, blood or component thereof from one (1) or more human beings, living or death, to another human being, is not liable as the result of any such activity except for his or her own negligence or misconduct.

§ 35-5-111. Eye enucleation; persons eligible to perform enucleation; certification requirements.

(a) A licensed funeral director or undertaker as defined in W.S. 33-16-301, a registered nurse licensed to practice in this state, a physician's assistant certified in Wyoming or an ophthalmic technician certified by the American Board of Ophthalmology may, upon certification of competence under subsection (b) of this section, enucleate eyes for a gift in accordance with W.S. 35-5-101 through 35-5-109 after proper determination of death by a physician. For purposes of this subsection, proper determination of death does not mean the execution and registration of a formal death certificate.

(b) To perform eye enucleation under subsection (a) of this section, a qualified funeral director, undertaker, registered nurse, physician's assistant or ophthalmic technician shall first successfully complete a course in eye enucleation and receive certification of competence from a medical school in the United States or from an ophthalmologist licensed to practice in the United States and certified by the American Board of Ophthalmology. The certificate shall provide:

(i) The date of satisfactory completion of required course work; and

(ii) The name, address and qualifications of the person or institution providing certification and the notarized signature of that person or authorized representative of the institution.

§ 35-5-112. Driver's license indication of anatomical organ donors; procedure.

(a) The motor vehicle division of the department of revenue and taxation shall adopt and implement a program whereby anatomical organ donors may be so identified by an appropriate decal, sticker or other marking to be affixed to the driver's license or identification card of the person.

(b) The division shall provide space on every application for a driver's license or renewal thereof in which the applicant may indicate his desire to have the marking provided in subsection (a) of this section on his driver's license. In addition, any person whose license has not expired or who has already obtained a license may have the marking affixed by the division upon request.

(c) The division shall publish the existence of the program along with information regarding the procedures for having the marking affixed to a license.

(d) The division shall notify its counterparts in each of the other states as to the existence of the program and the significance of the marking.

(e) No provision of this act [section] shall be so construed to modify or repeal any provisions of the Uniform Anatomical Gift Act [§§ 35-5-101 to 35-5-109], and the actual donation of an anatomical organ shall be in conformity with and subject to all provisions of the Uniform Anatomical Gift Act.

Appendix A

To make an anatomical donation if you are an adult, fill out a copy of the Uniform Donor Card, always carry the card on your person, and make your wishes known to your friends, relatives, and doctor. If you are a minor, fill out the Anatomical Gift by a Living Minor Donor form instead (page 208). The Anatomical Gift by Next of Kin or Other Authorized Person form is used to make a gift from the body of a dying or deceased loved one. The fourth form in this Appendix, the Anatomical Gift by a Living Donor, is similar to the Uniform Donor Card. It is included here because some states, such as Delaware, specify this form in their laws instead of the Uniform Donor Card.

Uniform Donor Card of

_____(Print or type name of donor)

In the hope that I may help others, I hereby make this anatomical gift, if medically acceptable, to take effect upon certification of my death. The words and marks below indicate my desires.
I give: (1) []any needed organs or parts;
(2) []the following organs, tissues, or parts only

_____
(3) []For the following purposes only _____.
(transplantation, therapy, medical research or education)
(4) []my body for anatomical study if needed.
Signed by the donor and the following two witnesses in the presence of each other:

_____
Signature of Donor

_____
Date of Birth of Donor

_____
City and State

_____
Date Signed

_____
Witness

_____
Witness
This is a legal document under the Uniform Anatomical Gift Act or similar laws.

Instructions: Check box 1 if the gift is unrestricted, i.e., of any organ, tissue, or part for any purpose specified in the Anatomical Gift Act (transplantation, therapy, research or education); do not check box 2, 3, or 4. If the gift is restricted to specific organ(s), tissue(s), or part(s) only, e.g., heart, cornea, kidneys, etc., check box 2 and write in the organ(s) or tissue(s) to be given. If the gift is restricted to one or more of the purposes listed, e.g., transplant, therapy, etc., check box 3 and write in the purpose for which the gift is made. If you wish to donate your entire body to a medical school, you should check box 4 (unlike the other choices, the exercise of this option usually requires an agreement with a medical school before a gift is made, however).

Anatomical Gift by Next of Kin or Other Authorized Person

I hereby make this anatomical gift from the body of _____ (name) who died on _____ (date) in _____ (city and state).

   The marks in the appropriate squares and the words filled into the blanks below indicate my relationship to the deceased according to the following order of priority and indicate my desires respecting the gift.

  1. I am the surviving:
  a. []spouse;
  b. []adult son or daughter;
  c. []parent;
  d. []adult brother or sister;
  e. []guardian;
  f._____ authorized to dispose of the body:

  2. I give: []the body of deceased; []any needed organs or parts; []the following organs or parts only_____;

  3. To the following person (or institution):_____(insert the name of a physician, hospital, research or educational institution, storage bank or individual);

  4. For the following purposes: []any purpose authorized by law; []transplantation; []therapy; []medical research and education.

Dated_____ City and State_____

_____
Signature of Survivor

_____
Address of Survivor

This is a legal document under the Uniform Anatomical Gift Act or similar laws.

Instructions: Fill in the name of the deceased on the first line and the date of death and place of death on the second line. Next indicate your relationship to the deceased by checking the appropriate square. Under item (2), check "[]the body of the deceased" if you wish to donate the entire body to a medical school (unlike the other choices, the exercise of this option usually requires an agreement with a medical school before a gift is made). Check "[]any needed organs or parts" if the gift is unrestricted, i.e., of any organ, tissue, or part. Check "[]the following organs or parts only" if the gift is restricted to specific organ(s), tissue(s), or part(s) only, e.g., heart, cornea, kidney, etc. Write in the organ(s) or tissue(s) to be given in the blank. It is not necessary to fill our item (3) unless you want to specify a particular recipient of the gift; if so, fill in the name of the recipient in the blank space. Under item (4), check the first box ("[]any purpose authorized by law") if the gift is unrestricted. If the gift is restricted to one or more of the purposes listed, check the appropriate box(es).

Anatomical Gift by a Living Donor

I am of sound mind and 18 years or more of age.

I hereby make this anatomical gift to take effect upon my death. The marks in the appropriate squares and words filled into the blanks below indicate my desires.

I give: []my body; []any needed organs or parts;[]the following organs or parts only_____;

To the following person or institutions: [ ]the physician in attendance at my death; [ ]the hospital in which I die; [ ]the following named physician, hospital, storage bank or other medical institution _____; []the following individual for treatment_____;
for the following purposes:[]any purpose authorized by law; []transplantation; []therapy; []research; []medical education.

Dated_____City and State_____

Signed by the Donor in the presence of the following who sign as witnesses.

_____
Signature of Donor

_____
Address of Donor

_____
Witness

_____
Witness

This is a legal document under the Uniform Anatomical Gift Act or similar laws.

Instructions: Check "[]my body" if you wish to donate your entire body to a medical school (unlike the other choices, the exercise of this option usually requires an agreement with a medical school before a gift is made). Check "[]any needed organs or parts" if you wish to make an unrestricted anatomical gift of any organ, tissue, or part. If the gift is restricted to specific organ(s), tissue(s), or part(s) only, e.g., heart, cornea, kidneys, etc., check "[]the following organs or parts only" and write in the organ(s) or tissue(s) to be given. If you wish to name a specific recipient of the gift, check the appropriate square in the next section and fill in the blank space, where applicable. If the purpose of the gift is unrestricted, check "[]any purpose authorized by law." If the purpose for which the gift is made is restricted, check the appropriate specific purpose(s) desired.

Anatomical Gift by a Living Minor Donor

I am of sound mind and under 18 years of age.

I hereby make this anatomical gift to take effect upon my death with the parental consent of the undersigned. The marks in the appropriate squares and the words filled into the blanks below indicate my desires.

I give: []my body; []any needed organs or parts; []the following organs or parts only_____

To the following person or institutions []the physician in attendance at my death; []the hospital in which I die; []the following named physician, hospital, storage bank or other medical institution_____; []the following individual for treatment_____;
for the following purposes; []any purpose authorized by law; []transplantation; []therapy; []research; []medical education.

Dated_____City and State_____

The undersigned parent or other person authorized by law grants permission for the above anatomical gift.

Signed by the Donor and the person giving parental consent in the presence of the following who sign as witnesses.

Signature of Donor_____
Address of Donor_____
Signature of Parent or other Person Authorized by Law_____
Address of Consenting Party_____
Witness_____
Witness_____

This is a legal document under the Uniform Anatomical Gift Act or similar laws.

Instructions: Check "[]my body" if you wish to donate your entire body to a medical school (unlike the other choices, the exercise of this option usually requires an agreement with a medical school before a gift is made). Check "[]any needed organs or parts" if you wish to make an unrestricted anatomical gift of any organ, tissue or part. If the gift is restricted to specific organ(s), tissue(s), or part(s) only, e.g., heart, cornea, kidneys, etc., check "[]the following organs or parts only" and write in the organ(s) or tissue(s) to be given. If you wish to name a specific recipient of the gifts, check the appropriate square in the next section and fill in the blank space, where applicable. If the purpose of the gift is unrestricted, check "[]any purpose authorized by law." If the purpose for which the gift is made is restricted, check the appropriate purpose(s) desired. In addition to the signature and address of the donor, the signature and address of the parent or other consenting party is required. If your state law requires the approval of both parents (see your state law requirements in Chapter 4), both parents must sign the document. Space is provided for the signatures of two witnesses, although these are ordinarily optional (see your state law requirements in Chapter 4). If your state laws do not presently allow anatomical gifts by minors, you may still want to fill out a form of gift, since the laws are subject to revision, and many states are expected to rewrite their laws to permit donations by minors in the near future.

Appendix B

Amended Uniform Anatomical Gift Act (1987)

NOTE: Words or phrases enclosed in square brackets [ ] indicate instances in which each state is to supply its own appropriate terms.

SECTION 1. **Definitions.** As used in this [Act]:

(1) "Anatomical gift" means a donation of all or part of a human body to take effect upon or after death.

(2) "Decedent" means a deceased individual and includes a stillborn infant or fetus.

(3) "Document of gift" means a card, a statement attached to or imprinted on a motor vehicle operator's or chauffeur's license, a will, or other writing used to make an anatomical gift.

(4) "Donor" means an individual who makes an anatomical gift of all or part of the individual's body.

(5) "Enucleator" means an individual who is [licensed] [certified] by the [State Board of Medical Examiners] to remove or process eyes or parts of eyes.

(6) "Hospital" means a facility licensed, accredited, or approved as a hospital under the law of any state or a facility operated as a hospital by the United States government, a state, or a subdivision of a state.

(7) "Part" means an organ, tissue, eye, bone, artery, blood, fluid, or other portion of a human body.

(8) "Person" means an individual, corporation, business trust, estate, trust, partnership, joint venture, association, government, governmental subdivision or agency, or any other legal or commercial entity.

(9) "Physician" or "surgeon" means an individual licensed or otherwise authorized to practice medicine and surgery or osteopathy and surgery under the laws of any state.

(10) "Procurement organization" means a person licensed, accredited, or approved under the laws of any state for procurement, distribution, or storage of human bodies or parts.

(11) "State" means a state, territory, or possession of the United States, the District of Columbia, or the Commonwealth of Puerto Rico.

(12) "Technician" means an individual who is [licensed] [certified] by the [State Board of Medical Examiners] to remove or process a part.

SECTION 2. **Making, Amending, Revoking, and Refusing to Make Anatomical Gifts by Individual.**

(a) An individual who is at least [18] years of age may (i) make an anatomical gift for any of the purposes stated in Section 6(a), (ii) limit an anatomical gift to one or more of those purposes, or (iii) refuse to make an anatomical gift.

(b) An anatomical gift may be made only by a document of gift signed by the donor. If the donor cannot sign, the document of gift must be signed by another individual and by two witnesses, all of whom have signed at the direction and in the presence of the donor and of each other, and state that it has been so signed.

(c) If a document of gift is attached to or imprinted on a donor's motor vehicle operator's or chauffeur's license, the document of gift must comply with subsection (b). Revocation, suspension, expiration, or cancellation of the license does not invalidate the anatomical gift.

(d) A document of gift may designate a particular physician or surgeon to carry out the appropriate procedures. In the absence of a designation or if the designee is not available, the donee or other person authorized to accept the anatomical gift may employ or authorize any physician, surgeon, technician, or enucleator to carry out the appropriate procedures.

(e) An anatomical gift by will takes effect upon death of the testator, whether or not the will is probated. If, after death, the will is declared invalid for testamentary purposes, the validity of the anatomical gift is unaffected.

(f) A donor may amend or revoke an anatomical gift, not made by will, only by:

    (1) a signed statement;

    (2) an oral statement made in the presence of two individuals;

    (3) any form of communication during a terminal illness or injury addressed to a physician or surgeon; or

    (4) the delivery of a signed statement to a specified donee to whom a document of gift had been delivered.

(g) The donor of an anatomical gift made by will may amend or revoke the gift in the manner provided for amendment or revocation of wills, or as provided in subsection (f).

(h) An anatomical gift that is not revoked by the donor before death is irrevocable and does not require the consent or concurrence of any person after the donor's death.

(i) An individual may refuse to make an anatomical gift of the individual's body or part by (i) a writing signed in the same manner as a document of gift, (ii) a statement attached to or imprinted on a donor's motor vehicle operator's or chauffeur's license, or (iii) any other writing used to identify the individual as refusing to make an anatomical gift. During a terminal illness or injury, the refusal may be an oral statement or other form of communication.

(j) In the absence of contrary indications by the donor, an anatomical gift of a part is neither a refusal to give other parts nor a limitation on an anatomical gift under Section 3 or on a removal or release of other parts under Section 4.

(k) In the absence of contrary indications by the donor, a revocation or amendment of an anatomical gift is not a refusal to make another anatomical gift. If the donor intends a revocation to be a refusal to make an anatomical gift, the donor shall make the refusal pursuant to subsection (i).

SECTION 3. **Making, Revoking, and Objecting to Anatomical Gifts, by Others.**

(a) Any member of the following classes of persons, in the order of priority listed, may make an anatomical gift of all or a part of the decedent's body for an authorized purpose, unless the decedent, at the time of death, has made an unrevoked refusal to make that anatomical gift:

    (1) the spouse of the decedent;

    (2) an adult son or daughter of the decedent;

    (3) either parent of the decedent;

    (4) an adult brother or sister of the decedent;

    (5) a grandparent of the decedent; and

    (6) a guardian of the person of the decedent at the time of death.

(b) An anatomical gift may not be made by a person listed in subsection (a) if:

    (1) a person in a prior class is available at the time of death to make an anatomical gift;

    (2) the person proposing to make an anatomical gift knows of a refusal or contrary indications by the decedent; or

(3) the person proposing to make an anatomical gift knows of an objection to making an anatomical gift by a member of the person's class or a prior class.

(c) An anatomical gift by a person authorized under subsection (a) must be made by (i) a document of gift signed by the person or (ii) the person's telegraphic, recorded telephonic, or other recorded message, or other form of communication from the person that is contemporaneously reduced to writing and signed by the recipient.

(d) An anatomical gift by a person authorized under subsection (a) may be revoked by any member of the same or a prior class if, before procedures have begun for the removal of a part from the body of the decedent, the physician, surgeon, technician, or enucleator removing the part knows of the revocation.

(e) A failure to make an anatomical gift under subsection (a) is not an objection to the making of an anatomical gift.

SECTION 4. **Authorization by [coroner] [medical examiner] or [local public health official].**

(a) The [coroner] [medical examiner] may release and permit the removal of a part from a body within that official's custody, for transplantation or therapy, if:

(1) the official has received a request for the part from a hospital, physician, surgeon, or procurement organization;

(2) the official has made a reasonable effort, taking into account the useful life of the part, to locate and examine the decedent's medical records and inform persons listed in Section 3(a) of their option to make, or object to making, an anatomical gift;

(3) the official does not know of a refusal or contrary indication by the decedent or objection by a person having priority to act as listed in Section 3(a);

(4) the removal will be by a physician, surgeon, or technician; but in the case of eyes, by one of them or by an enucleator;

(5) the removal will not interfere with any autopsy or investigation;

(6) the removal will be in accordance with accepted medical standards; and

(7) cosmetic restoration will be done, if appropriate.

(b) If the body is not within the custody of the [coroner] [medical examiner], the [local public health officer] may release and permit the removal of any part from a body in the [local health officer's] custody for transplantation or therapy if the requirements of subsection (a) are met.

(c) An official releasing and permitting the removal of a part shall maintain a permanent record of the name of the decedent, the person making the request, the date and purpose of the request, the part requested, and the person to whom it was released.

SECTION 5. **Routine inquiry and required request; search and notification.**

(a) On or before admission to a hospital, or as soon as possible thereafter, a person designated by the hospital shall ask each patient who is at least [18] years of age: "Are you an organ or tissue donor?" If the answer is affirmative the person shall request a copy of the document of gift. If the answer is negative or there is no answer and the attending physician consents, the person designated shall discuss with the patient the option to make or refuse to make an anatomical gift. The answer to the question, an available copy of any document of gift or refusal to make an anatomical gift, and any other relevant information, must be placed in the patient's medical record.

(b) If, at or near the time of death of a patient, there is no medical record that the patient has made or refused to make an anatomical gift, the hospital [administrator] or a representative designated by the [administrator] shall discuss the option to make or refuse to make an anatomical gift and request the making of an anatomical gift pursuant to Section 3(a). The request must be made with reasonable discretion and sensitivity to the circumstances of the family. A request is not required if the gift is not suitable, based upon accepted medical standards, for a purpose specified in Section 6. An entry must be made in the medical record of the patient, stating the name and affiliation of the individual making the request, and of the name, response, and relationship to the patient of the person to whom the request was made. The [Commissioner of Health] shall [establish guidelines] [adopt regulations] to implement this subsection.

(c) The following persons shall make a reasonable search for a document of gift or other information identifying the bearer as a donor or as an individual who has refused to make an anatomical gift:

(1) a law enforcement officer, fireman, paramedic, or other emergency rescuer finding an individual who the searcher believes is dead or near death; and

(2) a hospital, upon the admission of an individual at or near the time of death, if there is not immediately available any other source of that information.

(d) If a document of gift or evidence of refusal to make an anatomical gift is located by the search required by subsection (c)(1), and the individual or body to whom it relates is taken to a hospital, the hospital must be notified of the contents and the document or other evidence must be sent to the hospital.

(e) If, at or near the time of death of a patient, a hospital knows that an anatomical gift has been made pursuant to Section 3(a) or a release and removal of a part has been permitted pursuant to Section 4, or that a patient or an individual identified as in transit to the hospital is a donor, the hospital shall notify the donee if one is named and known to the hospital; if not, it shall notify an appropriate procurement organization. The hospital shall cooperate in the implementation of the anatomical gift or release and removal of a part.

(f) A person who fails to discharge the duties imposed by this section is not subject to criminal or civil liability but is subject to appropriate administrative sanctions.

SECTION 6. **Persons Who May Become Donees; Purposes for Which Anatomical Gifts May be Made.**

(a) The following persons may become donees of anatomical gifts for the purposes stated:

(1) a hospital, physician, surgeon, or procurement organization, for transplantation, therapy, medical or dental education, research, or advancement of medical or dental science;

(2) an accredited medical or dental school, college, or university for education, research, advancement of medical or dental science; or

(3) a designated individual for transplantation or therapy needed by that individual.

(b) An anatomical gift may be made to a designated donee or without designating a donee. If a donee is not designated or if the donee is not available or rejects the anatomical gift, the anatomical gift may be accepted by any hospital.

(c) If the donee knows of the decedent's refusal or contrary indications to make an anatomical gift or that an anatomical gift by a member of a class having priority to act is opposed by a member of the same class or a prior class under Section 3(a), the donee may not accept the anatomical gift.

SECTION 7. **Delivery of document of gift.**

(a) Delivery of a document of gift during the donor's lifetime is not required for the validity of an anatomical gift.

(b) If an anatomical gift is made to a designated donee, the document of gift, or a copy, may be delivered to the donee to expedite the appropriate procedures after death. The document of gift, or a copy, may be deposited in any hospital, procurement organization, or registry office that accepts it for safekeeping or for facilitation of procedures after death. On request of an interested person, upon or after the donor's death, the person in possession shall allow the interested party to examine or copy the document of gift.

SECTION 8. **Rights and Duties at Death.**

(a) Rights of a donee created by an anatomical gift are superior to rights of others except with respect to autopsies under Section 11(b). A donee may accept or reject an anatomical gift. If a donee accepts an anatomical gift of an entire body, the donee, subject to the terms of the gift, may allow embalming and use of the body in funeral services. If the gift is of a part of a body, the donee, upon the death of the donor and before embalming, shall cause the part to be removed without unnecessary mutilation. After removal of the part, custody of the remainder of the body vests in the person under obligation to dispose of the body.

(b) The time of death must be determined by a physician or surgeon who attends the donor at death or, if none, the physician or surgeon who certifies the death. Neither the physician or surgeon who attends the donor at death nor the physician or surgeon who determines the time of death may participate in the procedures for removing or transplanting a part unless the document of gift designates a particular physician or surgeon pursuant to Section 2(d).

(c) If there has been an anatomical gift, a technician may remove any donated parts and an enucleator may remove any donated eyes or parts of eyes, after determination of death by a physician or surgeon.

SECTION 9. **Coordination of Procurement and Use.**

Each hospital in this State, after consultation with other hospitals and procurement organizations, shall establish agreements or affiliations for coordination of procurement and use of human bodies and parts.

SECTION 10. **Sale or Purchase of Parts Prohibited.**

(a) A person may not knowingly, for valuable consideration, purchase or sell a part for transplantation or therapy, if removal of the part is intended to occur after the death of the decedent.

(b) Valuable consideration does not include reasonable payment for the removal, processing, disposal, preservation, quality control, storage, transportation, or implementation of a part.

(c) A person who violates this section is guilty of a [felony] and upon conviction is subject to a fine not exceeding [$50,000] or imprisonment not exceeding [five] years, or both.

SECTION 11. **Examination, Autopsy, Liability.**

(a) An anatomical gift authorizes any reasonable examination necessary to assure medical acceptability of the gift for the purposes intended.

(b) The provisions of this [Act] are subject to the laws of this State governing autopsies.

(c) A hospital, physician, surgeon, [coroner], [medical examiner], [local public health officer], enucleator, technician, or other person, who acts in accordance with this [Act] or with the applicable anatomical gift law of another state [or a foreign country] or attempts in good faith to do so is not liable for that act in a civil action or criminal proceeding.

(d) An individual who makes an anatomical gift pursuant to Section 2 or 3 and the individual's estate are not liable for any injury or damage that may result from the making or the use of the anatomical gift.

SECTION 12. **Transitional Provisions.** This [Act] applies to a document of gift, revocation, or refusal to make an anatomical gift signed by the donor or a person authorized to make or object to making an anatomical gift before, on, or after the effective date of this [Act].

SECTION 13. **Uniformity of Application and Construction.** This [Act] shall be applied and construed to effectuate its general purpose to make uniform the law with respect to the subject of this [Act] among states enacting it.

SECTION 14. **Severability.** If any provision of this [Act] or its application thereof to any person or circumstance is held invalid, the invalidity does not affect other provisions or applications of this [Act] which can be given effect without the invalid provision or application, and to this end the provisions of this [Act] are severable.

SECTION 15. **Short Title.** This [Act] may be cited as the "Uniform Anatomical Gift Act (1987)."

SECTION 16. **Repeals.** The following acts and parts of acts are repealed:

(1)
(2)
(3)

SECTION 17. **Effective Date.** This [Act] takes effect_____.

Appendix C

NATIONAL ORGAN TRANSPLANT ACT

Public Law 98-507
98th Congress

An Act

To provide for the establishment of the Task Force on Organ Transplantation and the Organ Procurement and Transplantation Network, to authorize financial assistance for organ procurement organizations, and for other purposes.
Be it enacted by the Senate and House of Representatives of the United States of America in Congress assembled, That this Act may be cited as the "National Organ Transplant Act."

TITLE I—TASK FORCE ON ORGAN PROCUREMENT AND TRANSPLANTATION

ESTABLISHMENT AND DUTIES OF TASK FORCE

Sec. 101. (a) Not later than ninety days after the date of the enactment of this Act, the Secretary of Health and Human Services (hereinafter in this title referred to as the "Secretary") shall establish a Task Force on Organ Transplantation (hereinafter in this title referred to as the "Task Force").
(b)(1) The Task Force shall—
  (A) conduct comprehensive examinations of the medical, legal, ethical, economic, and social issues presented by human organ procurement and transplantation.
  (B) prepare the assessment described in paragraph (2) and the report described in paragraph (3), and
  (C) advise the Secretary with respect to the development of regulations for grants under section 371 of the Public Health Service Act.
(2) The Task Force shall make an assessment of immunosuppressive medications used to prevent organ rejection in transplant patients, including—
  (A) an analysis of the safety, effectiveness, and costs (including cost-savings from improved success rates of transplantation) of different modalities of treatment;
  (B) an analysis of the extent of insurance reimbursement for long-term immunosuppressive drug therapy for organ transplant patients by private insurers and the public sector;
  (C) an identification of problems that patients encounter in obtaining immunosuppressive medications; and
  (D) an analysis of the comparative advantages of grants, coverage under existing Federal programs, or other means to assure that individuals who need such medications can obtain them.
(3) The Task Force shall prepare a report which shall include—

(A) an assessment of public and private efforts to procure human organs for transplantation and an identification of factors that diminish the number of organs available for transplantation;

(B) an assessment of problems in coordinating the procurement of viable human organs including skin and bones.

(C) recommendations for the education and training of health professionals, including physicians, nurses, and hospital and emergency care personnel, with respect to organ procurement;

(D) recommendations for the education of the general public, the clergy, law enforcement officers, members of local fire departments, and other agencies and individuals that may be instrumental in affecting organ procurement;

(E) recommendations for assuring equitable access by patients to organ transplantation and for assuring the equitable allocation of donated organs among transplant centers and among patients medically qualified for an organ transplant;

(F) an identification of barriers to the donation of organs to patients with special emphasis upon pediatric patients, including an assessment of—

(i) barriers to the improved identification of organ donors and their families and organ recipients;

(ii) the number of potential organ donors and their geographical distribution;

(iii) current health care services provided for patients who need organ transplantation and organ procurement procedures, systems, and programs which affect such patients;

(iv) cultural factors affecting the facility with respect to the donation of the organs; and

(v) ethical and economic issues relating to organ transplantation needed by chronically ill patients;

(G) recommendations for the conduct and coordination of continuing research concerning all aspects of the transplantation of organs;

(H) an analysis of the factors involved in insurance reimbursement for transplant procedures by private insurers and the public sector;

(I) an analysis of the manner in which organ transplantation technology is diffused among and adopted by qualified medical centers, including a specification of the number and geographical distribution of qualified medical centers using such technology and an assessment of whether the number of centers using such technology is sufficient or excessive and of whether the public has sufficient access to medical procedures using such technology; and

(J) an assessment of the feasibility of establishing, and of the likely effectiveness of, a national registry of human organ donors.

MEMBERSHIP

Sec. 102. (a) The Task Force shall be composed of twenty-five members as follows:
(1) Twenty-one members shall be appointed by the Secretary which:

(A) nine members shall be physicians or scientists who are eminent in the various medical and scientific specialties related to human organ transplantations;

(B) three members shall be individuals who are not physicians and who represent the field of human organ procurement;

(C) four members shall be individuals who are not physicians and who as a group have expertise in the fields of law, theology, ethics, health care financing, and the social and behavioral sciences;

(D) three members shall be individuals who are not physicians or scientists and who are members of the general public; and

(E) two members shall be individuals who represent private health insurers or self-insurers.

(2) The Surgeon General of the United States, the Director of the National Institutes of Health, the Commissioner of the Food and Drug Administration, and the Administrator of the Health Care Financing Administration shall be ex officio members.
(b) No individual who is a full-time officer or employee of the United States may be appointed under subsection (a)(1) to the Task Force. A vacancy in the Task Force shall be filled in the manner in which the original appointment was made. A vacancy in the Task Force shall not affect its powers.
(c) Members shall be appointed for the life of the Task Force.
(d) The Task Force shall select a Chairman from among its members who are appointed under subsection (a)(1).
(e) Thirteen members of the Task Force shall constitute a quorum, but a lesser number may hold hearings.
(f) The Task Force shall hold its first meeting on a date specified by the Secretary which is not later than thirty days after the date on which the Secretary establishes the Task Force under section 101. Thereafter, the Task Force shall meet at the call of the Chairman or a majority of its members, but shall meet at least three times during the life of the Task Force.
(g)(1) Each member of the Task Force who is not an officer or employee of the United States shall be compensated at a rate equal to the daily equivalent of the annual rate of basic pay in effect for grade GS-18 of the General Schedule under section 5332 of title 5, United States Code, for each day (including travel time) during which such member is engaged in the actual performance of duties as a member of the Task Force. Each member of the Task Force who is an officer or employee of the United States shall receive no additional compensation.
(2) While away from their homes or regular places of business in the performance of duties for the Task Force, all members of the Task Force shall be allowed travel expenses, including per diem in lieu of subsistence, at rates authorized for employees of agencies under sections 5702 and 5703 of title 5, United States Code.

SUPPORT FOR THE TASK FORCE

Sec. 103. (a) Upon request of the Task Force, the head of any Federal agency is authorized to detail, on a reimbursable basis, any of the personnel of such agency to the Task Force to assist the Task Force in carrying out its duties under this Act.
(b) The Secretary shall provide the Task Force with such administrative and support services as the Task Force may require to carry out its duties.

REPORT CENTER

Sec. 104. (a) The Task Force may transmit to the Secretary, the Committee on Labor and Human Resources of the Senate, and the Committee on Energy and Commerce of the House of Representatives such interim reports as the Task Force considers appropriate.
(b) Not later than seven months after the date on which the Task Force is established by the Secretary under section 101, the Task Force shall transmit a report to the Secretary, the Committee on Labor and Human Resources of the Senate, and the Committee on Energy and Commerce of the House of Representatives on its assessment under section 101(b)(2) of immunosuppressive medications used to prevent organ rejection.

(c) Not later than twelve months after the date on which the Task Force is established by the Secretary under section 101, the Task Force shall transmit a final report to the secretary, the Committee on Labor and Human Resources of the Senate, and the Committee on Energy and Commerce of the House of Representatives. The final report of the Task Force shall include—
(1) a description of any findings and conclusions of the Task Force made pursuant to any examination conducted under section 101(b)(1)(A),
(2) the matters specified in section 101(b)(3), and
(3) such recommendations as the Task Force considers appropriate.

TERMINATION

Sec. 105. The Task Force shall terminate three months after the date on which the Task Force transmits the report required by section 104(c).

TITLE II—ORGAN PROCUREMENT ACTIVITIES

Sec. 201. Part H of title III of the Public Health Service Act is amended to read as follows:

"PART H—ORGAN TRANSPLANTS

"ASSISTANCE FOR ORGAN PROCUREMENT ORGANIZATIONS

"Sec. 317. (a)(1) The Secretary may make grants for the planning of qualified organ procurement organizations described in subsection (b).
"(2) The Secretary may make grants for the establishment, initial operation, and expansion of qualified organ procurement organizations described in subsection (b).
"(3) In making grants under paragraphs (1) and (2), the Secretary shall—
   "(A) take into consideration any recommendations made by the Task Force on Organ Transplantation established under section 101 of the National Organ Transplant Act, and
   "(B) give special consideration to applications which cover geographical areas which are not adequately served by organ procurement organizations.
"(b)(1) A qualified organ procurement organization for which grants may be made under subsection (a) is an organization which, as determined by the Secretary, will carry out the functions described in paragraph (2) and—
   "(A) is a nonprofit entity.
   "(B) has accounting and other fiscal procedures (as specified by the Secretary) necessary to assure the fiscal stability of the organization,
   "(C) has an agreement with the Secretary to be reimbursed under title XVIII of the Social Security Act for the procurement of kidneys.
   "(D) has procedures to obtain payment for non-renal organs provided to transplant centers,
   "(E) has a defined services area which is a geographical area of sufficient size which (unless the service area comprises an entire State) will include at least fifty potential organ donors each year and which either includes an entire standard metropolitan statistical area (as specified by the Office of Management and Budget) or does not include any part of such an area,

"(F) has a director and such other staff, including the organ donation coordinators and organ procurement specialists necessary to effectively obtain organs from donors in its service area, and

"(G) has a board of directors or an advisory board which— "(i) is composed of—

"(I) members who represent hospital administrators, intensive care or emergency room personnel, tissue banks, and voluntary health associations in its service area,

"(II) members who represent the public residing in such area,

"(III) a physician with knowledge, experience, or skill in the field of histocompatibility,

"(IV) a physician with knowledge or skill in the field of neurology, and

"(V) from each transplant center in its service area which has arrangements described in paragraph (2)(G) with the organization, a member who is a surgeon who has practicing privileges in such center and who performs organ transplant surgery,

(ii) has the authority to recommend policies for the procurement of organs and the other functions described in paragraph (2), and

(iii) has no authority over any other activity of the organization.

"(2) An organ procurement organization shall—

"(A) have effective agreements, to identify potential organ donors, with a substantial majority of the hospitals and other health area entities in its service area which have facilities for organ donations,

"(B) conduct and participate in systematic efforts, including professional education, to acquire all usable organs from potential donors

"(C) arrange for the acquisition and preservation of donated organs and provide quality standards for the acquisition of organs which are consistent with the standards adopted by the Organ Procurement and Transplantation Network under section 372(b)(2)(D),

"(D) arrange for the appropriate tissue typing of donated organs,

"(E) have a system to allocate donated organs among transplant centers and patients according to established medical criteria,

"(F) provide or arrange for the transportation of donated organs to transplant centers,

"(G) have arrangements to coordinate its activities with transplant centers in its service area.

"(H) participate in the Organ Procurement Transplantation Network established under section 372,

"(I) have arrangements to cooperate with tissue banks for the retrieval, processing, preservation, storage, and distribution of tissues as may be appropriate to assure that all usable tissues are obtained from potential donors, and

"(J) evaluate annually the effectiveness of the organization in acquiring potentially available organs.

"(c) for grants under subsection (a) there are authorized to be appropriated $5,000,000 for fiscal year 1985, $8,000,000 for fiscal year 1986, and $12,000,000 for fiscal year 1987.

"ORGAN PROCUREMENT AND TRANSPLANTATION NETWORK

"Sec. 372. (a) The Secretary shall by contract provide for the establishment and operation of an Organ Procurement and Transplantation Network which meets the requirements of subsection (b). The amount provided under such contract in any fiscal year may not exceed $2,000,000. Funds for such contracts shall be made available from funds available to the Public Health Service from appropriations for fiscal years beginning after fiscal year 1984.

"(b)(1) The Organ Procurement and Transplantation Network shall carry out the functions described in paragraph (2) and shall—

"(A) be a private nonprofit entity which is not engaged in any activity unrelated to organ procurement, and

"(B) have a board of directors which includes representatives of organ procurement organizations (including organizations which have received grants under section 371), transplant centers, voluntary health associations, and the general public.

"(2) The Organ Procurement and Transplantation Network shall—

"(A) establish in one location or through regional centers—

"(i) a national list of individuals who need organs, and

"(ii) a national system, through the use of computers and in accordance with established medical criteria, to match organs and individuals included in the list, especially individuals whose immune system makes it difficult for them to receive organs,

"(B) maintain a twenty-four hour telephone service to facilitate matching organs with individuals included in the list,

"(C) assist organ procurement organizations in the distribution of organs which cannot be placed within the service areas of the organizations,

"(D) adopt and use standards of quality for the acquisition and transportation of donated organs,

"(E) prepare and distribute, on a regionalized basis, samples of blood sera from individuals who are included on the list and whose immune system makes it difficult for them to receive organs, in order to facilitate matching the compatibility of such individuals with organ donors,

"(F) coordinate, as appropriate, the transportation of organs from organ procurement organizations to transplant centers,

"(G) provide information to physicians and other health professionals regarding organ donation, and

"(H) collect, analyze, and publish data concerning organ donation and transplants.

"SCIENTIFIC REGISTRY

"Sec. 373. The Secretary shall, by grant or contract, develop and maintain a scientific registry of the recipients of organ transplants. The registry shall include such information respecting patients and transplant procedures as the Secretary deems necessary to an ongoing evaluation of the scientific and clinical status of organ transplantation. The Secretary shall prepare for inclusion in the report under section 376 an analysis of information derived from the registry.

"GENERAL PROVISIONS RESPECTING GRANTS AND CONTRACTS

"Sec. 374. (a) No grant may be made under section 371 or 373 or contract entered into under section 372 or 373 unless an application therefore has been submitted to, and approved by, the Secretary. Such an application shall be in such form and shall be submitted in such manner as the Secretary shall by regulation prescribe.

"(b)(1) In considering applications for grants under section 371—

"(A) the Secretary shall give priority to any applicant which has a formal agreement of cooperation with all transplant centers in its proposed service area,

"(B) the Secretary shall give special consideration to organizations which met the requirements of section 371(b) before the date of the enactment of this section, and

"(C) the Secretary shall not discriminate against an applicant solely because it provides health care services other than those related to organ procurement.

The Secretary may not make a grant for more than one organ procurement organization which serves the same service area.

"(2) A grant for planning under section 371 may be made for one year with respect to any organ procurement organization and may not exceed $100,000.

"(3) Grants under section 371 for the establishment, initial operation, or expansion of organ procurement organizations may be made for two years. No such grant may exceed $500,000 for any year and no organ procurement organization may receive more than $800,000 for initial operation or expansion.

"(c)(1) The Secretary shall determine the amount of a grant made under section 371 or 373. Payments under such grants may be made in advance on the basis of estimates or by the way of reimbursement, with necessary adjustments on account of underpayments or overpayments, and in such installments and on such terms and conditions as the Secretary finds necessary to carry out the purposes of such grants.

"(2)(A) Each recipient of a grant under section 371 or 373 shall keep such records as the Secretary shall prescribe, including records which fully disclose the amount and disposition by such recipient of the proceeds of such grant, the total cost of the undertaking in connection with which such grant was made, and the amount of that portion of the cost of the undertaking supplied by other sources, and such other records as will facilitate an effective audit.

"(B) The Secretary and the Comptroller General of the United States, or any of their duly authorized representatives, shall have access for the purpose of audit and examination to any books, documents, papers, and records of the recipient of a grant under section 371 or 373 that are pertinent to such grant

"(d) For purposes of this part:

"(1) The term "transplant center" means a health care facility in which transplants of organs are performed.

"(2) The term "organ" means the human kidney, liver, heart, lung, pancreas, and any other human organ (other than corneas and eyes) specified by the Secretary by regulation and for purposes of section 373; such term includes bone marrow.

"ADMINISTRATION

"Sec. 375. The Secretary shall, during fiscal years 1985, 1986, 1987, and 1988, designate and maintain an identifiable administrative unit in the Public Health Service to—

"(1) administer this part and coordinate with the organ procurement activities under title XVIII of the Social Security Act,

"(2) conduct a program of public information to inform the public of the need for organ donations,

"(3) Provide technical assistance to organ procurement organizations receiving funds under section 371, the Organ Procurement and Transplantation Network established under section 372, and other entities in the health care system involved in organ donations, procurement, and transplants, and

"(4) one year after the date on which the Task Force on Organ Transplantation transmits its final report under section 104(c) of the National Organ Transplant Act, and annually thereafter through fiscal year 1988, submit to Congress an annual report on the status of organ donation and coordination services and include in the report an analysis of the efficiency and effectiveness of the procurement and allocation of organs and a description of problems encountered in the procurement and allocation of organs.

"REPORT

"Sec. 376. The Secretary shall annually publish a report on the scientific and clinical status of organ transplantation. The Secretary shall consult with the Director of the National Institutes of Health and the Commissioner of the Food and Drug Administration in the preparation of the report."

TITLE III—PROHIBITION OF ORGAN PURCHASES

Sec. 301. (a) It shall be unlawful for any person to knowingly acquire, receive, or otherwise transfer any human organ for valuable consideration for use in human transplantation if the transfer affects interstate commerce.
(b) Any person who violates subsection (a) shall be fined not more than $50,000 or imprisoned not more than five years, or both.
(c) For purposes of subsection (a):
(1) The term "human organ" means the human kidney, liver, heart, lung, pancreas, bone marrow, cornea, eye, bone, and skin, and any other human organ specified by the Secretary of Health and Human Services by regulation.
(2) The term "valuable consideration" does not include the reasonable payments associated with the removal, transportation, implantation, processing, preservation, quality control, and storage of a human organ or the expense of travel, housing and lost wages incurred by the donor of a human organ in connection with the donation of the organ.
(3) The term "interstate commerce" has the meaning prescribed for it by section 201(b) of the Federal Food, Drug and Cosmetic Act.

TITLE IV—MISCELLANEOUS

BONE MARROW REGISTRY DEMONSTRATION AND STUDY

Sec. 401. (a) Not later than nine months after the date of enactment of this Act, the Secretary of Health and Human Services shall hold a conference on the feasibility of establishing and the effectiveness of a national registry of voluntary bone marrow donors.
(b) If the conference held under subsection (a) finds that it is feasible to establish a national registry of voluntary donors of bone marrow and that such a registry is likely to be effective in matching donors with recipients, the Secretary of Health and Human Services, acting through the Assistant Secretary for Health, shall, for purposes of the study under subsection (c), establish a registry of voluntary donors of bone marrow. The Secretary shall assure that—

(1) donors of bone marrow listed in the registry have given an informed consent to the donation of bone marrow; and

(2) the names of the donors in the registry are kept confidential and access to the names and any other information in the registry is restricted to personnel who need the information to maintain and implement the registry, except that access to such other information shall be provided for purposes of the study under subsection (c).

If the conference held under subsection (a) makes the finding described in this subsection, the Secretary shall establish the registry not later than six months after the completion of the conference.

(c) The Secretary of Health and Human Services, acting through the Assistant Secretary for Health, shall study the establishment and implementation of the registry under subsection (b) to identify the issues presented by the establishment of such a registry, to evaluate participation of bone marrow donors, to assess the implementation of the informed consent and confidentiality requirements, and to determine if the establishment of a permanent bone marrow registry is needed and appropriate. The Secretary shall report the results of the study to the Committee on Energy and Commerce of the House of Representatives and the Committee on Labor and Human Resources of the Senate not later than two years after the date the registry is established under subsection (b).

Approved October 19, 1984.

Appendix D

OMNIBUS BUDGET RECONCILIATION ACT OF 1986

(Selected Sections)

Sec. 9318. HOSPITAL PROTOCOLS FOR ORGAN PROCUREMENT AND STANDARDS FOR ORGAN PROCUREMENT AGENCIES.

(a) IN GENERAL.—Title XI of the Social Security Act is amended by inserting after section 1137 the following new section:

"HOSPITAL PROTOCOLS FOR ORGAN PROCUREMENT AND STANDARDS FOR ORGAN PROCUREMENT AGENCIES

"**Sec. 1138.(a)(1)** The Secretary shall provide that a hospital meeting the requirements of title XVIII or XIX may participate in the program established under such title only if—

"(A) the hospital establishes written protocols for the identification of potential donors that—

"(i) assure that families of potential organ donors are made aware of the option of organ or tissue donation and their option to decline,

"(ii) encourage discretion and sensitivity with respect to the circumstances, views, and beliefs of such families, and

"(iii) require that an organ procurement agency designated by the Secretary pursuant to subsection (b)(1)(F) be notified of potential organ donors; and

"(B) In the case of a hospital in which organ transplants are performed, the hospital is a member of, and abides by the rules and requirements of, the Organ Procurement and Transplantation Network established pursuant to section 372 of the Public Health Service Act (in this section referred to as the 'Network').

"(2) For purposes of this subsection, the term 'organ' means a human kidney, liver, heart, lung, pancreas, and any other human organ or tissue specified by the Secretary for purposes of this subsection.

"(b)(1) The Secretary shall provide that payment may be made under title XVIII or XIX with respect to organ procurement costs attributable to payments made to an organ procurement agency only if the agency —

"(A)(i) is a qualified organ procurement organization (as described in section 371(b) of the Public Health Service Act) that is operating under a grant made under section 371(b) of such Act, or (ii) has been certified or recertified by the Secretary within the previous two years as meeting the standards to be a qualified organ procurement organization (as so described);

"(B) meets the requirements that are applicable under such title for organ procurement agencies;

"(C) meets performance-related standards prescribed by the Secretary;

"(D) is a member of, and abides by the rules and requirements of, the Network;

"(E) allocates organs, within its service area and nationally, in accordance with medical criteria and the policies of the Network; and

"(F) is designated by the Secretary as an organ procurement organization payments to which may be treated as organ procurement costs for purposes of reimbursement under such title.

"(2) The Secretary may not designate more than one organ procurement organization for each service area (described in section 371(b)(1)(E) of the Public Health Service Act) under paragraph (1)(F)."

(b)EFFECTIVE DATES—(1) Section 1138(a) of the Social Security Act shall apply to hospitals participating in the programs under titles XVIII and XIX of such Act as of October 1, 1987.

(2) Section 1138(b) of such Act shall apply to costs of organs procured on or after October 1, 1987.

Sec. 9335. PAYMENT RATES FOR RENAL SERVICES AND IMPROVEMENTS IN ADMINISTRATION OF END STAGE RENAL DISEASE NETWORKS AND PROGRAM.

* *

(c) COVERAGE OF IMMUNOSUPPRESSIVE DRUGS.—

(1) IN GENERAL.—Section 1861(s)(2) of the Social Security Act (42U.S.C.1395x(2)(2) is amended—

(A) by striking "and" at the end of subparagraph (H)(ii),

(B) by inserting "and" at the end of subparagraph (I), and

(C) by inserting after subparagraph (I) the following new subparagraph:

"(J) immunosuppressive drugs furnished, to an individual who receives an organ transplant for which payment is made under this title, within 1 year after the date of the transplant procedure;".

(2) EFFECTIVE DATE.—The amendments made by paragraph (1) shall apply to immunosuppressive drugs furnished on or after January 1, 1987.

* *

Appendix E

GLOSSARY

Azathioprine. One of the major immunosuppressive drugs, sold under the brand name Imuran, that is employed to prevent the body from rejecting a transplanted organ.

Cadaveric. Pertaining to a dead body whose heart beat has stopped.

Crossmatch. Testing which determines whether there is a substance in the blood of a potential organ recipient which will react against the cells of the donor.

Cyclosporine. An immunosuppressive drug, sold under the brand name Sandimmune, that helps to prevent organ rejection in transplant recipients.

Decedent. Someone who has died, according to the legal definition of death. A decedent, although technically dead, may have his or her heart beat and other vital functions maintained indefinitely by artificial means.

Donee. One who receives a gift.

Donor. One who makes a gift.

Dura. One of the some twenty-five tissues and organs that can now be transplanted, the dura is the hard covering of the brain which can be used in surgery to repair wounds from serious head injuries or from surgical removal of tumors.

Encouraged voluntarism. The type of system of organ and tissue donation in the United States, whereby anatomical gifts come through voluntary acts of conscience of individuals or their next of kin. Also see **Presumed consent laws** below, regarding the other major, contrasting legal approach to organ donation found in a number of other countries.

Entire body donation. The donation of one's complete body to a medical or dental school for the purpose of teaching and research. If one chooses to donate one's entire body, then donation of individual organs for transplantation is not possible.

Extrarenal. Pertaining to organs of the body other than the kidney. The heart, liver, and pancreas, for example, are all extrarenal organs of the body.

Eye Enucleation. The removal of the eyeball in such a way that it comes out clean and whole.

Histocompatability. The degree to which organ or tissue taken from a donor matches the tissue type of the transplant recipient, as determined by technical markers.

Immune System. The body's natural defense system against germs, viruses, and other foreign substances. The body cannot separate "good" intruders from "bad" and attempts to destroy anything different from its own tissue, including transplanted organs. The regular use of immunosuppressive drugs to prevent rejection must therefore accompany organ transplants. As an undesirable side effect, these drugs also lower the body's resistance to viruses and germs.

Immunosuppressive Drugs. Drugs that are designed to prevent the body from rejecting a transplanted organ or tissue. Cyclosporine is the immunosuppressive drug most often used today because of its high rate of effectiveness.

Living, related donor. A living, blood relative who gives up one of his or her kidneys to be transplanted into the body of someone in the family whose kidneys have failed. Living, related donor transplants have a much higher rate of success than those involved unrelated donors. Of those transplants involving a living, related donor, a patient's brothers or sisters usually provide better tissue matches than those from a parent or child (blood tests determine the degree of compatability of donor and recipient tissue).

Match. See crossmatch.

National Organ Transplant Act. Signed into law in October of 1984, this federal Act (Public Law 98-507) mandated a comprehensive review of the medical, legal, ethical, social, and economic issues involved in human organ procurement and transplantation. The National Task Force on Organ Transplantation authorized by this Act conducted a year-long examination and made a series of recommendations designed to strengthen the ability of the nation's health care system to provide organ transplants. See Chapter 3 for the in-depth findings of the Task Force and Appendix C for the text of the Act.

Non-immigrant alien. An individual who is not a citizen of the United States and who does not live in this country. The practice of wealthy non-immigrant aliens purchasing organs from Americans for transplantation is under increasing scrutiny and possible legal sanction.

Organ procurement agencies. Organizations which coordinate activities involved in the recovery of donated organs for transplant purposes. Their principal roles include preserving donated organs, making arrangements for transporting organs, and tissue typing of donated organs. They also provide information about donation and transplantation and participate in educational activites to encourage anatomical gifts.

Paramount. Above others in rank, authority, power, or jurisdiction. Many state anatomical gift laws declare that the donee's rights are paramount to the rights of others; in other words, the donee's rights are superior to and take precedence over the rights of other interested parties.

Prednisone. This immunosuppressive drug is a steroid, taken in conjunction with other anti-rejection drugs to prevent organ rejection.

Presumed consent laws. Laws in effect in some countries, such as France, which permit removal of organs or tissues after death unless the deceased or a family member has objected. In the United States, the principle of presumed consent is applied primarily to the donation of corneas but not to major organs. The removal of corneas is permitted in certain cases under the jurisdiction of a coroner or medical examiner (some twenty-six states and the District of Columbia currently allow such removal).

Renal. Pertaining to the kidney. For example, there currently are more than ten times as many renal transplants performed annually as heart transplants.

Rejection. The natural response of the body to any foreign materials, including transplanted organs. This immune response is kept in check in most cases of transplanted organs or tissues by the use of immunosuppressive drugs, such as cyclosporine and prednisone.

Required request. Procedures mandated by state and federal laws, requiring hospitals routinely to ask for organ donations from all families of dying patients, unless there exists a compelling reason not to do so.

Routine inquiry. Another term for "required request."

Uniform Anatomical Gift Act. The 1968 act (revised in August, 1987) approved by the National Conference of Commissioners on Uniform State Law and the American Bar Association which has served as a model for state legislation on organ and tissue donation in the United States for the past twenty years. Almost every state's laws on anatomical gifts, with the exception of Utah and Wisconsin's, closely parallel point by point this model act.

Uniform Determination of Death Act. The model act which establishes the standard legal definition of death as the irreversible cessation of brain function. This definition of death has been legally adopted by 40 states and the District of Columbia to date.

Uniform Donor Card. A form, usually in the shape of a card that can easily be carried in the pocket, which allows one to make a gift of one's organs and tissues after death and to specify the terms of the gift. This form is legally binding in all fifty states and the District of Columbia. A copy of this form appears in Appendix A.

Xenographs. Across-the-species transplants, such as that attempted in the case of Baby Fae. Research in the use of xenographs is one possible direction that transplantation may take in the future, given the present scarcity of human organs available for transplantation.

Appendix F

SUPPORT SERVICES

Ambassadors for Corneal Transplants
Lions Eye Bank of Delaware Valley
Wills Eye Hospital, 9th and Walnut Streets
Philadelphia, Pennsylvania 19107
(215) 569-3937

The Ambassadors for Corneal Transplants provide a network of support for individuals who face corneal transplant surgery. Persons who have already received corneal transplants have organized to counsel others who are awaiting such surgery. In addition to counseling, the volunteers of this organization also engage in fund raising, public education, and commentary on state and federal legislation affecting transplantation.

American Association of Tissue Banks
1350 Beverly Road, Suite 220-A
McLean, Virginia 22101

The American Association of Tissue Banks is a scientific, not-for-profit national organization founded in 1976 to facilitate the availability of transplantable tissues of uniform high quality. The Association publishes standards to ensure that the conduct of tissue banking meets acceptable technical and ethical norms as well as technical manuals to guide the recovery, processing, preservation, and distribution of transplantable tissue. Specific guidelines include screening for AIDS and Hepatitis, maintenance of asepsis, sterile procurement, labeling, storage, donor selection criteria, required testing, and record keeping. AATB also carries out a program of inspection and accreditation to ensure professional standards. The Association sponsors important scientific exchange of information through meetings, seminars, and workshops and supports promotional and educational programs for the purpose of stimulating tissue donation.

American Council on Transplantation
700 N. Fairfax Street, Suite 505
Alexandria, Virginia 22314
(703) 836-4301

The Council provides the only national forum for discussion and formulation of public policy regarding transplantation. Its four divisions, the Organ Retrieval and Networking Forum, the Patient and Family Issues Forum, the Professional Education Forum, and the Public Education Forum address specific areas: (1) optimization of processes of donation and retrieval of organs and tissues; (2) search for solutions to the social, ethical, psychological, and economic problems of transplant patients and their families; (3) educational programs for health professionals to help them understand the transplantation process, the needs of donor families, and how to become more effective in encouraging organ and tissue donation; (4) development of methods and programs to encourage the public to become potential donors and to donate organs and tissues of loved ones as the opportunity arises; conduct of studies on the perspectives of minorities about organ and tissue donation and transplantation. Current individual membership dues are $15.00 ($25.00 for a family). ACT through its Patient and Family Issues Forum offers transplant patients and their families the opportunity to meet with other interested and involved individuals. It publishes a newsletter, *Transplant Action,* six times a year, which is intended to foster a better understanding of the many complex issues of organ and tissue transplantation.

American Kidney Fund
6110 Executive Boulevard
Rockville, Maryland 20852
(301) 881-3052
National Toll Free: (800) 638-8299
Maryland Toll Free: (800) 492-8361

The Fund provides financial assistance to kidney patients for treatment-related expenses, including transportation, special dietary needs, and living expenses. In 1987, it awarded direct financial aid grants to over 4,300 patients, as well as assistance to 920 In-Center Emergency Funds. Its revenues also support programs in community services, public and professional education, kidney donor development, and research. It provides organ donor cards as well as educational materials such as brochures, videocassettes, and slides that deal with the topics of donation and transplantation. The AKF has available an excellent brochure which presents basic facts about living, related donors (individuals giving one of their kidneys to a family member in need of a transplant). The publication describes in detail the experiences of 536 persons of all ages and incomes, ethnic backgrounds and religious beliefs, who have donated a kidney.

American Liver Foundation
998 Pompton Avenue
Cedar Grove, New Jersey 07009
(800) 223-0179 or (412) DONORS 7

Through its twenty-five chapters and national radio and T.V. campaigns, the American Liver Foundation carries on a year around program encouraging organ donation. As part of its services to liver patients and their families, it offers a full range of support services and networking assistance. It provides information on transplantation, including educational programs, lectures and discussion groups, aids in helping individuals find the right specialist, and counsels patients about financial options. It serves as trustee for transplant funds, providing professional administration without charge, and advises on fund raising. As the largest private contributor to liver research, the Foundation encourages promising young researchers to enter the field of liver research through programs of student and postdoctoral fellowships, many of which relate to transplantation. The Foundation actively seeks members and volunteers to assist in its ongoing educational and support programs for people of all ages, with all types of liver diseases.

Anatomical Gift Association
(312) 733-5283

The agency to contact if you live in Illinois and want to donate your entire body to a medical school upon death. Individuals living in other states who wish to make this type of donation should directly contact the department of surgery at a local medical or dental school. Most states require a signed, separate body donation form, obtainable from the particular school accepting your gift, in addition to your Uniform Donor Card specifying donation of the entire body.

Children's Liver Foundation
76 S. Orange Avenue, Suite 202
South Orange, New Jersey 07079
(201) 761-1111

This non-profit foundation provides support for families of children with liver disease, maintaining an information referral network whereby parents and families can meet and share common experiences and problems. It also guides families in the areas of insurance, Medicaid, and CHAMPUS coverage of medical costs of transplants, fund raising, and referral to other support organizations. The foundation supports research in pediatric liver disease through grants for liver disease research and participates in public and professional education through pamphlets, lectures, public service announcements, and symposia. It is active in legal reform and has been instrumental in the passage of "required request" legislation and laws mandating screening of infants for galactosemia in a number of states. One of its chief goals is to educate the lay public, medical professional, and Washington about pediatric liver disease, organ donation, and organ transplantation.

Children's Transplant Foundation
PO Box 2106
Laurinburg, North Carolina 28352
(919) 276-7171; after hours: (919) 276-2722

In spite of its name, this organization, originally started in 1981 on behalf of children undergoing liver transplants, works with adults as well as children, providing both financial assistance and emotional support to all types of transplant patients and their families. Through arrangements with private major corporations which allow use of their jets, it is able to supply transportation to transplant centers for evaluation and treatment as well as for the transplant operation itself. It serves as a patient advocate, intervening with private insurance companies and state Medicaid programs to help obtain payment. It is able to provide financial assistance with certain medical care expenses ancillary to the transplant itself. It also maintains family residences at two transplant centers for families who cannot afford lodging and food and hopes to open similar facilities at other transplant centers in the future.

Consortium of Registered Nurses for Eye Acquisition (CORNEA)
1511 K Street, NW, Suite 830
Washington, DC 20005-1401
(202) 628-4280

A non-profit organization designed to promote the role of nurses in the transplantation process, CORNEA was formed in 1983 to support eye banks and health care facilities in their efforts to increase organ and tissue donation. Working with hospital administrators and giving inservice programs, CORNEA has developed model programs for obtaining donations in hospitals. A direct increase of organ and tissue donations occur at locations with CORNEA programs. CORNEA collaborates with other nursing and transplant organizations, including the Eye Bank Association of America, to advance organ and tissue donation.

232 Support Services

The Deafness Research Foundation
342 Madison Avenue
New York, New York 10017
(212) 684-6556

The Foundation supports research regarding temporal bones. The temporal bone is the part of the skull containing the structures of hearing and balance—the middle and inner ear. As a fund-raising organization for research, the Foundation gives monies to different institutions and individuals involved in promising new research on hearing impairments. It supports the National Temporal Bone Banks program, administered by four regional centers, which actively seek persons with ear disease or hearing loss to make an anatomical gift of their internal ear structures for scientific study after their death. See separate listings for Eastern (and National) Center of the National Temporal Bone Bank, Midwestern Center, Southern Center, and Western Center. While volunteers are not needed, the Foundation does hire high school students. Private financial donations to support research in this area are accepted.

Department of Health & Human Services
See listing under **Office of Organ Transplantation.**

Eastern (and National) Center of the National Temporal Bone Bank
Massachusetts Eye and Ear Infirmary
243 Charles Street
Boston, Massachusetts 02114
(617) 573-3700

This regional center seeks persons living in the eastern part of the United States with ear disease or hearing loss to make an anatomical gift of their internal ear structures for scientific study upon their death. Files of each donor's hearing and medical records are maintained at the regional center and kept up-to-date for later comparison with the microscopic findings in the donated temporal bones. This method of study contributes to the understanding of the process of diseases affecting hearing and to the development of treatments for such disorders. The following states are served by this center: Connecticut, Maine, Massachusetts, New Hampshire, New Jersey, New York, Pennsylvania, Rhode Island, and Vermont. To make a pledge to donate your temporal bones, contact the regional center serving your state, whereupon you will be sent a donor packet. There is no age limit for donors. The study of your temporal bones is scientifically useful if you have any type of ear problem, such as deafness, dizziness, facial palsy, infection, tumor, or injury. Temporal bone donation does not interfere with other kinds of organ donation.

Eye Bank Association of America
1511 K Street, NW, Suite 830
Washington, DC 20005-1401
(202) 628-4280

The Eye Bank Association, established in 1961 by the American Academy of Ophthalmology, is a non-profit organization of 93 eye banks in 42 states. The EBAA is dedicated to the restoration of sight through the promotion and advancement of eye banking. Through the efforts of EBAA, Congress continues to recognize March as National Eye Donor Month. Among its many professional and educational activities, the EBAA is involved in establishing and maintaining quality control in eye banking; creating research programs to improve methods of sight restoration; increasing public awareness of organ and tissue donation, and eye banking; providing physicians, nurses, and others with professional development programs. It hold a yearly educational conference, scientific session and annual meeting to offer up-to-date medical, professional, societal and other information on corneal and general transplantation. The EBAA has initiated programs to assist Latin American cities in developing eye banks. It is allied with CORNEA and Ambassadors for Corneal Transplants (see above).

The Eye-Bank for Sight Restoration, Inc.
210 East 64 Street
New York, New York 10021-7498
Administration: (212) 980-6700
Laboratory: (212) 838-9211

The world's first transplantation agency, founded in 1944 by Dr. R. Townley Paton, the Eye-Bank originally popularized the donor pledge card and provided donated eye tissue on a national basis. Patterned after its example, other agencies involving eyes as well as other organs and tissues were established. Today, the Eye-Bank serves eleven counties in the Southern Tier of New York State, including New York City. Its new Hispanic Outreach program, designed to increase the number of donors among the Spanish-speaking communities in its jurisdiction, provides a model for other cities and states with large Hispanic populations. Its Spanish-language videotape, "Ilumina una vida," is made available to various community groups. Since its founding, it has provided tissue for almost 30,000 corneal transplants.

The Florida Gift of Life Foundation
1301 S. Andrews Avenue, Suite 101
Ft. Lauderdale, Florida 33316
(305) 355-5722

The Foundation establishes academic and corporate gift programs to support transplant recipients. It sponsors donor awareness programs and a speakers' bureau and serves as a professional vehicle for families involved in fund raising. It also provides financial assistance for expenses ancillary to the transplant operation itself.

The Living Bank
PO Box 6725
Houston, Texas 77265
National 24-hour Hotline
1-800-528-2971
In Texas call
(713) 528-2971
Information during working hours
(713) 961-9431

The Living Bank is the world's largest multi-organ donor registry and referral service. A non-profit, non-medical facility, the Living Bank does not store donated organs or perform transplant surgery. A copy of its donor application is available by writing or calling. Upon submission, the information regarding your wishes will be stored on computer disk, available by phone 24 hours a day. A wallet card containing the phone number of the Living Bank and a summary of your donor registration will be sent to you, to be carried with your driver's license. When your death is imminent or has occurred, Living Bank personnel, when notified by phone, will find suitable recipients for your specified donated organs, if medically acceptable, or your entire body if you have so indicated. The Living Bank stresses that its registration does not conflict with others, since all such organizations, including organ banks, medical schools, hospitals, and driver's license bureaus, work together to facilitate organ and tissue transplantation. The Living Bank makes available by mail a number of audiovisual resources free of charge. Videotapes produced for a general audience such as "Chords—A Song of Life" and "The Gift of Life" provide comprehensive overviews of anatomical donation through interviews with transplant recipients and families as well as related medical personnel. Videotapes directed at medical professionals ("The Vital Link") and law enforcement personnel ("Police Training") are also available upon request.

Medic Alert
PO Box 1009
Turlock, California 95381-1009
1-800-344-3226
This organization provides members with metal bracelets or necklaces engraved with the special medical conditions of the wearer, such as "Diabetes—Insulin Dependent." In addition, emblems may also be marked "Organ Donor." A hotline number on the back of the emblem gives emergency personnel 24-hour access to your emergency medical records at Medic Alert headquarters. Each member also receives a wallet card with personal and medical information in addition to that engraved on the emblem. The basic $20 fee provides lifetime membership.

Midwestern Center of the National Temporal Bone Bank
University of Minnesota
PO Box 396 UMHC
Minneapolis, Minnesota 55455
(612) 624-5466
See the main listing for Eastern (and National) Center of the National Temporal Bone Bank. The following states are served by this center: Illinois, Indiana, Iowa, Kansas, Michigan, Minnesota, Missouri, Nebraska, North Dakota, Ohio, Oklahoma, South Dakota, and Wisconsin.

National Burn Victim Foundation
308 Main Street
Orange, New Jersey 07050
(201) 731-3112
The National Burn Victim Foundation provides emotional support and counseling for burn victims and their families and sponsors a wide variety of other burn-related services, support systems, and educational programs. Insofar as organ and tissue donations are concerned, the foundation serves as a referral agency regarding donations to skin banks.

National Heart Assist and Transplant Fund
519 W. Lancaster Avenue
Haverford, Pennsylvania 19041
(215) 527-5056
Established five years ago, this organization provides social, emotional, and financial counseling for heart transplant patients and their families. It advises individuals regarding sources of money,

political contacts, church and community groups willing to help, and insurance coverage available. It provides encouragement as well as technical expertise so that family and friends of patients know how to go into the community and ask for donations and advises how to set up fund-raising programs and attain non-profit status. Due to contact with most of the transplant centers throughout the United States, the Fund is in a position to offer advice to patients as to centers closer to home, existing support groups, alternative payment opportunities, status of state and federal coverage for heart transplantation as well as specific requirements within the centers in patient selection criteria. It has in some cases actually matched patients with centers where all expenses were paid. The Fund has also provided needy patients with grants to help cover the costs of medication, transportation, living expenses, home care, and other disease-related charges. The group is involved in education to increase donor awareness through public talks and school presentations, and it provides films and other educational materials to those wishing to give presentations within their community. It fields questions on all aspects of the heart transplant process. It welcomes inquiries and accepts financial donations, in the form of a monetary tribute to an individual, an outright donation, a service, or a bequest in a will, from those interested in supporting its work of providing assistance to heart transplant patients.

National Kidney Foundation, Inc.
30 East 33rd Street
New York, New York 10016
(800) 622-9010
(212) 889-2210

The National Kidney Foundation conducts a variety of programs in research, public and professional education, and community and patient services. In the latter category, it provides information and referral services for kidney patients and their families, drug banks, support groups, summer camps for children on dialysis and transplantation, transportation services, counseling and screening, and direct financial assistance to needy patients. The Foundation produces numerous publications on kidney and urinary tract diseases and hypertension and provides speakers to address patient and community groups. In regard to professional education, it sponsors scientific sessions, forums, and post graduate courses. Each year it conducts two major public education campaigns, the New Year's Resolution Campaign (to sign a donor card) and National Organ and Tissue Donor Awareness Week. The National Kidney Foundation actively seeks donations to support its services from both individuals and corporations. It relies on volunteers to sustain its many programs.

The New York Firefighters Skin Bank
At New York Hospital
525 E. 68th Street
New York, New York 10021
(212) 472-7546

Because of the New York firefighters' support of the work of the skin bank, which opened some eleven years ago, the New York Hospital chose to reflect this involvement in the name of the bank. The bank procures, processes, and distributes transplantable skin for burn victims and surgical patients. Since this is the only skin bank in the Southern tier of New York, most requests for skin are local, although anyone in the United States can receive tissue from the bank. With the completion of planned computer tissue bank registration in the near future, the range of the bank's service area will become more national in scope.

North American Transplant Coordinators Organization (NATCO)
5000 Van Nuys Blvd., Suite 400
Sherman Oaks, California 90405
(818) 995-7338
Coordinators of this organization conduct an ongoing educational campaign to inform both the public and hospital personnel about the benefits of and new advances in organ donation and transplantation. NATCO sponsors workships, seminars, and an annual training course on procurement for transplant coordinators. It publishes a newsletter and holds an annual conference with exhibits.

Office of Organ Transplantation
Department of Health & Human Services
Public Health Service
Health Resources and Services Administration
Rockville, Maryland 20857
Created in order to implement the National Organ Transplant Act of 1984, the Office of Organ Transplantation is responsible for (1) developing and maintaining a grant program to help improve the organ procurement system in this country; (2) providing technical assistance to organ procurement organizations receiving federal funds; (3) conducting an information program to inform the public of the need for organ donations; (4) serving as a source of information on the activities of states, private sector, and voluntary organizations; (5) establishing and maintaining a national computerized network for organ matching, the Organ Procurement and Transplantation Network, and a Scientific Registry of organ transplant recipients; and (6) providing policy guidance, technical liaison, and leadership and promoting cooperative efforts with individuals and organizations in the health care systems involved in organ donations, procurement, and transplantation.

Pittsburgh Transplant Foundation
5743 Center Ave.
Pittsburgh, Pennsylvania 15206
(412) 366-6771
Originally affiliated with the University of Pittsburgh, the Foundation has recently become an independent organ procurement agency serving transplant centers in Pittsburgh as well as other centers throughout the country. Involved in public and professional education, it conducts seminars on anatomical donation and sponsors educational programs for health professionals in regional hospitals. The Foundation provides speakers for medical groups and publishes a newsletter as well as pamphlets and protocols.

Regional Organ Bank of Illinois, Inc.
800 S. Wells Street, Suite 190
Chicago, Illinois 60607
Business: (312) 431-3600
24-Hour Donor Hotline: (312) 431-7624
The thrust of ROBI is threefold: organ and tissue procurement; histocompatibility testing; and public and professional education. ROBI staff members are available to assist hospital personnel in Illinois in making legally required requests for organ donations from the next of kin of dying patients. ROBI's Director of Education is responsible for the development and implementation of public and

professional education in organ donation. Each year, ROBI conducts professional seminars on organ donation and transplantation. It has developed a special project to involve the black community more fully in organ donation. It makes available a variety of brochures, pamphlets, posters, and other support materials for governmental agencies as well as for individuals. Its speakers' bureau can be utilized by school, civic, social, and religious organizations. ROBI cooperates with the United Network for Organ Sharing in offering organ and tissue to recipients nation-wide, according to tissue type and medical need. It plans to make increasing use of volunteers in the future.

S.O.U.N.D.
Blessing Hospital
Attn: Jan Web
1005 Broadway
Quincy, Illinois 62301
(217) 223-5811, Ext. 1405

A support group for potential donors and transplant recipients and their families, S.O.U.N.D. promotes public awareness about organ donation and transplantation.

Southern Center of the National Temporal Bone Bank
Baylor College of Medicine
Neurosensory Center—Room A 523
Houston, Texas 77030
(713) 790-5470

See main listing for Eastern (and National) Center of the National Temporal Bone Bank. The following states are served by this center: Alabama, Arkansas, Delaware, Florida, Georgia, Kentucky, Louisiana, Maryland, Mississippi, North Carolina, South Carolina, Puerto Rico, Tennessee, Texas, Virginia, Washington D.C., and West Virginia.

Transplant Recipients International Organization (TRIO)
244 N. Bellefield
Pittsburgh, Pennsylvania 15213

Headquartered in Pittsburgh, this organization is expanding rapidly throughout the world. More than one hundred cities have requested chapters; seven have been established to date. TRIO provides support services for persons who plan to undergo transplant or who have already done so. Members of the organization, who have been transplanted themselves, make personal visits to candidates for transplantation in order to listen, answer questions, and quell anxieties. Contact the organization about membership and volunteer activities.

United Network for Organ Sharing (UNOS)
3001 Hungary Spring Road
Richmond, Virginia 23228
(800) 446-2726
(804) 289-5380

The National Organ Transplant Act of 1984 legislated that a national Organ Procurement and Transplant Network for organ matching be established. The contract for this network was awarded to the United Network for Organ Sharing, which maintains a computerized, consolidated registry of all potential organ recipients, according to tissue type and medical need.

Western Center of the National Temporal Bone Bank
UCLA School of Medicine
31-24 Rehabilitation Center
Los Angeles, California 90024
(213) 825-4710
See the main listing for Eastern (and National) Center of the National Temporal Bone Bank. The following states are served by this center: Alaska, Arizona, California, Colorado, Hawaii, Idaho, Montana, Nevada, New Mexico, Oregon, Utah, Washington, and Wyoming.

The publisher solicits information from organizations involved in the field of organ donation and transplantation which are not listed here and wish to be included in a future edition of this book.

Bibliography

For Further Reading and Reference

Bouressa, F.G. & O'Mara, R.J. (1987). Ethical dilemmas in organ procurement and donation. *Critical Care Nursing Quarterly,* 10(2), 34-47.
Presents an excellent overview of ethical dilemmas arising from the harvesting of donated organs and the need to provide health care workers as well as the general public with more guidance in this area.

Callender, C.O., Bayton, J.A., Yeager, C., and Clark, J.E. (1982). Attitudes among blacks toward donating kidneys for transplantation: A pilot project. *Journal of the National Medical Association,* 74 (8), 807-809.
This article explores the reasons behind the statistics which show that blacks are among those least likely to donate their own organs or those of a loved one.

Cardiac transplantation. (1985). *Heart and Lung,* 14, 484-504.
A series of four articles treats various aspects of heart transplantation, including indications for transplantation and patient selection, postoperative management with immunosuppressive drugs, side effects, and ethical issues. Written from a nursing perspective but containing helpful insights for the layman as well.

Creighton, H. (1985). Organ transplantation, Part 1. *Nursing Management,* 16(9), 16 and 18.
Provides an overview of various aspects of organ transplantation, with particular reference to the Report of the Massachusetts Task Force on Organ Transplantation.

_____. (1985). Organ transplantation, Part 2. *Nursing Management,* 16(10), 20 and 22.
Considers the various approaches to allocation of organs in light of need and scarcity. Also examines the stance of the Roman Catholic Church, Protestant Christianity, and Judaism on organ donation and transplantation.

From here to transplant. . .Introductory information for patients and families. (1987). Alexandria, Virginia: American Council on Transplantation.
This very helpful booklet provides a wide variety of information for persons planning to undergo a transplant operation, from financing issues to social concerns.

Gabriel, Roger. (1982). *A patient's guide to dialysis and transplantation.* Boston: Kluwer Academic.
Although dated, explains dialysis and transplantation from a patient's perspective.

Giving your kidney. Columbia, Missouri: Missouri Kidney Program (also available from the American Kidney Fund).

This brochure presents basic facts about living, related donors (individuals giving one of their kidneys to a family member in need of a transplant). It describes in detail the experiences of 536 persons of all ages and incomes, ethnic backgrounds and religious beliefs, who have donated a kidney, analyzing both the positive and negative aspects of their experiences.

Gutkind, Lee. (1988). *Many sleepless nights: The world of organ transplantation.* New York: Norton.
Describes the dramas revolving around organ retrieval, transplant surgery, and the use of immunosuppressive drugs at a large urban hospital (Pittsburgh's Presbyterian-University Hospital).

Holcombe, A. Bone marrow harvest... Booklet to educate donor. (1987). *Oncology Nursing Forum,* 14(2), 63-65.
Discusses the relatively new treatment of bone marrow transplantation (BMT) and explains, with detailed illustrations, the process of bone marrow harvesting for a transplant for oneself in the future, for one's brother or sister, or for one's identical twin. The purpose of BMT is to eradicate a disease such as a solid tumor malignancy through lethal doses of chemotherapy and/or radiation and then to "rescue" the patient from the resulting bone marrow toxicity through the infusion of either a donor's or one's own marrow.

Maier, Frank. (1988). A second chance at life. *Newsweek,* September 12, 52-61.
The former chief of the Chicago bureau of *Newsweek* tells his personal story of having a liver transplant, with humor and passion.

Miller, Thomas and Jayne. (1988). *Baby James: A Legacy of Love and Family Courage.* San Francisco: Harper & Row.
Recounts the ordeals and adventures of one family, whose fourteen-month-old adopted son had a successful heart transplant operation but subsequently died four and a half months later from organ rejection.

Rice, H.J. (1987). When the transplant patient is your husband. *RN,* 50(8), 55-58.
Examines the psychological and social factors at work in the relationship between a nurse and her husband when the husband has a transplant operation.

Schanbacher, B. & Hasselman, E. (1986). Management of the diabetic transplant recipient. *American Nephrology Nurses' Association Journal,* 13(4), 187-90.
Explains the special precautions for diabetic patients undergoing transplant surgery.

Schoenberg, L., Golden, D., Ota, B., and Wideman, C. (1984). Using cyclosporine in renal transplantation. *American Nephrology Nurses' Association Journal,* 11(6), 9-12.
Considers the side effects of immunosuppressive drug therapies in the case of kidney transplants.

Secretary of Department of Health and Human Services. (1987). *The status of organ donation and coordination service: Report to the Congress for fiscal year 1987.*
Contains results of many statistical studies on transplantation and donation, along with a kind of state-of-the-art analysis of the field.

Simmons, Robert, et al. (1987). *Gift of life: The effect of organ transplantation on individual, family and societal dynamics.* New Brunswick, New Jersey: Transaction Books.
　Explores the psychosocial dynamics of organ transplantation.

Solomon, S.B. Organ transplant law raises thorny questions. (1985). *Nursing and Health Care*, 6(1), 19-20.
　Examines behind-the-scenes activities leading up to the passage of the National Organ Transplant Act and the implications of this new law for public policy and clinical practice. Calls for a widening discussion of ethics, technology, and resource allocation in this area.

Tooke, M.C. Elders, J. & Johnson, D.E. (1986). Corneal transplantation. *American Journal of Nursing*, 86, 685-7.
　Describes pre-and post-operative care for corneal transplant surgery patients and describes the actual surgical procedures involved, which restore sight to nearly 95 per cent of those undergoing this type of operation.

Williams, V. (1987). Parkinson's disease: autotransplantation of adrenal medulla to caudate nucleus of the brain. *Journal of Neuroscience Nursing*, 19(3), 174.
　Describes briefly the new technique of brain implants to treat Parkinson's disease through the removal of a portion of one's adrenal gland and its implantation in the brain.

Yomtoob, Parichehr & Schwartz, Ted. (1986). *The gift of life: One family's story.* New York: St. Martin.
　Presents a personal account of one family's experience when a family member undergoes transplantation.

Index

A

Aborted fetuses
    See Fetuses
Accreditation, 229
Administrator of the Health Care Financing Administration, 16, 217
Advancement of dental science, 12, 212
Advancement of medical science, 12, 212
AIDS, 229
Alabama, anatomical gift laws, 27-30
Alaska, anatomical gift laws, 30-32
Alzheimer's disease, 1, 4
Ambassadors for Corneal Transplants, 229, 233
Amendment of anatomical gift, 9-10, 16
    donee specified and document delivered, 13, 16
    made by will, 13, 210
    not made by will, 210
    not refusal to make another gift, 210
American Academy of Ophthalmology, 232
American Association of Tissue Banks, 229
American Bar Association, 2, 9, 228
American Council on Transplantation, 229
American Kidney Fund, 230
American Liver Foundation, 230
Amish, 2, 4
Anatomical Gift Association, 8, 230-231
Anatomical gift by a living donor
    instructions for filling out form, 207
    model form, 207
Anatomical gift by a living minor donor, 8
    instructions for filling out form, 208
    model form, 208
Anatomical gift by next of kin or other authorized person
    instructions for filling out form, 206
    model form, 206
Anatomical gift not revoked by donor
    irrevocable, 210
Anatomical gift of part
    not refusal to give other parts, 210
Anatomical gift
    definition of, 209
    limits on, 209
    refusal of, 209
Anatomical gifts
    need for, 1, 7
Arizona, anatomical gift laws, 32-36
Arkansas, anatomical gift laws, 36-39
Autopsy laws, 10, 14, 16, 213
Azathioprine, definition of, 226

B

Bank or storage facility, definition of, 11
Baptists, 4
Bayton, J.A., 239
Blacks
    See Organ donation
    See Transplants
Bone
    See Transplants
Bone marrow
    See Transplants
Bone marrow donors
    national registry, 222-223
Bone Marrow Harvest (booklet to educate donors), 240
Bouressa, F.A., 239
Bracelets
    See Medic Alert
Brain death, 14, 228
Brain "implants"
    See Transplants
Brochures
    See Educational materials
Buddhism, 4
Burn-related services, 234-235

C

CHAMPUS, 231
CORNEA, 231
Cadaveric, definition of, 226
California, anatomical gift laws, 39-42
Callender, C.O., 239
Callender, Dr. Clive, 5
Camps
    See Support services,
    Summer camps
Children as donors
    See Organ donation, children
Children's Liver Foundation, 231
Children's Transplant Foundation, 231
Children's transplants
    See Transplants
The Christian Church, 4

Christian Scientists, 4
Church of Christ, 4
    See also United Church of Christ
Church of Jesus Christ of Latter-Day Saints, 4
Civil liability
    See Liability
Clark, J.E., 239
Colorado, anatomical gift laws, 42-47
Coma, 5
Commissioner of the Food and Drug Administration, 16, 217, 222
Committee on Energy and Commerce, 217
Committee on Labor and Human Resources, 217
Community services, 230
Conflicts of interest, safeguards against, 5, 10
Connecticut, anatomical gift laws, 47-50
Consortium of Registered Nurses for Eye Acquisition, 231
Cook, Robin, 5
Corneal transplant surgery
    See Transplants, eye
Coroner
    authorized to release part, 211
    right to remove part, 10
Creighton, H., 239
Criminal liability
    See Liability
Criteria of donation
    legal competence, 15
    mental competence, 14
    minimum age, 14
Crossmatching, definition of, 226
Custody of body after removal of gift, 14, 16, 213
Cyclosporine, 3, 240
    definition of, 226

D

Deafness Research Foundation, 232
Death
    definition of, 6, 10, 14, 16, 226, 228
    time of, 14, 16
Decedent, definition of, 11, 14, 209, 226
Definitions of terms
    See Uniform Anatomical Gift Act, definitions of terms
Delaware, anatomical gift laws, 50-53
Delivery of document of gift, 13
    Connecticut, 15
    not necessary, 13, 15, 212
    to expedite procedures, 13, 15, 212
Dental education, 12, 212
Department of Health & Human Services, 240

    See also Office of Organ Transplantation
Deposit of document of gift
    See Registry services
Diabetes, 1, 240
Dialysis, 235, 239
Dietary expenses
    See Support services
Director of the National Institutes of Health, 222
Disciples of Christ
    See Christian Church
District of Columbia, anatomical gift laws, 53-56
Document of gift, definition of, 209
Donation
    authorizes examination, 12
    See also Organ donation
Donee, 9-10, 12, 15, 212
    acceptance of gift, 13, 213
    acceptance of gift of entire body, 13
    attending physician, 13, 15
    attending physician, barred from removal part, 13
    attending physician, barred from transplant part, 13
    attending physician, transfer of gift to third party, 15
    authorization of surgeon for organ removal, 13, 210
    bank, 12
    college, 12, 212
    definition of, 226
    dental school, 12, 15, 212
    hospital, 12, 15, 212
    individual, 12, 15, 212
    medical school, 12, 15, 212
    not specified, 13, 15, 212
    physician, 12, 212
    procurement organization, 212
    rejection of gift, 13, 212-213
    rights of, 12, 16
    specified, 13, 212
    specified but not available, 13, 15, 212
    storage facility, 12, 15
    storage facility, nonprofit, 15
    surgeon, 12, 212
    when *must* refuse gift, 212
    university, 12, 212
Donee not specified
    procurement organization to be notified, 212
Donee specified
    to be notified by hospital of impending gift, 212
Donor
    See Organ donor
Donor families, needs of, 229

Driver's license
    See Manner of donation
Dura, definition of, 226
    See also Transplants

E

Eastern Center of the National Temporal Bone Bank, 232
Education, role of, 7, 12, 212
Educational materials
    brochures, 230, 237
    conferences, 236
    courses, 235-236
    discussion groups, 230
    eye, 232-233
    films, 235
    forums, 235
    heart, 235
    kidney, 230, 235
    lectures, 230-231
    liver, 230-231
    newsletters, 236
    pamphlets, 231, 236, 237
    posters, 237
    protocols, 236
    public service announcements, 231
    scientific sessions, 235
    seminars, 236, 237
    slides, 230
    speakers, 233, 235, 237
    symposia, 231
    urinary tract disease, 235
    videotapes, 6, 230, 233-234
    workshops, 236
Educational programs, 230
    clergy, 216
    community groups, 7
    community organizations, 1, 6
    family units, 2, 18
    fire departments, 216
    Hispanic, 1
    hospital staffs, 1
    law enforcement personnel, 7, 216, 234
    libraries, 1-2, 6
    medical professionals, 1, 7, 18, 216, 229-231, 233-237
    medical schools, 1
    minority groups, 2, 7, 18
    nurses, 2
    nursing schools, 1
    physicians, 2
    primary schools, 1-2, 18
    public, 1, 7, 216, 229-231, 233-237
    religious groups, 1-2, 6, 18
    secondary schools, 1-2, 18
Elders, J., 240
Embalming, 13
Emergency medical records
    See Medic Alert
Emergency rescuers
    duty to search for document of gift, 212
    role, 11
Encouraged voluntarism, 2, 226
Entire body donation, 8, 13, 15, 230-231, 234
    definition of, 226
Enucleator, definition of, 209
Episcopal Church, 4
Ethical issues
    See Transplants
Ethnic minorities
    See Organ donation, ethnic minorities
    See Transplants, ethnic minorities
Examination
    See Donation
Extrarenal, definition of, 226
Eye
    See Organ donation
    See Transplants
Eye Bank Association of America, 231-233
Eye banking, 231-233
    Latin America, 233
    See also Tissue banking
Eye Donor Month
    See National Eye Donor Month
Eye enucleation, 10
    definition of, 226
Eye-Bank for Sight Restoration, Inc., 6, 233

F

Failure to discharge duties
    administrative sanctions, 212
    not subject to liability, 212
Faith of Our Patients, 4
Fellowships, 230, 232
Fetuses
    organ donation, 14
    use in transplantation, 14
Filing of document of gift
    See Registry services
Financial counseling
    See Support services
Financial grants
    See Support services

Firemen
- duty to search for document of gift, 212
- role, 11

Florida Anatomical Gift Act, 7
Florida Gift of Life Foundation, 233
Florida, anatomical gift laws, 56-61
From Here to Transplant . . . Introductory Information for Patients and Families, 239
Fund raising
- See Support services

Funeral services
- See Memorial services

G

Gabriel, Roger, 239
Galactosemia, 231
Georgia, anatomical gift laws, 61-66
Golden, D., 240
Good faith performance
- See Liability, protection against

Greek Orthodox Church, 4
Gift of Life: The Effect of Organ Transplantation on Individual, Family and Societal Dynamics, 240
The Gift of Life: One Family's Story, 241
Giving Your Kidney, 239-240
Guardian, donation by
- See Next of kin

Gutkind, Lee, 2, 240
Gypsies, 4

H

Hasselman, E., 240
Hawaii, anatomical gift laws, 66-68
Heart donation
- See Organ donation, heart

Heart transplants
- See Transplants, heart

Hepatitis, 229
Hinduism, 4
Hispanic outreach programs, 233
- See also Educational programs
- See also Organ donation, Hispanic outreach programs

Histocompatibility, 219, 236
- definition of, 227
- testing, 236

Holcombe, A., 240
Hormonal therapy, 1
Hospital, definition of, 11, 209
Hospital protocols
- See Standards

Hospitals
- affiliation with procurement agency, 11
- duty to search for document of gift, 212
- required notification of contents of document of gift, 21

Howard University Hospital's Transplant Center, 5
Huntington's disease, 1, 4

I

Idaho, anatomical gift laws, 69-71
Illinois, anatomical gift laws, 71-74
"Ilumina Una Vida," 6
Immune system, definition of, 227
Immunosuppressive drugs, 1-3, 16, 215, 239-240
- coverage by Social Security Act, 225
- definition of, 227

Imuran, 226
Independent Conservative Evangelical Church, 4
Indiana, anatomical gift laws, 74-78
Insurance reimbursement
- for transplantation, 216

Interstate commerce, definition of, 222
Iowa, anatomical gift laws, 78-80
Islam, 4

J

Jehovah's Witnesses, 2, 4
Johnson, D.E., 240
Judaism, 2, 4, 239

K

Kansas, anatomical gift laws, 81-83
Kentucky, anatomical gift laws, 83-86
Kidney transplants
- See Transplants

L

Law enforcement personnel
- duty to search for document of gift, 212
- See also Educational programs, law enforcement personnel
- role, 11

Lectures
- See Educational materials

Legal liability

See Liability
Legal reform, 231
Legislation, 240
    federal, 1, 5, 7, 11, 228
    required request, 1, 7, 10, 211,
      224-225, 228, 231, 236
    required request, when waived, 211
    routine inquiry, 10
    state, 1-2, 5-9, 11, 14, 228
Liability
    protection against, 10, 14, 16, 213
Liver disease, 230
    children, 231
Liver transplants
    See Transplants
Living Bank, 233-234
Living donor
    See Anatomical gift by a living donor
Living expenses
    See Support services
Living, related donor, 230, 240
    definition of, 227
Louisiana, anatomical gift laws, 87-91
Lutheran Church, 4

M

Maier, Frank, 240
Maine, anatomical gift laws, 92-95
Manner of donation
    card, 13, 15
    driver's license, 15-16, 210
    driver's license, canceled, 210
    driver's license, expired, 210
    driver's license, revoked, 210
    driver's license, suspended, 210
    other than will, 13, 15, 210
    will, 12, 15, 210
    will, invalid for testamentary purposes, 210
    will, not probated, 210
    will, probated, 210
    will, problems with, 15
Many Sleepless Nights: The World of Organ Transplantation, 2, 240
Maryland, anatomical gift laws, 96-99
Massachusetts Task Force on Organ Transplantation
    Report, 239
Massachusetts, anatomical gift laws, 100-103
Medic Alert, 234
Medicaid, 7, 11, 224, 231
Medical education, 1, 4, 12, 212

Medical examiner
    See Coroner
Medical school
    certification, 2
    curricula, 2
Medicare, 2, 7, 11, 224-225
Memorial services, 9, 13, 16, 213
Metal bracelets
    See Medic Alert
Metal necklaces
    See Medic Alert
Methodists, 4
Michigan, anatomical gift laws, 104-107
Midwestern Center of the National Temporal Bone Bank, 234
Minnesota, anatomical gift laws, 108-111
Minor donor, 15
    See also Anatomical gift by a living minor donor
    See also Organ donation, children
Mirós, Gilda, 6
Mississippi, anatomical gift laws, 113-116
Missouri, anatomical gift laws, 116-120
Montana, anatomical gift laws, 120-124
Mormons
    See Church of Jesus Christ of Latter-Day Saints
Moslem donors, 4
Mutilation of body
    forbidden to donee, 14, 16, 213

N

NATCO
    See North American Transplant Coordinators Organization
National Burn Victim Foundation, 234
National Center of the Temporal Bone Bank
    See Eastern Center of the Temporal Bone Bank
National Conference of Commissioners on Uniform State Law, 2, 9-10, 228
National Eye Donor Month, 232
National Heart Assist and Transplant Fund, 234
National Kidney Foundation, 4, 236
National Organ and Tissue Donation Awareness Week, 235
National Organ Transplant Act, 2, 16, 236, 237, 240
    definition of, 227
    Task Force, 1-2, 16, 215, 227
    Task Force, assessments of, 215
    Task Force, composition of, 216
    Task Force, report of, 215, 217
    text of, 215
National organ-sharing system
    See Organ Procurement and

National registry
    Transplantation Network
    donors, 216
National Temporal Bone Banks Program, 232
Nebraska, anatomical gift laws, 124-127
Necklaces
    See Medic Alert
Networking opportunities
    See Support services
Nevada, anatomical gift laws, 127-130
New Hampshire, anatomical gift laws, 131-132
New Jersey, anatomical gift laws, 133-135
New Mexico, anatomical gift laws, 136-138
New Year's Resolution Campaign, 235
New York Firefighters Skin Bank, 235
New York Hospital, 235
New York, anatomical gift laws, 139-140, 142-143
Next of kin, donation by, 7, 9-12, 15, 210, 236
    adult brother or sister, 12, 210
    adult son or daughter, 12, 210
    See also Anatomical gift by next of kin or other authorized person
    consent not required, 210
    donation refused, 12
    Florida law, 15
    grandparent, 210
    guardian, 210
    other authorized person, 12
    other form of communication reduced to writing and signed, 211
    other recorded message, 13, 211
    parent, 12, 210
    parents of minor, 15
    recorded telephonic message, 211
    revocation prior to removal of part, 211
    rights, 9, 14, 213
    spouse, 12, 210
    survivor out of country, 15
    survivor out of town, 15
    telegraphic message, 13, 15, 211
    telephonic message, 13, 15
    when disallowed, 210, 212
    written document, 13, 15, 211
Non-immigrant alien, definition of, 227
North American Transplant Coordinators Organization, 236
North Carolina, anatomical gift laws, 144-147
North Dakota, anatomical gift laws, 148-150
Nursing school
    certification, 2
    curricula, 2

O

O'Mara, R.J., 239
Office of Organ Transplantation, 236
Ohio, anatomical gift laws, 151-154
Oklahoma, anatomical gift laws, 156-159
Omnibus Budget Reconciliation Act of 1986, 2, 224-225
Oregon, anatomical gift laws, 159-162
Organ, definition of, 221-222
Organ donation
    barriers to, 16
    black community, 1, 5-6, 237, 239
    children, 2, 8
    emblems of, 234
    ethnic background, 230
    ethnic minorities, 5-7, 230, 239
    eye, 4, 6, 231-233
    fear of premature removal, 5
    federal legislation, 229
    financial incentives, 7
    France, 7, 227
    heart, 1
    Hispanic outreach programs, 6
    kidney, 3, 239
    lack of information, 5-6
    mistrust of doctors, 5
    model hospital program, 231
    motivation, 7-8
    overview, 1-2
    placement of organs, 234
    professional education, 2, 18
    public education, 2, 18
    racial pride, 5
    racism, fear of, 5
    religious views, 1, 4-6, 230, 239
    research, 16
    skin, 234-235
    state legislation, 229
    statistics, 1, 3, 5-7, 239-240
    temporal bones, 232
Organ donor, 14
    age limit, 1
    cards, 10
    definition of, 11, 209, 226
    heart, 1
    families, needs of, 230, 237
    need for, 1
    pool, expansion of, 1
    selection criteria, 209, 229
Organ procurement, 216, 240
    coordination, 213, 216
    hospital protocols, 224
    quality assurance, 229

Organ procurement agencies, 16, 215, 224, 236-237
    definition of, 209, 227
    grant program, 218, 220-221, 236
    standards, 224
Organ Procurement and Transplantation Network, 16, 215, 219-220, 224, 236, 237
Organ Retrieval and Networking Forum, 229
Organ transplantation
    See Transplants
Orthodox Judaism
    See Judaism
Ota, B., 240

P

Pamphlets
    See Educational materials
Paramedics
    duty to search for document of gift, 212
    role, 11
Paramount, definition of, 227
Parkinson's disease, 1, 4, 14, 241
Part, definition of, 11, 209
Patient and Family Issues Forum, 229
Patient selection criteria, 235
A Patient's Guide to Dialysis and Transplantation, 239
Paton, Dr. R. Townley, 233
Pennsylvania, anatomical gift laws, 162-166
Person, definition of, 12, 15, 209
Physician to remove organ(s)
    See Surgeon to remove organ(s), designated by donor
Physician to remove organ(s) not designated
    See Surgeon to remove organ(s) not designated
Physician who certifies death
    may not remove part, 14, 213
    may not remove part (except Wyoming), 16
    may not remove part, exception, 213
    may not transplant part, 14, 213
    may not transplant part (except Wyoming), 16
    may not transplant part, exception, 213
Physician, definition of, 12, 209
Pittsburgh Transplant Foundation, 236
Pituitary glands
    See Transplants
Posters
    See Educational materials

Prednisone
    definition of, 227
Presbyterian-University Hospital, 2
Presbyterians, 4
Presumed consent laws, 2, 7
    definition of, 228
Procurement
    See Organ procurement
Procurement organization, definition of, 209
    See also Organ procurement agencies
Professional education
    medical schools, 2
    nursing schools, 2
Professional Education Forum, 229
Protestant Christianity, 239
Public Education Forum, 229
Public policy
    See Support services
Public service announcements
    See Educational materials
Purchase of organs
    exclusions, 213
    forbidden, 213
    penalty, 213, 222
Purposes for which anatomical gifts may be made, 12, 15, 212

R

Race
    influence on transplant success, 3, 5
Racial pride
    See Organ donation, racial pride
Racism
    See Organ donation, racism
Recipients of anatomical gifts
    See Donee
Reform Judaism
    See Judaism
Refusal of gift, 10, 13, 212-213
Refusal to donate
    documented, attached to driver's license, 210
    documented, oral statement, 210
Regional Organ Bank of Illinois, 236
Registry services
    anatomical board, 15
    bank, 13, 15
    county clerk's office, 15
    See also Delivery of document of gift
    department of health services, 15
    department of highway safety and motor vehicles, 15

hospital, 13, 15, 212
New Mexico, 16
obligation to produce document for examination upon death of donor, 13, 15-16, 212-213
procurement organization, 212
registrar of vital statistics, 15
registry office, 13, 15, 212
state office, 15
storage facility, 13, 15
See also Support services
Rejection of organ
definition of, 228
Religious views
See Organ donation
See Transplants
Renal, definition of, 228
Research, 1, 4, 12, 212
ear disease, 232
hearing loss, 232
kidney, 230, 235
liver, 230
pediatric liver disease, 231
sight restoration, 232
transplantation, 25, 216
Restorative surgery, 1, 4
Revocation of anatomical gift, 9-10, 16
by parent of minor, 15
by spouse, 15
document not delivered, 13, 16
donee specified and document delivered, 13
made by will, 13, 210
not made by will, 210
not refusal to make another gift, 210
Rhode Island, anatomical gift laws, 166-169
Rice, H.J., 240
Roman Catholic Church, 4, 6, 239
Routine inquiry
See Legislation
Rush-Presbyterian-St. Luke's Medical Center, 4

S

S.O.U.N.D., 237
Safekeeping of document of gift
See Registry services
Sale of organs
exclusions, 213
forbidden, 11, 213, 222
penalty, 213, 222
Sandimmune, 226
Schanbacher, B., 240
Schoenberg, L., 240

Schwartz, Ted, 241
Scientific registry
organ transplant recipients, 220, 236
Secretary of Health and Human Services, 215, 222
annual report on organ transplantation, 222
Seventh-Day Adventists, 4
Simmons, Robert, 240
Skin
See Transplants
Skin banks, 235
Skin transplants
See Transplants
Slides
See Educational materials
Solomon, S.B., 240
South Carolina, anatomical gift laws, 169-171
South Dakota, anatomical gift laws, 172-174
Southern Center of the National Temporal Bone Bank, 237
Spanish-speaking donors
See Educational programs, Hispanic
See Hispanic outreach programs
See Organ donation, Hispanic outreach programs
Standards
hospitals, 2, 11
organ procurement agencies, 2, 20-21, 229
State anatomical gift laws
See name of particular state
State, definition of, 12, 209
The Status of Organ Donation and Coordination Service: Report to the Congress for Fiscal Year 1987, 240
Stillborn fetuses
See Fetuses
Storage of document of gift, 9
See also Registry services
Summer camps
See Support services
Support services
academic gift programs, 233
corporate gift programs, 233
dietary expenses, 230
donors, 2, 8, 229-230, 233-234, 237
financial counseling, 230-231, 234-235,
financial grants, 230-231, 233, 235-236
food, 231
fund raising, 229-232, 233-235
home care, 235
living expenses, 230-231
medication, 235

networking opportunities, 229, 231, 234-235
patient advocate, 231
psychological counseling, 231, 234-235, 239
public policy, 2, 229
referral to other organizations, 231, 233, 235, 236
referral to specialists, 230, 235
registry services, 8, 233, 234
screening, 235
summer camps, 235
transplant recipients, 2, 8, 229-231, 234-235, 237
transportation, 230-231, 235-236
trustee for transplant funds, 230
volunteers, 2, 8, 229-230, 235-236
Surgeon General of the United States, 16, 217
Surgeon to remove organ(s)
designated by donor, 13, 210
designated by donor but not available, 13, 210
Surgeon to remove organ(s) not designated, 13, 210
Symposia
See Educational materials

T

TRIO
See Transplant Recipients International Organization
Task Force
See National Organ Transplant Act
Technician, definition of, 209
Temporal bones
See Organ donation
Tennessee, anatomical gift laws, 175-177
Texas Medical Association
Committee on Medicine and Religion, 4
Texas, anatomical gift laws, 179-180
Therapy, 10, 12, 212
Tissue banking, 229
See also Eye banking
Tooke, M.C., 240
Transplant center, definition of, 221
equitable allocation, 216
Transplant families
needs of, 234-235, 237
Transplant Recipients International Organization, 237
Transplantation technology, 18, 216
Transplants, 12, 212

advances, 1, 3
public education, 18
black community, 1, 5-6
bone, 1, 3-4
bone marrow, 240
brain "implants", 1, 4
children, 3
criteria for, 6
dura, 3
economic factors, 16, 229
equitable access, 16, 216
ethical issues, 229, 239
ethnic minorities, 5, 7, 230
eye, 1, 3-4, 6, 229, 231-233, 240
heart, 1, 3, 234-235, 239
kidney, 1, 3, 5-6, 230, 240
kidney, living relative as donor, 3, 5
legislation, federal, 229
legislation, state, 229
liver, 1, 3
personal account, 241
pituitary glands, 3
professional education, 18
psychological issues, 229
reimbursements, 18
religious views, 1, 4-6, 239
research, 16
skin, 1, 3-4, 234-235
social issues, 229, 240
statistics, 3, 240
Transportation
See Support services
Trustee for transplant funds
See Support services
24-hour hotlines, 231, 233, 234, 236

U

UNOS
See United Network for Organ Sharing
Uniform Anatomical Gift Act, 2, 9, 11, 14-16
definition of, 228
definitions of terms, 11, 14-15, 209
severability of invalid provisions, 213
text of, 11-14
uniformity of interpretation, 14, 213
Uniform Anatomical Gift Act, amended, 2, 10, 14
text of, 209-214
Uniform Determination of Death Act, 14, 18-19
definition of, 228
Uniform Donor Card, 8, 231, 233

definition of, 228
instructions for filling out, 205
model form, 205
United Church of Christ, 4
See also Church of Christ (Independent)
United Methodists
See Methodists
United Network for Organ Sharing, 237
University of Pittsburgh, 236
Utah, anatomical gift laws, 181-182

V

Valuable consideration, definition of, 222
Vanderbilt University, 4
Vermont, anatomical gift laws, 183-184
Videotapes
See Educational materials
Virginia, anatomical gift laws, 185-189
Volunteers
See Support services

W

Washington, anatomical gift laws, 189-192
West Virginia, anatomical gift laws, 192-197
Western Center of the National Temporal Bone Bank, 238
Wideman, C., 240
Will, donation by
See Manner of donation
Williams, V., 241
Wisconsin, anatomical gift laws, 197-200
Witnesses to donation, 8, 10, 13, 15, 209
California, 15
Utah, 15
Wyoming, anatomical gift laws, 200-201, 203

X

xenographs, 1

Y

Yeager, C., 239
Yomtoob, Parichehr, 241

LIBRARY USE ONLY
DOES NOT CIRCULATE